International Marketing

International Marketing

Javed Shaikh

RANDOM

RANDOM PUBLICATIONS

NEW DELHI (INDIA)

International Marketing

ISBN 978-93-5111-348-5

Published in 2014 in India by

Reprint 2019

RANDOM PUBLICATIONS

4376-A/4B, Gali Murari Lal, Ansari Road
New Delhi-110 002
Phone : +91-11-43580356, +91-11-23289044
e-mail: randomexports@gmail.com, sales@randompublications.com,
info@randompublications.com

Type Setting by : Keystoneprintads, Delhi-110051
Printed at : Mehra Printers, Delhi-110 092

Preface

Marketing is the process of focusing the resources and objectives of an organisation on environmental opportunities and needs. It is a universal discipline. However, markets and customers are different and hence the practice of marketing should be fine tuned and adjusted to the local conditions of a given country. The marketing man must understand that each person is different and so also each country which means that both experience and techniques obtained and successful in one country or countries. Every country has a different set of customers and even within a country there are different sub-sets of customers, distribution channels and media are different. If that is so, for each country there must be a unique marketing plan.

International Marketing can be defined as exchange of goods and services between different national markets involving buyers and sellers. According to the American Marketing Association, "International Marketing is the multinational process of planning and executing the conception, prices, promotion and distribution of ideal goods and services to create exchanges that satisfy the individual and organizational objectives."

I would like to thank my team for standing beside me throughout my career and writing this book. My special thanks go to "Random Publications" who have published the book.

— *Javed Shaikh*

Contents

1

Understanding the International Marketing Environment

GLOBAL TRADE SYSTEM

The cease of the Uruguay Round in 1994 saw the establishment of a new trading system and related agreements under the auspices of the World Trade Organization. The WTO oversees implementation of the agreements by which member countries, especially those that are developed, reduce tariff rates over a wide range of products. They have made tradeweighted tariff cuts that average 40 per cent on industrial products. The WTO also tightens rules on non-tariff barriers by expecting members to replace NTBs with bound tariff rates. The UR has converted all NTBs for agricultural products into bound tariffs, which have to be cut by an average of 35 per cent. These developments have helped to open potential new markets for emerging agriculture- and resource-based Central Asian countries. However, as the international trading system becomes more rule-based, it will also be highly competitive. Therefore, new export approaches will be needed.

TRADE CHARACTERISTICS OF CENTRAL ASIA

The export base of Central Asian economies is narrow, comprised mainly of oil and gas, minerals, base metals and cotton. Furthermore, many of the products exported are in their unprocessed forms. Most exports from the Central Asian economies depend on the Russian Federation and other members of the Commonwealth of Independent States. However, efforts have been made to extend markets beyond the Russian Federation and the CIS to the United Kingdom of Great Britain and Northern Ireland, Germany, Turkey, the Republic of Korea and China. Central Asian economies will have to focus on the use of new marketing tools as one priority export-related issue over the next five years in order to meet the following objectives:

- Diversifying the number of markets for their products
- Developing downstream products for export

Central Asian economies formerly had access to materials, machinery, equipment, consumer goods and foodstuffs from a limited number of supply sources, mainly the Russian Federation and some of the other CIS countries. As a result, Central Asian economies developed strong trade links with the Russian Federation and the CIS and could use these links to increase their exports.

However, as the Russian Federation opens its market as a preparation for joining the WTO, Central Asian countries will find increased competition. Therefore, they will have to develop ways to enhance their competitiveness. Central Asian countries are aware of the need for adjustment to the international market environment. They also need to be aware of the major events that have taken place that may influence their trade policies.

DECLINING SIGNIFICANCE OF TRADE CONCESSIONS FOR DEVELOPING COUNTRIES

Previously, developed countries allowed certain exports of developing countries to enter their markets either tariff-free or at preferential tariff rates. For example, under the Lomé Convention, the European Union grants preferential treatment to imports from countries in Africa, the Caribbean and the Pacific. Similarly, Australia and New Zealand grant preferential treatment to imports from Pacific Island nations. However, following the cease of the UR and the subsequent reduction of tariff rates by developed countries, such preferential rates will become marginalized. Furthermore, quota restrictions on imports will gradually be lifted. *For example, trade in textiles had been governed by the Multifibre Arrangement, which is a series of bilateral import quotas for textiles and garments produced by developing economies.* The MFA has now been replaced by the new Agreement on Textiles and Clothing. Items covered under the MFA are to be liberalized under ATC.

The liberalization of the multilateral trade system will create export opportunities for Central Asia countries, because it allows them to compete on an equal footing in new markets. However, such new markets will require the use of different marketing strategies.

THE AFTERMATH OF THE ASIAN ECONOMIC CRISIS

The Asian economic crisis, which started in July 1997 spread throughout the region, and extended as far as the Russian Federation and parts of Latin America, resulting in the severe financial collapse of their currencies and financial systems. The impact was greater in the emerging Asian economies, especially in South-East Asia and the Republic of Korea. Heavy debt burdens, massive corporate failures and declining production and output have been common characteristics among the Asian economies hit by the crisis.

The subsequent fall in demand, especially for commodities, had a serious impact on countries with highly commodity dependent economies. The decline in commodity prices reduced real incomes of producers, especially in developing countries of Africa and Latin America. Japan, the world's second largest economy, also went into recession during the later part of 1998. The Japanese banking system was burdened by corporate debt from the 1980s.

If it continues, the crisis would have severe effects on countries that export oil and raw material commodities. However, the situation in Asia has stabilized and optimism slowly returning to the region. With the exception of Indonesia and Hong Kong, China, the rest of Asia was expected to register positive growth in 1999. Japan's economy also rebounded, achieving 1.9 per cent growth during the first quarter of 1999. The recovery of Asian economies would include increased demand for commodities like cotton, grain, and minerals, creating export opportunities for Central Asian countries. They need to market their products as well as attract Asian investors from Japan and the newly-industrialized Asian economies to invest in downstream production for subsequent export from Central Asian countries back to their home countries.

PRIVATE SECTOR AND PUBLIC SECTOR COOPERATION

Central Asian economies already have existing state trading entities that focus on export and trading. However, changes in the international trade environment make it important for the government to consult with the private sector about the assistance they will need in order to adapt. Governments should have feedback mechanisms and dialogues with the private sector to ensure that rules and regulations facilitate business development.

An example would be the establishment of industry advisory groups that include people from the public and private sector. Similarly, economic agencies should develop channels for feedback as well as information for disseminating to the business community. The regulatory framework should be friendly and relevant to business and should not block business development.

The process of two-way communication will also help in providing appropriate assistance for exports and product development and will enable companies in Central Asian countries to compete. The right institutions to implement policies need to be set up and nurtured. Private and public sector interactions will influence the bureaucracy to have pro-business attitudes.

State trading enterprises could be restructured to do trading for production companies in the private sector. This form of collaboration between the private and public sector will help the small and medium-sized enterprises in Central Asian countries to persuade STEs to export their products to new markets with minimum transaction costs.

DEVELOPING TRADE CAPACITY

Central Asian economies are well endowed with abundant natural resources such as oil, gas and metals, as well as commodities like cotton, grain, and cereals. These natural resources create the potential to develop horizontal and vertical industrial linkages, which can help to broaden the export base. The republics of the former Soviet Union were traditional markets for the exports of Central Asian economies. However, when the Russian economy opened, the result was more foreign competition for Central Asian countries. Therefore, Central Asian countries have had to adopt two new approaches:

- Upgrade the quality of their exports in order to compete in the Russian market
- Diversify into other export markets.

The Central Asian governments need to increase their efforts to develop institutions designed to have more efficient trade activities. Trade efficiency can be defined as the effective facilitation and promotion of both exports and imports without friction and at the appropriate cost. Without trade efficiency, export sectors and the supporting physical infrastructure would be unable to help improve economic development of the country.

THE NEED FOR A TRADE PROMOTION ORGANIZATION

Government institutions should be designed and created in order to provide support for the business community, which will build productive capacity, upgrade industrial and agrotechnology, and expand exports and markets. There is therefore an urgent need to create a trade promotion organization. If a TPO is given the right direction and managed effectively, it can play an important, catalytic role in developing and promoting the country's exports. The TPO can also performance as an advisor and facilitator for the government's trade development strategies. TPOs are generally created to be the government's instrument for export promotion and development. However, a TPO could have an expanded role if the government thinks that it would be a suitable complement to help implement the national trade policy. TPOs could help to restructure selected STEs to become export development arms for non-exporting companies.

POLITICAL FACTORS

- The political stability of the nation. Is it a democracy, communist, or dictatorial regime?
- Monetary regulations. Will the seller be paid in a currency that they value or will payments only be accepted in the host nation currency?

ECONOMICAL FACTORS

- Consumer wealth and expenditure within the country.

- National interests and inflation rate.
- Are quotas imposed on your product.
- Are there import tariffs imposed.
- Does the government offer subsidies to national players that make it difficult for you to compete?

SOCIAL FACTORS

- *Language*: Will language be a barrier to communication for you? Does your host nation speak your national language? What is the meaning of your brand name in your host country's language?
- *Customs*: What customs do you have to be aware of within the country? This is important. You need to make sure you do not offend while communicating your message.
- *Social factors*: What are the role of women and family within society?
- *Religion*: How does religion affect behaviour?
- *Values*: what are the values and attitudes of individuals within the market?

TECHNOLOGICAL

- The technological infrastructure of the market.
- Do all homes have access to energy
- Is there an Internet infrastructure. Does this infrastructure support broadband or dial up?
- Will your systems easily integrate with your host countrys?

THE LEGAL, POLITICAL/TRADE ENVIRONMENT

The legal/political aspect is very important in global marketing. "International law" can be defined as rules and principles that states and nations consider binding upon themselves. This raises two interesting characteristics of international law. The first is that "law" belongs to individual nations and international law only exists to the degree that individual nations are willing to relinquish their rights. The second is the lack of an adequate international judicial and administrative framework or a body of law which would form the basis of a truly comprehensive international legal system.

The international business is also subject to political decrees made by governments both in "home" and "host" countries. Home governments can apply pressure not to deal with disapproved parties. These measures may take the refusal to grant an export licence, or withdrawal of export guarantee cover. The host government may take measures like taxation, ownership controls, operating restrictions or expropriation.

LAWS, RULES, AND STANDARDS

All agricultural exports operate within an institutional environment, which is made up of a set of political, social and legal ground rules. These ground rules form the laws of all production, exchange and distribution and give rise to certain expectations and assurances about the actions of others, and give order and stability to the means of doing business. The most important rules in any system are those defining, allocating and enforcing property rights, and rules and conventions defining allowable and non-allowable forms of cooperation and competition (standards, rules of contract, fair trading etc.). Well defined and enforced systems regarding property rights are essential. Articulated ownership and rights to use, trade and alter assets is vital to market development, since this assigns to individuals the right to benefits and losses in production and marketing activities.

Rules and conventions specifying entry conditions and boundaries on cooperative and competitive policies also facilitate exchange and coordination. The establishment and enforcement of standards can reduce transaction costs by increasing the available information to buyers and consumers. Standards may include basic weights, measures, quality grades and contract forms. Quality standards may be mandatory or voluntary and minimum or multiple grades. These standards help where trade is at a distance. The EU has a strict set of standards regarding horticultural products. For example, including hygiene, quality and certificates of origin.

Licensing also facilitates marketing agencies and producers by reducing transaction costs. This occurs when the criteria for licensing revolves around asset holdings, financial solvency and so on. Performance standards are built in to maintain the licensing agreement. Increasingly, consumer and trading bodies like the EU are enforcing the disclosure of more and more information. Particularly, these efforts revolve around packaging, labelling and information, for example, pesticides used on horticultural produce.

As this trend to disclosure of information grows, along with the phenomenon of product liability, regulations regarding certain tests or inspection of products, handling and processing procedures may be enforced. So may ingredient and nutrition information. This is becoming an increasingly important issue as food products become more complex and varied. One of the problems with this noble effort to inform the consumer is that producers may lose their competitive differentiation advantage through divulging information to competitors. The EU has gone to extraordinary lengths to inform the consumer, issuing directives on product descriptions and pricing. For example the EU directive on the pricing of cabbages runs to hundreds of pages and, what constitutes "chocolate" and a "sausage" to name but two products, is quite revealing. The following case proves the point. The EU is also very strict, as is the USA, on food additives or flavour substitutes. It is particularly so for any substance which may have long term harmful effects. The EU produces "E numbers" standards for product additives and artificial colorants or flavourings.

Issues

Most issues in the legal/political environment centre around the following:

- "Institutional environment" - made up of political, social and legal ground rules within which the global marketer must operate.
- Property rights - patents, trademarks.
- Taxation - what taxation plans will be faced abroad?
- Recourse - possibility and length of action with the possibility of image damaging necessitating arbitration.
- Movement of equity and expropriation threats - often necessitating protocols or the signing of trade frameworking agreements.

Efforts to regulate the international legal system include individual country efforts, like the USA International Trade Commission and the GATT system. The GATT system is a set of norms and procedures which member governments have accepted to create order and predictability in international trade relations.

The three basic principles are:

1. Nondiscrimination - each member country must treat the trade of all other member countries equally
2. Open markets which are encouraged by GATT through a prohibition of all forms of protection except customs tariffs,
3. Fair trade which prohibits export subsidies on manufactured products and limits the use of export subsidies on primary products.

None of these principles is fully realised, simply because it is impossible to "police" all sovereign governments and dictate what is or is not tariff or non tariff discriminating. The need to systematically evaluate the legal/political environment cannot be overemphasized. This can be done by reference to the appropriate embassy or government agency or via magazines like "Foreign Affairs" and even by reference to a domestic agency in the host country.

THE POLITICAL ENVIRONMENT

Checks can be made on the legal/political system as to its ideology, nationalism, stability and international relations.

- *Ideology*: A country's ideological leaning may be capitalism, socialism, a mixture or other form. In the last years remarkable changes have been taking place in the ideologies of many countries. The most dramatic example has been the collapse of the communist USSR and Eastern Europe and its replacement with market led policies and ideologies. Similarly, many African countries are abandoning their centrist leanings in favour of market led economies. For example, Zimbabwe and Tanzania.

- *Nationalism*: Whilst, primarily a phenomenon of the developing countries, Yugoslavia has shown it is not entirely so. Nationalism can lead to expropriation of foreign held assets.
- *Stability*: Changes in regime, violence and cultural divisions based on language or other factors can lead to a very uncertain environment in which to conduct business. The current uncertainty in Liberia and Rwanda, the violence of Somalia and Yugoslavia increase the risk and diminish the confidence of doing business in these countries.
- *International relations*: In general international relations have improved over the last twenty years. The development of GATT, NATO and the EU have gone a long way to reduce the element of "foreigness".
- *Expropriation*: Expropriation is an extreme form of political action. It may occur for a number of reasons, including the desire to retain national assets, as a "hostage" situation in international disputes, for example the seizure of Union Carbide's assets after the Bhopal disaster in India. Other government activity, which affects capital investment includes joint venturing insistence and repatriation of funds. "Partnering" remains widespread (inward investment in tandem with a domestic company) as does restrictions on repatriation of funds. In Zimbabwe, for example, HJ Heinz, the multinational food agent, has entered into partnership with Olivine industries. Over time, even if initially the investment is not favourable, the Government may relax its conditions as it sees the benefits.

  If expropriation is a real possibility then the investor should seek to minimise risk by:

  - Relatively rapid depreciation of assets and repatriation of funds by manipulated transfer prices
  - Establish a local supply infrastructure so that any adverse action damages the host economy
  - Raise as much investment capital in the country as possible
  - Retain control of critical inputs and minimise local stocks of these.

However these measures may increase the risk of expropriation or reduce the potential success of the venture.

Incentives: Many countries try to reduce perceived risk by promoting inward investment through the provision of tax breaks, free ports, enterprise zones etc., which are not tied as in partnering.

The key is to look at what the disadvantages are. If the government mainly wishes to attract the mobile investor, or overcome say poor local skills, one has to assess what would happen if the plan was withdrawn once the capital had been committed. Similarly if viability depends on incentives rather than real return on investment, the question is, is the venture really worth it?

Assessing Political Vulnerability

Political vulnerability should be assessed by using a systematic checklist.

Such a checklist should include the following:

- The firm's own country's relations with other countries
- Sensitivity of the product or industry
- Size and location of operation - the bigger the more vulnerable
- Visibility of firm - is it high profile say via advertising?
- Host country's political situation
- Company behaviour - is it a good corporate citizen?
- Contribution to host country, *for example, employment*
- Localisation of operations
- Subsidiary dependence.

Depending on the answers to these checkpoints, the amount of risk, real or perceived, can be assessed and fed into the investment discussion.

Marketing Implications

Political factors give rise to a number of marketing implications.

These include the following:

- Is the product ever subject to political debate regarding adequacy of supply, *for example, oil?*
- Is the product a critical input for other industries, *for example, cement?*
- Is the product socially or politically sensitive, *for example, food?*
- Is the product of national defence significance?
- Is the product taking a disproportional amount of capital repayment?
- Is the product leading to the locus of control being held outside of the host country?

Again, the answers to these questions will enable the marketer to assess the degree to which the product being marketed has to be priced and resourced, so as to either avoid or reduce the risk of expropriation or other political reactions.

THE LEGAL ENVIRONMENT

The international legal framework is somewhat confused. Most controls or regulations revolve around export and import controls, transfer pricing, taxes, regulation of corrupt practices, embargoed nations, antitrust, expropriation and distribution of equity, patents and trademarks. The following touches on a number of these issues and in particular the import/ export regulations.

International Law

To many, the supreme body is the International Court of Justice, situated in The Hague, Holland. Here a number of international disputes may be taken for ultimate adjudication. However, a series of other bodies and legislation exists.

- *FCN*: (Friendship, Commerce and Navigation) and Tax Treaties primarily US based and concerned with giving protection of trading rights and avoiding double taxation.
- *IMF* and *GATT* and concerned with member nations international trade restrictions and dumping.
- *UNCITRAL*: (UN) international trade law commission set up with the intent to provide a uniform commercial code for the whole world, particularly international sales and payments, commercial arbitration and shipping legislation. Works with international chambers of commerce and Governments.
- *ISO:* (International Standards Organisation) often works with ILO, WHO etc. and contains technical committees working on uniform standards.
- Patents and trademarks there is no such thing as international patent. The most important patent agreement is the International Convention for the Protection of Industrial Property, first signed in 1983 and now honoured by 45 countries. The treaty provides that if a filee files in a signatory country within one year of the first filing, the filee will be afforded the date of the first filing for priority purposes.

  A patent cooperation treaty (PCT) and a European Patent Convention are also in effect. The PCT has 39 countries including the USA, Japan and Brazil. The EU convention covers 15 countries and gives patent protection in all 15 if signified in one.
- Air transport is covered mainly by IATA (International Air Transport Authority), ICAA (International Civil Aviation Authority) and ITU (International Telecommunication Company).
- Codes of conduct, like those in the OECP, are not technical law but important. Member countries produce guidelines for

multinational enterprises covering aspects of general policy, disclosure of information, competition, financing, taxation, employment and industrial relations.

- Recourse arbitration is an attempt to reduce disputes by consultation. Some of the most widely used are the International Chamber of Commerce, the American Arbitration Association, the London Court of Arbitration and the Liverpool Cotton Exchange.

Marketing Implications

The implications of international law on marketing operations are legion.

The principle ones are as follows:

- *Product decisions*: Physical, chemical, safety, performance, packaging, labelling, warranty
- *Pricing decisions*: Price controls, resale price maintenance, price freezes, value added systems and taxation
- *Distribution*: Contracts for agents and distribution, physical distribution, insurance
- *Promotion*: Advertising codes of practice, product restriction, sales promotion
- *Market research*: Collection, storage and transmission of data.

TERMS OF ACCESS

One particular area where legal/political effects are felt by international marketers is in the terms of access. The phrase "terms of access" refers to all the conditions that apply to the importation of goods from a foreign country. The major instruments covered by this phrase include import duties, import restrictions or quotas, foreign exchange regulations and preference arrangements.

Tariff Systems

Tariff systems provide either a single rate of duty for each item applicable to all countries, or two or more rates, applicable to different countries or groups of countries.

Tariffs are usually grouped into two classifications:

- *Single-column tariff*: The single-column tariff is the simplest type of tariff and consists of a schedule of duties in which the rate applies to imports from all countries on the same basis.
- *Two-column tariff*: Under the two-column tariff, the initial single column of duties is supplemented by a second column of "conventional" duties which show reduced rates agreed through tariff negotiations with other countries. The conventional rates, for example those agreed upon

by "convention", are supplied to all countries enjoying MFN (most favoured nation) treatment within the framework of GATT. Under GATT, nations agree to apply their most favourable tariff or lowest tariff rate to all nations who are signatories to GATT, with some substantial exceptions.

Preferential Tariff

A preferential tariff is a reduced tariff rate applied to imports from certain countries. GATT prohibits the use of preferential tariffs with the major exceptions of historical preference plans, such as the British Commonwealth preferences and similar arrangements that existed before the GATT convention; preference plans that are part of a formal economic integration treaty, such as free-trade areas or common markets; and the granting of preferential access to industrial country markets to companies based in less-developed countries.

Types of Duty

Customs duties are of two different types. They are calculated either as a specific amount per unit or specific duty, or as a percentage of the value of the goods or ad valorem, or as a combination of both of these methods.

- *Ad valorem duties*: This duty is expressed as a percentage of the value of goods. The definition of customs value varies from country to country. Therefore an exporter is well advised to secure information about the valuation practices applied to his product in the country of destination. A uniform basis for the valuation of goods for customs purposes was elaborated by the Customs Cooperation Council in Brussels and was adopted in 1953. In countries adhering to the Brussels convention on customs valuation, the customs value is landed CIF cost at the port of entry. This cost should reflect the arm's-length price of the goods at the time the duty becomes payable. Major trading nations that are not members of the Brussels convention on customs valuation are the USA and Canada, which use FOB costs as the basis of valuation, and Japan, which uses CIF value.
- *Specific duties:* These duties are expressed as a specific amount of currency per unit of weight, volume, length or number of other units of measurements; for example, fifty US cents per pound, one dollar per pair, twenty-five cents per square yard. Specific duties are usually expressed in the currency of the importing country, but there are exceptions, particularly in countries that have experienced sustained inflation. In the Chilean tariff, rates are given in gold pesos and, therefore, must be multiplied by an established conversion factor to obtain the corresponding amount of escudos.

- *Alternative duties*: In this case both ad valorem and specific duties are set out in the custom tariff for a given product. Normally, the applicable rate is the one that yields the higher amount of duty, although there are cases where the lower is specified.
- *Compound or mixed duties*: These duties provide for specific plus ad valorem rates to be levied on the same substances.
- *Anti-dumping dunes*: The term dumping refers to the sale of a product at a price lower than that normally charged in a domestic market or country of origin. To offset the impact of dumping, most countries have introduced legislation providing for the imposition of antidumping duties if injury is caused to domestic producers. Such duties take the form of special additional import charges designed to cover the difference between the export price and the "normal" price, which usually refers to the price paid by consumers in the exporting countries. Anti-dumping duties are almost invariably applied to substances that are produced in the importing country.

Other Import Charges

Variable import levies: Several countries, including Sweden and the European Union, apply a system of variable import levies to their imports of various agricultural products. The objective of these levies is to raise the price of imported products to the domestic price level.

- *Temporary import surcharges*: Temporary surcharges have been introduced from time to time by certain countries, such as the UK and the USA, to provide additional protection for local industry and, in particular, in response to balance of payments deficits.
- *Compensatory import taxes:* In theory these taxes correspond with various international taxes, such as value-added taxes and sales taxes. Such "border tax adjustments" must not, GATT, amount to additional protection for domestic producers or to a subsidy for exports. In practice, one of the major tax inequities today is the fact that manufacturers in value-added tax (VAT) countries do not pay a value added tax on sales to non-VAT countries such as the USA while USA manufacturers who pay income taxes in the USA must also pay VAT taxes on sales in VAT countries. For example, EU imposition of a tax on imported horticultural products.
- *Adaptation to meet local requirements:* The impact of adaptation to conform to local safety and other requirements can be crippling. For example, a Jaguar car made in the UK and sold in Japan would be three times its UK value. An alternative approach to the Japanese market would be to begin with the Japanese customer to identify

the customer's wants and needs and to design a product for that market or to adapt the design to a world design that would fit the needs and wants in both the domestic and the Japanese markets. The implementation of such a programme would involve major marketing investments by the Jaguar Motor Company in establishing distribution, advertising and promotion, training and developing organisations to market the car in Japan. It would also involve significant expenditures in designing the car to appeal to the needs of the Japanese customer.

The Kennedy Round and the General Agreement on Tariffs and Trade (GATT)

A major development of the 1960s was a series of agreements negotiated in the 1963-67 period, popularly known as the "Kennedy Round". During these negotiations, tariff concessions on nonagricultural products by the four largest industrial participants -the USA, the UK, Japan, and the EEC - averaged slightly more than 35 per cent and covered about $20 billion of trade. On agricultural products, excluding grains, the average reduction by the major industrial countries amounted to about 20 per cent and affected about one-half of the dutiable imports. Tariff reductions under the agreement took place in five equal instalments. The first was concluded on January 1, 1968 and the last on January 1, 1972. Over 60 thousand items were involved, representing approximately $40 billion in world trade annually.

At the cease of the Kennedy Round negotiations, tariffs on dutiable nonagricultural products averaged 9.9 per cent in the USA, 8.6 per cent in the EEC, 10.8 per cent in the UK and 10.7 per cent in Japan. A second "Tokyo Round" of trade negotiations was undertaken by the 97 nation GATT in the 1970s. The target in these negotiations, which were still under way in 1979, was to achieve another 35 per cent tariff reduction. The latest GATT round, the so called Uruguay Round, was long held up over subsidy wranglings between the EU and the USA. However in early 1994, an agreement was concluded, but is yet to be ratified by all signatories.

When the European Union and the USA agreed to bury their differences (primarily over subsidies and trade in television and films) on Tuesday 14 December 1992, the way was cleared for the signing of the eighth General Agreement on Tariffs and Trade (GATT) in April 1994 in Morocco, only two days before the deadline. Whilst only 20 countries took part in the first round signed in Geneva in 1947, the current round boasts 116 participants. After failing to meet two deadlines in 1990 and 1991, many thought the Uruguay round would never be concluded. However, completion of the North American Free Trade Agreement (NAFTA) and the hints of the development of a similar trading block in the Asian-Pacific Region (APEC), helped focus the minds of the negotiators.

The principal aim in the early days of GATT was to cut tariffs and to this end average tariffs have fallen from almost 40% to 4.7% and now it will be as little as 3% if the Uruguay round succeeds. GATT has, over the years, gradually gone into other areas. The Kennedy Round introduced rules against dumping exports, the Tokyo Round made it harder for countries to manipulate technical standards, import licences and customs regulations in order to keep imports out. GATT basically stands to defuse trade tension between countries and smaller countries enjoy better access to larger countries' markets through GATT than they could if they had negotiated by themselves.

The new package, which covers ten times the value of the previous seven GATT Rounds put together, touches on more than four billion Sterling Pounds worth of International Trade, nearly twenty times the size of UK's annual budget. Economists reckon that the Uruguay Round will add about $270 billion to world income within a decade and boost global trade by more than 12%. The deal also creates a powerful international bureaucracy, the World Trade Organisation (WTO) to police world trade and performance as a bulwark against a return to the economic protectionism which proceeded war in the 1930s. But not all countries will gain. Africa will be a net loser, with Nigeria down by $1,0 billion. Other fears are that Africa will lose out on agricultural prices but textiles will get a boast. The proposed effects are shown in figure.

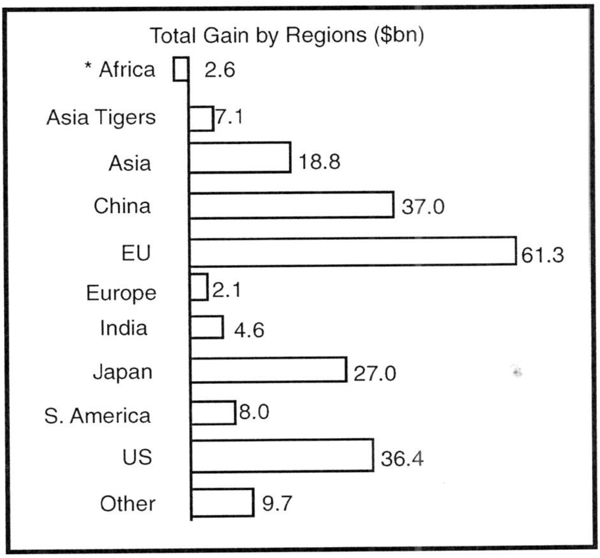

Fig. Total in Agriculture $73 Billion; Textiles $85 Billion Services $29 Billion; Other $23 Billion Total $209.4 Billion

NON-TARIFF BARRIERS

With the success of the Uruguay Round tariff negotiations, attention has naturally turned to the remaining non-tariff obstacles to trade.

A non-tariff trade barrier is defined by economists as any measure, public or private, that causes internationally traded goods and services to be allocated in such a way as to reduce potential real-world income.

Potential real-world income is the attainable level when resources are allocated in the most economically efficient manner. To the businessman a non-tariff barrier is any measure, other than tariffs, that provides a barrier or obstacle to the sale of his products in a foreign market.

The major non-tariff trade barriers are as follows:

- *Quotas and trade control*: These are specific limits and controls. The trade distortion of a quota is even more severe than a tariff because once the quota has been filled, the price mechanism is not allowed to operate. The good is simply unavailable at any price. "State trading" refers to the practice of monopolising trade in certain commodities. In communist countries all commodities are monopolised, but there are many examples of non-communist government monopolies: the Swedish government controls the import of all alcoholic beverages and tobacco products, and the French government controls all imports of coal.
- *Discriminatory government and private procurement policies*: These are the rules and regulations that discriminate against foreign supplies and are commonly referred to as "Buy British" or "Buy American" policies.

RESTRICTIVE CUSTOMS PROCEDURES

The rules and regulations for classifying and valuing commodities as a basis for levying import duties can be administered in a way that makes compliance difficult and expensive.

SELECTIVE MONETARY CONTROLS AND DISCRIMINATORY EXCHANGE RATE POLICIES

Discriminatory exchange rate policies distort trade in much the same way as selective import duties and export subsidies. Selective monetary policies are definite barriers to trade. For example, many countries from time to time require importers to place on deposit at no interest an amount equal to the value of imported goods. These regulations in effect raise the price of foreign goods by the cost of money for the term of the required deposit.

RESTRICTIVE ADMINISTRATIVE AND TECHNICAL REGULATIONS

These include anti-dumping regulations, size regulations and safety and health regulations. Some of these regulations are intended to keep out foreign foods while others are directed towards legitimate domestic objectives. For example, the safety and pollution regulations being developed in the United States for automobiles are motivated almost entirely by legitimate concerns about highway safety and pollution. However, an effect of the regulations, particularly on smaller foreign manufacturers, has been to make it so expensive to comply with US safety requirements that they have withdrawn from the market.

In 1969 GATT published a 276 page report listing non-tariff barriers to trade. This report, which listed such obscure items as an Italian sanitary tax on foreign snake poison, is already out of date.

Packaging or pesticide regulations often erect a hurdle for exports, but not insurmountably so. The EU has strict hygiene requirements for imports of horticultural produce for Africa which require strict observance. Producers of restrictive administrative regulations are incredibly creative in establishing barriers to trade.

This can be seen in the following case: The example emphasizes how difficult it is to deal with non-tariff barriers to trade. The Mexicans could protest the decisions of the US Department of Agriculture, but the Florida growers who were competing with the Mexican growers, in effect, wrote their own regulations. They maintained that the regulations worked for the benefit of everyone: growers on both sides of the border and the consumer. A strong case could be made for the harm done by these regulations to Mexican growers and US consumers, but the mechanism for hearing this case did not really exist. The Mexican growers could influence this decision by pressuring the US government through diplomatic channels, or try to appeal directly to consumers and thereby influence legislative and administrative action in government. An important test of a ruling or regulation is whether it has a greater impact on foreign producers. If this is the case, and there is no apparent social benefit for consumers, the ruling is a non-tariff barrier.

TARIFF CLASSIFICATION

Before World War II specific duties were widely used and the tariffs of many countries, particularly those in Europe and Latin America, were extremely complex. Since the war the trend has been towards the conversion to ad valorem duties. Tariff administration has been simplified by the adoption by a large number of countries of the Brussels nomenclature (BTN). This nomenclature was worked out by an international committee of experts under the sponsorship of the Customs Cooperation Council, which in 1955 produced a convention that entered into force in 1959.

The rules of this convention are now being applied by most GATT countries. Approximately two-thirds of all world trade is now conducted under tariffs based on the BTN system. It is significant, however, that among major trading nations neither the USA nor Canada uses the BTN.

The BTN groups substances mainly according to the material from which they are made. For less-developed countries, it is both easy to use and applicable to the goods they produce. An additional advantage of the BTN is its widespread use. A common basis for the classification of goods facilitates comparison of duties applied by different countries and simplifies international tariff negotiations. In spite of the progress made in simplifying tariff procedures, the task of administrating a tariff presents an enormous problem. Even a tariff schedule of several thousand items cannot clearly describe every product that enters into international trade. The constant flow of new products and new materials used in manufacturing processes introduces new problems. Often, two or more alternative classifications must be considered in assessing the rate on a particular substance depending upon how it is used or its component material.

The classification of a product can make a substantial difference in the duty applied. There are two important implications of this fact for export marketers. The first is that exporters should seek the most favourable classification for their products in order to minimise the duty levied in the importing country. The second is that the difficulties of classification raise serious questions about the accuracy of data on international trade patterns. When using international trade data, it is important to bear in mind the enormous problems posed by classification and recognize that the numbers in trade reports may often reflect hasty and arbitrary classifications that distort the true picture of the trade flow.

Evidence of the inaccuracy of grade classification practices is provided by frequent failure of import and export figures of the same commodity to reconcile between two countries. Some clever marketers seek to get their products reclassified in order to get a lower tariff structure.

WINDS OF CHANGE

The emergence of Japan in the 1970s and 80s, coupled with more trade between developing countries, harmed the balance of payments of the Western economies. Coupled with oil shocks and debt crises, attitudes to trade changed somewhat in the 1980s. In effect free trade was reversed. The Industry and Development Global Report made a series of observations showing that whilst expansion of demand was there, it was patchy and therefore in some sectors excess occurred. Coupled with plans like the CAP of the EU (Common Agricultural Policy of the European Union) which produced "mountains" of butter, sugar, etc., this excess led to downward pressure on prices which newly emerging nations may be better equipped to deal with if raw materials are banned in country.

The growth of economic unions like the EU which are limited multilateral organisations have undermined the strength of GATT agreements but only in so far as non-tariff barriers are concerned. Such non-tariff barriers may merely be devices to soften up foreign rivals and force them into regulatory voluntary restrictions on trade.

The main non-tariff barriers of recent times have been countervailing duty and anti-dumping. Protectionist measures like these can reduce global opportunities in direct ways (imposition of quotas, Health and Safety Standards, etc.), affect the attractiveness of marketing offers to intermediaries by affecting market price (tariffs), volume (voluntary restraints) and uncertainty ("proved" dumping cases) or they reduce opportunities by affecting the attractiveness of your offer to end users (cancelling out price advantages).

Anti-dumping is the worst form of protection because anti-dumping creates uncertainty for producers and intermediaries, one needs not be "guilty" to be penalized for it. Anyone entering the industry after a charge of dumping against it will face the highest rate of levy. They can be fined and therefore be driven away and as a result consumers will suffer. In order to circumvent protection, options include avoiding certain commodities or industries, teaming up with local contacts, producing from inside the market or self regulation.

The legal/political system is a minefield, with few international standards or regulations to fall back on. Thankfully, for many agricultural products and agribusinesses like timber, fish, livestock and so on, the rules are fairly well defined. However, change can occur very quickly. The imposition of a transport levy by the South Africans affected Zimbabwe's drought relief programme costs, and the increase of duties by 40% by the same country are hitting Zimbabwe's clothing exports there very hard. Zimbabwe and Botswana, who enjoy large beef quotas with the EU, can be affected overnight by a ban. On a number of occasions the EU has imposed a ban on beef exports from Zimbabwe because of a so called "foot and mouth" outbreak in Zimbabwe, Although minor in scale, its consequences can be major for the industry. Marketers are beholden to always keep a constant watch on changes which are and could occur in the legal/political environment.

COUNTRY RISK ANALYSIS

Country risk refers to the risk of investing in a country, dependent on changes in the business environment that may adversely affect operating profits or the value of assets in a specific country. *For example, financial factors such as currency controls, devaluation or regulatory changes, or stability factors such as mass riots, civil war and other potential events contribute to companies' operational risks.* This term is also sometimes referred to as political risk, however country risk is a more general term, which generally only refers to risks affecting all companies operating within a particular country.

Political risk analysis providers and credit rating agencies use different methodologies to assess and rate countries' comparative risk exposure. Credit rating agencies tend to use quantitative econometric models and focus on financial analysis, whereas political risk providers tend to use qualitative methods, focusing on political analysis. However, there is no consensus on methodology in assessing credit and political risks.

2

The Global Economic Environment is Changing Rapidly

AN OVERVIEW

In the past fifty years the global economy has changed rapidly. Particularly marked has been the development of world economic integration and standardised products. Coca Cola, Nissan and Marlboro cigarettes are examples of products which serve nearly every market.

Generally there have been four major changes:

- Capital movements rather than trade have become the driving force of the global economy
- Production has become "uncoupled" from employment
- Primary products have become "uncoupled" from the industrial economy and,
- The world economy is in control - individual nations are not, despite the large world economic share of the USA and Japan.

Taking each of these changes in turn, world trade is about some US$ 3 trillion, however, capital movements are much higher. The London Eurodollar market is worth about US$ 75 trillion per annum and foreign exchange transactions are US$ 35 trillion per annum.

Another change is the decoupling of employment from production. Employment is in decline whilst manufacturing output is growing or remaining static at 20-25% of GNP. Sectors such as agriculture, are achieving higher productivity through mechanisation but this is at the expense of employment. Still another change is the decoupling of the primary product market from the industrial economy. Many commodity prices have collapsed, *for example tea,* yet industrial economies have been relatively affected. Unfortunately the prime producers have been dramatically affected.

Finally, the most significant change is the change of focus from domestic to the world economy as the chief economic unit. This has been grasped by Japan and Germany, but not really by the USA, or Africa. These factors have repercussions on exporting by developing countries. Firstly with developing countries' emphasis on the export of primary products, they are at the mercy of world supply and demand movements, with the resultant fluctuations in prices.

Depressed world market prices can have a deleterious effect on developing economies. Secondly the rapid globalisation and focus away from domestic economies has created global competition and in turn, this has pushed up quality. Generally speaking, unless developing countries can break into non-comittally based products they are being further left behind in the global economic stakes. However positively, whilst developed worlds concentrate on industrial and service products it leaves opportunities for developing countries to export more food based products.

GLOBAL ECONOMY

The development of the global economy can be traced back many hundreds of years when traders from the east and west came together to exchange goods. However, the growth of the modern global economy is marked by a number of features as follows:

Legacy of Mercantilism 1500-1750

The prevalent wisdom was one of nationalism, that is, that one nation prospered at the expense of another. Nations like the UK, Netherlands and later France and Germany, with powerful navies which ruled the waves in the West, and the traders of the East, dominated that area. Over time, nationalism gave way to bullionism, where gold and silver, rather than other raw materials, became the basis of wealth. Still later, domination took another form, where countries were believed to be powerful if they had a favourable balance of trade - an excess of exports over imports. Mercantilism died with the development of the United Nations (UN) and the General Agreement on Tariffs and Trade (GATT), along with Adam Smith's tome on the "Wealth of Nations" which advocated market forces as the principal driving force to development and wealth.

World Trade

Economic progress is linked to world trade and those who preach trade restrictions are denying this fact. Countries like the old communist bloc have not developed as fast as those with more outward orientation. The same can be said of African nations, where the inability to industrialise and export in volume has locked them into, generally, primary product producers. Economic Structural Adjustment Programmes (ESAP) are supposed to remedy this situation by giveng "command economies" a market oriented focus.

Another argument concerns whether marketing has relevance to the process of economic development. Less developed countries (LDCs) have traditionally focused on production and domestic income generation. Also, marketing addresses itself to needs and wants and it could be argued that where LDCs' productive capabilities are far less than unsatisfied needs and wants, then marketing is superfluous. However, adopting "marketing" could lead to the more efficient and effective use of productive and marketing resources and it may be able to focus on current needs and find better solutions.

For example, techniques developed in the West for optimising transport resources could well be transferred to effect. Similarly, adopting new methods of marketing may give better results. A good example is the Cold Storage Company of Zimbabwe (CSC). By changing from the current system of marketing cattle (the CSC takes in cattle, at fixed prices and slaughters) to an auction system by description, all actors in the system could benefit. Decisions in product, price, communications and merchandising can stimulate economic development. Changing from fixed price systems to market based pricing could lead to the faster achievement of development objectives (for example "higher incomes"). In current drought conditions in Africa, governments could well benefit from advertising other forms of nutritious food, for example, fish, rather than let the populace be left uninformed and disgruntled about the lack of maize.

Composition of World Trade

Agriculture, minerals, fuels and manufactured goods figure most in world trade. However shifts are occurring.

Table Shift in Commodity Trade -% of World Trade

Product	1980	1985%	1988%
Agriculture	22.5	1	14
Minerals	14	-5	14
Fuel	41	-3.5	1
Manufactures	17	4.5	1

Interestingly enough, those economies which have divested themselves of agriculture (or made it more efficient) and invested in manufacturing are those which have shown spectacular growth. Table compares Zimbabwe with Thailand.

Patterns of Trade

Most industrialised nations trade with each other. This had led to their continued domination. particularly the USA, Western Europe and Japan which between them have 66% of world GNP and trade. In 1985 industrialised trade to other industrialised countries accounted for 47% of trade, next came developing countries to industrialised and finally industrialised to developing countries (13%). Political influences can also be seen between trading partners, for example Zimbabwe's trade with China.

Marketers need to identify trading patterns between nations and product trading patterns. East-West trade and West to the former communist bloc is likely to grow at the expense of North-South trade.

Table. Structure of Production

			Distribution of GDP %							
Country	GDP $ m		Agriculture		Industry		Manufacturing		Services	
	1970	1992	1970	1992	1970	1992	1970	1992	1970	1992
Zimbabwe	1415	5350	15	22	36	35	21	30	49	43
Thailand	7087	110337	26	12	25	39	16	28	49	49

This pattern is repeated throughout Africa and Asia in general.

Comparative Costs - comparative Advantage

Price has been called the immediate basis for international trade - cheaper prices based on different cost structures, especially labour. Countries trade because they produce and export goods in which they enjoy a greater comparative advantage and import goods in which they have a least comparative advantage.

Balance of Payments

This is the measure of all economic transactions between one nation and another. The balance of payments is made up of the current account, showing trade in goods and services; and the capital account, which shows financial transactions. In 1989, after official transfers, the USA had a US$ 109,242 million deficit on its current account, Japan had a $ 131,400 million surplus, Tanzania a $ 778,5 million deficit and Zimbabwe a $ 2,783 million deficit. The balance of payments account helps marketers select the location of supply for foreign markets and the selection of markets. The capital account may show the nations which have control restrictions and hence be difficult to deal with. In this regard, African nations are generally disadvantaged.

Government Policy

This refers to the government measures and regulations which have a bearing on trade - tariffs, quotas, exchange controls and invisible tariffs. These can cause formidable barriers to marketers and will be dealt with at length later.

World Institutions

Institutions like GATT and the United Nations Conference on Trade and Development (UNCTAD) have been of help to countries in their development. GATT had over 120 members and associated and accounted for 80% of world trade. Its intention was to create a general system of preferences and negotiate tariffs for members' products on a nondiscriminant basis and provide a forum for consultation.

The Kennedy Round of the 1960s was superseded by the Tokyo round of the 1970s and that by the current Uruguay round signed in 1994. UNCTAD furthers the development of emerging nations. It seeks to improve the prices of primary goods exports through commodity agreements. It also established a tariff preference system favouring developing nations.

Regionalism

Regionalism is a major and important trade development. Some regional groupings have either market (EU) or command (China) or mixed economies (former communist countries and The Preferential Trade Area (PTA) and The Southern African Development Community (SADC). With these developments, free trade zones have occurred (all internal barriers abolished) economic unions (the EU), export pricing zones (Mauritius) and other plans.

The major regional economic organisations are: Acuerdo de Cartegna (Andean Group), Association of South East Nations (ASEAN), Asian Pacific Rim countries (APC), Caribbean Community and Common Market (CARICOM), Central American Common Market (Mercado Comùn Centro Americano), Council of Arab Economic Unity, Economic Community of West African States (ECOWAS), the European Union (EU), Latin American Integration Association, Organisation Commune Africane et Mauricienne, Preferential Trade Area (PTA) and the Southern African Development Conference (SADC). A principal collapse has been the Council for Economic Assistance (COMECON) with the disappearance of the communist bloc in Eastern Europe. Of these blocs, the EU (reporting 33% of world trade) and EFTA are very important. To counteract the growing power of the EU, the USA and Canada have entered into an agreement with Mexico as a willing partner and created the North American Free Trade Agreement (NAFTA).

These blocs are of various form, power, influence and success. ASEAN is a collaboration of industry and agriculture, PTA in tariffs. SADC and PTA have had historically little impact but are now beginning to grow in importance in view of the normalisation of South Africa. The EU, North American Union and the Pacific Rim Union will pose the greatest power blocs in future years. Many developing countries have entered into trading blocks as a reaction against loss of developed country markets or as a base to build economic integration and markets. The development of trading blocs can bring headaches and advantages to trade. It is worth comparing the European Union, a relatively well developed bloc, with SADC and the PTA which are well developed.

The International Financial System

Global financing operations based on the gold standard gave rise to instability, so Bretton Woods, post World War II, saw the nascence of the International Monetary Fund (IMF) and World Bank. The IMF deals with the International Monetary System. Involved countries joined IMF to establish a par value for other countries in terms of the US dollar and maintain it with +/- one per cent of that value.

The system fell down because large corporations were holding more funds than banks and so a "float" set in. IMF began to fade somewhat. However it still lends, on a short term basis, to countries with payment problems to help them continue trading. The World Bank, or International Bank for Reconstruction and Development (IBRD) deals with international capital. It provides long term capital to aid economic development. Currently it has about US$ 22 billion annually for this operation. The role of the World Bank has often been criticised especially on its conditionalities for loans to Africa in funding structural adjustment and trade liberalisation programmes. However many developing countries require institutional funding to help them with trade and balance payment problems.

Other major lenders include the EU and bilateral donors and agencies who have provided money for developmental projects. A principal donor is the United States Agency for International Development (USAID).

The United States of America

Since the Gulf War of 1991, the USA has played an increasingly important role in the economic affairs of the world. Since that time, itself, and its agency USAID, have increasingly flexed their muscles. However, the balance of economic power in recent years, has shifted towards the Pacific rim, especially Japan and the Asian Tigers.

Individual Economies

Whilst the global factors have aided the development of a world economy, marketers must consider carefully individual economies. A study of these helps answer the questions - how big is the market and what is it like? Currently there are over 200 individual countries in the world.

Size of Market

General indications of market size include population (growth rates and distribution) and income (distribution, per capita, GNP).

- *Population*: In general, the larger the population, the bigger the market. However there is no correlation between income level and population. China has 2 billion plus people, India 1 billion, Zimbabwe 8 million. However, they do not have the same income per capita as the USA or UK. In 1993 the USA population of 252.2 million, the UK 57.4 million and Africa 400 million, were respectively 6%, 1.5% and 9% of the world's population. However the USA and UK had an infinitely higher GNP per capita income than Africa, US$ 22,520, UK $17,300 and Africa $ 270 respectively.

Different countries experience different population growth rates. In the early 90s, the UK had an annual growth rate of 0.1%, the Ivory Coast 6%, and Africa in general, 3% per annum. Low income countries and oil rich countries have the largest growth rates. Growth rates have a dual edge - they are good for sales but bad for world resources. The world population, currently standing at 5 billion is experiencing a rapid growth rate. It is expected to reach 7 billion by the end of the century. The strain on world resources is likely to be very large. The distribution of the population is also important. Different age groups have different needs and population density should mean good market potential, the higher the better. The Netherlands have 1000 persons per square mile, Bangladesh 1,791 but the USA only 65 persons per square mile. However, the USA spends more per capita than Bangladesh

- *Income*: No one has yet been able to assess accurately the impact of the AIDS pandemic on world population and economic activity. South Africa estimates AIDS will cost South African industry R16.7 billion by the year 2000. Suffice to say, unless a cure or prevention is found, it could be serious, especially in Africa and South East Asia, the world's "hot spots"

Income is the most important variable affecting market potential. Markets are not markets without money to spend. Interestingly, there is an inverse correlation between GNP per capita and income elasticity of demand for food. Asia has a 0.9 income elasticity of demand and the USA 0.16.

The distribution of income is very uneven. In Kenya the lowest 20% of the population receive less then 3% of national resource. This bimodal distribution of income means marketers must analyse two economies in a country. Per capita measures have therefore, many limitations. Per capita judges a country's level of economic development and its degree of modernisation and progress in health, education and welfare. Half of the world's population lives with an average per capita income of only US$ 270. Per capita is usually reflected in US dollars and is only valid for comparison if exchange rates are equal. Exchange rates reflect international goods and services in a country but not domestic consumption.

Another limitation of per capita measures is the lack of comparability with the figures themselves. The US budget contains food, clothing and shelter. In many of the less developed nations these items may be largely self provided and therefore not reflected in national income tables. Also in the UK, snow equipment is included, and this is not, obviously, in Africa and parts of Asia.

Other limitations are that sales of goods are not well correlated with per capita income and if there is great unevenness in income distribution, per capita figures are less meaningful. Product saturation can be equally troublesome in affecting market potential. A vacuum cleaner in the Netherlands has a 95% household penetration rate, but only 7% in Italy.

Gross National Product is a better indicator of potential than Gross Domestic Product as GDP includes more than "product". World GNP figures reveal the concentration of wealth in the three nations, the USA, Japan and Western Europe. Africa trails far behind.

However, when evaluating markets it is wise to consider individual product areas. For example, Belgium's GNP is better than India's but India's, consumption of steel is 3 times that of Belgium's.

Table GDP and GNP of Selected Countries

	GDP US$ bn	% of World	GNP US$ bn	% of World
USA	5670	35	3000	29
UK	903	6	540	5
Africa	322	3	220	3

The United Nations International Comparison Project (ICP) developed a sophisticated method for measuring total expenditure, which has been used to derive more reliable and directly comparable estimates of per capita income. The World Bank has published a comparison of ICP findings with its own Atlas figures based on the exchange rate conversion. The use of exchange rates tends to distort real income or standard of living measures.

The Nature of Economy

More than money makes up an economy's economic environment. Natural resources -raw materials now and in the future are important. If synthetic gold or tobacco were developed or, in the case of the latter, became unfashionable, Zimbabwe's economy would be ruined. Topography may produce two, three or more submarkets in a country.

Zambia, for example, has "rural" and "urban" areas with different needs and wants. Extremes of climate - like the Southern African drought in 1992 can devastate economies and derail any economic development plans and exports. Simply, products are not available to export, because they are being consumed by the domestic economy.

The Nature of Economic Activity

Economic activity is often correlated to the type of economic activity. Various methods have been derived to classify economies.

Stages of Market Development

Global markets are at different stages of development which can be divided into five categories based on the criterion of gross national product per capita.

- *Preindustrial countries*: Incomes less than USS 400 GNP per capita. Limited industrialisation, low literacy rates, high birth rates, heavy reliance on foreign aid, political instability. Parts of Sub-Saharan Africa. Little market potential.
- *Less developed countries*: Per capita between US$ 401 and US$ 1,635. Early stages of industrialisation, growing domestic market, mature product markets, increasing competitive threat.
- *Developing countries*: Per capita income between US$ 1,636 and US $ 5,500. Decrease in percentage of agricultural workers, industrialisation, rising wages, high literacy rates, lower wage rates than developed countries, formidable competitors.
- *Industrialised countries* - per capita income between US$ 5,501 and US$ 10,000. Moving towards post industrialisation, high standard of living.
- *Advanced countries*: Per capita income in excess of US$ 10,000. Post industrialisation, information processors, knowledge based, less machine based. Product opportunities are in new products, innovations and raw materials plus fresh foods.

World Bank Classification

The World Bank has drawn up a classification of economies based on GNP per capita.

- Low income economies, China and India, other low-income-GNP per capita income of between US$ 675 or less, 41 nations including Tanzania, Kenya, Zambia and Malawi.
- Middle income economies, lower middle income, GNP per capita of between US$ 676 and US$ 2,695, 40 nations including Zimbabwe, Mexico and Thailand.
- Upper middle income, GNP per capita of between US$ 2,676 and US$ 8,355, 17 nations including Brazil, Portugal and Greece.
- High income economies, OECD members and others, GNP per capita of between US$ 8,356 or more, 24 nations including UK and the USA.
- Other economies - communist bloc.

Mozambique and Switzerland are the two extreme ends of the spectrum with US$ 80 per capita and US$ 29,880 per capita respectively.

Rostow: Whilst economic in nature, Rostow produced a five stage model of economic takeoff:

- Stage 1 traditional society, little increase in productivity, no modern science application systematically, low level of literacy
- Stage 2 the preconditions of takeoff, modern techniques in agriculture and production, developments in infrastructure and social institutions

- Stage 3 the takeoff, normal growth patterns, rapid agricultural and industrial modernisation, good social environment.
- Stage 4 the drive to maturity, modern technology applied to all fronts, international involvement, can produce anything
- Stage 5 the age of high mass consumption, production of durable goods and services, large amounts of

These classifications enable marketers to assess where and how to operate in countries which may display the stage characteristics. For example African exporters would look to stage 4 and 5 economies to obtain the greatest revenue opportunities for other produce.

Another way to assess the market alternatives to a potential global marketer is to look at the origin of its national product - is it farm or factory generated? Farm workers tend to have low incomes. Input-output tables provide other insights into a country's potential, that is, what inputs go into a particular industry's output? What combination of labour, materials and equipment?

Infrastructure

Infrastructure is a very important element in considering whether to market in a country or not. Transportation, for example, is vital. Zambia and Zimbabwe are landlocked and have relatively poor transport facilities. Tanzania, whilst having direct access to the coast, has also a relatively poor internal rural infrastructure. Chaos can therefore ensue, especially during the rainy season. Without being able to get produce to the point of exportation, countries will suffer poor export performance accordingly. Energy consumption shows the overall industrialisation of a society as does its infrastructure. The less energy is consumed, the less likely the development of the market resulting in a not too attractive market proposition.

Communications are essential. India has only some 10 million telephones to a population of 1 billion people. Media availability is important. Zambia has 680 radios per 1000 population, France 2,059 per 1000. Malawi has no domestic television service but access to satellite television. Commercial infrastructure is also vital - banks, accountants, advertising agencies and other services. Without these " transaction " facilities, exporting cannot take place.

Urbanisation

Differences exist between "urban" and "country" dwellers. City dwellers may have more income, more developed communications and access to new products. Developing countries tend to suffer from rural drift, but without the accompanying incomes characteristic of developed countries. So when assessing market opportunities widespread urbanisation is no guarantee of a good market potential.

Other

Inflation causes havoc with economies and foreign exchange. For example Zambia has an unofficial inflation rate of over 100%, which makes it difficult and expensive to access capital for investment and obtain pre-export finance. The role of Government is essential. Some encourage joint ventures and investment, others do not.

The number of international companies operating in an economy can be both good and bad. Japan's investment in the USA and UK is high, creating jobs, but gives rise to negative feelings because access to Japan is not so easy. This has led to calls for protectionism. Similarly, flows from developed countries to less developed ones are generally one way. This leads to instability in the underdeveloped country because it has no "hostage" leverage. Repatriation or transfer of dividends can be an issue which can detract from investment if negative facilities exist. This can seriously undermine economic development and trade.

Many African countries are undergoing structural adjustment and trade liberalisation programmes. In some cases, these have met with limited success. They can create market opportunities, but they also can cause internal economic upheavals for long periods of time, detracting from investment by outsiders and limiting the export opportunities, especially if interest rates rise, as is often the case.

The economic environment is one of the major determinants of market potential and opportunity. Careful analysis of this, particularly income and the stage of economic development is essential. Failure to do so will lead, at best, to sub optimal opportunity and, at worst, to disaster. Less developed countries like Africa, are at a disadvantage, due to their primary material export dependence. It behoves these nations in the continent to derive policies and strategies for rapid industrialisation, or forever to be at the mercy of world demand and prices.

INTERNATIONAL MONETARY SYSTEM

Historically, any commodity that was generally accepted as a medium of exchange could be used as money. Various objects have been used as money over time, including human skulls, cows, wine, shells, and mainly metals. Even today in the Yap island of the Pacific, large stones (fei) are used as money.

Cows were used as money in ancient Greece or Hellas, Egypt, China, Italy, and Britain. In Southern Sudan, even today, people use cattle and goats as a standard of value. Thus, "a reasonably sound wife costs about 40 head of cattle, with perhaps a few goats and chickens thrown in."

From recent discoveries in Dispilio, near Kastoria, Greece, the most ancient signs of written words, fishing and other instruments, and vases were dated back to 5260 B.C. Also, shapes of coins, similar to talents used in ancient Greece and Rome and existing now in the Museum of Heracleion, Crete, were found to belong to the same ancient times. Such discoveries put an end to the myths about the Phoenician alphabet and the Indo-European race. Hellenes were living in that area and the rest of Greece at that time. The research continues and is financed by the European Union. Moreover, human fossil bones and tools were discovered by French and Greek archeologists in Triglia, Halkidikis, as ancient as 11–12 million years old, compared to 2.5-million-year-old tools found in Africa.

Lending operations for commodities predates money itself, as for example during the Minoan and Mycenean civilizations, when values were expressed in terms of cows and oxen. Also, the Code of Hammurabi deals with mortgages and debts. However, the use of coins and other monetary units, away from the inefficient barter system, later necessitated the establishment of banks.

In addition to cattle, during the Homeric period, certain pieces of gold called talents were used as money. Recent research in Mycenae discovered a copper ingot 2.5 feet long in a shape of ox-hide, dated around the fourteenth century B.C. Moreover, certain pieces of gold were in circulation but were expressed mainly in terms of cows.

An alternative name to euro, suggested in the European Union, was the talent, used in ancient Greece and classical Rome, which are considered as the common roots of the EU member states. It was considered as a hard currency with a value of 26 kg of silver.

In ancient Sparta, large iron disks were introduced by Lycurgus as money units. The Spartan monetary units had a face value higher than the intrinsic or metal value. This system of debased money is used even today by advanced money societies. Later, gold and silver were deposited by the Lacedaemonians with the Arcadians for safekeeping.

Silver coins replaced previous tortoise-shell currency in Corinth, the island of Aegina, and mainly Athens. They were stamped to indicate their value on the one side, and with an owl on the other side. Aristotle, commodities have a use value and an exchange value measured in drachmas, which can be used for exchanges and storage of wealth. Plato proposed, in the Laws, that token money be used for domestic transactions and gold and silver for transactions with foreigners. In that way, money was internationalized by the Hellenes at that time. However, Aristophanes noted in "The Frogs" that "in our Republic bad citizens are preferred to good, just as bad money circulates while good money disappears." This concept is very near to Gresham's law, after Sir Thomas Gresham, Queen Elizabeth's Chancellor of the Exchequer.

As domestic and foreign trade increased, mainly between Athens-Piraeus and Phoenicia, Egypt, Sicily, and other neighbouring countries, banking transactions developed. A number of arcades, the most famous called Degma, were used for exhibitions and exchanges of commodities from all the markets of the eastern Mediterranean and beyond. Moreover, regulations similar to our antitrust laws were enacted by the city government.

Other important monetary units used in ancient times were the Pu money, in the shape of a shirt, as well as knives and other metallic instruments, in China around 700 B.C. Also, the first paper or parchment money was issued in China in 140 B.C. In Egypt, the first coinage was established under the Ptolemies at the end of the fourth century B.C.

Money and credit opened new freedoms and opportunities during the period of the Roman Empire. Financiers and profiteers flourished while trade enterprises were growing, and money interest began to play an important role in trade and finance. The Romans used a common currency to help military cooperation and to stimulate free economic transactions with the regions under their domain. Such common currencies were used later by the United States and the European Union.

Copper bars or ingots were the first monetary units in ancient Rome. Silver coins, called denarii, similar to those previously used in Greece and mostly debased, were introduced after 269 B.C. Furthermore, with the use of gold later, three metals were used together and serious problems of trimetalism or bimetalism appeared as the relative values of the various metals changed over time. During the Roman Empire, the creation of a new commercial class, the patricians, increased transactions in the cities and necessitated a body of laws that later had a profound influence on legal and economic institutions, including banks and other financial firms. The recognition of juristic or artificial persons by the Roman laws was important for the creation and expansion of the corporate form of modern enterprises. The Romans, with their efficient administration of justice and the security of life and property, created many trading, financial, and shipping centres in their dominion and promoted international transactions.

Nevertheless, Rome suffered at times from too little or too much gold and silver and the frequent debasement of its metal money. The rudimentary banking system was inadequate to deal with price changes in the absence of a paper or check system. Moral corruption, slavery, and decline of the silver and gold mines of Spain and Greece were the main reasons for the fall of the Roman Empire.

During the Byzantine Empire and the Middle Ages, gold was the main currency used, but there were problems of debasement of currencies and price fluctuations, mainly from changes in the supplies of gold and silver. Tax reductions and other administrative reforms stimulated trade and made Constantinople, the capital of Byzantium, a commercial and financial centre for southeastern Europe and the Middle East. However, commercially minded Venetians, who were better organized in foreign trade and finance, managed to settle in a number of ports around the Balkan and other areas and to control customs revenue and banking activities.

In competition with the Genoese, another commercial people, they exploited the lucrative trade and financial markets of the Golden Horn, the Black Sea, and other neighbouring regions. In the Middle Ages, early financial operations were carried on by monasteries, but any interest was considered immoral by Church law and was considered unnatural by Aristotle. After the Renaissance, modern banking activities were conducted at the old Fairs and monasteries and by the Lombard bankers in England, as well as by financial houses such as the Bardi, the Medici, the Peruzzi, and the Strozzi of Italy, based mainly in Florence, and the Fuggers and the Rothschilds in Germany. They were exempted from the ban on usury and made loans to kings and even to the Pope. Goldsmiths or jewelers in Lombard Street and other places accepted deposits for safekeeping, giving the proper receipts, which were payable to the bearer. The depositors could hand the receipts over to their creditors, performing the same functions as in modern banking. Thereafter, important banks appeared, such as the Bank of Sweden, the Bank of France, and the German Reichs Bank.

The British silver coin initially was a pound of standard silver. Also, the French livre was one pound of silver, and both represented one of the early international monetary units. Other countries, mainly Mexico, China, and India, developed a silver standard.

During the period of Mercantilism, emphasis was given:

- On foreign trade as a means of accumulating precious metals, primarily gold and silver, as the most desirable form of national wealth,
- On the supremacy of the state over the individual. Gold and silver could be used to finance trade or pay large armies for foreign wars or be retained as luxuries.

As Columbus said, with gold one can get even souls into paradise. The state should support foreign trade and establish colonies to increase national wealth. Commercial expansion occurred by monopolies, such as the Merchant Adventurers, the Eastland Company, the Muscovy Company, and the East India Company.

Towards the end of the Mercantilistic period, the physiocratic school appeared in France. The school was based on the natural order, which prevailed over all the economic activities in a harmonious way, similar to that of the planetary system. This laissez-faire system was further developed by Adam Smith and other classical economists and is considered as the basis of capitalism. Later, Eugen Von Böhm Bawerk and other Austrian economists stressed the justification of interest payment, based mainly on the productivity of capital, which helps the worker and the entrepreneur to increase production. The gold standard, first introduced in Britain in 1821, was also adopted by Portugal (1854), Germany (1871), and other European countries later. Britain abandoned gold from 1914 to 1925 and permanently in 1931.

During the classical gold era, roughly from 1870 to 1914, there was a high capital mobility, mainly from Britain, France, and Germany (about 3–9 per cent of the GDP) to Australia, Canada, New Zealand, and Sweden. Such capital flows were used primarily for investment but also as official reserves (gold and foreign exchange), mainly by the United States, Russia, India, Belgium, and Sweden. A similar phenomenon can be observed in our day with the capital flow in emerging nations, which is used primarily for reserve holdings. In all these cases, the role of investment banks in 1870–1914 was important in stimulating global capital flows, as it is now.

MONETARY SYSTEMS IN THE AMERICAS

In the Western Hemisphere, the Incas, covering most of the coast and Highlands of western South America, had no monetary system of any kind, whereas in the American colonies, coins brought over by European immigrants and Indian wampums (ornamental cloth) were initially used as money. Corn was mainly used as a medium of exchange (1631) in Massachusetts, whereas tobacco and rice were used in the south. In order to facilitate trade with the Spanish colonies, the Spanish silver dollars, or fractions of them, were also used in the Americas. After George Washington's inauguration (1789) as the first president of the United States, gold and silver full-bodied coins were used.

In the United States, for practical purposes, silver was used from 1792 to 1834 and primarily gold from 1834 on, although the Coinage Act of 1792 provided for a mint and stipulated that the principal coin would be the $10 Eagle (weighing 270 grains and containing 247.5 grains of pure gold out of 480 grains in a troy ounce). In 1837, the price of an ounce of gold was fixed by the U.S. Congress at $20.67. In 1832 and later, Robert Owen of England introduced a paper money in "the Owenite communities in America," mainly in Cincinnati, Tennessee, and Ohio, with nominal values in labour hours. These labour notes entitled "National Equitable Labour Exchanges," based on the utopian teachings of Charles Fourier of France, were short-lived, primarily because of the difficulties in exchanges.

Nevertheless, bank notes and U.S. Treasury notes were mostly used because they were less costly and more convenient than gold. But "In issuing paper money...it is only necessary that its quantity should be regulated." Moreover, international payments were made in bills of exchange, comparable to postdated checks. Thus, a U.S. exporter would receive gold or more usually bills of exchange from the importers of other countries and sell them for U.S. dollars in New York or other cities. Because of the Civil War and the increase in prices, payments in gold in the United States were suspended in December 1861. The convertibility of gold for the dollar was restored at $20.67 in January

1879 and remained so until 1933. The pure gold standard system was introduced in 1900 in order to avoid relative price fluctuations in the prevailing bimetalic system of gold and silver. The United States managed to hang onto gold during World War I, but prices increased by more than double from 1914 to 1920, and then by 1932 they fell more than they had risen.

However, new discoveries of gold led to changes in prices and economic instability. Also, when a country had a deficit in the balance of payments, a net outflow of gold would take place, and under a gold standard system, money supply and eventually prices would be reduced, with the possibility of a recession or depression and unemployment. Ceteris paribus, lower prices would lead to more exports and less imports, thereby restoring the balance-of-payments equilibrium. The opposite is expected in countries with surplus in the balance of payments, which would lead to a net inflow of gold, an increase in money supply and prices, less exports and more imports until the balance-of-payments equilibrium is restored. Metals, primarily gold and silver, were used as money mainly in international transactions by different societies. Metals are generally accepted as money because they are homogeneous commodities, easily portable, divisible, storable, and relatively scarce and have a cost to produce and a value in industrial use. In 1933, the United States abandoned the pure gold standard system, in which anybody could get gold. In its place, the gold reserve system was introduced, in which a certain percentage of the money supply was kept in gold. The price of gold was determined at $35 per ounce in January 1934, but in practice, it was used only for the settlement of international transactions. In March 1973 the price of gold was left to the free market of supply and demand.

The Bank of North America, established by the Continental Congress in 1781, and the Bank of the United States, established by Alexander Hamilton in 1791, were the first U.S. banks. In order to manage money and credit more effectively, the Federal Reserve Bank ("Fed"), as an institution independent of the federal government.

INTERNATIONAL MONETARY FUND

The most effective international organizations, formed by agreements among a large number of nations, are the International Monetary Fund (IMF), the International Bank for Reconstruction and Development or World Bank, and the General Agreement on Tariffs and Trade (GATT), recently named the World Trade Organization (WTO). The IMF and the World Bank were established by forty-four countries at Bretton Woods, New Hampshire (United States), in July 1944, whereas the GATT was negotiated in Havana, Cuba, and established in Geneva in 1948.

The International Monetary Fund (IMF), which is a pool of central-bank reserves and national currencies, was established at Bretton Woods in 1944 under the auspices of the United Nations, but it actually started operations on March 1, 1947. In order to facilitate international finance and help correct fundamental balance-of-payments disequilibriums, it tied all currencies to gold and hence to each other. The IMF, with headquarters in Washington, D.C., was created to help finance balance-of-payments deficits and to reform the international monetary system towards mutual cooperation and freely convertible currencies among the member nations. The waves of devaluations in the currencies of a number of countries before World War II, mainly in 1931–1936, as a way to increase exports and reduce imports at the expense of their trading partners (beggar-thy-neighbour policies) was the rationale of the creation of the IMF. These policies resulted in frequent changes in exchange parities, economic instability, and high unemployment.

The IMF makes its own stock of currencies available (gives loans) to the members. It functions as a pool of currencies or an international clearing institution, using the assigned quotas of the member countries to arrange international payments. Also, it provides short-term loans and advice to member countries, primarily emerging nations, with balance-of-payments difficulties. Member nations were committed to keep their currencies within plus or minus 1 per cent of parity, although further changes in exchange rates were permitted if needed. From that standpoint, the system can be characterized as an "adjustable peg" exchange rate system. Moreover, because the dollar, being the key currency, was convertible into gold (1/35 ounce of gold), every currency had a gold value related to the dollar, which may be considered as a yardstick of value. The Bretton Woods system then may also be characterized as a gold exchange standard system.

Each member nation was responsible to subscribe to the capital of the IMF, paying one fourth in gold and three fourths in its currency (in demand notes), depending mainly on its share of world trade. The member countries were responsible to sell their currencies to the IMF, which could also borrow currencies from its members and their subscribed quotas. Initially the IMF had a total quota of $8.8 billion, but that was increased gradually to about $260 billion (198 billion Special Drawing Rights or SDRs) and 182 members presently. Immediately after World War II, the United States had about 33 per cent of the voting power in the IMF and 35 per cent in the World Bank, because of its dominant economic position. Thereafter, the U.S. voting power steadily declined to the current levels of less than 20 per cent in the IMF and around 17 per cent in the World Bank. As we enter a new millennium, international institutions, mainly the IMF, are expected to play a more important role in regulating financial cooperation and reducing tensions among member nations, particularly between rich and poor nations, which have heavy debts.

Nevertheless, gold is an expensive reserve asset, as human resources are used to dig it in distant areas and bury it in heavily guarded places in central banks or in the IMF in Washington. That is why Robert Triffin of Yale

University suggested that central bank deposits with the IMF be denominated in a new international unit of account or a form of paper gold. A similar system was proposed by John M. Keynes, as an alternative to the U.S. plan for the IMF at Bretton Woods in 1944. Moreover, the use of gold for the determination of money supply may lead to excessive liquidity and global inflationary pressures, when excessive amounts of gold are available, as well as to inadequate liquidity, when not enough gold is available, resulting in recessions or even depressions, as happened with the severe recession of 1907 (rich man's panic) and the Great Depression of the 1930s.

Although the Bretton Woods system performed well in the 1950s, the fact that the United States had large deficits in its balance of payments in the 1960s increased the dollar reserves of other countries and consequently the demand for gold, forcing the United States to apply first voluntary controls and then mandatory controls to capital outflows. At the same time, Japan, West Germany, and other European countries with surpluses refused to revalue their currencies, suggesting that the United States eliminate its balance-of-payments deficits. In an attempt to further discourage European companies from raising capital in the United States, the interest-equalization tax was imposed in the mid-1960s to equalize the cost of raising funds in the United States, where interest rates were lower. Moreover, the U.S. Treasury issued medium-term bonds with an exchange-rate guarantee, known as Roosa bonds, to discourage foreign central banks from cashing their excess dollars for gold. Also, U.S. short-term interest rates were raised to attract foreign funds, but long-term interest rates remained low to encourage domestic investments, a policy known as "operation twist." Nevertheless, the "dollar glut" continued in the 1960s, mainly because of the U.S. trade deficits, in contrast to the "dollar shortage" in the 1950s.

In 1969, a special quota (of $10 billion) was created by the IMF to be used for automatic drawings. They are Special Drawing Rights (SDRs), which are gradually replacing gold as a reserve asset. The acceptance of SDRs is an obligation for members, subject to some limitations. Each member can buy currencies directly from other countries up to the amount allocated by the IMF, without going through the regular Fund operations. In the case of SDRs the IMF acts as an intermediary or guarantor. Although large amounts of SDRs are allocated to developed countries, a growing number of emerging nations receive SDR allocations lately.

The IMF carries on its books $5 billion gold, but at market prices the gold the fund owns is worth more than $30 billion. Therefore, the fund can write off some $8 billion that forty poor countries owe it, but under conditions that would not give them incentives for further borrowing with the expectation of not paying back future loans.

Each member paid one fourth of its quota in gold or in dollars and the rest in its own currency. This pool may be considered as an extension of the central-bank reserves and aimed at stable exchange rates. It was accepted that drawings of member countries could be made on permission, as Harry D. White, the U.S. representative, insisted, and not automatically, as John M. Keynes, the British representative, suggested.

The quotas, which are revised every five years to reflect economic changes of members, determine the number of votes and the borrowing limits of the member countries. The United States has almost 20 per cent of the total voting power, followed by Germany and Japan with 5.7 per cent each, and then Britain and France with 5.1 per cent each. These five developed countries with more than 40 per cent voting power dominate the IMF, which operates as a central bank for central banks. Member governments select governors, who constitute the highest governing body of the Fund and meet every September in Washington, whereas power is vested in the Board of Executive Directors (some twenty persons).

A member of the Fund can borrow 25 per cent of its quota without restrictions (gold tranche) and higher amounts with restrictions (credit tranches), but repayments are normally to be made within three to five years. Approximately, the quotas (in billions of Special Drawing Rights or SDRs) (one SDR is equal to about $1.3) are: 27 for the United States; 8 each for Germany and Japan; 7 each for Britain and France; 5 for Saudi Arabia; 4 each for Canada, Italy, and Russia; 3 each for Belgium, China, India, and Netherlands; 2 each for Australia and Brazil; and close to 2 each for Mexico, Spain, and Venezuela, and so on.

The U.S. official reserve assets in March 1998 were $69.35 billion, $30.22 billion of which were foreign currencies, $11.05 billion gold, $10.11 billion holdings of IMF SDRs, and $17.98 billion was the reserve position, that is, the U.S. ability to draw foreign currencies from the IMF. As the cure for sick economies, the IMF usually prescribes tough austerity measures, which lead to deep cuts in public spending, tight credit, high unemployment, sharp currency depreciation, severe stock market decline, and even social unrest. Some of these symptoms occurred in Mexico and the Southeast Asian countries.

Some countries blame Washington and other Western capitals for their strong influence on the IMF. Such austerity measures may result in high unemploy-ment, and many people blame IMF for worsening their misery and for losing their jobs (arguing that IMF stands for I'M Fired?). Moreover, the loans from the IMF are relatively small compared to about $2 trillion traded daily in the international currency market. Although it provided more than $150 billion for the Asian and Mexican bailouts lately, as a lender of last resort, it is criticized that in its effort to save weak economies, it discourages the private sector and the related governments to take the necessary painful fiscal and monetary measures to correct the problems of crony capitalism. That is why the U.S. Congress is skeptical on providing additional financing for the IMF.

WORLD TRADE ORGANIZATION

The World Trade Organization (WTO) is an organization that intends to supervise and liberalize international trade. The organization officially commenced on January 1, 1995 under the Marrakech Agreement, replacing the General Agreement on Tariffs and Trade (GATT), which commenced in 1948. The organization deals with regulation of trade between participating countries; it provides a framework for negotiating and formalizing trade agreements, and a dispute resolution process aimed at enforcing participants' adherence to WTO agreements which are signed by representatives of member governments and ratified by their parliaments. Most of the issues that the WTO focuses on derive from previous trade negotiations, especially from the Uruguay Round.

The organization is currently endeavoring to persist with a trade negotiation called the Doha Development Agenda (or Doha Round), which was launched in 2001 to enhance equitable participation of poorer countries which represent a majority of the world's population. However, the negotiation has been dogged by "disagreement between exporters of agricultural bulk commodities and countries with large numbers of subsistence farmers on the precise terms of a 'special safeguard measure' to protect farmers from surges in imports. At this time, the future of the Doha Round is uncertain."

The WTO has 153 members, representing more than 97% of total world trade and 30 observers, most seeking membership. The WTO is governed by a ministerial conference, meeting every two years; a general council, which implements the conference's policy decisions and is responsible for day-to-day administration; and a director-general, who is appointed by the ministerial conference. The WTO's headquarters is at the Centre William Rappard, Geneva, Switzerland. The WTO's predecessor, the General Agreement on Tariffs and Trade (GATT), was established after World War II in the wake of other new multilateral institutions dedicated to international economic cooperation - notably the Bretton Woods institutions known as the World Bank and the International Monetary Fund.

A comparable international institution for trade, named the International Trade Organization was successfully negotiated. The ITO was to be a United Nations specialized agency and would address not only trade barriers but other issues indirectly related to trade, including employment, investment, restrictive business practices, and commodity agreements. But the ITO treaty was not approved by the United States and a few other signatories and never went into effect. In the absence of an international organization for trade, the GATT would over the years "transform itself" into a de facto international organization.

The GATT was the only multilateral instrument governing international trade from 1948 until the WTO was established in 1995. Despite attempts in the mid 1950s and 1960s to create some form of institutional mechanism for international trade, the GATT continued to operate for almost half a century as a semi-institutionalized multilateral treaty regime on a provisional basis.Seven rounds of negotiations occurred under the GATT. The first real GATT trade rounds concentrated on further reducing tariffs.

Then, the Kennedy Round in the mid-sixties brought about a GATT anti-dumping Agreement and a part on development. The Tokyo Round during the seventies was the first major attempt to tackle trade barriers that do not take the form of tariffs, and to improve the system, accepting a series of agreements on non-tariff barriers, which in some cases interpreted existing GATT rules, and in others broke entirely new ground. Because these plurilateral agreements were not accepted by the full GATT membership, they were often informally called "codes". Several of these codes were amended in the Uruguay Round, and turned into multilateral commitments accepted by all WTO members. Only four remained plurilateral (those on government procurement, bovine meat, civil aircraft and dairy products), but in 1997 WTO members agreed to terminate the bovine meat and dairy agreements, leaving only two.

Well before GATT's 40th anniversary, its members concluded that the GATT system was straining to adapt to a new globalizing world economy. In response to the problems identified in the 1982 Ministerial Declaration (structural deficiencies, spill-over impacts of certain countries' policies on world trade GATT could not manage etc.), the eighth GATT round - known as the Uruguay Round - was launched in September 1986, in Punta del Este, Uruguay.

It was the biggest negotiating mandate on trade ever agreed: the talks were going to extend the trading system into several new areas, notably trade in services and intellectual property, and to reform trade in the sensitive sectors of agriculture and textiles; all the original GATT substances were up for review. The Final Act concluding the Uruguay Round and officially establishing the WTO regime was signed during the April 1994 ministerial meeting at Marrakesh, Morocco, and hence is known as the Marrakesh Agreement.

The GATT still exists as the WTO's umbrella treaty for trade in goods, updated as a result of the Uruguay Round negotiations. GATT 1994 is not however the only legally binding agreement included via the Final Act at Marrakesh; a long list of about 60 agreements, annexes, decisions and understandings was adopted.

The agreements fall into a structure with six main parts:

- The Agreement Establishing the WTO
- Goods and investment - the Multilateral Agreements on Trade in Goods including the GATT 1994 and the Trade Related Investment Measures

- *Services*: The General Agreement on Trade in Services
- Intellectual property — the Agreement on Trade-Related Aspects of Intellectual Property Rights (TRIPS)
- Dispute settlement (DSU)
- Reviews of governments' trade policies (TPRM)

The topmost decision-making body of the WTO is the Ministerial Conference, which usually meets every two years. It brings together all members of the WTO, all of which are countries or customs unions. The Ministerial Conference can take decisions on all matters under any of the multilateral trade agreements. The inaugural ministerial conference was held in Singapore in 1996.

Disagreements between largely developed and developing economies emerged during this conference over four issues initiated by this conference, which led to them being collectively referred to as the "Singapore issues". The second ministerial conference was held in Geneva in Switzerland. The third conference in Seattle, Washington ended in failure, with massive demonstrations and police and National Guard crowd control efforts drawing worldwide attention. The fourth ministerial conference was held in Doha In Persian Gulf nation of Qatar. The Doha Development Round was launched at the conference. The conference also approved the joining of China, which became the 143rd member to join.

The fifth ministerial conference was held in Cancún, Mexico, aiming at forging agreement on the Doha round. An alliance of 22 southern states, the G20 developing nations (led by India, China and Brazil), resisted demands from the North for agreements on the so-called "Singapore issues" and called for an end to agricultural subsidies within the EU and the US. The talks broke down without progress.

The sixth WTO ministerial conference was held in Hong Kong from 13 December – 18 December 2005. It was considered vital if the four-year-old Doha Development Agenda negotiations were to move forward sufficiently to conclude the round in 2006. In this meeting, countries agreed to phase out all their agricultural export subsidies by the end of 2013, and terminate any cotton export subsidies by the end of 2006. Further concessions to developing countries included an agreement to introduce duty free, tariff free access for goods from the Least Developed Countries, following the Everything But Arms initiative of the European Union — but with up to 3% of tariff lines exempted. Other major issues were left for further negotiation to be completed by the end of 2010. The WTO General Council, on 26 May 2009, agreed to hold a seventh WTO ministerial conference session in Geneva from 30 November–3 December 2009.

A statement by chairman Amb. Mario Matus acknowledged that the prime purpose was to remedy a breach of protocol requiring two-yearly "regular" meetings, which had lapsed with the Doha Round failure in 2005, and that the "scaled-down" meeting would not be a negotiating session, but "emphasis will be on transparency and open discussion rather than on small group processes and informal negotiating structures". The general theme for discussion is "The WTO, the Multilateral Trading System and the Current Global Economic Environment"

The WTO launched the current round of negotiations, the Doha Development Agenda (DDA) or Doha Round, at the fourth ministerial conference in Doha, Qatar in November 2001. The Doha round was to be an ambitious effort to make globalization more inclusive and help the world's poor, particularly by slashing barriers and subsidies in farming. The initial agenda comprised both further trade liberalization and new rule-making, underpinned by commitments to strengthen substantial assistance to developing countries.

The negotiations have been highly contentious and agreement has not been reached, despite the intense negotiations at several ministerial conferences and at other sessions. Disagreements still continue over several key areas including agriculture subsidies.

FUNCTIONS

Among the various functions of the WTO, these are regarded by analysts as the most important:

- It oversees the implementation, administration and operation of the covered agreements.
- It provides a forum for negotiations and for settling disputes.

Additionally, it is the WTO's duty to review and propagate the national trade policies, and to ensure the coherence and transparency of trade policies through surveillance in global economic policy-making. Another priority of the WTO is the assistance of developing, least-developed and low-income countries in transition to adjust to WTO rules and disciplines through technical cooperation and training. *The WTO is also a centre of economic research and analysis*: regular assessments of the global trade picture in its annual publications and research reports on specific topics are produced by the organization. Finally, the WTO cooperates closely with the two other components of the Bretton Woods system, the IMF and the World Bank.

PRINCIPLES OF THE TRADING SYSTEM

The WTO establishes a framework for trade policies; it does not define or specify outcomes. That is, it is concerned with setting the rules of the trade policy games. Five principles are of particular importance in understanding both the pre-1994 GATT and the WTO:

- *Non-Discrimination*: It has two major components: the most favoured nation (MFN) rule, and the national treatment policy. Both are embedded in the main WTO rules on goods, services, and intellectual property, but their precise scope and nature differ across these areas. The MFN rule requires that a WTO member must apply the same conditions on all trade with other WTO members, *i.e.* a WTO member has to grant the most favourable conditions under which it allows trade in a certain product type to all other WTO members. "Grant someone a special favour and you have to do the same for all other WTO members." National treatment means that imported goods should be treated no less favourably than domestically produced goods (at least after the foreign goods have entered the market) and was introduced to tackle non-tariff barriers to trade (e.g. technical standards, security standards *et al.* discriminating against imported goods).

- *Reciprocity*: It reflects both a desire to limit the scope of free-riding that may arise because of the MFN rule, and a desire to obtain better access to foreign markets. A related point is that for a nation to negotiate, it is necessary that the gain from doing so be greater than the gain available from unilateral liberalization; reciprocal concessions intend to ensure that such gains will materialise.
- *Binding and enforceable commitments*: The tariff commitments made by WTO members in a multilateral trade negotiation and on accession are enumerated in a schedule (list) of concessions. These schedules establish "ceiling bindings": a country can change its bindings, but only after negotiating with its trading partners, which could mean compensating them for loss of trade. If satisfaction is not obtained, the complaining country may invoke the WTO dispute settlement procedures.
- *Transparency*: The WTO members are required to publish their trade regulations, to maintain institutions allowing for the review of administrative decisions affecting trade, to respond to requests for information by other members, and to notify changes in trade policies to the WTO. These internal transparency requirements are supplemented and facilitated by periodic country-specific reports (trade policy reviews) through the Trade Policy Review Mechanism (TPRM). The WTO system tries also to improve predictability and stability, discouraging the use of quotas and other measures used to set limits on quantities of imports.
- *Safety valves*: In specific circumstances, governments are able to restrict trade. There are three types of provisions in this direction: substances allowing for the use of trade measures to attain noneconomic objectives; substances aimed at ensuring "fair competition"; and provisions permitting intervention in trade for economic reasons. Exceptions to the MFN principle also allow for preferential treatment of developing countries, regional free trade areas and customs unions.

ORGANIZATIONAL STRUCTURE

The General Council has multiple bodies which oversee committees in different areas, and they are the following:

- *Council for Trade in Goods*: There are 11 committees under the jurisdiction of the Goods Council each with a specific task. All members of the WTO participate in the committees. The Textiles Monitoring Body is separate from the other committees but still under the jurisdiction of Goods Council. The body has its own chairman and only ten members. The body also has several groups relating to textiles.
- *Council for Trade-Related Aspects of Intellectual Property Rights*: Information on intellectual property in the WTO, news and official records of the activities of the TRIPS Council, and details of the WTO's work with other international organizations in the field.
- *Council for Trade in Services*: The Council for Trade in Services operates under the guidance of the General Council and is responsible for overseeing the functioning of the General Agreement on Trade in Services (GATS). It is open to all WTO members, and can create subsidiary bodies as required.
- *Trade Negotiations Committee*: The Trade Negotiations Committee (TNC) is the committee that deals with the current trade talks round. The chair is WTO's director-general. The committee is currently tasked with the Doha Development Round.

The Service Council has three subsidiary bodies: financial services, domestic regulations, GATS rules and specific commitments. The General council has several different committees, working groups, and working parties. There are committees on the following: Trade and Environment; Trade and Development (Subcommittee on Least-Developed Countries); Regional Trade Agreements; Balance of Payments Restrictions; and Budget, Finance and Administration. There are working parties on the following: Accession. There are working groups on the following: Trade, debt and finance; and Trade and technology transfer.

Voting System

The WTO operates on a one country, one vote system, but actual votes have never been taken. Decision making is generally by consensus, and relative market size is the primary source of bargaining power. The advantage of consensus decision-making is that it encourages efforts to find the most widely acceptable decision. Main disadvantages include large time requirements and many rounds of negotiation to develop a consensus decision, and the tendency for final agreements to use ambiguous language on contentious points that makes future interpretation of treaties difficult.

In reality, WTO negotiations proceed not by consensus of all members, but by a process of informal negotiations between small groups of countries. Such negotiations are often called "Green Room" negotiations (after the colour of the WTO Director-General's Office in Geneva), or "Mini-Ministerials", when they occur in other countries.

These processes have been regularly criticised by many of the WTO's developing country members which are often totally excluded from the negotiations.. Richard Harold Steinberg (2002) argues that although the WTO's consensus governance model provides law-based initial bargaining, trading rounds close through power-based bargaining favouring Europe and the United States, and may not lead to Pareto improvement.

DISPUTE SETTLEMENT

In 1994, the WTO members agreed on the Understanding on Rules and Procedures Governing the Settlement of Disputes (DSU) annexed to the "Final Act" signed in Marrakesh in 1994. Dispute settlement is regarded by the WTO as the central pillar of the multilateral trading system, and as a "unique contribution to the stability of the global economy". WTO members have agreed that, if they believe fellow-members are violating trade rules, they will use the multilateral system of settling disputes instead of taking action unilaterally.

The operation of the WTO dispute settlement process involves the DSB panels, the Appellate Body, the WTO Secretariat, arbitrators, independent experts and several specialized institutions.

ACCESSION AND MEMBERSHIP

The process of becoming a WTO member is unique to each applicant country, and the terms of accession are dependent upon the country's stage of economic development and current trade regime. The process takes about five years, on average, but it can last more if the country is less than fully committed to the process or if political issues interfere. As is typical of WTO procedures, an offer of accession is only given once consensus is reached among interested parties.

Accession Process

A country wishing to accede to the WTO submits an application to the General Council, and has to describe all aspects of its trade and economic policies that have a bearing on WTO agreements. The application is submitted to the WTO in a memorandum which is examined by a working party open to all interested WTO Members. After all necessary background information has been acquired, the working party focuses on issues of discrepancy between the WTO rules and the applicant's international and domestic trade policies and laws. The working party determines the terms and conditions of entry into the WTO for the applicant nation, and may consider transitional periods to allow countries some leeway in complying with the WTO rules.The final phase of accession involves bilateral negotiations between the applicant nation and other working party members regarding the concessions and commitments on tariff levels and market access for goods and services. The new member's commitments are to apply equally to all WTO members under normal non-discrimination rules, even though they are negotiated bilaterally. When the bilateral talks conclude, the working party sends to the general council or ministerial conference an accession package, which includes a summary of all the working party meetings, the Protocol of Accession (a draft membership treaty), and lists ("schedules") of the member-to-be's commitments. Once the general council or ministerial conference approves of the terms of accession, the applicant's parliament must ratify the Protocol of Accession before it can become a member.

Members and Observers

The WTO has 153 members (almost all of the 123 nations participating in the Uruguay Round signed on at its foundation, and the rest had to get membership). The 27 states of the European Union are represented also as the European Communities. WTO members do not have to be full sovereign nation-members. Instead, they must be a customs territory with full autonomy in the conduct of their external commercial relations. Thus Hong Kong became a GATT contracting party, and the Republic of China (ROC) (commonly known as Taiwan, whose sovereignty has been disputed by the People's Republic of China or PRC) acceded to the WTO in 2002 under the name of "Separate Customs Territory of Taiwan, Penghu, Kinmen and Matsu" (Chinese Taipei).

A number of non-members (30) are observers at WTO proceedings and are currently negotiating their membership. As observers, Iran, Iraq and Russia are not yet members. Russia is the biggest economy outside WTO and after the completion of Russia's accession, Iran would be the biggest economy outside the WTO. Observers must start accession negotiations within five years of becoming observers. Some international intergovernmental organizations are also granted observer status to WTO bodies. 14 states and 2 territories so far have no official interaction with the WTO.

AGREEMENTS

The WTO oversees about 60 different agreements which have the status of international legal texts. Member countries must sign and ratify all WTO agreements on accession. A discussion of some of the most important agreements follows. The Agreement on Agriculture came into effect with the establishment of the WTO at the beginning of 1995. The AoA has three central concepts, or "pillars": domestic support, market access and export subsidies.

The General Agreement on Trade in Services was created to extend the multilateral trading system to service sector, in the same way the General Agreement on Tariffs and Trade (GATT) provides such a system for merchandise trade. The Agreement entered into force in January 1995. The Agreement on Trade-Related Aspects of Intellectual Property Rights sets down minimum standards for many forms of intellectual property (IP) regulation. It was negotiated at the end of the Uruguay Round of the General Agreement on Tariffs and Trade (GATT) in 1994.The Agreement on the Application of Sanitary and Phytosanitary Measures - also known as the SPS Agreement was negotiated during the Uruguay Round of the General Agreement on Tariffs and Trade, and entered into force with the establishment of the WTO at the beginning of 1995. Under the SPS agreement, the WTO sets constraints on members' policies relating to food safety (bacterial contaminants, pesticides, inspection and labelling) as well as animal and plant health (imported pests and diseases). The Agreement on Technical Barriers to Trade is an international treaty of the World Trade Organization. It was negotiated during the Uruguay Round of the General Agreement on Tariffs and Trade, and entered into force with the establishment of the WTO at the end of 1994. The object ensures that technical negotiations and standards, as well as testing and certification procedures, do not create unnecessary obstacles to trade". The Agreement on Customs Valuation, formally known as the Agreement on Implementation of Article VII of GATT, prescribes methods of customs valuation that Members are to follow. Chiefly, it adopts the "transaction value" approach.

INTERNATIONAL MONETARY FUND

The International Monetary Fund (IMF) is the international organization that oversees the global financial system by following the macroeconomic policies of its member countries, in particular those with an impact on exchange rate and the balance of payments. It is an organization formed with a stated objective of stabilizing international exchange rates and facilitating development through the enforcement of liberalising economic policies on other countries as a condition for loans, restructuring or aid. It also offers highly leveraged loans, mainly to poorer countries. Its headquarters are in Washington, D.C., United States.

The International Monetary Fund was created in July 1944, originally with 45 members, with a goal to stabilize exchange rates and assist the reconstruction of the world's international payment system. Countries contributed to a pool which could be borrowed from, on a temporary basis, by countries with payment imbalances. The IMF was important when it was first created because it helped the world stabilize the economic system. The IMF works to improve the economies of its member countries.

The IMF describes itself as "an organization of 186 countries, working to foster global monetary cooperation, secure financial stability, facilitate international trade, promote high employment and sustainable economic growth, and reduce poverty". With the exception of Taiwan, North Korea, Cuba, Andorra, Monaco, Liechtenstein, Tuvalu and Nauru, all UN member states participate directly in the IMF. Member states are represented on a 24-member Executive Board and all members appoint a Governor to the IMF's Board of Governors.

The International Monetary Fund was conceived in July 1944 during the United Nations Monetary and Financial Conference. The representatives of 45 governments met in the Mount Washington Hotel in the area of Bretton Woods, New Hampshire, United States, with the delegates to the conference agreeing on a framework for international economic cooperation. The IMF was formally organized on December 27, 1945, when the first 29 countries signed its Articles of Agreement. The statutory purposes of the IMF today are the same as when they were formulated in 1943.

The IMF's influence in the global economy steadily increased as it accumulated more members. The number of IMF member countries has more than quadrupled from the 44 states involved in its establishment, reflecting in particular the attainment of political independence by many developing countries and more recently the collapse of the Soviet bloc. The expansion of the IMF's membership, together with the changes in the world economy, have required the IMF to adapt in a variety of ways to continue serving its purposes effectively.

In 2008, faced with a shortfall in revenue, the International Monetary Fund's executive board agreed to sell part of the IMF's gold reserves. On April 27, 2008, IMF Managing Director Dominique Strauss-Kahn welcomed the board's decision of April 7, 2008 to propose a new framework for the fund, designed to close a projected $400 million budget deficit over the next few years. The budget proposal includes sharp spending cuts of $100 million until 2011 that will include up to 380 staff dismissals.

At the 2009 G-20 London summit, it was decided that the IMF would require additional financial resources to meet prospective needs of its member countries during the ongoing global financial crisis. As part of that decision, the G-20 leaders pledged to increase the IMF's supplemental cash tenfold to $500 billion, and to allocate to member countries another $250 billion via Special Drawing Rights.

As of May 2010 Hungary ($11.6 billion), Romania ($12.5 billion) and Ukraine (the IMF granted a $16.4-billion loan to Ukraine in 2008, of which the government has so far received $10.6 billion) are the largest borrowers of the fund.

In 1995, the International Monetary Fund began work on data dissemination standards with the view of guiding IMF member countries to disseminate their economic and financial data to the public. The International Monetary and Financial Committee (IMFC) endorsed the guidelines for the dissemination standards and they were split into two tiers: The General Data

Dissemination System (GDDS) and the Special Data Dissemination Standard (SDDS). The International Monetary Fund executive board approved the SDDS and GDDS in 1996 and 1997 respectively and subsequent amendments were published in a revised "Guide to the General Data Dissemination System". The system is aimed primarily at statisticians and aims to improve many aspects of statistical systems in a country. It is also part of the World Bank Millennium Development Goals and Poverty Reduction Strategic Papers.

The IMF established a system and standard to guide members in the dissemination to the public of their economic and financial data. Currently there are two such systems: General Data Dissemination System (GDDS) and its superset Special Data Dissemination System (SDDS), for those member countries having or seeking access to international capital markets.

The primary objective of the GDDS is to encourage IMF member countries to build a framework to improve data quality and increase statistical capacity building. This will involve the preparation of metadata describing current statistical collection practices and setting improvement plans. Upon building a framework, a country can evaluate statistical needs, set priorities in improving the timeliness, transparency, reliability and accessibility of financial and economic data. Some countries initially used the GDDS, but lately upgraded to SDDS.

Two criticisms from economists have been that financial aid is always bound to so-called "Conditionalities", including Structural Adjustment Programmes (SAP). It is claimed that conditionalities (economic performance targets established as a precondition for IMF loans) retard social stability and hence inhibit the stated goals of the IMF, while Structural Adjustment Programmes lead to an increase in poverty in recipient countries.

The IMF sometimes advocates "austerity programmes," increasing taxes even when the economy is weak, in order to generate government revenue and balance budget deficits. Countries are often advised to lower their corporate tax rate. These policies were criticized by Joseph E. Stiglitz, former chief economist and Senior Vice President at the World Bank, in his book Globalization and Its Discontents. He argued that by converting to a more Monetarist approach, the fund no longer had a valid purpose, as it was designed to provide funds for countries to carry out Keynesian reflations, and that the IMF "was not participating in a conspiracy, but it was reflecting the interests and ideology of the Western financial community".

Argentina, which had been considered by the IMF to be a model country in its compliance to policy proposals by the Bretton Woods institutions, experienced a catastrophic economic crisis in 2001, which some believe to have been caused by IMF-induced budget restrictions — which undercut the government's ability to sustain national infrastructure even in crucial areas such as health, education, and security — and privatization of strategically vital national resources. Others attribute the crisis to Argentina's misdesigned fiscal federalism, which caused subnational spending to increase rapidly. The crisis added to widespread hatred of this institution in Argentina and other South American countries, with many blaming the IMF for the region's economic problems. The current — as of early 2006 — trend towards moderate left-wing governments in the region and a growing concern with the development of a regional economic policy largely independent of big business pressures has been ascribed to this crisis.

Another example of where IMF Structural Adjustment Programmes aggravated the problem was in Kenya. Before the IMF got involved in the country, the Kenyan central bank oversaw all currency movements in and out of the country. The IMF mandated that the Kenyan central bank had to allow easier currency movement. However, the adjustment resulted in very little foreign investment, but allowed Kamlesh Manusuklal Damji Pattni, with the help of corrupt government officials, to siphon off billions of Kenyan shillings in what came to be known as the Goldenberg scandal, leaving the country worse off than it was before the IMF reforms were implemented. In an interview, the former Romanian Prime Minister Tãriceanu stated that "Since 2005, IMF is constantly making mistakes when it appreciates the country's economic performances". In September 2007 the IMF said "given the Irish economy's strong fundamentals and the authorities' commitment to sound policies, the Directors expected economic growth to remain robust over the medium term". Seventeen months later in April 2009 the New York Times quoted Nobel prize-winning economist, Paul Krugman, who identified Ireland as a model for the worst-case scenario for the global economy.

Overall the IMF success record is perceived as limited. While it was created to help stabilize the global economy, since 1980 critics claim over 100 countries (or reputedly most of the Fund's membership) have experienced a banking collapse that they claim have reduced GDP by four per cent or more, far more than at any time in Post-Depression history. The considerable delay in the IMF's response to any crisis, and the fact that it tends to only respond to them (or even create them) rather than prevent them, has led many economists to argue for reform. In 2006, an IMF reform agenda called the Medium Term Strategy was widely endorsed by the institution's member countries.

The agenda includes changes in IMF governance to enhance the role of developing countries in the institution's decision-making process and steps to deepen the effectiveness of its core mandate, which is known as economic surveillance or helping member countries adopt macroeconomic policies that will sustain global growth and reduce poverty. On June 15, 2007, the Executive Board of the IMF adopted the 2007 Decision on Bilateral Surveillance, a landmark measure that replaced a 30-year-old decision of the Fund's member countries on how the IMF should analyse economic outcomes at the country level.

3

International Trade Barriers: Tariff and Non-Tariff

TARIFF AND NON-TARIFF BARRIERS

TARIFFS AND TARIFF RATE QUOTAS

Tariffs, which are taxes on imports of commodities into a country or region, are among the oldest forms of government intervention in economic activity. They are implemented for two clear economic purposes. First, they provide revenue for the government. Second, they improve economic returns to firms and suppliers of resources to domestic industry that face competition from foreign imports.

Tariffs are widely used to protect domestic producers' incomes from foreign competition. This protection comes at an economic cost to domestic consumers who pay higher prices for import competing goods, and to the economy as a whole through the inefficient allocation of resources to the import competing domestic industry. Therefore, since 1948, when average tariffs on manufactured goods exceeded 30 per cent in most developed economies, those economies have sought to reduce tariffs on manufactured goods through several rounds of negotiations under the General Agreement on Tariffs Trade (GATT).

Only in the most recent Uruguay Round of negotiations were trade and tariff restrictions in agriculture addressed. In the past, and even under GATT, tariffs levied on some agricultural commodities by some countries have been very large. When coupled with other barriers to trade they have often constituted formidable barriers to market access from foreign producers. In fact, tariffs that are set high enough can block all trade and performance just like import bans.

Round of negotiations were trade and tariff restrictions in agriculture addressed. In the past, and even under GATT, tariffs levied on some agricultural commodities by some countries have been very large. When coupled with other barriers to trade they have often constituted formidable barriers to market access from foreign producers. In fact, tariffs that are set high enough can block all trade and performance just like import bans.

Round of negotiations were trade and tariff restrictions in agriculture addressed. In the past, and even under GATT, tariffs levied on some agricultural commodities by some countries have been very large. When coupled with other barriers to trade they have often constituted formidable barriers to market access from foreign producers. In fact, tariffs that are set high enough can block all trade and performance just like import bans.

ISSUES

In the Uruguay round of the GATT/WTO negotiations, members agreed to drop the use of import quotas and other non-tariff barriers in favour of tariff-rate quotas. Countries also agreed to gradually lower each tariff rate and raise the quantity to which the low tariff applied. Thus, over time, trade would be taxed at a lower rate and trade flows would increase.

Given current U.S. commitments under the WTO on market access, options are limited for U.S. policy innovations in the 2002 Farm Bill vis a vis tariffs on agricultural imports from other countries.

Providing higher prices to domestic producers by increasing tariffs on agricultural imports is not permitted. In addition, particularly because the U.S. is a net exporter of many agricultural commodities, successive U.S. governments have generally taken a strong position within the WTO that tariff and TRQ barriers need to be reduced.

Non-Tariff Trade Barriers

Countries use many mechanisms to restrict imports. A critical objective of the Uruguay Round of GATT negotiations, shared by the U.S., was the elimination of non-tariff barriers to trade in agricultural commodities (including quotas) and, where necessary, to replace them with tariffs – a process called tarrification.

Tarrification of agricultural commodities was largely achieved and viewed as a major success of the 1994 GATT agreement. Thus, if the U.S. honours its GATT commitments, the utilization of new non-tariff barriers to trade is not really an option for the 2002 Farm Bill.

Domestic Content Requirements

Governments have used domestic content regulations to restrict imports. The intent is usually to stimulate the development of domestic industries. Domestic content regulations typically specify the percentage of a product's total value that must be produced domestically in order for the product to be sold in the domestic market (Carbaugh).

Several developing countries have imposed domestic content requirements to foster agricultural, automobile, and textile production. They are normally used in conjunction with a policy of import substitution in which domestic production replaces imports.

Domestic content requirements have not been as prevalent in agriculture as in some other industries, such as automobiles, but some agricultural examples emphasize their effects. Australia used domestic content requirements to support leaf tobacco production. In order to pay a relatively low import duty on imported tobacco, Australian cigarette manufacturers were required to use 57 per cent domestic leaf tobacco. Member countries of trade agreements also use domestic content rules to ensure that nonmembers do not manipulate the agreements to circumvent tariffs. For example, North American Free Trade Agreement (NAFTA) rules of origin provisions stipulate that all single-strength citrus juice must be made from 100 per cent NAFTA origin fresh citrus fruit.

Again, as is the case with other trade barriers, it seems unlikely that introducing domestic content rules to enhance domestic demand for U.S. agricultural commodities is a viable option for the 2002 Farm Bill.

Import Licenses

Import licenses have proved to be effective mechanisms for restricting imports. Under an importlicensing plan, importers of a commodity are required to obtain a license for each shipment they bring into the country. Without explicitly utilizing a quota mechanism, a country can simply restrict imports on any basis it chooses through its allocation of import licenses. Prior to the implementation of NAFTA, for example, Mexico required that wheat and other agricultural commodity imports be permitted only under license. Elimination of import licenses for agricultural commodities was a critical objective of the Uruguay Round of GATT negotiations and thus the use of this mechanism to protect U.S. agricultural producers is unlikely an option for the 2002 Farm Bill.

Import State Trading Enterprises

Import State Trading Enterprises (STEs) are government owned or sanctioned agencies that performance as partial or pure single buyer importers of a commodity or set of commodities in world markets. They also often enjoy a partial or pure domestic monopoly over the sale of those commodities. Current important examples of import STEs in world agricultural commodity markets include the Japanese Food Agency (barley, rice, and wheat), South Korea's Livestock Products Marketing Organization, and China's National Cereals, Oil and Foodstuffs Import and Export Commission (COFCO).

STEs can restrict imports in several ways. First, they can impose a set of implicit import tariffs by purchasing imports at world prices and offering them for sale at much higher domestic prices. The difference between the purchase price and the domestic sales price simply represents a hidden tariff.

Import STEs may also implement implicit general and targeted import quotas, or utilize complex and costly implicit import rules that make importing into the market unprofitable. Recently, in a submission to the current WTO negotiations, the United States targeted the trade restricting operations of import and export STEs as a primary concern. A major problem with import STEs is that it is quite difficult to estimate the impacts of their operations on trade, because those operations lack transparency. STEs often refuse to provide the information needed to make such assessments, claiming that such disclosure is not required because they are quasi-private companies. In spite of these difficulties, the challenges provided by STEs will almost certainly continue to be addressed through bilateral and multilateral trade negotiations rather than in the context of domestic legislation through the 2002 Farm Bill.

Technical Barriers to Trade

All countries impose technical rules about packaging, product definitions, labeling, etc. In the context of international trade, such rules may also be used as non-tariff trade barriers. For example, imagine if Korea were to require that oranges sold in the country be less than two inches in diameter. Oranges grown in Korea happen to be much smaller than Navel oranges grown in California, so this type of "technical" rule would effectively ban the sales of California oranges and protect the market for Korean oranges. Such rules violate WTO provisions that require countries to treat imports a nd domestic products equivalently and not to advantage products from one source over another, even in indirect ways. Again, however, these issues will likely be dealt with through bilateral and multilateral trade negotiations rather than through domestic Farm Bill policy initiatives.

Exchange Rate Management Policies

Some countries may restrict agricultural imports through managing their exchange rates. To some degree, countries can and have used exchange rate policies to discourage imports and encourage exports of all commodities. The exchange rate between two countries' currencies is simply the price at which one currency trades for the other. For example, if one U.S dollar can be used to purchase 100 Japanese yen (and vice versa), the exchange rate between the U.S. dollar and the Japanese yen is 100 yen per dollar. If the yen depreciates in value relative to the U.S. dollar, then a dollar is able to purchase more yen. A 10 per cent depreciation or devaluation of the yen, for example, would mean that the price of one U.S. dollar increased to 110 yen.

One effect of currency depreciation is to make all imports more expensive in the country itself. If, for example, the yen depreciates by 10 per cent from an initial value of 100 yen per dollar, and the price of a ton of U.S. beef on world markets is $2,000, then the price of that ton of beef in Japan would increase from 200,000 yen to 220,000 yen. A policy that deliberately lowers the exchange rate of a country's currency will, therefore, inhibit imports of agricultural commodities, as well as imports of all other commodities. Thus, countries that pursue deliberate policies of undervaluing their currency in international financial markets are not usually targeting agricultural imports.

Some countries have targeted specific types of imports through implementing multiple exchange rate policy under which importers were required to pay different exchange rates for foreign currency depending on the commodities they were importing. The objectives of such programmes have been to reduce balance of payments problems and to raise revenues for the government. Multiple exchange rate programmes were rare in the 1990s, and generally have not been utilized by developed economies.

Finally, exchange rate policies are usually not sector-specific. In the United States, they are clearly under the purview of the Federal Reserve Board and, as such, will not likely be a major issue for the 2002 Farm Bill. There have been many calls in recent congressional testimony, however, to offset the negative impacts caused by a strengthening US dollar with counter-cyclical payments to export dependent agricultural products.

Precautionary Principle, Sanitary and Phytosanitary Barriers to Trade

The precautionary principle, or foresight planning, has recently been frequently proposed as a justification for government restrictions on trade in the context of environmental and health concerns, often regardless of cost or scientific evidence.

It was first proposed as a household management technique in the 1930s in Germany, and included elements of prevention, cost effectiveness, and ethical responsibility to maintain natural systems.

In the context of managing environmental uncertainty, the principle enjoyed a resurgence of popularity during a meeting of the U.N. World Charter for Nature (of which the U.S. is only an observer) in 1982. Its use was re-endorsed by the U.N. Convention on Bio-diversity in 1992, and again in Montreal, Canada in January 2000.

The precautionary principle has been interpreted by some to mean that new chemicals and technologies should be considered dangerous until proven otherwise. It therefore requires those responsible for an activity or process to establish its harmlessness and to be liable if damage occurs. Most recent attempts to invoke the principle have cited the use of toxic substances, exploitation of natural resources, and environmental degradation.

Concerns about species extinction, high rates of birth defects, learning deficiencies, cancer, climate change, ozone depletion, and contamination with toxic chemicals and nuclear materials have also been used to justify trade and other government restrictions on the basis of the precautionary principle.

Thus, countries seeking more open trading regimes have been concerned that the precautionary principle will simply be used to justify nontariff trade barriers. For example, rigid adherence to the precautionary principle could lead to trade embargoes on products such as genetically modified oil seeds with little or no reliance on scientific analysis to justify market closure. Sometimes, restrictions on imports from certain places are fully consistent with protecting consumers, the environment, or agriculture from harmful diseases or pests that may accompany the imported product. The WTO Sanitary and Phytosanitary (SPS) provisions on technical trade rules specifically recognize that all countries feel a responsibility to secure their borders against the importation of unsafe products.

Prior to 1994, however, such barriers were often simply used as excuses to keep out a product for which there was no real evidence of any problem. These phony technical barriers were just an excuse to keep out competitive products. The current WTO agreement requires that whenever a technical barrier is challenged, a member country must show that the barrier has solid scientific justification and restricts trade as little as possible to achieve its scientific objectives. This requirement has resulted in a number of barriers being relaxed around the world.

It should be emphasized that WTO rules do not require member countries to harmonize rules or adopt international standards - only that there must be some scientific basis for the rules that are adopted. Thus, any options for sanitary and phytosanitary initiatives considered in the 2002 Farm Bill must be based on sound science and they do not have to be harmonized with the initiatives of other countries.

4

World Transfer Pricing and International Marketing

AN OVERVIEW

A small operation managed by a few individuals was the typical beginning of a large corporation with a hundred operating affiliates dispersed around the world. Decision making was highly centralized and lines of communication were short.

As the company grew, the founding management team found it more difficult to keep matters under control. This problem was greatly exacerbated when operations within the company became physically separated. Centres of activity in different locations called for a different style of management. Funneling of all decisions from diverse locations through a small group of individuals, who no longer possess the necessary intimate awareness of the circumstances surrounding each decision, is a surefire prescription for stifling growth.

Growth is the name of the game for modern corporations. Growth entails individual operating affiliates taking appropriate action to enhance productivity, market share, and the scope of a company's product line. It has been found that operating affiliates physically separated from the parent organization can best achieve these objectives under a decentralized style of management.

Responsibility now falls on the shoulders of the manager of an operating affiliate to make the necessary decisions that will lead to improved financial results, the universal measure of performance. The parent organization takes on a new role as coordinator and monitor of activities now that responsibility for operations has been transferred to the operating units. Far from playing a passive role, the parent organization focuses its attention on optimizing the performance of its semiautonomous operating affiliates. To do this, the parent organization must establish, and articulate, a set of strategic goals and allocate limited corporate resources to the various operating affiliates to best achieve these goals. It must ensure that the short-term action plans of the operating affiliates are in accord with its long-term plans.

Top management positions in the operating affiliates must be filled with individuals capable of leading their affiliates in the right direction and an incentive system must be set up to induce managers to orient their thinking to the goals of the company. Finally, the parent organization must set up a financial reporting and control system to monitor its global operations, to provide necessary information for the making of decisions and to evaluate the performance of the affiliate managers.

Although operating affiliates appear to be semiautono-mous units in that they are given a wide spectrum of decision-making responsibility in managing their local operations, they are not independent centres of corporate activity. They are often united in manufacturing and marketing a common product line, in the course of which they routinely buy and sell finished goods, components, or raw materials from one another. These intra company exchanges of goods, components, and raw materials require a transfer price. The parent organization sets the transfer price after considering various factors with an eye on optimizing corporate perfor-mance as a whole.

Transfer prices are often not negotiated and agreed on by the actual buyers and sellers of the goods and components being shipped between operating affiliates. Yet transfer prices directly affect the revenue and cost of goods sold, and therefore, the profitability of the operating affiliates. Because the affiliate managers are monitored by a financial reporting and control system that scrutinizes their financial results, one can expect that affiliate managers have an entirely different perspective on transfer pricing than the executives of the parent organization. Transfer pricing can easily embroil executives of the parent organization and the managers of operating affiliates in endless disputes. Some firms have even established an administrative panel for reviewing transfer prices to resolve sharp differences of opinion between those responsible for managing operating affiliates and those responsible for setting transfer prices.

TRANSFER PRICES AND TAXES

A global company with operations in many nations must deal with a new dimension of complexity in establishing transfer prices, which is not present when a company operates solely within the confines of a single nation. A company whose operations are within a single nation pays the same taxes on profits regardless of the transfer pricing policy. The consolidation process, whether for financial or tax accounting purposes, eliminates intra company transactions to arrive at either a book profit or a before-tax profit. When a company transacts business through affiliate companies in different nations, however, transfer pricing provides a mechanism for shifting taxable profits between tax jurisdictions.

Tax authorities in various nations are concerned with the notion that transfer pricing, often set by parent organizations outside their jurisdiction, is based on minimizing taxes paid in their jurisdictions. There certainly is an element of truth in this contention, but there are other considerations in administering transfer prices than minimizing taxes. The setting of transfer prices provides a way of moving funds internationally for a variety of purposes, of circumventing currency exchange controls that threaten to choke the operations of a company, of minimizing the deleterious impact of other artificial barriers to trade such as duties and tariffs, and of reducing currency risk exposure.

A transfer pricing policy attempts to satisfy a multiple set of objectives. Some of these objectives call for high transfer prices, whereas others require low transfer prices. A company must select what it considers to be an optimal transfer price, which is a compromise price for best achieving divergent objectives. This optimal transfer price may not be the one that minimizes taxes on profits. The selected transfer price may not be satisfactory both to the local tax authority and to the manager of an affiliate if it reduces the reported profitability of the affiliate. However, setting the transfer price is critical to optimizing the financial performance of the corporation as a whole, given the conditions that prevail at a point in time.

MINIMIZING TAXES

Tax authorities of most countries have guidelines or controls that are expected to be complied with in setting transfer prices. Management is not free to arbitrarily select transfer prices without having to substantiate their transfer price decisions. Nevertheless, there is still an element of choice where a selected transfer price may reduce the tax burden of a company. Suppose that a company consists of a parent organization and two operating affiliates—one in nation A, where the tax rate on profits is 30 per cent, and one in nation B, where the tax rate on profits is 40 per cent. The tax is applied to each affiliate's gross margin for illustrative purposes. The affiliate in nation A makes a product that is entirely sold through the affiliate in nation B. Two cases are considered—a low and a high transfer price.

Table. Case I-Low Transfer Price

	Nation A	Nation B	Consolidated
	Tax 30%	Tax 40%	
Sales	$2000	$3200	$3200
Cost of Goods Sold	1500	2000	1500
Gross Margin	500	1200	1700
Tax	150	480	630
Net Income	$350	$720	$1070

Everything made in a factory in nation A is sold through a marketing organization in nation B. Therefore, total sales in nation A, calculated on the basis of an administered transfer price, is also the cost of goods sold in nation B. Sales in nation B of $3,200 is the net consolidated sales for the company, because all goods produced in nation A are sold in nation B. The actual cost of manufacturing the goods in nation A is $1,500. Because nation B does not add value to the goods, the consolidated cost of goods sold for the company is also $1,500. The consolidated tax is the sum of the $150 and the $480 paid to the tax authorities of nations A and B, respectively. The consolidated net income is $1,070, the sum of the net incomes of the two affiliates.

Suppose that the transfer price is increased from $2,000 to $2,500 for goods shipped between the two affiliates. Consolidated sales, cost of goods sold, and gross margin are unaffected by the change in the transfer price, because it is netted out in the consolidation process. Taxes paid in each nation are no longer the same because of the change in the transfer price. In case II, the increase in the transfer price shifts the profit to Nation A, which has the lower tax rate. The affiliate in nation A earns more taxable income and pays more in taxes than in case I. The affiliate in nation B earns less taxable income and pays less in taxes in case II than in case I. The net effect, as seen by comparing case II with case I, is that the company as a whole is paying less in taxes, which increases its consolidated net income.

It is true that had the two nations the same tax rate, the total taxes paid by the company, and the consolidated net income, would not be affected by changes in the transfer price. Even so, transfer prices determine what portion of total taxes are to be paid to the tax authority in nation A and to the tax authority in Nation B. Although the parent organization may be relatively insensitive concerning to whom it pays taxes, needless to say, the tax authorities are very much concerned as to which is collecting taxes. The problem is compounded, from the point of view of a tax authority, because the transfer price is probably set by a parent organization not under its jurisdiction. The importance of transfer pricing to both managers and tax authorities can be appreciated when it is realised that between 40 per cent and 60 per cent of international trade involves goods moving between affiliates of the same company. Corporate decisions on transfer prices do have a meaningful impact on what a tax jurisdiction collects.

There are nations, islands, and localities where tax authorities exhibit little interest in transfer prices. Ireland, Puerto Rico, and other nations or areas designated as free trade zones or having special tax privileges may not tax corporate profits, or have a very low tax rate. These nations or locales are interested in companies building plants on their soil for the social benefits that accrue from employment of individuals who might otherwise be unemployed. Companies operating in such nations or locales can substantially decrease their overall tax rate. The effective reduction in tax rates depends on the transfer prices of imported components and semifinished goods and the transfer prices of exported finished goods. Granting tax concessions is one way for a nation to attract companies. At this time, eastern European nations offer tax incentives but do not have a prescribed accounting methodology to calculate profits, which makes it impossible to quantify the tax benefit. More than one company has set up an operation in eastern Europe to later discover that the government had a much different version in mind of the nature of the tax benefits than the investors anticipated. Such shortsightedness by government officials has a deleterious impact on attracting other companies.

Many nations are discovering that viewing business solely as a way to fill the public coffers may not be in their long-term best interests. Within the United States, states with high corporate tax rates have experienced companies moving to states with low corporate tax rates.

The higher they raise their corporate tax rates, the less they collect in taxes. As once companies moved from one state to another, now they move from one nation to another. In selecting a potential site, a businessman considers many factors, of which taxes are but one. Some of these are social and political stability; a system of commercial law to resolve disputes; a set of acceptable accounting practices (both to assess tax liabilities and evaluate tax incentives); a labour force with the requisite skills and will to work; and an infrastructure of transportation, communication, and utility and social (education, medical care) services.

There are more locations that offer good potential sites for factories than before. Managers no longer feel that their factories must be anchored to one nation and have learned to manage far-flung operations.

Nations must now compete for factories. Tax authorities in developed nations are beginning to realise that they may end up collecting less tax revenue in their eagerness to collect more tax revenue by raising tax rates. The United States was forced to repeal a luxury tax on pleasure boats because pleasure boat construction virtually ceased with the passage of the new tax. New Jersey was forced to repeal a sales tax on trucks when truck selling companies moved their operations to nearby Pennsylvania. In both cases, tax revenues fell when tax rates were raised, and the tax authorities were forced to rescind tax increases. In a global economy, companies are mobile and will relocate to avoid especially burdensome taxes.

INTERNATIONAL FUNDING

Businesses operating in hard currency nations have the advantage of being able to transfer and convert currencies as necessary. Many nations, however, have currencies that lack convertibility, the so-called soft currencies. Transfer pricing provides a means of moving funds from one country to another, when direct currency convertibility is not possible.

If a nation has an affiliate that completes the manufacturing process and sells its output within that nation, funds can be moved out of that nation by increasing the transfer price for goods imported by the affiliate.

The same objective can be accomplished by increasing the charges for services rendered by the parent organization to the affiliate, such as selling and administrative (SandA) fees, research and development (RandD) expenses, financial charges on transferred assets, and royalties for rights to patents and dividends. Sometimes currency exchange controls focus on the amount of dividends that can be paid by an affiliate to its parent. A quasi-dividend can be paid by raising the transfer price of goods moving into the nation or by increasing corporate fees, financial charges, and royalty payments.

Some nations with severe restrictions on dividend outflows will permit increases in transfer prices and service fees. These quasi-dividend payments are allowed because the local government recognizes that few companies can afford the luxury of investing in a nation that prohibits the company from earning a return on its investment. However, actions such as these that drain funds out of a soft currency nation eventually result in some sort of currency exchange restriction. This often results in affiliate profits accumulating in a currency that may not be particularly desirable. Sometimes currency exchange restrictions can be bypassed by the affiliate making an investment, or lending funds, to an affiliate in another nation.

CONTROLLING REPORTED PROFITS

Shifts in transfer prices, corporate administrative fees, and other parent company charges to an affiliate are means of managing the affiliate's reported profitability. It may be in the interest of a parent organization to lower the reported profitability of an affiliate for reasons other than tax minimization.

These include deflecting union demands for higher wages, reducing political pressure to nationalize or expropriate a profitable affiliate, and dissuading potential competitors from entering the market. Lowering profitability is also a way to counter price controls that limit profitability. If a government has set price controls based on the cost of production plus a limited markup for profits, increases in the transfer price of goods sent to the affiliate lowers the profit margin of goods sold in that nation. This may permit goods to be sold at government decreed profit margins with the company as a whole still able to earn its normal profits.

A few nations have tax rates that are linked to profitability. The greater the profitability, the higher the tax rate. The logic behind this taxation policy is that there is a level of profits on investment that seems"excessive" to the government. Such excessive profitability should be punished by the government, and there is no greater punishment than taking away the excess profits through a higher tax rate. By increasing the transfer price of goods being imported into the nation, the degree of profitability is decreased, lowering the tax rate and, presumably, restoring respectability in the eyes of the government. Alternatively, it may be in the interests of the parent organization to enhance the profitability of an affiliate. This may be done by lowering the transfer price

of imported goods. One reason for enhancing the profitability of an affiliate is to provide sufficient financial resources to the affiliate for it to withstand price cutting by competitive companies. Improving an affiliate's profitability, even at the cost of paying more in taxes, may allow the affiliate to borrow needed funds for operation from local banks and other financial institutions, to improve its credit rating to qualify for lower interest loans and to fund capital outlays from its own resources.

CIRCUMVENTING EXCHANGE CONTROLS

Governments with soft currencies often limit the amount of their currency that companies operating in their nations can exchange for other currencies. Their motivation is to discourage the selling of the domestic soft currency and the buying of a hard currency, which would exert downward pressure on the value of the local currency. In other words, exchange controls are set up to keep a soft currency from becoming softer.

From the point of view of a parent organization, restricting hard currency outflows inhibits an affiliate's ability to pay for imported components or other items necessary for its operations. Transfer prices for the needed components can be kept artificially low to expand the volume of goods that are being imported into a soft currency nation. This sustains an affiliate's manufacturing operation without exceeding government decreed restrictions on converting soft currency to hard currency. But there is an adverse consequence because such a course of action results in a parent corporation accumulating even larger amounts of soft currency. These holdings of soft currency are constantly losing purchasing power through inflation.

The soft currency cannot be converted to a more desirable currency because of currency exchange restrictions and the soft currency, which has little value within the nation, has no value outside the nation. One of the knottiest problems associated with an operating affiliate in a soft currency nation is funding of hard currency imports necessary for its operation and obtaining a hard currency return on a hard currency investment.

Some companies will not set up an operation in a soft currency nation unless there is a prearranged means to earn hard currency to pay for hard currency imports and to provide a hard currency return on a hard currency investment.

Pepsi Cola struck a barter deal for producing its soft drink in the former Soviet Union. Its soft ruble revenue, net of soft ruble expenses, is exchanged for Russian built tankers, which are then sold for hard currencies. Oil companies will not set up operations in the Commonwealth of Independent States, and other soft currency nations, unless they receive a share of the output, which is shipped out of the nation and sold for hard currency.

The easiest way for a company to earn hard currency in a soft currency nation would be to export a portion of its output to hard currency nations. However, most soft currency nations do not permit the hard currency revenue to remain with the company. The hard currency revenue is exchanged for an equivalent amount of soft currency, which is then credited to the exporter's bank account.

In essence, the national government receives the hard currency revenue from exports and pays soft currency to the exporter. Sometimes international banks are at fault for imposing this condition on a nation as a means to guarantee repayment of international debt. Regardless of whether the nation or the international banks impose this condition, it is self-defeating because the economic development of a developing nation is held back by the inability of companies to earn sufficient hard currency to justify their investments.

MINIMIZING DUTIES AND TARIFFS

Duties and tariffs imposed on goods imported into a nation can be reduced by lowering the transfer price. This is the exact opposite of reducing taxes on profits by increasing the transfer price. Because the tariff rate is usually less than the tax rate on profits, lowering transfer prices to reduce import tariffs often results in a higher tax on profits.

In some nations, however, tariffs on certain imported goods and commodities are not set by a corporate-determined transfer price but by an internationally posted price. This can be done only for generic goods (steel) or commodities (oil), where there is an active market with published and verifiable prices. Sometimes tax authorities will reference costs not to a "transfer price" cost but to an internationally agreed standard. One example of this is tanker rates in the oil business. An oil company can manage the profitability, and therefore, the tax liability, of a refinery by the transfer price associated with international tanker transportation for moving oil to and from a refinery.

The tax authorities of many nations and the oil companies have agreed to a panel of experts determining a fair and representative tanker rate that is used for the computation of taxes independent of the transfer price, or internal cost, that oil companies charge for shipping oil among their affiliates. This eliminates arguments between tax authorities and oil companies concerning the appropriate shipping charge.

Determining the optimal transfer-pricing policy is further complicated when a nation in which an affiliate operates has an export subsidy programme or provides a tax credit on the value of exports. It may be advantageous to lower transfer prices to an affiliate whose output is exported to third parties or other affiliates in other nations to take advantage of these tax incentives.

The optimal transfer price depends on the nature of the export subsidy or tax credit, the volume of the affiliate's output that is exported from the nation, the relationship between taxes on profits and the generation of tax credits and on the capacity of the affiliate to utilize the tax credit or export subsidy.

The nature of the taxes paid in a nation in the form of income taxes, duties and tariffs on imported goods, and export subsidies or tax credits on exported goods influence the setting of transfer prices.

There is no hard and fast rule on whether a high or a low transfer-pricing policy is best for a company. The particular circumstances of a company's operations in a nation and the nature of taxes and subsidies determine the best transfer-pricing policy.

A transferpricing system integrated into a financial reporting and control system should be capable of analyzing "what" if scenarios to evaluate the effect of different transfer-pricing policies.

REDUCING CURRENCY EXCHANGE RISK

Changes in currency exchange rates result in transaction and translation gains and losses. More importantly, they affect the competitive position of an affiliate. If an affiliate manufactures and markets its goods in a nation, and imports components from another nation, a revaluation of the currency where the finished goods are being sold relative to the currency of its purchased components reduces manufacturing costs.

This makes the affiliate more competitive and profitable. A devaluation, on the other hand, increases the cost of imported components, making the affiliate less competitive and less profitable.

Reality is much more complex than this simple example because affiliates may export and import components and finished goods to and from a variety of nations. Changes in exchange rates benefit some affiliates and hurt others, and it may not be obvious because of the nature of buying and selling of goods and services.

It is possible that a change in currency exchange rates that is adverse to a particular affiliate may be beneficial to the company as a whole because of the nature of the net exposure of the company to the affected currencies. Adjustments to transfer prices may affect currency holdings before an anticipated change in exchange rates takes place and may be able to restore a company's competitive position after the change has taken place.

Therefore, a financial reporting and control system should have the capacity to assess changes to both transfer prices and currency exchange rates to enable the parent organization to respond both to anticipated changes in currency exchange rates and to subsequent shifts in its competitive position.

TRANSFER PRICING AND JOINT VENTURES

A joint venture partner, a local partner owning a portion of an affiliate, and a minority shareholder are going to be as interested in transfer pricing as the local tax authority. Less often, a partnership is structured on the basis of a claim, or royalty, on revenue. More often, it is a claim on profits.

If one party to a venture or partnership can influence revenue, costs, and profitability through transfer pricing, then the other party or partner, or a minority shareholder, will be deservedly concerned. One way to manage transfer pricing with regard to having partners or minority shareholders is to formalize the setting of transfer prices in some verifiable manner such as a set markup above costs, another is to reference transfer prices to an observable market transaction.

Either way minimizes the opportunity for one party to a partnership or joint venture to manipulate transfer prices to its advantage. If the partners, participants, and minority shareholders feel that their interests are vulnerable by virtue of the other party to a business venture controlling transfer prices, then they may not contribute to the venture that which was expected of them.

Avoiding these problems can be more easily said than done. Some years ago, Ford Motor Company purchased the minority shares of its partially owned subsidiaries because the company felt that it could not administer transfer pricing in a way that was fair to all concerned.

Some managements have made the strategic decision not to enter into joint ventures, or have local partners or minority shareholdings in corporate affiliates, where they can manage the profitability of the venture through transfer prices. Sometimes, the solution for a problem is to avoid the problem.

TRANSFER PRICING AND MANAGERIAL PERFORMANCE EVALUATION

It may be in the interest of the corporation as a whole to transfer in components that are more highly priced than those an affiliate can purchase from other sources. It may be in the interest of the corporation as a whole to transfer goods made in one affiliate to another affiliate for less than what the affiliate can sell them for to third parties. Although the corporation may gain by such a set of transfer prices for goods moving among affiliates, it does not serve the interests of the affiliate managers if they are subsequently judged on profitability. This dichotomy of purpose in establishing a transfer-pricing policy for the good of the whole company, yet holding managers of affiliates accountable for profits that are contaminated, so to speak, by transfer prices has not been successfully addressed when transfer prices are different from market prices.

In fact, this is one potent argument in favour of companies having transfer pricing policies based on the market price for comparable goods. If transfer prices are set at the price for goods exchanged between unrelated parties, then there is no dichotomy of purpose in setting transfer prices and measuring performance. Managers of affiliates can be judged in an unbiased fashion on the profitability of their operations because they are buying and selling at market prices—the same prices that would prevail if they were independent companies.

The disadvantage of letting the market set transfer prices is that the parent corporation can no longer utilize transfer pricing as a means to pursue the overall optimization of the financial performance of the corporation. One possible approach to the dysfunctional aspects of setting transfer prices at other than market prices and measuring management performance of affiliates is to isolate and separately state the amount of inter company "profit" or "loss" that each affiliate is experiencing in its transactions with other affiliates. This approach provides the parent organization with information on whether an affiliate is suffering from unwarranted decreased profitability or enjoying unwarranted increased profitability because of transfer pricing.

SETTING TRANSFER PRICES BY COST OF PRODUCTION

There are two general approaches for setting transfer prices: the cost of production and market prices associated with third party, or unrelated, transactions. The cost-of-production approach bases the price of goods to be transferred between affiliates on the variable cost of production, an allowance for fixed costs that are general in nature and are apportioned over the entire product line, and an allowance for fixed costs that can be apportioned among the individual products.

This latter category usually includes research and development costs and selling and administrative costs. The remaining components may include financial fees and royalties associated with tangible and intangible assets to be apportioned to individual products and the selection of an appropriate profit margin.

The variable cost of production includes labour, material, and other direct costs that are consumed in the production of an item. If the policy of the company is to hire and fire (lay off) factory workers as production rises and falls, then labour is a variable cost. If a company is reluctant to let go of their workers when sales decline, then factory labour should be considered part of fixed costs. Factory labour costs are usually part variable and part fixed. Other variable costs can be the unit financing and utility costs associated with machinery and processes used in the manufacture of a particular product and unit shipping costs. These costs can also be treated as fixed costs depending on how the company's cost accounting system is set up.

Fixed costs are all costs not included in variable costs. Fixed costs are the financing or depreciation costs of the factory; the overhead costs of marketing, accounting, and supervision; the cost of inventories, warehouses, insurance, utilities, communication, property taxes, and other non-variable cost items.

Fixed costs may not be entirely fixed in that there is some variation as production levels change. For instance, bonuses, which would be considered part of the fixed costs of having an executive suite, rise and fall with profits, which are related to production levels. The number of staff personnel in marketing, accounting, engineering, and other overhead functions can vary with the production level.

Some elements of fixed costs are allocated in the transfer price setting mechanism in a way that fairly apportions the fixed cost burden among the various products. Other elements of fixed costs can be apportioned more on the basis of the benefit derived by an individual product. One of these is research and development, where the allocation can be made over a product line in proportion to the degree of RandD expenditures associated with the development of an individual product.

Although there is general agreement that this is a fair way to apportion RandD expenses of successful undertakings, there is lack of agreement on how to apportion RandD expenses for failed projects.

Some maintain that the allocation of expenses associated with failed RandD projects should be apportioned to all products on the basis that every product should bear the risk of failed RandD efforts. Others object on the grounds that had the RandD effort succeeded, a particular product might not have benefited. Therefore, it makes no sense for the transfer price to contain the cost of a failed RandD effort, which, had it succeeded, would not be part of the transfer price of the product.

The question as to the proper treatment of failed RandD projects is not an internal accounting matter. Tax authorities are interested in who takes the write off of a failed RandD project. In the United States, the Internal Revenue Service (IRS) is concerned whether a transfer price contains a provision for failed RandD expenditures.

If a transfer price contains only that portion of RandD expenditures that were successful with regard to a particular product, then failed RandD projects of a U.S. corporation are being written off solely against U.S. income. A portion of the tax loss write-off is passed on to the tax authority of another nation by including an element of failed RandD expenditures in the transfer price.

Another fixed cost element that can be separated and apportioned in a different manner than general fixed costs are services provided to an individual product.

These may be coordination and control expenses associated with a product; costs for enhancing the efficiency of operations for manufacturing the product or expanding the scope of its market; and the costs of recruiting and training of management and operations personnel associated with manufacturing, marketing, and repairing or servicing the product. The allocation of these service costs to individual products provides another element in deriving their transfer prices.

The derivation of the transfer price also includes elements for tangibles and intangibles associated with a product. Tangibles are the plant, equipment, and other physical assets dedicated to the manufacture of the product. Part of the transfer price provides a financial return for tangibles based on their value. Intangibles represent the technical knowledge and expertise and applicable patents that can be allocated to a particular product. The transfer price also contains an element that provides a company with a return on intangibles.

Intangible costs within a transfer price cannot be capriciously determined by management because intangible costs affect taxable profits. For this reason, the IRS has established guidelines for determining the intangible cost element in a transfer price.

An intangible cost element must be present if there are intangible costs associated with the manufacture or marketing of a product and must be so identified. Intangible costs can be proportioned in relation to the income attributable to the intangibles by units of production, sales, net or gross profits, or other reasonable methods. The fee for intangible property incorporated in a transfer price must be similar to what would have been arranged with an independent third party.

The last part of the cost approach in setting transfer prices is determining the proper profit margin on the goods made by one affiliate and shipped to another. This may be the average profit margin for the company as a whole or a profit margin associated with a specific product line. Regardless, the stipulated profit margin must be reconciled in some manner with the profitability of the company or a product line to satisfy the tax authorities.

The need for reconciliation of the profit and the various cost elements of the transfer price with the tax authorities sometimes results in the tax group within the finance department of a company being responsible for administering transfer prices.

However, this choice may hinder general management from using transfer prices as a means to achieve corporate objectives. The chief advantage of the cost of production approach for setting transfer prices is that the costs are available and are subject to quantification. For this reason, the production cost approach has been more common in the past than the market price approach.

The chief disadvantage is that there is no real incentive for an affiliate to improve its manufacturing process, to enhance its efficiency, or to take steps to lower costs. Mistakes, errors, inefficiencies in manning or machinery, management inattention to detail, worker carelessness, and excessive remuneration of white and blue collar workers alike may all be incorporated in the determination of costs and passed on to the affiliates in the transfer price. Another disadvantage is that both the tax authority and the affiliates may object to the nature of the apportionment of RandD, SandA, tangibles, and intangibles among the various products and the assigned profit margin.

SETTING TRANSFER PRICES BY MARKET PRICES

The disadvantages associated with the cost-of-production method of setting transfer prices can be mostly avoided by referencing transfer prices to third party transactions for identical, or nearly identical, products.

If an affiliate can obtain the item being purchased from a third party for a certain price, then that price can be the basis for setting the transfer price. The proponents of market-oriented transfer prices maintain that letting the market set the transfer price is inherently more fair than a production-cost-based system because one affiliate is not supporting the inefficiencies of another.

If an affiliate receives only the global competitive price for its products, then there is an incentive for it to take whatever actions are needed to correct the inefficiencies in its operations that are resulting in higher costs.

In a truly decentralized operation, managers are expected to make their decisions on an independent basis, and unrelated companies are permitted to compete for the business of an affiliate, along with other affiliates. The parent organization does not set transfer prices and has little or no influence over the decisions made by the managers of the affiliates. No favour or special consideration is shown to fellow affiliates in the competitive process of selecting suppliers for components and goods. The hope, of course, is that everyone is kept on his or her competitive toes to produce salable goods at the lowest possible cost.

This managerial philosophy, where each affiliate is treated as an independent company, is sometimes referred to as the small business unit (SBU) management philosophy. The disadvantage is that, although each affiliate is focused on optimizing its operations, the end result may be suboptimal performance of the corporation as a whole.

Suppose that affiliate X produces all of a component (part X) for a number of widget manufacturing affiliates. Total demand for part X is 2 million per year.

Affiliate X has $10 million in fixed annual costs, which include a profit margin on the investment in manufacturing facilities plus a return on the RandD investment for the development of part X. The variable costs for manufacturing part X is $5. The transfer price based on the fixed and variable costs of affiliate X supplying all other affiliates with part X is $10.

Table. Volume Of Sales: 2,000,000

Fixed Costs	$10,000,000
Variable Costs at $5 per Unit	10,000,000
Total Costs	$20,000,000
Transfer Price Based on Cost of Making 2,000,000	$10.00

Affiliate A is free to cut its best deal and obtains a quote of $9.50 from another company. Affiliate A does what is best for maximizing its profits and purchases 200,000 part X's from a third party for $9.50 rather than pay $10 to affiliate X. Affiliate X has lost a contract for 200,000 part X's and now operates on a basis of a sales volume of 1,800,000 per year.

Table. Volume Of Sales: 1,800,000

Fixed Costs	$10,000,000
Variable Costs at $5 per Unit	9,000,000
Total Costs	$19,000,000
Transfer Price Based on Cost of Making 1,800,000	$10.56

The remaining affiliates must pay a higher price because there is less sales volume to cover the fixed costs of affiliate X. The increase in transfer price to cover the fixed and variable costs is essentially equivalent to treating fixed costs as a component of variable costs, which it is not. Nevertheless, affiliate X must cover all its costs. When affiliate X announces the increase in price, affiliate B concludes a deal with a third party at $9.75 causing another loss of 200,000 for affiliate X.

Table. Volume Of Sales: 1,600.000

Fixed Costs	$10,000,000
Variable Costs at $5 per Unit	8,000,000
Total Costs	$18,000,000
Transfer Price Based on cost of Making 1,600,000	$11.25

Now it's time for affiliate C to say goodbye to affiliate X, as it maximizes its profit by reducing the cost of part X by paying $10.50 to another outside source. This is higher than the $10 price that applied when all the affiliates received part X from affiliate X. It is clear from the continuation of this exercise that, as each affiliate maximizes its profits by cutting costs, the corporation as a whole is being sub optimized. Even if the various affiliates do not pay more than an average price of $10 per unit for part X in purchasing all part X's from outside sources, the global company is stuck with an affiliate with no sales and a fixed annual cost of $10 million that represents, in large measure, financing costs on plant and equipment.

It is highly likely that the fixed costs in affiliate X contain an allowance for RandD expenses and product development that have to be recouped in the operation of a company, but do not have to be recouped by another company if it is essentially manufacturing a copy of part X. Copying is fairly common in global commerce because patent protection is limited to the nation issuing the patent. Global companies often obtain patents in a number of nations, but this may not be possible for all nations.

A company may manufacture a copy of a product in one of these nations. Although it is true that affiliate X is free to pursue patent infringement action against sales in a particular nation where it has patent protection, the time involved in enforcement proceedings and the legal expenses may make such protection prohibitively expensive. Furthermore, there is no internationally recognized legal structure to handle patent infringements.

In addition to RandD expenses, the fixed costs of affiliate X may also contain a service element for the benefit of the affiliates purchasing its output that may not be provided by third parties. By each affiliate "doing its own thing," the RandD and service costs cannot be covered. One principal problem associated with using market reference points for transfer pricing is that the affiliates may be shipping components and parts that are not readily available from other firms.

Most components and parts are specifically designed for a company's product line and are not available from third parties unless contracted for by an affiliate. Market prices for similarly designed components that cannot be actually used in the company's product line may not be relevant. Moreover, the quality inherent in third-party quotes for similar parts may not be up to the standards imposed on products made within a global corporate family.

There is no easy answer as to which approach for determining transfer prices should be followed. Both have their adherents and detractors. Either approach restricts transfer prices to something related to third-party, or market, transactions or to the cost of manufacture. Surveys have shown that nations seem to exhibit cultural preferences as to which approach to follow and as to what motivates companies in setting transfer prices.

Companies in some countries favour costbased transfer prices, whereas companies in other nations favour market-based transfer prices. U.S. based corporations have historically preferred setting transfer prices by the cost approach because the necessary data is available, whereas the necessary data for setting transfer prices on the basis of market transactions may not be available. Oftentimes, market quotes for uniquely designed parts and components may have to be derived rather than observed because there are no market transactions for the precise item.

Should General Motors set its transfer price on carburetors being shipped to Europe based on its cost of production or on what Toyota charges its U.S. transplants? The two carburetors are not the same and do not have the same cost of production. Furthermore, there may not be a data base available for prices for carburetors sold between related and unrelated parties from which to derive a market price.

Preferences change with time. Surveys done in the 1970s indicated that the preponderance of U.S. companies were motivated by tax minimization in setting transfer prices. More recent surveys indicate that companies are more interested in setting transfer prices on the basis of measuring the performance of affiliate managers and of providing reliable and unbiased information for the making of decisions.

This change in attitude in U.S. companies may be the result of the United States becoming a relative tax haven compared to other nations. Its corporate tax rate of 34 per cent, plus state taxes, is less than in many other industrialized nations, where tax rates range between 40 per cent and 55 per cent. A U.S. company's total tax bill may, in fact, be reduced by allocating more profits to the United States. Regardless of changes in attitudes as to what is important in setting transfer prices, the essential point is that there is no unanimity on which approach to use and on what motivates companies in setting transfer prices.

Up to this point, an important assumption has been that the parent company has real control over transfer prices to manage corporate cash flows and the profits reported by affiliates and to overcome artificial barriers to trade in the form of custom duties, currency exchange, and price controls. Some recent surveys suggest that competitive forces and market conditions within a nation seem to be more important in setting transfer prices than decisions made by a parent organization. If transfer prices are being set by exogenous commercial forces, then the presumption that a parent organization is able to achieve optimal financial performance of a global family of affiliates through the careful orchestration of transfer pricing is being challenged.

TAX CONSIDERATIONS

Taxation and transfer pricing are intimately entwined, because transfer pricing of goods, parts, and components moving in and out of a nation has a direct impact on taxes on profits and on the amount of duties and tariffs paid to the tax authority. The discussion on transfer pricing based on the cost-of-production approach shows an intimate involvement with the tax authority in the methodology for calculating various elements of the transfer price. There is little uniformity on taxation among nations. Taxes range from taxation of a corporation's activities to the "water's edge" or on its global earnings, the so-called "unitary tax." The state of California invented the unitary tax in the 1930s when movie companies in California began moving out of the state to avoid state taxes. A unitary tax was applied against the global earnings of a company and the tax was determined by the proportion of a company's sales, property, and payroll within the state to its global sales, property, and payroll. The resulting tax had no relation to the degree of profitability of a company's operation in California. A company could operate at a loss in California and still pay a tax based on its global profits.

Needless to say, both foreign governments and multinational companies have vigourously fought the unitary tax. A number of court decisions confirmed or restricted unitary taxation over the years. Ultimately, opposition to the unitary tax succeeded. In November 1991, Alaska was the last state to abandon having a company's state tax liability based on the global earnings of the company. The unitary tax still exists in a truncated form, where earnings are restricted to the "water's edge." The state tax is calculated on the portion of a company's activities within a state as compared to its activities within the United States.

Although most other countries limit their assessment on what is to be taxed to the operations of a company within their jurisdiction, there is no universal agreement as to what constitutes revenue and expenses in the calculation of taxable income and no uniformity on tax rates. Every nation decides what is subject to taxation and the applicable tax rates. The complexity of tax regulations, in general, and the diversity of tax laws among nations are such that it is necessary for an affiliate to retain the technical expertise necessary to understand and comply with local tax regulations. The parent organization must retain the technical knowledge for its own tax jurisdiction and have sufficient knowledge of tax matters elsewhere to coordinate tax planning among the various affiliates.

The vigour with which tax payments are enforced varies among nations. Some countries with seemingly high tax rates permit an underground economy to flourish without much in the way of enforcing tax payments. The other side of the coin is the willingness of companies to adhere to tax laws. In some nations, a businessman who scrupulously follows the tax laws and pays what is owed to the tax authority will find himself at a competitive disadvantage.

NATURE OF TAXES

Taxes can be direct or indirect. The United States relies more on direct taxation, which is applied to each taxable entity. A U.S. corporation is taxed at 34 per cent on its profits. If a corporation pays a dividend to its shareholders, then the next taxable entity, the individual, pays a tax, which may be 28 per cent or more. This is double taxation. Some nations, such as Germany, have two corporate tax rates on profits—one for retained profits and the other for distributed profits in the form of dividends. A lesser tax rate applies to profits that are distributed to shareholders to reduce the degree of double taxation.

Europe relies more on indirect taxes—particularly, the value added tax (VAT). The VAT is basically a tax applied to each stage of the production process and is not directly associated with the degree of profitability. Indeed, only a small portion of a VAT is associated with profits. Suppose that a company's manufacturing operations has the following financial results.

Wages, rents, interest, profit	$400,000
Outside purchases of goods and services for which VAT has already been paid	600,000
Total sales	$1,000,000

The additive method is to apply the VAT rate, say 10 per cent, to all costs associated with the production of goods, including profit and excluding purchases of goods and services from third parties for which the VAT has already been paid. In this case, $400,000 of a company's activities falls into this category resulting in a VAT of $40,000. A simpler method of calculation is to take the gross sales of the company ($1,000,000), subtract all purchases of goods and services for which VAT has already been paid ($600,000), and apply the VAT rate to the balance ($400,000). Either method yields the same result. The VAT is essentially equivalent to a national sales tax, because every company associated with the production and marketing of goods and providing services pays a tax on whatever value it adds to the goods or services. The value added tax, like a sales tax, is a tax on consumption, whereas U.S. taxes are on income and profits.

Value added tax rates vary widely from country to country and according to the nature of the business. Certain European countries have low VAT rates (5 per cent) for business transactions associated with food and high VAT rates (40 per cent) for luxury products. Others attempt to have one rate that applies to most forms of commerce. Because the VAT is not paid on items that have already been exposed to a value added tax, and with the European economy becoming more integrated, there is a powerful incentive for the European Community to harmonize VAT rates and coordinate the handling of VAT payments for products or components shipped between members of the European Community.

The amounts of value added by a company are frequently disclosed in European financial statements. In the excerpt from the British company, the company had gross revenues of 3,213 million pounds in 1987 of which 919.1 million pounds represents added value by the company. Of the total of 919.1 million pounds of added value, 496.8 million pounds was paid to the company's employees, 157.1 million pounds was paid in taxes to government tax authorities, and the remainder was paid to the internal and external providers of capital.

U.S. TAXATION OF GLOBAL COMPANIES

Nations have different ways of taxing global companies domiciled within their jurisdiction. If a parent corporation is domiciled in the United States, it does not pay taxes in the United States on profits earned by incorporated affiliates in other nations, unless the nation is considered a tax haven. This, in the United States, is known as Subpart F income, which will be discussed later under rein voicing centres. Unlike an incorporated affiliate, a branch of a U.S. company located in a foreign nation is taxed directly on its earnings regardless of whether the earnings are remitted to the home office or not. The taxes paid on remitted and unremitted earnings are not the same, in that unremitted earnings have to be translated to U.S. dollars before a tax liability can be assessed, and therefore, are influenced by changes in currency exchange rates. Taxes can also be calculated on the basis of the increase in the net worth of the branch, which can also be affected by changes in currency exchange rates. Sometimes a U.S. company will first open a branch operation in another country to permit startup losses to flow back to the parent organization. When the branch becomes profitable, it may be reorganized as a wholly owned subsidiary, reducing the company's overall tax liability.

U.S. based companies usually operate in the global market through operating affiliates whose stock is owned by the parent corporation. The parent corporation pays U.S. taxes only on the profits generated from dividends, royalties, and other service payments and fees paid by a non-U.S. domiciled affiliate to the parent organization. Taxes paid on profits by affiliates in their nations of domicile can be treated either as a tax credit or a tax deduction by the parent organization in the calculation of its U.S. taxes. To the degree that a tax paid on profits to a foreign government is treated as a tax credit, the net effect of a company paying taxes on its profits in a foreign country is that these taxes are essentially paid for by the U.S. government foregoing an equivalent amount of U.S. source based tax revenue.

Obviously, taxes paid to foreign governments must pass certain criteria set forth by the Internal Revenue Service to be considered for a tax credit. Foreign tax credits apply to taxes paid on foreign source profits calculated in a conventional way as U.S. source profits. Tax credits are also available for foreign government withholding taxes on dividends, interest payments, and royalties paid by a foreign-based affiliate to a U.S. parent company. There is a maximum permissible limit on tax credits linked to the ratio of foreign source income to total worldwide income multiplied by the tax liability of U.S. operations. This effectively limits the foreign tax credit to the U.S., not the foreign, tax rate. A company doing business in a nation with a higher tax rate on profits than in the United States does not receive a tax credit equal to the taxes paid to the foreign government. The tax credit is based on the U.S. tax rate. With U.S. tax rates being lower than in most other industrialized nations, U.S. based global companies are not being fully compensated by tax credits on foreign income taxes. This may provide an incentive to shift taxable income back to the United States through changes in transfer prices.

The U.S. tax authorities permit a credit for taxes paid on profits to other nations under the notion of tax equity and tax neutrality. The principle of tax equity implies that a U.S. taxpaying entity with an operation in another nation should not pay more in taxes than having the operation domiciled in the United States.

Were the equity principle absolutely true, a U.S. taxpaying entity would be indifferent, or neutral, to whether the operation was located in another nation or in the United States. Some maintain that the U.S. tax code does not adhere to the tax neutrality principle because a company doing business in New York City does not obtain a tax credit on its federal taxes for taxes paid to the state and city of New York on profits made in their jurisdiction.

A company with an affiliate in another nation not only receives a tax credit, which neutralizes its foreign and U.S. income taxes, but does not have to pay U.S. taxes on its foreign source earnings until those earnings are remitted to the parent in the form of a dividend, a royalty payment, or an equivalent thereof.

As long as foreign source profits remain in the coffers of the affiliate, no taxes are due to the U.S. government, even though, under special circumstances, the affiliate may lend these funds to the parent company. Deferral of dividend payments is essentially an interest-free loan made by the U.S. government to the foreign affiliate of a U.S. parent company on the amount of U.S. taxes due if, and when, these funds are repatriated to the U.S. parent. The principles of equity and neutrality built into the U.S. tax code were designed to provide an incentive for U.S. firms to invest overseas as part of the national policy of rebuilding war-torn nations. U.S. companies would be better off confining their activities within the United States, and would not invest in foreign affiliates, if the profits of these foreign affiliates were exposed to double taxation.

Qualified foreign taxes, which cannot be utilized as tax credits, may be used as a tax deduction. A tax deduction is not as valuable as a tax credit. Tax deductions apply when there is not sufficient U.S. taxes to be shielded by tax credits, or where the overall limitation on tax credits has been exceeded. Tax deductions can be carried back or carried forward, whichever is more useful.

REIN VOICING CENTRES

Some companies have set up rein voicing centres to manage all intra company trading of products. A rein voicing centre is at a single location, buying the output of the manufacturing affiliates and selling it to the marketing affiliates. Each affiliate receives or pays in its own currency, thus concentrating all intra company transaction currency exposure at the rein voicing centre. The centre possesses the necessary data to assess the net currency exposure of intra company transactions and can enter into appropriate currency hedges. The centre may also receive better quotes from currency exchange dealers because all intra company currency exchange transactions are done at one location.

The rein voicing centre can mark up the price of all products flowing through the centre to cover its administrative expenses. If there is little or no profitability associated with the operations of a rein voicing centre, it does not matter where the rein voicing centre is located from a tax viewpoint. However, it is possible to increase the markup to the point where corporate profit can be diverted from the nations where the goods are manufactured and marketed to the nation where the rein voicing centre is located. Now the location of the rein voicing centre is critical from a tax viewpoint.

In the 1960s, the U.S. government became concerned with the accumulation of profits in rein voicing centres located in tax havens. Tax havens were characterized as nations imposing no, or a very low, tax on profits, having a high degree of bank secrecy, and little or no currency controls. These nations consider financial activities of importance to their economy, provide modern communication facilities, and promote themselves as offshore financial centres. Bahamas, Bermuda, Cayman Islands, Liberia, Panama, and Vanuatu have been identified as tax havens.

It is possible to "run" a rein voicing centre through these nations without a physical presence of personnel or products. Profits can be easily diverted to tax havens by increasing the markup on selling prices, thus reducing tax liabilities to the nations where the products are manufactured and marketed. If the criteria for determining a tax haven is satisfied, then the income earned by a rein voicing centre, or any corporate entity in the declared tax haven, is deemed Subpart F income. This income flows directly to the U.S. parent corporation and is taxed as though the income was earned in the United States.

TAXATION IMPACT ON TRANSFER PRICING

Companies operating in the United States are guided by Section 482 of the Internal Revenue Code when setting transfer prices. Specifically, the IRS, through the Secretary of the Treasury, has the right to "distribute, apportion, or allocate gross income, deductions, credits, or allowances... between or among... businesses, if he determines that such distribution, apportionment, or allocation is necessary in order to prevent evasion of taxes. The IRS has been granted wide latitude to do whatever it wants if the IRS deems that dealings between a U.S. parent and its affiliates do not meet its standards. For instance, the IRS can reallocate income and deductions if loans have been made between a parent corporation and an affiliate at an unrealistic interest rate.

Unrealistic interest rates are those that would not occur for similar transactions between unrelated third parties. This also applies to charging for services and use of property, and transfers of tangible and intangible property including lease payments and royalties. A reference to IRS guidelines has already been made in discussing RandD and intangible costs in setting transfer prices by the production cost approach. Basing transfer pricing on published data rather than corporate derived prices is another example of the close working relationship, voluntary or not, between tax authorities and managers responsible for transfer prices.

In general, the IRS standard for determining transfer pricing, and other dealings between a parent and its affiliates, is whether it is an "arm's-length" transaction—one that would occur between a company and a third party having no affiliation other than the commercial transaction under consideration. This is independent of whether the transfer price is based on the cost of production or on market prices. If the transfer price between affiliates is seemingly out of line with a price that would have been charged to an unrelated party, then the IRS has the right to reallocate income or deductions according to what it feels to be the appropriate transfer price.

The IRS specifies various methods for establishing an appropriate transfer price. The preferred one is the comparable uncontrolled price method where prices are the same for goods sold to affiliated and to nonaffiliated companies. The price for goods sold to an unrelated third party establishes the transfer price for goods transferred to an affiliate.

This method does not work when goods are not sold to third parties, but are totally transferred between affiliates. Under these circumstances, the second method for setting the transfer price is the resale price method. This is the price for which the company would sell the item to an unspecified third party. The third party would add the same comparable value as the affiliate and sell the completed product with an appropriate markup. By netting the market price of the appropriate markup and the value added to the product by an affiliate, one can "back into" an appropriate transfer price from the point of view of the tax authority. The third method is the "cost plus" method, where the IRS permits three different ways of allocating costs (full absorption, direct cost, and incremental cost). All these methods leave some margin of discretion as to what is the appropriate transfer price.

If all these fail, as they frequently do for high-technology products, customised components, or subassemblies, then so-called fourth methods are permitted, such as determining transfer pricing on the basis of a predetermined profit for the foreign firm's operations and, through a netting process of accounting for applicable costs, establishing an appropriate transfer price.

Regardless of the methodology, the burden of proof in supporting a transfer price is with the taxpayer, not the IRS. To confuse matters more, there have been occasions when the tax courts have rejected the notion of arm's-length transfer pricing in settling tax disputes between corporations and the IRS.

OTHER NATIONS' POLICIES CONCERNING TRANSFER PRICING

The tax authority in Canada views transfer pricing of goods similar to the way the United States does. Transfer pricing for services differs in that it is based on a pro rata sharing of actual incurred costs between the parent corporation and its affiliate, and not necessarily at an arm's-length price.

Tax authorities in Japan follow a system comparable to that of the United States. German tax code provisions permit the reallocation of domestic source income if revenue or income has been shifted to another nation through a transaction that is different from those that would have been entered into by unrelated parties. In other words,

transfer pricing should be arm's-length, although the code is not specific in defining arm's-length pricing. The United Kingdom is similar to Germany in not specifically defining arm's-length pricing. The Inland Revenue may adjust taxable income based on fairness and arm's-length criteria. Disputes between corporations and Inland Revenue agents are frequently settled by negotiation, resulting in some sort of compromise between the two parties. This is unlike in Germany, where the adjustments made by the tax authorities are considered final, and unlike in the United States, where adjustments are litigated in tax courts.

Tax authorities in many nations are currently taking a much closer look at transfer pricing practices. Recently, the U.K. Inland Revenue recast the accounts of one non-British company operating in the United Kingdom and assessed back taxes of nearly 2 billion pounds. In the United States, there is growing political pressure for the IRS to take more vigourous action against foreign-owned companies operating through U.S. based affiliates.

This pressure stems from the realization that the aggregate expenses for foreign-owned businesses operating in the United States exceed aggregate revenues. This means that, in the aggregate, foreign-owned subsidiaries are claiming to operate at a loss, although individual foreign-owned subsidiaries may be paying taxes on profits. Some foreign-owned affiliates operating in the United States have a twenty-year string of consecutive losses. This is not considered a realistic appraisal of performance because there are few profit-motivated foreign-based parent companies that would support twenty years of successive losses were they real.

Poor or nonexistent profits for foreign-based affiliates operating in the United States are blamed on transfer pricing. Transfer price manipulation is felt to have resulted in tax underpayments of between $12 and $50 billion. Legislation was passed in 1989 to require foreign-owned businesses in the United States to keep records, in English, of transactions with foreign related parties. Much of this legislation has to do with substantiating transfer pricing on either a cost or arm'slength transaction with an unrelated third party. A growing risk associated with manipulating transfer prices for the purpose of tax minimization.

The risk is that the tax authorities will recast the company's statements with their own version of the proper transfer price, thus exposing a company to the risk of double taxation. Most nations have entered into tax treaties with various other nations with regard to taxing of affiliates of parent organizations domiciled in the treaty nations. These treaties determine withholding taxes on dividends, interest, and royalties; relief from double taxation; and the types of taxes and organizations covered by the treaty. Overall exposure to taxation can be reduced by judicious structuring of the legal corporate entities of a parent company and its affiliates in accordance with the provisions of these treaties.

Some of these treaties contain formal agreements for the mutual examination of the tax returns of affiliates of a parent company. The tax returns of affiliates and parent organizations are exchanged and examined by the tax authorities to determine correct tax liabilities, detect tax avoidance maneuvers, scrutinize trans- fer pricing practices, and exchange information useful to the tax authorities. These treaties also provide a forum for one tax authority to complain about the actions taken by another, when these actions are deemed detrimental to its interests.

Recent developments in international cooperation of tax authorities include the establishment of a formal agreement on transfer prices. The mutual agreement of various nations to reference a published source for tanker rates in determining oil company tax liabilities is an example of this. Australia and the United States are attempting to grant "advance determinations" of the proper transfer price for Australian companies dealings with their U.S. affiliates. A recent survey has shown that about half of IRS tax examinations of multinational companies involve transfer prices. If a mutually agreeable methodology could be arranged between a company and the IRS, many of these tax examinations could be eliminated.

The IRS is attempting to develop a procedure whereby a company and the IRS would mutually agree to a transfer-pricing agreement covering the distribution of finished goods, sales of raw materials and components, general and administrative expenses, and managerial and technical services. If the taxpayer develops an acceptable transfer-pricing methodology, then the taxpayer and the IRS would enter into an advance-pricing agreement. The IRS would limit its examinations to an audit to ensure that the taxpayer has complied with the agreement.

However, the taxpayer is obliged to submit pricing data of independent transactions, or an adequate substitute, to show that the transfer price possesses the necessary attributes of an arm's-length transaction. The taxpayer is also responsible to show that the agreed transfer-pricing methodology is generating acceptable transfer prices from an arm's-length perspective.

The preference of tax authorities in many nations for arm's-length transfer pricing may act as an inducement to switch from the cost-of-production to the market price approach in setting transfer prices because, presumably, they are one and the same. The financial and taxation departments of multinational, or global, companies must deal daily with what are considered to be the most pressing issues in international accounting today. Those involved with transfer pricing must measure the consequences of their transfer-pricing decisions both on corporate profits and on current and potential tax liabilities. Potential tax liabilities, stemming from tax authorities rejecting management's transfer price decisions, and substituting their own, are enormous. This must weigh heavily on the shoulders of those responsible for setting transfer prices.

5

International Marketing Planning and Communication Policy

INTERNATIONAL COMMUNICATION POLICY

The Internet today has reached a level of political importance where some form of governance policy is needed. The problem is to determine which policies to govern which aspects of the Internet.

From one perspective, the Internet does not exist: It is merely a conglomeration of linked individual networks which has no formal corporeal existence. From this perspective, there is no need for any policy save laissez-faire. What may need to be governed are specific pieces, since there is no whole.

From another perspective, the elements of the Internet constitute a conceptual whole, the ultimate commons, where no part can function well without all other parts operating well. From this perspective, some form of overall governance is essential, which without a whole, there will be no parts.

The issue of what kind of communications policy should govern the Internet, if any. It looks at the interface between telecommunications technology, content, economics and law that constitutes the policy problematique. It focuses on the policy issue that has placed the problematique in bold relief: the issue of how to assign domain names. It looks at the implications of this for different approaches to governance.

It uses the "R word": regulation of the Internet. It starts from the premise that, because the elements of the Internet are of public interest, there will be regulation. The issue is who will regulate, what, and on which basis..

TECHNOLOGICAL DIMENSIONS

At the heart of the matter are the technological dimensions, the characteristics of the Internet that define the need and the prospects for governance. In telecommunications terms, these technological dimensions constitute a new paradigm for looking at policy.

A New Network Paradigm

Although telephone switching systems have matured to the point that hundreds of millions of connections a day can be set up and maintained by the network, their essential characteristic remains a continuous full-time pathway between two points at any one time.

Packet switching represents a significantly different communications model. The content, once put into digital form, is divided into small well-defined groups of coded data, each with an identifying numerical address. Anything that can be digitized can be sent as a packet. To the Internet, a packet is a packet is a packet, whether it carries numbers, words, digitized sounds or digitized pictures. It became possible, and the U.S.

Defence Department's Arpanet actualized the possibility, to send an unlimited number of packets over the same circuit with different addresses. Routers, rather than switches, became the key to delivering the packets to the intended destination. Controlled by software and microprocessors, the router inspects the address of a packet and sends it on its way on a full-time circuit to another router to an eventual end point. As the Arpanet evolved from an X.25 network into the TCP/IP network that undergirds the Internet, the designers reserved 32 bits for the packet address which are represented in decimal notation in a format xxx.xxx.xxx.xxx, where each group of x's can range from 0 to 255.

The innovation of a Domain Name Server in 1984, prior to the creation of the Web in 1998-89, provided synonyms for the somewhat inscrutable digit strings of the actual address. The actual addresses of the packets remained the digit strings but they were replaceable by more or less scrutable alphabetic equivalents stored on a DNS server file which permitted the lookup of the alphabetic name from a numerical address and vice versa. Thus was born the web site name, a new entity and a new property right in a new and legally ambiguous sphere.

The telephone system addressing system started in the simplest possible fashion with Sally asking an operator to connect her to Harry. Under the direction of the Bell System-affiliated companies and by agreement with the non-Bell operating companies, the present U.S. ten digit area code-exchange-line number system evolved over decades into a national standard. By contrast, the Internet addressing plan was designed from its day of creation by engineers and scientists as a logical and comprehensive construct to meet their needs for low cost data communication. The integrity of the plan was guaranteed by its sponsorship by the US Department of Defence and by later private sector successors.

The alphabetic names associated with numeric addresses were divided into domains, a limited typology of alpha addresses that enabled the routers to do their lookups efficiently. To find the numeric twin of the Internet address of "UN.ORG," for instance, the router need not search through every entry in its address table, just the addresses ending in ".ORG." These suffixes as the first level of searching and selecting are known as top level domains: the current set includes.COM.MIL.ORG and.NET, corresponding to net addresses for entities in commercial, military, non-profit and network administration endeavors.

Internet addresses are conceptually very different from telephone numbers. In the U.S., Canada and the Caribbean, most area codes denote a geographic place with boundaries identifiable with governmental jurisdictions: nations, states, cities. The exchange part of the phone number is traditionally associated with a specific place with a street address, the central office, from which the wires emerge to connect the telephone user over the "last mile" to the network. The place-centered nature of the phone system numbering plan is beginning to break down with the rise of wireless cellular systems, the widespread use of ghostly 800 and 888 numbers which may be answered here one minute and there the next. Nonetheless, jurisdiction can be established in all cases. Internationally, the country code, city code numbering system links phone number to place to jurisdiction.

Internet Communications

Internet addresses have no fixed location. They are purely conceptual. There is no central office. The routers which direct packets to the packet address at rates between 100,000 and 500,000 a second can know only the next logical point in a routing table and which outbound circuit is available to carry the packet. Packets are free to traverse the globe on countless circuits to geographically indeterminate end points. The technology provides assurance that the packets are reassembled in the right order and are very likely not corrupted by data errors.

A further distingnet addresses is that neither the sender nor the receiver of a packet is a paying customer for the packet. Telephony requires two paying customers to complete a call, each of whom is a paying for the privilege and each of whom has at a minimum a billing address and usually a street address in a city, a state/province and country. The Internet senders and receivers are inherently tied neither by the billing process nor the technology to place.

We have identified the technical underpinnings of novel realities which have led to major policy debates which are far from resolved. From inside the Internet, names for addresses are structured but purely arbitrary, the technology is indifferent to content, and the sender/receiver dyad is unlocatable in a conventional spatial sense.

Technology and Property: Intellectual Property: Names, Sounds, Pictures, Words, and Ideas

Names have value; legal ownership and the right of exclusivity for patents, trademarks, service marks and copyrights for sound/picture/literary content are well-established in Western law. The treaties underlying the World Intellectual Property Organization have extended the principles, if not the practices, to a wide spectrum of countries. A substantial body of commercial law and practice guarantees that recourse is available to a party which believes its property rights have been infringed upon. A variety of adjudicatory mechanisms are available to resolve disputes and provide redress at a national level.

The Internet poses a challenge due to its indeterminate ubiquity. Infringement becomes possible from any corner of the globe, that is, from any address on the Internet. If content can be digitized it can be not only pirated, but it can also be disseminated globally with no impediment. No court, mediation board or arbitrator can be presumed to exist with authoritative jurisdiction even if the infringer can be definitively identified. The efforts of the United States to halt the active commerce in pirated compact disks and software in China are illustrative of the difficulty of maintaining ownership of intellectual content; absent any overarching jurisdiction, diplomatic pressure had to be brought to bear in a bilateral context of numerous other foreign policy issues. The Internet raises the very real specter of massive evapouration of assets. The Internet is not an inherently broadcast medium although it shares the ability of radio and television to simultaneously reach many people through Web sites either sought deliberately per occasion by the receiver or "pushed" by a Web application such as Pointcast. With the partial exceptions of short-wave radio and the direct broadcast satellites, the content of radio and television broadcasting since Marconi has been firmly under the thumb of governmental authority under the rationales of orderly spectrum allocation, revenue generation twinned with cultural uplift or outright thought control.

The potentially universal accessibility of content via the Web upsets the traditional regulatory model. In its blithe way, the Web does not care what it carries: hate, love, pornography, fraud, lies, truth, scholarship, charlatanry are all the same in the stream of bits and all equally accessible. The efforts of the German government to shut down Nazi-leaning, anti-Semitic Web sites by penalizing the Internet service provider was a kind of desperate grasping for any available handle since the real purveyors were to difficult to reach. The ease of establishing a Web site provides assurance that the extinction of one offender will not prevent recrudescence. On the horizon are technical developments which will make the Internet much more like a broadcast medium and even more subversive of government control: vastly increased circuit capacity through a technology known as "wave division multiplexing" and a redesign of the underlying Internet protocols to permit simultaneous transmission of the large amounts of data required for images.

Problems Resulting from the Technological Characteristics of the Internet

Creation and Destruction of Property Rights

The ownership of domain names is just one example of a new form of an old, satisfactorily, if not perfectly settled issue. A broader question is how to retain ownership of digital content once it has been digitized and made available on the Internet. The widespread availability of inexpensive copying machines a decade ago created a culture of book and substance copying to the great distress of conventional publishers. Law suits and clarifications of the copyright law resulted in a "fair use" doctrine which limits copying to personal use. "Fair use" on the Internet is much more difficult, if not impossible, to define. For one class of content creators, the issue is irrelevant: those for whom dissemination is more important than immediate financial gain. Scientists, scholars in the humanities and creative writers are increasingly bypassing paper-based media and are skipping directly to Internet publication. The effect on the lucrative business of scholarly publishing will be devastating as publishers watch their feedstock evapourate.

Trade in Services is an Increasingly Large Portion of World Trade

The Internet promises to expand this invisible trade exponentially and uncontrollably from the standpoint of sovereign authorities. Insurance is not the only thing that can be moved beyond existing regulatory measures. Software itself as well as music and visual content are becoming major elements in world trade, all moved silently through the Internet. Relying upon their semi-sovereign status as well as the global nature of the Internet, the Coeur d'Alene tribe of native Americans in Idaho have established an international lottery on the Internet doubly beyond the control of the U.S. and Idaho State governments.

The conventional telecommunications services which have constituted a growing share of world trade in invisibles have been a well-regulated, though recently contentious, affair both in governmental and commercial terms. Traffic is measured in minutes by the sending and recipient countries and companies and compensation is paid under international agreements much as banks settle funds flows.

Internet telephony, on the other hand, upsets these arrangements by bypassing the telephone companies call accounting systems almost entirely through the use of dedicated full-time circuits. Once the quality of service deficiencies are addressed and the last mile problem is solved, a very large piece of international trade will disappear from the scope.

Finally, some of the trade is in goods and services that are usually regulated in national commerce but where the nature of the Internet permits easy avoidance. Pornography and gambling are two examples where the fluidity of the Internet makes national control extremely difficult. The revenues generated in these two trades have not been estimated, but are clearly large.

Authenticity of Communications becomes Suspect on the Internet

Considerable effort is being devoted to security and encryption due to the anonymity of the Internet and the indeterminacy of the packet technology. Law enforcement and national security interests have butted up against the anxiety engendered by the lack of clear knowledge of where the Internet address is located and who is there. Authenticity anxiety is most powerfully felt when money is exchanged.

Privacy of Communication is a Reasonable Assumption in Circuit Switched Networks

Indeed, the almost total digitization of the telephone network and its reliance on extremely high speed multiplexing techniques drove the U.S. government to successfully press for the adoption of the Communications Assistance to Law Enforcement Act which obliges telephone companies and their suppliers to modify their equipment to support digital wiretaps in ways which have yet to be resolved. Privacy is not a reasonable assumption on the Internet.

Problem of Preserving National, Regional and Local Culture is Exacerbated by the Internet

Before the Internet achieved its current prominence, the dominance of U.S. mass media products in the world market was a major bargaining issue during the Uruguay round of trade negotiations with France and Canada holding out for significant restrictions. Substantively unrelated agricultural negotiations led to compromises which apparently satisfied the negotiators. The Internet players are not so easily identified and mollified as the Disney Corporation and Rupert Murdoch. The relatively low cost of entry and exit means that backyard moguls can become significant originators of cultural content available everywhere. A clash with local mores is inevitable in open societies and even more so in closed ones. The dominance of the English language on the Web is a thorn to cultural preservationists outside the English-speaking countries. Efforts are underway to make the Web multilingual but the most common ways of representing text digitally were designed for the Roman alphabet, especially as used in English.

Crime and Terrorism take on new Guises with the Availability of Inexpensive and Widely Available Instantaneous Global Communication

As evidenced by the mostly benign attacks by self-styled "hackers," the network and the computers connected to it themselves are potential targets for criminal enterprises that normally fall under the rubrics of theft, larceny and property destruction. Internet aside, as the normal business of daily life such as power distribution, financial systems, air traffic control become pervasively intertwined with automated systems, the potential for criminal and terrorist attack becomes acute.

The historical working commercial and international law has not been brought to bear on these issues or is inherently incapable of being applied.

ECONOMICS OF THE INTERNET

Had the Internet remained a vehicle for communication among highly specialized publics, such as the scientists and engineers who first used it, there would probably be no need to talk about governance. The "club-like" approach to maintaining system coherence and allowing for technological change worked well when there were only a limited number of actors and very few evident economic or social issues connected to the technologies. In fact, the technical management of the Internet could still be accomplished by the consensual approach were it not for the non-technical issues.

The telephone industry is a case in point. In the United States, non-governmental structures such as the American National Standards Institute, the Institute of Electrical and Electronic Engineers, the National Exchange Carriers Association as well as legacies of the monopoly era such as Bellcore have effectively set and maintained interoperability, accounting and settlement standards with little authoritative government input.

Standards-setting in these bodies is bottom up: companies with a compelling commercial need convene working groups to develop compromise standards which will ensure interoperability in the interest of establishing a wider market. Some commercial enterprises are able to set standards without the assistance of either voluntary groups or governmental authorities. Market dominance is the standard-setting mechanism. We do not need to cite the all-too-obvious examples. ISDN is an interesting case of an elegant, logically coherent and comprehensive construct built from first principles, top down. Although it is very important for the carriers, it is less so for consumers in the US; data networking largely ignores ISDN. Likewise, the OSI data communications model, while serving as a point of reference, has been bypassed by the semi-conformant TCP/IP model.

Growth causes problems because it increases the number of players. Many of these do not share the values of the technicians and academics who set up and were the first users of the Internet. The perspective of short-term profit is different, and often contradictory to, the perspective of long-term free and unregulated exchange of information.

Moreover, as the Net becomes more lucrative, there is an urge on the part of governments to tax it as a means of raising public revenue. Here the decentralized and borderless nature of the Internet makes it difficult to collect taxes fairly since it is easy to avoid them. While some of the major governments in the world talk of policies to ensure that the Internet is a tax-free zone, it is questionable how long that commitment will last.

CONTENDING APPROACHES TO REGULATING THE INTERNET

Ultimately there are three approaches to regulation of the Internet, a self-regulating market, national regulation or an international regime. Each has its own distinct features, and limitations.

Self-regulating Market

One version of this approach is Peter Huber's Law and Disorder in Cyberspace where he argues that the advance of technology is so rapid that no regulatory regime has had and can have any effect which is not detrimental. The maintenance of order in the "telecosm" should be maintained by private actors and private litigants, common law courts and the market. Against Huber, Stewart Baker has argued that judges are clumsy and retrograde makers of social policy. More to the point, in the international arena, the Anglo-Saxon common law tradition is non-existent and "the market" is a synonym for the global behemoths of Canada, the United States, the European Union and Japan.

A Market Guided by National Authorities

Just as the Federal Communications Commission has regulated the cable TV, telephone and broadcast industries in the US for almost 100 years, so also could it and its foreign counterparts regulate the Internet. Two obstacles are likely to obviate this option. First, the technology is mutating so quickly that even the FCC cannot keep up with the demands for new regulations in its traditional sphere. Second, the Internet lacks the choke points of easily identifiable parties to regulate. A comparison of the efficacy of customs collection from large ocean vessels with that from Caribbean drug runners in small fast boats which can land anywhere points up the difficulty of dealing with widely dispersed mobile targets.

An International Regime

The basis for an international umbrella to set policy and resolve disputes has been laid with the World Trade Organization which is responsible for administering trade agreements such as the General Agreement on Trade and Tariffs, the General Agreement on Trade in Services and the Agreement on Trade-Related Intellectual Property Rights. The emerging services of the Internet and the dilemmas they pose have not yet been addressed by the WTO, but the model has been established. We argue that an international convention with representation of an unprecedented kind can set the framework for international regulation of the Internet. The precedent has been established with both the Rio de Janeiro conference on the environment and the Beijing conference on women; both conferences drew their representation and their strength from a broad range of interests that went well beyond nation-states.

The three contending approaches are not mutually exclusive: they could co-exist by assigning one approach to one aspect of Internet policy and others to other aspects. For this to work, however, there would need to be an overarching understanding of which approach would be applied to which aspect and some means to ensure that the result of the approach in one aspect did not have a negative impact on another.

ASPECTS OF A COMMUNICATION POLICY

One way to look at communications policy is to break down communications itself into its component parts.

In an analytical sense, communication includes:

- A sender,
- A message,
- A channel or medium
- A receiver and
- Feedback.

Each component has its own regulatory dimension and its own constituency. The model emphasizes the complexity of the international regulatory problematique by suggesting the many agencies involved.

Table. Public Policy Issues in Communications, National and International

Communication aspect	National Issue	International Efforts	Constituencies
Sender	Universal service Non-discrimination Competition Trademarks Tax policy	Developing country access (UNDP/World Bank/ITU) Non-discrimination (UNHCHR) Competition in services (WTO) Authentication (UNCITRAL) Domain name registration (ITU/WIPO) Trademarks (WIPO)	E-commerce companies Software producers Electronic media Universities and libraries Netizens
Message	Content regulation Copyright	Norms for content regulation (UNHCHR) Copyright (WIPO)	Government censors Press, film, music industry; Civil libertarians
Medium	Telecom regulation Encryption policy Competition Public investment	Transmission standards and protocols (ITU) Satellite orbit slots (ITU) Competition WTO) Payments policy (ITU) Infrastructure investment (World Bank)	Telecommunications companies; Banks and financial service companies; Internet service providers
Receiver	Universal access	Universal access	User groups; Students and researchers
Feedback	Access to governance Interactivity Finance	Access to governance Interactivity	Non-governmental organizations Industry groups Developing country governments

It is no coincidence that the first two universal international organizations were concerned with communications: the Universal Postal Union and the, then, International Telegraph Union. Without some regulatory mechanism, communication flows over national borders could not be assured. Both institutions have endured (even though the ITU became the International Telecommunications Union) as what are now termed technical agencies of the United Nations system. The ITU has, through the domain-names controversy, become involved in Internet regulation, together with WIPO.

The question is, however, will the Internet change the parameters of international regulation, can the existing agencies perform the task and is there now a need for a conscious international communications policy?

Sender

The key issue for senders is to ensure access. In order to be a sender, one needs a method of identification. The need for order in identification is reflected in the discussions about how best to register domain names. In that sense, it is probably not surprising that the first large controversy in international regulation is in that area. Here the market mechanism has largely failed. The controversy also lays out in stark relief that there are many more significant parties to the question than just governments: individual and corporate senders, non-governmental organizations, channel providers and receivers as well.

A second issue for senders is the freedom to send messages. This is partly a matter of content but is also a matter of having a network on which any sender can expect to reach receivers. Here the question turns on whether reasonable access can be obtained to Internet service providers, with minimal regulation and reasonable cost, and whether receivers can be expected to be able to get the messages. This latter, again, is a matter of provision of the appropriate technology at a reasonable cost. The case in which Internet intermediaries in Austria were obliged to disconnect Internet sites in Iraq is an example of this issue. Cost is related to the degree of competition among senders, and here the work of the World Trade Organization in terms of increasing trade in services is relevant.

Organizations of senders are beginning to develop. These can be nationally-based, as many are, but they are increasingly transnational. This in itself is a new phenomenon. It creates the prospect of international non-governmental organizations of senders which need not be comprised, as are traditional NGOs, of federations of national affiliates.

Message

Issues of message relate to regulation of content. What messages should be allowed, who will determine whether they will be allowed and who will regulate this. The Internet developed as an almost free market for ideas, but many individuals and a few national authorities have found messages objectionable. The efforts at censorship of adult material by the German government through prosecution of CompuServe managers for alleged pornographic content. A similar issue can be said to have been raised by efforts to regulate the use of encryption technology.

Communications policy includes regulatory policy and there are already efforts to develop national regulatory norms that would be applicable to the Internet, most recently the German Information and Communication Services Bill. These are highly controversial, since restriction in one kind of content may set precedents for wider regulation. They also pose national constitutional questions, as was found in the case of the invalidation of the Communications Decency Law in the United States. They are also likely to be ineffective, since the borderless nature of the Internet makes applicability of national regulations highly problematic.

Medium

The medium or channel over which the message is sent has historically been the focus of communications regulation. Partly this was because the channel, which was a physical entity, could be regulated. Partly it was because communications channels, like frequencies or lines that passed over public lands, were inherently public goods. At the international level this aspect of regulation has been reflected in international standards for bandwidths, frequency allocations and exchange protocols. It has also been reflected in agreements on the allocation of geostationary orbit slots.

Ensuring competition among providers of media has been a concern. Just as many governments are privatizing their national telecommunications systems, mergers among main Internet pipe providers has raised the specter of monopoly and has produced some efforts at regulation, as is the case of European Commission scrutiny of the proposed MCI/WorldCom merger.

A new effort at regulation through the medium is found in an increasing effort to regulate content by regulating channel providers. These include the cases of the government of Austria shutting down an Internet service provider by confiscating its physical servers, or the libel action against America On-Line. The futility of this type of regulation has also been demonstrated.

Perhaps more importantly, telecommunications technology is increasingly intersecting with the recognized global commons, as satellite-based transmission technologies designed to increase bandwidth and ensure coverage begin to compete for scarce orbital slots.

The fact that two private corporations, Teldesic and a consortium of Motorola and others, intend to place large number of communications satellites in orbit will inevitably require some effort at regulation. Similarly, the increase of wireless transmission is already leading to regulatory efforts on a national basis and can be expected increasingly to enter international "space".

Receiver

As in the case of senders, the key issue for receivers of messages is access. One should be able to receive what the messages that one wishes and the Internet, with its packet delivery technology, facilitates this. Access, however, can be controlled by cost, by regulation or by technology. The largest obstacle, however, is access to service providers, particularly in the developing countries. Partly this is a matter of technology transfer, partly of cost. However, as events such as the World Bank/UNDP/Canada Global Knowledge '97 Conference showed, many of the technical solutions are available, if they can be disseminated.

The real question is cost, including those of national telecommunications. Here it is partly a matter of local assignment of costs, which is related to telecommunications monopolies and the issue of competition, partly it is a matter of how international prices are calculated. In the matter of postal rates, which may have an analogy with Internet rates, mechanisms have been put in place to adjust rates to both national and international reality in the public interest.

Feedback

The final aspect of communications is feedback. Here the interactive nature of Internet makes it perhaps the most complete communications system yet devised. How and whether feedback can be regulated is as yet an open question, although the well-publicized libel case against Matt Droan and America On-Line is beginning to indicate that there is an issue here. Similarly, the role of gatekeepers, including non-governmental organizations, in channeling feedback has yet to be explored. Each of the elements also describes a constituency or constituencies whose interests may conflict.

DOMAIN NAME DISPUTE AS AN EXAMPLE

Internet governance might have remained a dormant issue were it not for the domain name dispute. This issue stands at the interface between the technological issues of Internet management and the economic and social issues that have emerged. It affects most of the aspects of communications. Its resolution has placed competing models in stark relief. It has illuminated the problems of national versus international regulation and it has mobilized the distinctly different constituencies within the Internet.

Origins of the Problem

The assignment of names to domains in preference to numbers was a convenience for the early users of the Internet. The responsibility for assigning numbers was delegated by the United States government to an independent entity called the International Assigned Numbers Authority, headed by Prof. Jon Postel of the University of Southern California.

The IANA was primarily concerned with ensuring that duplicate numbers were not assigned and that assigned numbers were entered into a central directory. IANA assigned the country codes for domain names, including that for the United States.

The attachment of names to the numbers which were not country-specific, the generic top-level domain names for .com, .org and .edu was the responsibility of another entity, which was working under a subcontract from the National Science Foundation, as a result of competitive bidding. The entity was a private company, Network Solutions, Incorporated, functioning as InterNic. It is a commentary on the size of the Internet when the contract was issued that NSI began to register domain names that the NSF provided a subvention to NSI to cover the costs of what was in effect a free service.

As the Internet increased in size, the number of registrations increased dramatically. NSI made a decision to charge for site registration, a decision that was extremely unpopular among those persons who believed that the Internet should be, in effect, a free good.

The cost factor, plus some management problems in NSI caused by the sudden increase in volume, caused many Netizens to see NSI as a potential monopoly. NSI's policy of registering any name that was not duplicative also produced problems when trademarked names were appropriated by other persons. A number of entrepreneurs, sensing the potential growth of the Internet, registered blocks of names and, in some cases, resold them to the trademark holders in what was perceived as a form of extortion. Court cases based on trademark infringement began to emerge. As the number of domains registered under .com increased into the millions, a shortage of good names was perceived.

Among major constituency groups like the Internet Society, some of the major telecommunications companies and a growing group of Internet service providers, the problems with domain registration affected both the order and the procedures of the Internet. The NSF subcontract with Network Solutions was due to expire in 1998 and they decided to develop an alternative. In the tradition of informal governance, they formed what was called the International Ad-Hoc Committee to develop an alternative method of domain registry.

The resulting proposal, evolved under the "rough consensus" model that had traditionally governed Internet standards, included the creation of seven new top-level domains, the establishment of a large number of registrars, the creation of a central registry of names and numbers, the creation of a dispute resolution machinery and the establishment of an Internet policy institution. Significantly, it included an involvement of two international organizations, the ITU to register the registrars and the WIPO to manage the dispute resolution mechanism.

The proposal was embodied in a Memorandum of Understanding that was signed by a large number of parties at ITU headquarters in May 1997. Memoranda of Understanding were a common method within the ITU for establishing standards without a formal intergovernmental agreement, although their legitimacy was enforced by their status within the international telecommunications regime. The MoU created a mechanism that included a Policy Advisory Board, made up of representatives of the various Internet constituencies, a Policy Oversight Committee made up of elected representatives of constituency groups and a Council of Registrars, composed of those entities who were selected to register domain names, to oversee the domain name registration process. The net effect of the MoU would be to internationalize Internet governance, at least in terms of one of its central functions. While for the "Internet establishment", the MoU solved what was becoming a major problem, for others, including NSI, it constituted both a threat and an affront. A number felt that it gave too much power to international organizations. Others felt that it by-passed national regulatory mechanisms, especially in the United States. Still others felt than any regulation whatsoever threatened the open character of the Internet. Pressure was put on governments not to accept the MoU.

The United States government was put under particular pressure. As the government which had funded much, but not all, of the development of the Internet and which, through IANA and the NSI contract, maintained the root directory, it felt a particular responsibility. At the same time, the United States Federal Government was in a stage of trying to de-regulate industries. Cross-pressured, the United States delegation to the ITU did not sign the MoU and sent conflicting signals about its position.

Clearly unsure of its position, the United States government reverted to procedures that were used nationally when regulations were contemplated. The national entity concerned with telecommunications regulation, the National Telecommunications and Information Administration issued a request for comments on June 16, 1997 based on a series of specific questions about Internet governance in general and about detailed aspects of the domain name registration question. Some 282 distinct comments were received over the comment period in July and August 1997. Based on these, an advisor to the United States president began to prepare a proposal for management of the Internet.

The proposal was finally issued in what was called a "green paper", a draft policy statement. The Green Paper sought to resolve the dilemma by creating a new structure for domain name assignment through the devolution of the IANA function to a non-profit public corporation located in the United States, creating five new generic top-level domain names, undertaking a study of Internet governance and, as a transitional matter, extending the NSI registration contract until the details of the new system were worked out. The

Green Paper was also submitted for public comment on February 20, 1998. By the end of March 1998, over 500 distinct comments had been received. They ranged from short comments favouring one or another model through detailed, well-elaborated comments on specific issues raised in the Green Paper as well as on the Green Paper itself. They included comments from individuals and from the European Union.

An Empirical Analysis

The two sets of public comments on US government policy proposals for the Internet constitute a unique picture of the various issues in Internet governance and the major actors involved. The changes in perspective reflected in the six months between the first and second comment periods are also instructive. In order to observe these changes, we coded all of the distinct responses in terms of their perspective on the three contending approaches to regulation: acceptance of an international role, acceptance of the concept of self-regulation and attitude towards national regulation.

Our analysis of the first comments has already been reported in detail.1/ _ We included only one comment by each individual2/and, in the case of a number of identical communications sent by different persons, included the comment only once. As a result, the number of comments in our database is smaller than that reported by the NTIA.

Commenters and Constituencies

The pattern of commenters showed some change over the two periods, as can be seen from Table. The number of individuals commenting in their own right increased, while the comments from companies involved in web management decreased.

The individuals were different, however. While in the 1997 comments, a large proportion made non-substantial comments, or vented frustration about Network Solutions, in the 1998 comments, the focus was on the content of the Green Paper.

Table. Types of Commenters on NTIA Proposals

Type of respondent	July-August 1997	February-March 1998
Academic	*	2.1%
Business	19.2%	16.3%
Government	1.5%	1.0%
Individual	52.8%	63.6%
Institution	8.9%	9.5%
Web management	17.7%	7.4%
TOTAL	100.0%	100.0%
Number	282	513

Note:

*Not coded separately in 1997, included under individuals.

The most significant difference, however, was the proportion of comments coming from outside the United States. Only seven per cent of the commenters in the July-August request for proposals were from outside the United States, in the March 1998 round, they constituted at least 20 per cent.3/Perhaps more importantly, they were more heavily represented among the commenters from institutions, a category which includes a diverse group of entities ranging from industry associations through non-governmental organizations and user groups like the Internet Society. This included some of the quasi-official bodies like the Policy Advisory Board, the Policy Oversight Council and the Council of Registrars, all of which are mechanisms set up under the MoU.

Table. Type of Commenters by Origin, March 1998

Type	Non-US	US	Total
Academic	9.1%	90.9%	11
Business	15.5%	84.5%	84
Government	80.0%	20.0%	5
Individual	16.0%	84.0%	326
Institution	42.9%	57.1%	49
Web management	31.6%	68.4%	38
Total	20.1%	79.9%	513

A major criticism made of the Green Paper, in many of the comments, was its "US-centric" orientation. Many commenters noted that the Paper largely ignored the work of the CORE in Geneva, proposed a United States location for the central registry corporation and had little role for international organizations.

One of the dimensions that we coded in the responses, was whether they saw an international regulatory dimension for the Internet. Most of the international dimension were favourable to it, but commenters from outside the United States were much more likely to both mention and favour an international dimension.

This of course includes a large number of comments which explicitly favoured the CORE model. In terms of types of commenters, individuals were less likely to mention the international dimension, while institutions and web managers were much more likely to do so.

This was a much larger proportion for all categories than was found in the July-August 1997 comments, which focused on a more US-centric type of questions and which we coded differently.

In that round only about a quarter of the commenters mentioned the international dimension, although a group which were identified as more actively involved had similar proportions as institutions in the later round.

Table. Orientation to Iinternational Governance of the Internet, March 1998 comments

	Non-US	US	Total
Favour	71.8%	40.0%	46.4%
No mention	22.3%	55.4%	48.7%
Oppose	5.8%	4.6%	4.9%
Total	100.0%	100.0%	100.0%
Number	103	410	513

Table. "Eminent" Commenters in July-August 1997 who Mentioned International Nature of the Internet, by type

Type of Respondent	Percentage	Number
Business association	91%	11
Government	0%	1
Individual	67%	24
International organization	50%	2
ISP	57%	7
Large corporation	92%	12
NGO	90%	10
Small business	60%	5
Web management	67%	6
Grand Total	74%	78

While a lower proportion of commenters mentioned the concept of Internet self-governance as a model, almost all who did so favoured this approach. This was particularly true of commenters from outside the United States in contrast to those from inside the United States. Institutions were particularly likely to mention this and favour it as had also been the case in the July-August 1997 comments. The proportion mentioning self government in February-March 1998 was slightly higher than that in July-August 1997.

There was little support for a model based on national regulation of the Internet. Only about half of the comments mentioned national aspects of regulation at all, but of those who did so, opposition was clear, as can be seen from Table. In fact, there was little difference in this between commenters from outside and inside the United States.

Table. Mentions of National Regulation Issues

	Non-US	US	Total
Favour	6.8%	10.5%	9.7%
No mention	52.4%	56.1%	55.4%
Oppose	40.8%	33.4%	34.9%
Total	100.0%	100.0%	100.0%
Number	103	410	513

The comments elicited a number of different positions. Many commenters clearly favoured the CORE proposals. They included some of the CORE principals, registrars in waiting and persons wanting to register domains using the new generic top- level domain names, as well as persons looking for the combination of international self-government represented by CORE. Included were comments provoked by one of the CORE registrars. A few comments favoured the status quo of a U.S. government involvement and ancillary institutions. A large number of comments, particularly from the United States, accepted the Green Paper as a reasonable compromise and made comments on its structural aspects. Some of the commenters from outside the United States referred to mechanisms to ensure international representation on the board of the new company to replace IANA.

Many of the U.S. commenters were concerned that their particular constituency should be represented. To draw a picture of the comments, we sought to code the main policy focus of the comment. Some were merely statements for or against the main contending institutions, Network Solutions and CORE, others referred to structural aspects of the Green Paper proposals, while still others focused on the specific issue of trademarks and dispute resolution about them which may felt were not well treated in the proposals. Table shows this.

Table. Main policy Focus of Comment

Policy Focus	Per cent
None	32.4
Opposed to or critical of Network Solutions	9.4
Supportive of Network Solutions	1.0
Opposed to or critical of CORE	1.0
Supportive of CORE	10.9
Like status quo, no change is desirable	0.4
Trademark issues	6.0
Structural issues relating to Green Paper	24.0
Business or commerce issues	2.1
Technical issues in domain names	12.9
Total	513 cases

The analysis of comments shows a wide diversity of views. Of importance, however, is the increased international interest in Internet governance, all the more remarkable because comments on proposed rules in the United States usually elicit little attention. Clear also is the hostility felt outside the United States to any governance model that is US-centric. If there had been comments on issues other than domain names, a similar diversity of views could probably be found.

It is evident that while there is the beginning of a rough consensus on some general principles, there is no consensus on details. There is a general understanding that governance should be international and self-regulating, but no agreement on the mechanisms. There is a great deal of diversity of views on even the facts.

Some of the defenders of the status quo referred to the fact that the Internet had been created as a result of US government efforts, some critics of the Green Paper pointed out that many aspects of the Internet, including some of the early basic research, had been done outside the United States. There were differences of views on whether a single registry was needed, whether registrars should run registries, whether any of these would enhance or restrict competition.

It should be noted that the matter of domain names has only been widely discussed in the context of the NTIA request for comments. The CORE group undertook a wide-ranging and thorough consultation of those who they considered to be the constituencies of the Internet but it is obvious that they missed some key groups. The issue has not been discussed in any detail at the intergovernmental level and, apart from the links between domain names and intellectual property, little attention has been given to the other communications aspects of the Internet.

A REGIME OF NUANCED GOVERNANCE

While there is a general consensus favouring self-regulation with very limited public intervention, there is no consensus yet on most of the issues of how to bring this about. There has also been little examination of the larger picture, beyond domain names.

The percolating issues of Internet commerce, content regulation and extension of the Internet to widening publics, especially in the developing countries, are moving an increasing number of governments to consider the possibility of defining more clearly a comprehensive Internet regime. In the parlance of international relations theory, a regime is "a set of principles - explicit or implicit - norms, rules and decision-making procedures around which expectations of actors converge in order to coordinate actors' behaviour with respect to a concern to them all." Development of a regime usually follows a sequence of agreements, either tacit or formal. The first stage is to agree on what are termed principles, which are statements of fact.

In terms of the Internet, they would include statements about the nature of the technology involved, about the essential mechanisms for making the Net work. The second stage has to do with norms, statements about rectitude. In terms of the Internet they might include such norms as free and open access, avoidance of content control, responsibilities of senders, media and receivers and issues of payment and taxation. A third stage is to convert these norms and principles into operating rules and to set up whatever machinery might be necessary to enforce the rules and modify them as may be required.

Regimes take time to create. It can be argued that much has already been done to set the bases for an Internet regime and that, in some respects, its technological operation suggests that in that sense a regime is already present. But in terms of the non-technological issues of Internet governance, there is little that can be said to have been agreed.

There are some who would argue that a regime agreed by governments is not even necessary. Some argue that the Internet is essentially a private entity, not of the public interest, and therefore not needing government agreement. This is not a widely held view, however, and most would agree that the Internet is a public good or a public trust. The fact that individual governments are already trying, without much success, to regulate elements of the Internet suggests that any agreements to be legitimate will have to be made by governments. The issue, then, is what type of agreements, reached where.

Internet Charter Idea

The idea that there should be an international, intergovernmental agreement on the basis for Internet governance has already been presented by the European Commission. As a press release of February 4, 1998 stated:

Following a proposal of its members in charge of industrial affairs and telecommunication and external relations and trade policy, Martin Bangemann and Sir Leon Brittan, the European Commission today recommended in a communication to launch an international debate regarding global communications policy, to set a framework for international policy cooperation and to start a process which could lead to the adoption of an International Communications Charter. After a review of various policy issues relating to economic and social dimensions of the Internet, the communication concluded:

Although good progress has been achieved, the understandings and agreements arrived at within these fora consist either of principles, which are not necessarily compatible, or do not cover all elements of a comprehensive framework. Also, the process will now need to continue with as wide a participation of the international community as possible, including the developing countries.

An International Charter would:

- Be a multi-lateral understanding on a method of coordination to remove obstacles for the global electronic marketplace;
- Be legally non-binding
- Recognize the work of existing international organizations
- Promote the participation of private sector and relevant social groups
- Contribute to more regulatory transparency.

An International Charter would not therefore define the key issues to be solved as such, but contain an understanding on how a process of strengthened international coordination should be organized, with as wide as possible a participation of the international community. The Charter could be agreed by or in the course of 1999.

The difficulty with the European Commission proposal is that, by being non-binding, it may not be able to address the basic issues of governance, when these require formal decisions of government and, while serving as a reference document, it may lack the possibility of its own modification in the light of technological, economic and social changes relating to the Internet.

The EU proposal suggests either using an existing ministerial meeting or convening a special ministerial meeting to deal with the issue. The question here would be which ministers. As has been noted, the governance issues of the Internet cut across many of the traditional sectoral lines. It could be trade ministers, for example, or those in charge of telecommunications. It could involve law enforcement ministries. Choosing one ministry over another would imply a decision as to which sector is most important in Internet governance. Such a choice would also affect which of the organizations of the United Nations system would be primarily involved. There is clearly no consensus about which this might be at either the national or the international level.

Concept of a Framework Convention

What the European Union is proposing is the beginnings of a framework convention. Most international regimes are embodied in legally-binding multilateral treaties. However, these are increasingly sequential in nature, with treaties expanding and ramifying in an orderly way in response to further negotiation and new developments. It might be worthwhile to consider extending the EU proposal towards a framework convention rather than a non-binding document.

Example of the UNFCC

The current best example of a framework convention is the United Nations Framework Convention on Climate Change. This was a response to the dilemma of how to address the problems of global climate change, about which there was no initial consensus. As described by Paterson 6/, the process of agreeing on the climate change convention involved first reaching an agreement on the nature of the problem. This largely took place in technical forums, especially of the World Meteorological Organization. Then, when there was a consensus about the nature of the problem, it was possible to determine norms and determine procedures that could be followed subsequently to deal with the issue. The climate change convention was agreed relatively quickly and signed at the United Nations Conference on Environment and Development.

Subsequently, a series of protocols have elaborated details on how to address the identified issues, most recently at Kyoto in December 1997, and a process is in motion, following agreed and legally-binding procedures, to tie up other loose ends.

The climate change convention is a model of how to establish a regime in an environment where little is agreed beyond the existence of a problem, but which provides an element of order without which subsequent agreements might be difficult.

What would an Internet Framework Convention do?

An international framework convention on the Internet would have to do three things: it would have to define the nature of the problems through describing the technological elements and their linked economic and social issues; it would have to articulate basic norms about how the Internet is to be governed and it would have to establish a machinery for both monitoring compliance with the norms and determining future changes.

The task of sorting out the roles and responsibilities of the numerous national, international and private entities cannot be left to Darwinian processes at this point in the development of a global enabling technology. A framework convention is needed to allocate to existing authorities regulatory rights and responsibilities and to establish dispute resolution mechanisms at the international level.

Who Should be Involved?

The Internet is a unique public space. It involves governments but goes beyond them. It involves many different publics but also goes beyond any one of them. It cannot be controlled by coercion and therefore its governance implies legitimacy. Legitimacy is only achieved when all of the concerned parties accept a decision or a set of rules. The rough consensus approach that governed the Internet in its early days is an example.

For this reason, any framework convention needs to be based on agreements by governments but must go far beyond them to bring on board the many constituencies that currently exist or can be forecast. Negotiation of a framework convention would require the kind of government/civil society/international organization participation that any negotiation about the global commons needs, but in this case the participation of the different parties would need to be far more explicit than in previous negotiations.

MARKETING COMMUNICATION STRATEGY

A powerful marketing communication strategy should serve to make your business stand out from the crowd. This substance discusses several strategies to develop your own compelling core marketing communications piece.

You will have the components of an effective marketing communications kit, which can be placed inside a pocket folder with your logo on the front. This folder should be presented to anyone that has expressed an interest in your company's products or services. It will performance as a compelling sales tool to educate prospects on why they should do business with you.

COMPELLING STORY

Every small business owner should be able to tell a compelling story about their passions and why they started their business. After all, how can you expect to create passion in your customers if you're not able to convey your own business passion?

The Compelling Story is just that - an exciting and interesting story as to why you decided to create the business you did. This story must be personal and connect emotionally. A compelling story can create instant trust - and you won't stand a chance of selling your products or services to someone unless they trust you.

So, how do you go about creating your own compelling story? Here is a list of important criteria to keep in mind.

- Make it personal - Talk about the people you've touched
- Appeal to the emotions
- Create a story - make it fun to read
- Be passionate
- Incorporate your values

Your particular story is the perfect way to open your marketing communications folder and should be featured as the first item seen on the inside right pocket. Your story should not be longer than a single page.

COMPETITIVE SQUASH

The purpose of this one page document is to summarize why people should buy from you as opposed to your competition. You should summarize all the advantages of doing business with your company. Communicate your unique approach, the value customers get when they do business with you, and why your products and services are the best in your field. Don't be shy. This is your chance to show off. Don't make this one text heavy. Pick three or four things you wish to communicate and summarize them in a compelling way.

PROBLEM SOLVER

The purpose of this one page sheet is to show how you are able to solve the business problems of your customers. This is just another way of creating trust and interest.

In order to be effective, incorporate the following elements.

- Briefly summarize the main problem or problems of your target market
- Describe how your prospect's problems are solved once they purchase your solution
- Describe the steps needed to solve the particular problem

This should describe several specific customer types and demonstrate how their problems were alleviated with your products and services.

PRODUCT/SERVICE SUMMARY

Nothing difficult here - simply summarize the various products, services, and package options you offer and list the benefits of each.

Notice we said to summarize the benefits, not the features. This is an important distinction. Too many companies spend enormous amounts of time covering various product features. Instead, concentrate on the benefits of the product and how they will solve specific problems and issues.

DEVOTION PAGE

Can you feel the love? This is the page that summarizes your customer testimonials. A testimonial is proof that you have a track record of delivering what you promise. Make sure each testimonial focuses on a result that was achieved to help the customer with a specific issue.

Here are a few ideas for collecting customer testimonials:

- While customers may love your product or service, some may feel they don't have the time to write a testimonial. For customers with an established relationship, write one up on their behalf and present it to them for their approval. Be honest and tell them you want to use the testimonial on your website and related marketing materials.
- After you have completed the job and surpassed the customer's expectation, ask them face-to-face for a quick testimonial. Have them just write a sentence or two on a piece of paper. It will literally take them a minute or two to write. They will rarely refuse if you have provided value to them.
- Ask your customers to write the testimonial as if they were recommending your products and/or services to a friend. This will typically create more powerful and genuine copy.

Your summary of customer testimonials should fit on a single sheet of paper. If you have enough, use both sides of the sheet.

INFORMATIONAL SUBSTANCE

Here is where you can provide some free information to help your customer solve a problem. Write a 1-2 page substance on a topic that is important to your customer base. Keep it short. If it is a long substance, summarize it and then provide the web URL where they can view or download the entire document at no charge. By providing free information that is relevant and valuable, you will continue to build on the trust and interest you have established.

PROMOTIONAL MIX

There are seven main aspects of a promotional mix. These are:

- *Advertising*: Any paid presentation and promotion of ideas, goods, or services by an identified sponsor. Examples: Print ads, radio, television, billboard, direct mail, brochures and catalogs, signs, in-store displays, posters, motion pictures, Web pages, banner ads, and emails.
- *Personal Selling:* A process of helping and persuading one or more prospects to purchase a good or service or to performance on any idea through the use of an oral presentation. Examples: Sales presentations, sales meetings, sales training and incentive programmes for intermediary salespeople, samples, and telemarketing. Can be face-to-face or via telephone.
- *Sales promotion*: Media and non-media marketing communication are employed for a pre-determined, limited time to increase consumer demand, stimulate market demand or improve product availability. Examples: Coupons, sweepstakes, contests, product samples, rebates, tie-ins, self-liquidating premiums, trade shows, trade-ins, and exhibitions.
- *Public relations:* Paid intimate stimulation of supply for a product, service, or business unit by planting significant news about it or a favourable presentation of it in the media. Examples: Newspaper and magazine substances/reports, TVs and radio presentations, charitable contributions, speeches, issue advertising, and seminars.
- *Corporate image*: The Image of an organization is a crucial point in marketing. If the reputation of a company is bad, consumers are less willing to buy a product from this company as they would have been, if the company had a good image.
- Direct Marketing is often listed as a the fifth part of the marketing mix
- *Exhibitions*: Are try-outs. You make your product, and let potential buyers try the product, this way, you know directly what people see in your product. The downside, your competitor can see exactly what you are doing.

6

International Balance of Payments Financing and Adjustment

GAINS FROM INTERNATIONAL TRADE

More and more, we live in an interdependent world in which countries are not self-sufficient, but they trade with each other according to their comparative advantage. Exports and imports of goods and services and financial transactions have increased drastically since World War II.

The direct or indirect benefits of international trade and finance come primarily from the enlargement of the market and the specialization and more efficient employment of productive resources, as well as technological advances.

Each country has certain advantages, compared to other countries, that can be better exploited through foreign trade. When a country is able to supply another country with a cheaper commodity, it would be better for the latter country to import this commodity and concentrate instead on the production of other commodities in which it has some advantage. In this case, the first country has what is called an absolute cost advantage over the second country. This might be due to better climatic conditions, more advantageous soil and subsoil resources, cheaper labour or other factors of production, or better technology.

What matters most, though, is not the absolute but the relative cost. One country that may be able to produce two commodities, say jute and wheat, more cheaply than another country has an absolute advantage in both commodities. But if the production of jute is comparatively cheaper than wheatmore the first country can still benefit from trade by specializing in the production of jute and exchange some of it for the other country's wheat. And the second country will be better off by specializing in the production of wheat and exchanging some of it for jute. In this case, the first country has a comparative advantage in jute over wheat and an absolute advantage in both jute and wheat. Likewise, the opportunity cost of jute is equal to the amount of wheat to be given up to release resources for the production of a unit of jute.

The Multiplier Effect and Absorption

Additional investment (*dI*) in the economy would increase income (*dY*) by a multiple amount and the multiplier ($k = dY/dI$) depends on the marginal propensity to consume (*MPC*), that is, k = 1/1 – MPC = 1/MPS where MPS stands for the marginal propensity to save. For example, if MPC is 0.8 or the MPS 0.2, then k = 1/0.2 = 5, that is, each additional $1.00 invested would increase national income by $5.00, assuming no leakage in the spending rounds. In an open economy, the leakage of spending outside the economy into imports (*M*) is making the multiplier smaller depending on the marginal propensity to import (*MPM*). That is,

$$k = 1/\ (MPS + MPM)$$

Thus, assuming MPM = 0.2 and using the above example, we have,

$$k = 1/\ (0.2 + 0.2) = 1/0.4 = 2.5,$$

which is smaller than that without imports. The same thing would occur from additional government spending or exports, which increase the multiplier. National production (or gross domestic product, *GDP*) may be different than national expenditures for consumption (C), investment (*I*), and government spending (*G*). That is, total domestic output, or what an economy produces, may be different than total domestic expenditures (demand), or what it absorbs (*A*). The difference is net exports, that is, exports of goods and services (*X*) minus imports of goods and services (*M*). Then, total output is equal to total expenditures, or

$$GDP = C + I + G + (X - M)$$

As absorption, A, is equal to C + I + G, then GDP = A + X – M and GDP – A = X – M. If absorption or total domestic spending exceeds total domestic production, then the difference will be covered by imports. Depending on the elasticity of exports, a devaluation, ceteris paribus, is expected to increase exports if there is unemployment in the economy; but if there is full employment, the result would be inflation.

The Use of Geometry

The gains from foreign trade. Before international trade, country 1 produces and consumes at point A, where the indifference or consumers' preference curve meets the production possibility curve. After trade with other countries, production moves to point B as the country specializes in the production of commodity X for which it has a comparative advantage, that is, a comparative cost advantage. A straight line tangent to the production possibility curve at point B and the shift of the indifference curve I to indifference curve II indicate the gains of society from foreign trade from A to D. As a result, the country exports BC of commodity X and imports CD of Y.

Likewise, country 2 with a comparative advantage in the production of commodity Y would specialize in the production of commodity Y, exporting

B_2 C_2 of Y and importing C_2 D_2 of X. In a broad sense, a country has a comparative advantage in the production of a commodity if the exports of this country's commodity, as a percentage of total exports, is higher than its imports of this commodity. For example, the U.S. chemical exports are 12 per cent of total exports and imports are 6 per cent of total imports, the United States has a comparative advantage in chemicals, whereas Japan has a comparative advantage in cars with exports of more than 20 per cent of total and imports of only 3 per cent of total, respectively. Two countries with identical production possibility curves but different indifference curves (tastes). Before foreign trade, country 1 produces and consumes at point A and country 2 at point A_2. With foreign trade, the first country specializes in the production of commodity Y, where it has a comparative advantage, producing at point B, whereas country 2 specializes in the production of commodity X, producing also at point B. A straight line tangent to the production possibility curve at point B shows the higher consumption levels through the shift of the indifference curves from I to II for country 1 and from I_2 to II_2 for country 2. Both countries enjoy higher consumption at points D and D_2, respectively, because of trade between them. Country 1 exports BC of Y and imports CD of X, whereas country 2 exports BC_2 of X and imports C_2 D_2 of Y.

Two countries with the same taste, as the common indifference curve I indicates. The tangency of this curve on the production possibility curves at points A and B shows production and consumption of countries 1 and 2, respectively, before foreign trade. After trade, country 1 specializes in the production of commodity X, producing at point A_2, whereas country 2 specializes in the production of commodity Y, producing at point B_2, which are determined by a straight line tangent to the production possibility curves of country 1 and country 2, respectively. Both countries consume at point D on a higher indifference curve I_2, and country 1 exports A_2 C of X and imports CD of Y, whereas country 2 exports C2 B_2 of Y and imports C_2 D of X..

With foreign trade, the quantity of supply increases from Q_2, determined by the equilibrium of domestic demand and supply, to Q_3. Domestic demand is Q_1, total supply is Q_3, and the difference $Q_1 - Q_3$ is absorbed by exports, whereas additional production due to free trade is $Q_2 - Q_3$.

TERMS OF TRADE AND CURRENCY DEVALUATION

In general terms, the ratio of export prices to import prices is called the terms of trade. A distinction can be made between commodity or net-barter terms of trade, measured by the ratio of the export price index to import price index *(Px/Pm)100*; gross barter terms of trade, measured by the ratio of physical quantity index of exports to that of imports or *(Qx/Qm)100*; and income terms of trade, which can be derived by multiplying the price index of exports by the quantity index of exports and dividing by the price index of imports or *(Px·Qx)/Pm*. Finally, by multiplying net-barter by gross-barter terms of trade, the current-account terms of trade is derived or $(Px \cdot Qx)/(Pm \cdot Qm) \times 100$. The last expression is important because it incorporates both prices and quantities of exports and imports and, therefore, indicates whether a country has a deficit or a surplus in its trade balance. Thus, if the index of a current-account terms of trade is lower than 100, this means that total export proceeds are less than total import payments. Inversely, if it is higher than 100, the country is better off; at 100 there are no net gains or losses for the country from foreign trade. When productivity of exports (Rx) is also considered, we can measure the single factorial terms of trade $(Px/Pm)Rx$. When the productivity of both exports and imports (Rx/Rm) is considered, we have the double factorial terms of trade, that is $(Px/Pm)(Rx/Rm) \times 100$.

The reciprocal demands between two countries establish the terms of trade, which are affected by domestic costs. This principle can be explained with the help of what Alfred Marshall called the reciprocal demand curves, or offer curves. Thus, the offer curve of country X (say the United States) indicates how much steel the country demands from another country Y (say Japan) in exchange for wheat at different prevailing prices and vice versa for country Y.

Such offer curves can be used also for bundles of exportable goods in exchange for bundles of importable goods. After successive trade transactions between the two countries, the two offer curves meet at the equilibrium point E, where the amounts of wheat offered and steel demanded by country X equal the amounts of steel offered and wheat demanded by country Y; that is, where the reciprocal demands of the two countries are equal. The price ratio, which is measured by the slope of the ray 0A, shows the terms of trade. A change in the supply or demand against country X and in favour of country Y is reflected by the shift in Y's offer curve to a new position (Y2), establishing a new price ratio, 0B; that is, new terms of trade more favourable for Y and less favourable for X. Thus, at the price ratio 0A, one ton of steel was exchanged with one ton of wheat, whereas at 0B, the same one ton of steel is exchanged with more wheat (1.3 tons). This means that X's terms of trade deteriorated by 30 per cent in favour of Y.

Exports and imports react to exchange rate changes. Net exports, that is, exports minus imports, are expected to rise when the currency of a country depreciates and to fall when it appreciates, after a time lag. As the price of a currency, in terms of other currencies, rises, export prices increase and prices of imports fall. As a result, the volume of exports declines and that of imports rises, or the gross-barter (quantity) terms of trade decline. Ceteris paribus, this has a contractionary effect on domestic output and employment. This is so, because with a currency depreciation (devaluation) exports rise and imports fall, thereby improving the balance of trade and the economy of the country in question, and vice versa with a currency appreciation. An appreciation of the currency of country Y (Japanese yen) would shift its offer curve to Y_2 and the slope 0A to 0B, in which one ton of steel would be exchanged with 1.3 tons of wheat. Therefore, through the currency appreciation, the gross-barter or quantity terms of trade improves for country Y and deteriorates for country X, which is exchanging more of its product (wheat) for the same amount of steel.

The opposite is expected to occur with currency depreciation, as the prices of exports would be lower for other countries, without an equivalent currency depreciation, and foreign demand for exportable goods would increase. This would lead to deterioration of the net-barter or price terms of trade, but to the improvement of the gross-barter or quantity terms of trade. Therefore, the net effect on the balance of trade would depend on which index, the price index or the quantity index, would be higher, and this would be shown by the current-account terms of trade. The exchange rate depreciation (devaluation) is affected by the price elasticity of imports and exports. In order to pay for imports, foreign exchange is needed, which can be obtained by exports. The size of the devaluation of a currency depends on the price elasticity of demand for imports (*Epm*), which is determined by the percentage change in the quantity (*Q*) of imports (*m*) demanded over the percentage change in price (*P*) of imports, or, Epm = (dQm/Qm)/ (dPm/Pm)

Likewise, price elasticity of exports is equal to the percentage change in the quantity of supplied exports over the percentage change in price. In the case of devaluation of a currency, expectations are that the balance of trade would improve, depending on the international demand elasticity. Thus, if the price elasticity of demand for imports is 1.2, Epm nd that for exports is 0.7, Epx then a devaluation of the currency of the country by 20 per cent would improve the balance of trade by 38 per cent.

If the summation of the elasticities of imports and exports is higher than 1, ceteris paribus, there would be improvement in the balance of trade. In our example, Epm + Epx = 1.2 + 0.7 = 1.9. If this summation is equal to 1, there would be no change, but if it is less than 1, there would be deterioration in the balance of trade. For example, if the elasticity of imports is 0.4 and that of exports 0.5, then Epm + Epx = 0.4 + 0.5 = 0.9, and the balance of trade would be worse off.

Usually, the summation of the international demand elasticities is higher than 1, thereby ensuring improvement in the balance of trade following a devaluation or depreciation of a currency. This is so because a devaluation or depreciation of a currency means higher prices for imports and lower prices for exports, and therefore less imports and more exports, thereby improving the balance of trade of the country. Moreover, the income elasticity of imports (*Eym*) is determined by the percentage change in the quantity of imports demanded over the percentage change in national income (*Y*), or,

$$Eym = (dQm/Qm)/ (dY/Y)$$

Also, income elasticity of exports is equal to the percentage change in the quantity of supplied exports over the percentage change in national income.

DETERMINATION OF EXCHANGE RATES

Exchange rates, that is, prices of a currency in terms of other currencies, may be fixed or flexible. In the case of a fixed exchange rate, the central bank of a country determines the price of its currency versus the currencies of other countries. With flexible exchange rates, the price of a currency in terms of other currencies is determined by free market supply and demand. The price of the dollar in terms of euros, the new currency introduced by the European Union.

The equilibrium point (E), where the familiar down sloping demand (D) curve meets the upsloping supply (S) curve, indicates the price of the dollar in euros and the quantity of dollars demanded and offered at this price. If the price is higher than the equilibrium price, there would be more dollars supplied than demanded; that is a surplus of dollars. When the price is lower than the equilibrium price, there would be a shortage of dollars.

Ceteris paribus, in the case of surplus, there would be a pressure for lower prices, whereas in the case of shortage, there would be a pressure for higher prices, back to the equilibrium point. Globalization driven mainly by information technology and impressive financial development is revolutionizing production, constantly expanding markets, changing social conditions, and intensifying the interdependence of nations. In this type of globocracy and internetocracy, globocapitalism is subordinating politics and resulting in what Marx and Engels predicted more than a century ago, withering the state away, but voluntarily, not through the dictatorship of the proletariat.

With the liberalization of capital in a growing borderless world, huge amounts of money circle the planet instantly, replacing the use of letters of credit and other previous financial instruments. Nevertheless, there are arguments, mainly by Professor John Gray, that globalization, based on laissez-faire capitalism and Thatcherism, is a utopian idea, an Enlightenment thinking, which erodes social cohesion and imposes cultural imperialism that vests on British-American power.

It is an unstable, inequitable, and immoral neoliberal system, destroying the welfare state, traditional societies in emerging nations, and families everywhere. Varieties of capitalism and national variations, with state spending to avoid stagflation and high inequality, which prevails largely in Latin America and even in the United States, should be the economic goal, according to these arguments, because, in an analogy to Aristophanes and Gresham's law, under globalization, "bad capitalism drives out good."

It seems that, in spite of the disadvantages of globalization and neoliberalism, global-capitalism would prevail in the twenty-first century, because welfarism and state intervention lead to inefficiency and laziness.

The rise in the middle class and the spread of ownership in shares, as many countries follow the U.S. system in which over 50 per cent of Americans have investments in stocks, supports the argument of Joseph Schumpeter of the trend towards the system of people's capitalism or in practical terms "shareholder capitalism."

The evolution of the international monetary system went through a number of stages, from the use of different goods as money to the gold standard period, the interwar instability, and the Bretton Woods fixed exchange rates. The postwar trade deficits in many countries led to the dollar shortage up to the late 1950s, but severe competition from abroad turned the United States from a surplus to a deficit country and to a substantial gold drain from the U.S. reserves resulting in the post-1973 floating exchange rates.

The growing capital mobility made pegging exchange rates, that is, the price of a currency following the value of another hard currency, such as the dollar, difficult to maintain. The implication is that floating rates are expanding all over the world. Through arbitrage, equalization of spot and forward exchange rates can take place almost instantly, whereas foreign exchange options are rapidly growing worldwide.

Although international trade is, in principle, no different from domestic trade, the use of different currencies and different laws and regulations distinguish global from domestic trade and finances and require separate analysis. Some important international currency symbols are shown below.

Country	Currency	Symbol
Brazil	Real	R1
Australia	Dollar	A$
Canada	Dollar	C$
European Union	Euro	€
France	Franc	FF
Germany	Mark	DM
Greece	Drachma	Dr
India	Rupee	Rs
Japan	Yen	Y
Mexico	Peso	Ps
Saudi Arabia	Riyal	SR
Singapore	Dollar	S$
South Africa	Rand	R
Switzerland	Franc	SF
United Kingdom	Pound	£
United States	Dollar	$

The equilibrium (E1) of supply of and demand for dollars ($), in terms of yen, at a price of 80 yen per dollar and quantity 6 (say billion dollars). In case of shift in the demand curve from D1 to D2, the new exchange rate would be 100 yen per dollar and the quantity $8 (billion). This would be the result of an increase in the price of the dollar, through a depreciation of the yen. If the

U.S. Federal Reserve Bank (Fed) decided to reduce the price of the dollar, it can supply dollars to the market, thereby restoring the initial price. Changes in exchange rates affect foreign trade. Thus, as a result of the rising exchange rate (appreciation) of the dollar, above the rate of inflation, in the early 1980s, net exports (exports minus imports) fell sharply. The opposite occurred when the dollar began to fall after 1985 and net exports began to improve, but with a time lag of more than a year.

BALANCE OF PAYMENTS AND FOREIGN EXCHANGE

An accounting statement showing the transactions of the United States with all the other countries for a period of time. Positive figures (credit) show items that bring gains in foreign exchange. Negative figures (debit) indicate items that bring losses in foreign exchange. The U.S. balance of trade, that is, exports minus imports of merchandise, was negative since 1975, reaching a record deficit of $168.8 billion in 1998, some $64 billion with Japan and $ 56.9 billion with China. The balance of current accounts, which includes the balance of goods, services and investment income as well as unilateral transfers, reached a record deficit of $233 U.S. billion dollars in 1998. The previous record deficit was that in 1987 of $168 billion. Even higher current account deficits are predicted in the near future.

Ceteris paribus, under flexible exchange rates, the depreciation of a country's currency restores the trade equilibrium and eventually the balance of payments of the country in question. Countries with fixed exchange rates will face problems of excess supply and overvaluation of their currencies, then running balance-of-trade deficits. Once their reserves of foreign exchanges are depleted, their currencies, sooner or later, would be depreciated to correct the trade imbalance. The main reason of depreciation of a currency is inflation, which may be due to excess demand over supply, which may be the result of an increase in spending and in money supply (demand-pull inflation), or to higher costs due to an increase in wages and other costs (cost-push inflation). Demand-pull and cost-push inflation as a result of the shifts in the demand and supply curves, respectively. Moreover, inflation may be the result of structural rigidities and inflexibility in production, imports and income distribution (structural inflation), mainly in emerging nations.

The effects of a devaluation or depreciation upon the balance of trade of a country. As a result, the prices of imports of the country in question increase and those of exports decline. With inelastic demands, quantity for imports changes little, as does quantity for exports. Therefore, the balance of trade deficit and the demand for foreign currencies could increase for some time, as a result of the devaluation or depreciation, before improving later through long-run increases in the elasticity, as the J-curve shows. Indicates the equilibrium price after trade. Country 1 exports commodity Y and country 2 imports Y until the equilibrium price is reached in the middle graph. The relationship of foreign trade and national income. Investments (I) and exports (X) act as injections in the economy, increasing national income (Y), whereas savings (S) and imports (M) are considered as leakages. When S − M = I + X, then we have the equilibrium level of income. An increase in exports (X2) leads to a new equilibrium of income (Y2 2).

The relationship of balance of payments and foreign exchange. Suppose that U.S. buyers demand more European products. Ceteris paribus, this would lead to a deficit in the U.S. trade balance and a lower price of the dollar in terms of euros, from 1.2 to 1.0, as the supply curve would shift to S2. Assuming the same demand curve, the new equilibrium would be at point b at a price 1.0 and quantity 8, that is, a lower amount of euros per dollar and more dollars offered than at the previous equilibrium. Therefore, under flexible exchange rates, the depreciation of the dollar restores equilibrium to the foreign exchange market at point b.

PROBLEMS OF PROTECTIONISM AND THE WORLD TRADE ORGANIZATION

From time to time, protectionist measures, in the form of quotas, tariffs, or capital movements, are imposed by a number of governments around the world, which inhibit free trade and investment. Restrictions on imports of steel, cars, textiles, dairy products, fruits, and a host of other products, as well as on financial instruments and multinational companies, were and still are imposed by a number of developed and developing countries. For example, the United States wants to limit annual steel imports, mainly from Japan, Brazil, South Korea, India, Italy, France, Indonesia, and Russia, to about 29 million tons because unfairly they sell in the United States market at prices less than the cost. It is argued that protection may be needed for infant industries, mainly in developing countries. Alexander Hamilton, the first Secretary of the Treasury of the United States (1791), and Frederick List, a German political refugee in the United States, urged the use of tariffs to foster growth in U.S. manufacturing. Via internal economies of scale and cost reduction, as well as external economies, through backward and forward linkages with other industries, industrialization would improve. Moreover, through industrial protection, diversification in the domestic economy would be achieved, and overspecialization in agricultural or mining products in poor countries, which are easily exposed to cyclical fluctuations, would be avoided. However, it is doubtful if protection would be removed when the "infants" become "adults" able to compete in open markets.

Policymakers can move closer to the competitive ideal and maximize social welfare, reaching Pareto's optimum, by removing distortions to this ideal, thereby achieving the first-best solution. However, this may be difficult in practice because of the eventual side effects of such a policy. For example, removal or reduction of a tax on gasoline may increase the satisfaction of one group but reduce the welfare of society as a whole by increasing air pollution. If the adverse side effects of the first-best solution are excessive, then the second-best policy may be applicable through the introduction of another distortion to reduce or offset the effects of existing distortions, as for example, the shift from a gasoline tax reduction to an income tax reduction, as long as expected gains are greater than losses to society.

Similar evaluations of second-best policies can be made in the formations of common markets, regarding inner group benefits versus the rest of the world. In order to reduce protectionism and encourage free international trade, the General Agreement on Tariffs and Trade (GATT) came into existence in Geneva on January 1, 1948. Its main functions were to organize conferences for nondiscriminatory tariff reduction, enforce international agreements regarding prohibitive barriers (quotas, export subsidies, and the like), and to help improve the position of the poor member nations. Under the auspices of GATT, extensive negotiations for tariff reduction produced good results during the Kennedy Round (1962–1967) for industrial countries, but limited results for developing countries. Such reductions were sizable (up to 50 per cent), mainly for raw material and manufacturing goods. The Trade Expansion Act, which the U.S. Congress passed in 1961, authorizing the President to make across the board tariff cuts, influenced, to a large extent, the negotiations of the Kennedy Round. Because poor countries received little attention in their appeal for more trade and no aid, by the GATT, which was considered as the "rich countries' club," they supported the creation of the United Nations Conference for Trade and Development (UNCTAD). The main conferences of UNCTAD in Geneva in 1964 (attended by 122 countries), in New Delhi in 1968, in Nairobi in 1976, and so on, made suggestions to help poor nations improve exchange reserves and increase imports of capital goods. In order to end unfair trade practices mainly by Japan and to meet the European complaints as well as to reduce the pressure for import quotas by Congress, mainly in textiles, steel and agricultural products, the Nixon administration called for a new round of GATT negotiations. As a result, the Tokyo Round produced results similar to the Kennedy Round, cutting tariffs on manufacturing products by 36 per cent, on the average. The meeting of GATT members at Punda del Este, Uruguay, in 1986–1993, known as the Uruguay Round, produced new measures for trade liberalization through cuts in tariffs and subsidies, as well as for protection in intellectual property and elimination of dumping.

Particular attention was given to the interests of the developing countries, mainly Brazil and India, and the encouragement of foreign investment. In 1993, it was agreed by all member nations to reduce the subsidized agricultural exports by 21 per cent over six years, whereas restrictions on rice imports in South Korea and Japan were eliminated.

The United States, Australia, and Canada, as large exporters of farm products, want to liberalize trade of such products and they object to the EU Common Agricultural Policy (CAP). The World Trade Organization (WTO), which replaced GATT in 1995, extended its authority to agricultural products and services, whereas a vote of two thirds of members was enough to settle trade disputes rather than a unanimous vote as under GATT.In the meeting of the member nations in Seattle, United States, in November 1999, and in Washington in April 2000, developing countries complained against the industrialized countries that rich nations get benefits from the trade rules at their expense. They proposed to reintroduce subsidies that are needed to protect their native industries and to weaken antidumping measures that protect mainly U.S. producers from cheap imports.

Also, they proposed to delay the enforcement of intellectual property rights (copyrights, patents, trademarks), to shorten the ten-year restriction on imports by rich countries, and to avoid policies that harm the environment. Furthermore, it is argued that infant industries need protection until they become competitive through economies of scale and experience. Representatives of developing countries, environmentalists, and labour unionists argue that globalization and the WTO ignore core labour issues and environmental standards. As the argument goes, by reducing tariffs and supporting greater openness, the WTO encourages investment in countries with low wages, without the protection of the environment. Such problems would have more importance after China's membership in the WTO. Because of the rebellion by developing nations, the riots, and the infighting among the 135 member countries, the WTO conference in Seattle collapsed.

The argument of poor nations, mainly Brazil, India, and Egypt, was that Washington had tried to benefit the United Steelworkers, Boeing, Amazon.com, and other industries in this conference at their expense, whereas Europe and Japan emphasized their disputes over agriculture and steel. Nevertheless, open global markets foster the movement of capital, products, and people around the world. Moreover, free trade spurs competition, lowers prices, increases average wages, and improves the quality of life. However, globalization may increase inequality, which is poisoning democracy. Some countries unfairly subsidize exports to infiltrate and increase their shares in foreign markets. Japan did that for exports of steel and other products in the United States. Such policy forced the U.S. government not to allow the sale of Japanese steel at a lower price than that of American steel ("trigger price mechanism") and to establish quotas for the number of imported Japanese cars. Lately, the U.S. Department of Commerce complained that NEC and Fujitsu, both Japanese super-computer makers, sold their products on the American markets at prices well below fair values, thereby harming Silicon Graphics, a U.S. competitor. For that reason, and as a result of the International Trade Commission ruling, the United States imposed duties to compensate for the related damage.

EFFECTS OF CUSTOMS DUTIES

Although tariffs and other restrictions are in the domain of international economics, their growing importance for domestic fiscal and financial policies requires a brief review here. In taxed imports, through tariffs or customs duties, foreign suppliers have to sell their products at lower net prices, affecting domestic policies on subsidies, employment, and bankruptcies. The burden of product taxes is thus shifted to foreigners. Such a shifting runs counter to the international equity principle, according to which each country should pay its own taxes. However, other countries whose products are taxed use the principle of retaliation and impose their own taxes on products they import. The results of such protectionist policies are higher prices and lower quantities of products exchanged. Similar changes in prices may take place through taxes on exports, which burden foreign consumers.

Countries that enjoy monopolies or oligopolies in natural resources or products and dominate export markets may impose export taxes, thereby increasing the cost of exports. Again, the foreign consumers will pay more, free trade will be restricted, and conflicts among countries may arise, unless such policies are in harmony through mutual understanding or international agreements among the governments concerned. The government can use customs duties to collect revenue and, at the same time, to protect domestic production and employment, especially in infant industries. The amount of revenue from tariffs and the degree of protection depend on the elasticities of supply and demand for the commodity imported. The higher the elasticity of demand for imports, the more the decrease in the quantity of imports and the less the revenue from custom duties. The same holds true for the elasticity of supply. The supply and demand for a commodity that is partly produced domestically and partly imported (AG) to cover total demand. When a tariff per unit is introduced, total demand would be reduced, domestic production would be increased, and imports would be reduced to EF. The government would collect total revenue BCFE (revenue effect), that is, (EB) × (EF). The triangle ABE measures the benefits of tariffs to the producers (protective effect); the triangle CGF measures the sacrifice to the consumers (consumer effect) because of higher prices due to tariffs. Domestic producers produce more output by AB, and consumers demand less output by CG as a result of tariffs. The result is a payment of subsidies to domestic producers, which can be considered as an income transfer from the consumers to the producers of the import-competing good considered.

Some governments provide budget subsidies for certain products that can be unloaded to other countries at prices below the cost of production (dumping). To retaliate, other nations use antidumping and countervailing duty measures. Such subsidies and antidumping policies restrict free and fair trade among nations and increase the possibilities of protectionism, in addition to budgetary expenditure needed to pay for subsidiaries. Among the products subsidized are textiles, electronics, and primarily steel. Steelmakers in the United States complain against Japan and the EU and ask for quota restrictions; the Japanese complain against South Korea; EU steelmakers complain against Romania and Brazil; and those in developing countries, against industrial countries, accusing them of trying to keep the "new boys"— the Third World producers off the world markets.

To avoid protectionism and trade wars, many steelmakers and other producers ask for multilateral agreements among interested nations similar to that of cotton textiles in the 1960s, which allow developed countries to restrict textile imports from developing countries. However, steel users and primarily automakers and construction industries object to such agreements, which protect inefficient domestic manufacturers and push up prices. For the government, though, such agreements lead to less unemployment and more tax revenue.

An unwise policy of protectionism in the 1930s exacerbated the Great Depression of that period. Throughout the 1920s, U.S. exports increased, as did private loans to finance such exports to other countries. After the crash of 1929, average tariffs were raised to 40 per cent. Foreign firms could not sell their products to the United States and could not collect dollars to pay their loans. The tariffs of the 1930s walled out competition and walled in inefficiency. They cut back imports, but they reduced exports as well. The result of the beggar-thy-neighbour policy of protectionism reduced world industrial production by about 30 per cent and increased unemployment by more than 25 per cent, whereas world trade in manufactured goods declined by more than 40 per cent and overall government revenue from tariffs was reduced.

For some commodities, effective tariffs are relatively high in the United States, mainly for clothing, fabrics, milk, cheese, butter, cigars, cigarettes, plant, vegetables, olive oil, and other primarily agricultural products. Similar and even higher tariffs prevail in Japan and the EU countries. Tariff reductions and improvements in trade with the poor nations would also allow reduction in U.S. aid, which is a burden on the budget, and stop the cry of the poor nations for "trade, no aid."

Recently, the United States and the European Union had a "banana war" because the Europeans refused to open their markets to bananas produced mainly in central American countries and shipped by Chiquita Brands International and Dole Food, two American companies. In retaliation, the United States announced 100 per cent tariffs on some European products, such as cashmere sweaters, Mont Blanc pens, tapered candles. and bath products. The Europeans argue that the companies are American and influence politicians through generous contributions to both Democrats and

Republicans, but the bananas are produced elsewhere. However, the World Trade Organization ruled that Europe has to abide and negotiate a settlement in order to avoid retaliation.

LETTERS OF CREDIT AND BANKERS' ACCEPTANCES

In order to reduce foreign trade risks, exporters want assurances that they will receive payment for the products they sell. Normally, an importer applies to a commercial bank for a letter of credit (LOC) in which the bank guarantees payment to the exporter, at a specific time, with the presentation of required documents, mainly the bill of lading. The LOC may be revocable, that is, it can be changed by the parties or, usually, irrevocable, in which case it cannot be changed without the consent of the parties. Also, the LOC may be revolving, when it is used for many shipments for a period of time, or may be a standby LOC, when the bank, with a fee by the exporter, promises to pay the exporter in case the importer defaults. To facilitate trade financing and minimize currency risks, banks or other firms may buy invoices from exporters at a discount, collecting the invoices from the importers (factoring). Moreover, the exporters can sell the promissory notes, endorsed by importers' banks, to forfeiting banks with a discount.

These financial (forfeiting) devices are used by banks and other institutions to finance exports to emerging nations. Also, barter trade or counter trade can take place among traders of different countries to conserve foreign exchange and avoid tariffs and other restrictions. Bankers' acceptance is a time draft an exporter draws and presents, together with the shipment documents, to a bank for acceptance. The bank that accepts the draft usually pays the exporter before maturity at a discount and may rediscount it with the Federal Reserve Bank at the prevailing discount rate. At maturity, the bank will pay the holder of the draft the face value of the draft received from the importer a day earlier. Bankers' acceptances are used mainly for large amounts of trade between different countries, for which the importer pays a fee, usually 1.5 per cent of the draft value.

7

International Marketing Barriers and Trade Distortions

PROTECTION OF LOCAL INDUSTRIES

While countries generally do not mind exporting, they simply do not like imports. A survey of more than 28,000 people in twenty-three countries, even well-educated workers in poorer countries are against free trade. In addition, workers in the industries that face foreign competition tend to be against free trade. On the other hand, well-educated people in well-educated countries are more likely to favour trade. Why do nations impede free trade when the inhibition is irrational? One reason why governments interfere with free marketing is to protect local industries, often at the expense of local consumers as well as consumers worldwide. Regulations are created to keep out or hamper the entry of foreign made products.

Arguments for the protection of local industries usually take one of the following forms:

- Keeping money at home,
- Reducing unemployment,
- Equalizing cost and price,
- Enhancing national security, and
- Protecting infant industry.

KEEPING MONEY AT HOME

Trade unions and protectionists often argue that international trade will lead to an outflow of money, making foreigners richer and local people poorer. This argument is based on the fallacy of regarding money as the sole indicator of wealth. Other assets, even products, may also be indicators of wealth. For instance, it does not make sense to say that a man is poor just because he does not have much cash on hand when he owns many valuable assets such as land and jewellery. In addition, this protectionist argument assumes that foreigners receive money without having to give something of value in return. Whether local consumers buy locally made or foreign products, they will have to have money to pay for such products. In either case, they receive something of value for their money.

REDUCING UNEMPLOYMENT

It is standard practice for trade unions and politicians to attack imports and international trade in the name of job protection. The argument is based on the assumption that import reduction will create more demand for local products and subsequently create more jobs. Most economists see this kind of thinking as one-sided, though not completely without merits.

At the least, import reduction makes foreigners earn fewer dollars with which they can buy US exports. As a result, foreign demand for American products declines. In addition, foreign firms may refuse to invest in the USA. They are inclined to invest only when import demand is great enough to justify building and using local facilities.

Another problem with protectionism is that it may lead to inflation. Instead of using protective relief to gain or regain market share and for competitive investment, local manufacturers often cannot resist the temptation to increase their prices for quick profits. With higher prices at home, consumers become poorer and buy less, and the economy suffers. To make matters worse, other countries will often retaliate by refusing to import products. On a related subject, note that the establishment of foreign operations is not necessarily harmful to employment at home. In fact, jobs are often created rather than lost.

EQUALIZING COST AND PRICE

Some protectionists attempt to justify their actions by invoking economic theory. They argue that foreign goods have lower prices because of lower production costs. Therefore, trade barriers are needed to make prices of imported products less competitive and local items more competitive. This argument is not persuasive to most analysts for several reasons. First, to determine the cause of price differentials is unusually difficult.

Is it caused by labour, raw materials, efficiency, or subsidy? Furthermore, costs and objectives vary greatly among countries, making it impossible to determine exactly what costs need to be equalized. Second, even if the causes of price differentials can be isolated and determined, it is hard to understand why price and cost have to be artificially equalized in the first place. Trade between nations takes place due to price differentials; otherwise, there is no incentive to trade at all. Although the estimates of the cost of protection vary, they all point to the same conclusion: the costs to consumers are enormous.

While the US International Trade Commission ruled that imports hurt American steel-makers, the Consuming Industries Trade Action Coalition (CITAC) contended that quotas on steel imports could cost American manufacturers nine jobs for every job saved in the steel industry. Tariffs on imported steel would cost consumers between $2 billion and $4 billion and between 36,000 and 75,000 jobs. The steel industry conducted its own study which showed that American steel, due to overcapacity, could easily replace imports, thus adding less than $2 to the cost of each automobile.

In any case, the WTO also ruled in 2003 that steel tariffs imposed by the USA were illegal. If cost/price equalization is a desired end, then international trade may be the only instrument that can achieve it. For example, if wages are too high in one country, that country will attract labour from a lower-wage country. That process will increase the labour supply in the high-wage country, driving the wages down. On the other hand, the labour supply in the lower-wage nation will decrease, driving up wages. Thus, equalization is achieved.

ENHANCING NATIONAL SECURITY

Protectionists often use the patriotic theme. They usually claim that a nation should be self-sufficient and even willing to pay for inefficiency in order to enhance national security. That point of view has some justification–to a certain extent. Opponents of protectionism dismiss appeals to national security.

A nation can never be completely self-sufficient because raw materials are not found in the same proportion in all areas of the world. The USA itself would be vulnerable if the supply of certain minerals were cut off. Moreover, national security is achieved at the cost of higher product prices, and money could be used for something more productive to the national interest.

In addition, in the case of such scarce resources as oil, if the USA were to try to be self-sufficient, it would quickly use up its own limited resources. The country may be better off exploiting or depleting the resources of others. North Korea's brand of self-sufficiency, coupled with its defence budget, has virtually driven the nation to starvation.

PROTECTING INFANT INDUSTRY

The necessity to protect an infant industry is perhaps the most credible argument for protectionist measures. Some industries need to be protected until they become viable. South Korea serves as a good example. It has performed well by selectively protecting infant industries for export purposes. In practice, it is not an easy task to protect industries. First, the government must identify deserving industries. Second, appropriate incentives must be created to encourage productivity.

Finally, the government has to make sure that the resultant protection is only temporary. There is a question of how long an "infant" needs to grow up to be an "adult." A spoiled child often remains spoiled.A person taught to be helpless often wants to remain helpless or does not know how to stop being helpless. In a practical sense, there is no incentive for an infant industry to abandon protection and eliminate inefficiency.

GOVERNMENT: A CONTRIBUTION TO PROTECTIONISM

Government can be considered to be the root of all evil–at least as far as international trade is concerned. A government's mere existence, even without tariffs or any attempt to interfere with international marketing, can distort trade both inside and outside of its area. At the international level, different governments have different policies and objectives, resulting in different rates for income and sales taxes. Taxation is not the only cause of tax and income differences. Some governments allow cartels to operate. A cartel is an international business agreement to fix prices and divide markets, in addition to other kinds of cooperation. Such an arrangement is illegal in the USA, but it is permissible and even encouraged in many countries.

Australia and New Zealand, for example, allow livestock firms to cooperate with each other in exporting beef to the USA. Economic cooperation among governments yields economic benefits and problems by significantly affecting internal and external trade patterns. The CAP (Common Agricultural Policy) of the European Union is a good example. The CAP, with more than twenty price systems, was adopted to satisfy France's demand to protect its farmers as a condition for joining the European Community.The practice requires the EU to impose variable-levy tariffs on many imported farm products in order to raise prices to European levels so that EU farmers will not be undersold at home regardless of world prices. Furthermore, authorities agree to buy surplus produce to maintain high target prices.The practice encourages farmers to overproduce products, which are later often sold abroad at lower prices.

Based on the results of a number of studies, because of the CAP, the EU has experienced an average loss of GDP of about 1 per cent as well as a large redistribution of income to farmers from consumers and taxpayers. Many believe that the USA is the most liberal nation in promoting free trade. This notion is debatable. The USA achieves its protection goals through a variety of means. It has quotas on sugar, processed dairy products and clothespins. Interestingly, in terms of combined ad valorem tariff equivalents, US protection is highest on products exported by the least developed countries. Japan is the same with regard to agricultural products. In contrast, the Canadian and EU protectionist measures hurt the low- and middle-income exporters the most. In conclusion, governments everywhere seem to be the main culprits in distorting trade and welfare arrangements in order to gain some economic and political advantage or benefit. These governments use a combination of tariff and non-tariff methods. A discussion of the various kinds of tariff and non-tariff barriers and their marketing implications follows.

MARKETING BARRIERS TARIFFS

Tariff, derived from a French word meaning rate, price, or list of charges, is a customs duty or a tax on products that move across borders. Tariffs may be classified in several ways. The classification scheme used here is based on direction, purpose, length, rate, and distribution point. These classifications are not necessarily mutually exclusive.

DIRECTION IMPORT AND EXPORT TARIFFS

Tariffs are often imposed on the basis of the direction of product movement; that is, on imports or exports, with the latter being the less common one. When export tariffs are levied, they usually apply to an exporting country's scarce resources or raw materials.

PURPOSE PROTECTIVE AND REVENUE TARIFFS

Tariffs may be classified as protective tariffs and revenue tariffs. This distinction is based on purpose. The purpose of a protective tariff is to protect home industry, agriculture, and labour against foreign competitors by trying to keep foreign goods out of the country. The purpose of a revenue tariff, in contrast, is to generate tax revenues for the government. Compared to a protective tariff, a revenue tariff is relatively low. As in the case of the EU, it applies tariffs of up to 236 per cent on meat and 180 per cent on cereals, while its tariffs on raw materials and electronics rarely exceed 5 per cent.

LENGTH TARIFF SURCHARGE VERSUS COUNTERVAILING DUTY

Protective tariffs may be further classified just as to length of time. A tariff surcharge is a temporary action, whereas a countervailing duty is a permanent surcharge. When Harley-Davidson claimed that it needed time to adjust to Japanese imports, President Reagan felt that it was in the national interest to provide import relief. To protect the local industry, a tariff surcharge was used. In this particular case, the tariff achieved its purpose, and the company roared back. In 2002, it shipped 263,653 units, totaled $4.1 billion in sales, earned $580 million in profit, and captured 46 per cent of the North American heavyweight motorcycle market. More than 100,000 people rode their Harley-Davidson motorcycles to Wisconsin in 2003 to celebrate the company's 100- year anniversary. Countervailing duties are imposed on certain imports when products are subsidized by foreign governments. These duties are thus assessed to offset a special advantage or discount allowed by an exporter's government. Usually, a government provides an export subsidy by rebating certain taxes if goods are exported.

RATES SPECIFIC, AD VALOREM, AND COMBINED

How are tax rates applied? To understand the computation, three kinds of tax rates must be distinguished: specific, ad valorem, and combined.

Specific Duties

Specific duties are a fixed or specified amount of money per unit of weight, gauge, or other measure of quantity. Based on a standard physical unit of a product, they are specific rates of so many dollars or cents for a given unit of measure. Product costs or prices are irrelevant in this case. Because the duties are constant for low- and high-priced products of the same kind, this method is discriminatory and effective for protection against cheap products due to their lower unit value; that is, there is a reverse relationship between product value and duty percentage. As product price goes up, a duty when expressed as a percentage of this price will fall. On the other hand, for a cheap product whose value is low, the duty percentage will rise accordingly.

Ad Valorem Duties

Ad valorem duties are duties "according to value." They are stated as a fixed percentage of the invoice value and applied at a percentage to the dutiable value of the imported goods. This is the opposite of specific duties since the percentage is fixed but the total duty is not. Based on this method, there is a direct relationship between the total duties collected and the prices of products; that is, the absolute amount of total duties collected will increase or decrease with the prices of imported products. The strength of this method is that it provides continuous and relative protection against all price levels of a particular product. Such protection becomes even more crucial when inflation increases prices of imports. If specific duties were used, their effects lessen with time because inflation reduces the proportionate effect. Another advantage is that ad valorem duties provide an easy comparison of rates across countries and across products.

Combined Rates

Combined rates are a combination of the specific and ad valorem duties on a single product. They are duties based on both the specific rate and the ad valorem rate that are applied to an imported product. For example, the tariff may be 10 cents per pound plus 5 per cent ad valorem. Under this system, both rates are used together, though in some countries only the rate producing more revenue may apply. One important fact is that the average tariff rates affect the poor the most. After all, working-class consumers spend a large share of their income on the necessities of daily life, and many such necessities are imported. Affluent consumers, in comparison, are not bothered as much by tariffs because these necessities represent only a fraction of what they earn.

DISTRIBUTION POINT: DISTRIBUTION AND CONSUMPTION TAXES

Some taxes are collected at a particular point of distribution or when purchases and consumption occur. These indirect taxes, frequently adjusted at the border, are of four kinds: single-stage, value added, cascade, and excise.

Single-Stage Taxes

Single-stage sales tax is a tax collected at only one point in the manufacturing and distribution chain. This tax is perhaps most common in the USA, where retailers and wholesalers make purchases without paying any taxes by simply showing a sales tax permit. The single-stage sales tax is not collected until products are purchased by final consumers.

Value-Added Tax

A value-added tax (VAT) is a multi-stage, noncumulative tax on consumption. It is a national sales tax levied at each stage of the production and distribution system, though only on the value added at that stage. Its important feature is that it credits taxes paid by companies on their material inputs against taxes they must collect on their own sales. In other words, each time a product changes hands, even between middlemen, a tax must be paid, but the tax collected at a certain stage is based on the added value and not on the total value of the product at that point.

Sellers in the chain collect the VAT from a buyer, deduct the amount of VAT they have already paid on their purchase of the product, and remit the balance to the government. European Union customs officers collect the VAT upon importation of goods based on the CIF (cost, insurance, and freight) value plus the duty charged on the product. Even though VAT was first proposed in France in 1920, it was not until 1948 that the first recognizable VAT appeared in France. At that time, this tax was largely unknown outside the theoretical discussions. At present, more than 120 countries rely on it to raise $18 trillion or about a quarter of the world's tax revenue, affecting four billion people or 70 per cent of the world's population.

VAT is supposed to be nondiscriminatory because it applies both to products sold on the domestic market and to imported goods. The importance of the value-added tax is due to the fact that GATT allows a producing country to rebate the value-added tax when products are exported. Foreign firms trying to obtain a refund from European governments have found the refund process anything but easy. Since the tax applies to imports at the border but because it is fully rebated on exports, VAT may improve a country's trade balance. The evidence, however, offers a mixed picture. To strengthen VAT collections, a country should employ a single VAT rate, thus reducing administrative complexity. Value-added taxes should have few exceptions, and any exceptions should apply only to educational, medical, and social services. In addition, only exports should be zero-rated.

Cascade Taxes

Cascade taxes are collected at each point in the manufacturing and distribution chain and are levied on the total value of a product, including taxes borne by the product at earlier stages. Of the tax systems examined, this appears to be the most severe of all. For over thirty years, a now-defunct cascade system of taxation in Italy hurt the development of large-scale wholesale business there. Since the IGE was imposed each time the goods changed hands, Italian manufacturers minimized transfers of goods by selling products directly to retailers. The IGE was replaced by a value-added tax in 1973, and it was hoped by foreign manufacturers that the revival of wholesale organizations might facilitate imports of foreign consumer goods.

Excise Tax

An excise tax is a one-time charge levied on the sales of specified products. Alcoholic beverages and cigarettes are good examples. It is also common to levy excise taxes on motor vehicles, petroleum, and consumer durables. Excise taxes account for about 19 per cent of all tax revenues. These four kinds of indirect taxes are often adjusted at the border. Border taxes can be used to raise prices of imports or lower prices of exports.

Prices of imports are raised by charging imported goods with a tax usually borne by domestic products. For exported products, their export prices become more competitive when such products are relieved of the same tax that they are subject to when produced, sold, and consumed domestically.

MARKETING BARRIERS NON-TARIFF BARRIERS

Tariffs, though generally undesirable, are at least straightforward and obvious. Non-tariff barriers, in comparison, are more elusive or non-transparent. Tariffs have declined in importance, reaching the lowest level ever of about 4 per cent on average after fifty years and eight global rounds of trade negotiation. In the meantime, non-tariff barriers have become more prominent. Often disguised, the impact of non-tariff barriers can be just as devastating, if not more so, as the impact of tariffs.

There are several hundred types of non-tariff barriers. The US Trade Representative, countries use a variety of barriers that include non-scientific sanitary standards, customs procedures, and government monopolies. Japan's telecommunications, agriculture, and pharmaceuticals sectors have "structural rigidity, excessive regulation, and market access barriers."

China, on the other hand, has import standards and sanitary requirements that act as import barriers. China must act to improve the protection of intellectual property rights. Non-tariff barriers may be grouped into five major categories. Each category contains a number of different non-tariff barriers.

GOVERNMENT PARTICIPATION IN TRADE

The degree of government involvement in trade varies from passive to active. The types of participation include administrative guidance, state trading, and subsidies.

Administrative Guidance

Many governments routinely provide trade consultation to private companies. Japan has been doing this on a regular basis to help implement its industrial policies. This systematic cooperation between government and business is labeled "Japan, Inc."

To get private firms to conform to the Japanese government's guidance, the government uses a carrot and- stick approach by exerting the influence through regulations, recommendations, encouragement, discouragement, or prohibition. Japan's government agencies' administrative councils are influential enough to make importers restrict their purchases to an amount not exceeding a certain percentage of local demand. The Japanese government denies that such a practice exists, claiming that it merely seeks reports on the amounts purchased by each firm.

Government Procurement and State Trading

State trading is the ultimate in government participation, because the government itself is now the customer or buyer who determines what, when, where, how, and how much to buy. In this practice, the state engages in commercial operations, either directly or indirectly, through the agencies under its control. Such business activities are either in place of or in addition to private firms.

Although government involvement in business is most common with the communist countries, whose governments are responsible for the central planning of the whole economy, the practice is definitely not restricted to those nations. The US government, as the largest buyer in the world, is required by the Buy American Act to give a bidding edge to US suppliers in spite of their higher prices. The Government Procurement Act requires the signatory nations to guarantee that they will provide suppliers from other signatory countries treatment equal to that which they provide their own suppliers. This guarantee of "*national treatment*" means that a foreign government must choose the goods with the lowest price that best meet the specifications regardless of the supplier's nationality. The Code requires that technical specifications should not be prepared, adopted, or applied with a view to creating obstacles to international trade. The purchasing agency must adopt specifications geared towards performance rather than design and must base the specifications on international standards, national technical regulations, or recognized national standards, when appropriate.

Subsidies

GATT, subsidy is a "financial contribution provided directly or indirectly by a government and which confers a benefit." Subsidies may take many forms–including cash, interest rate, value-added tax, corporate income tax, sales tax, freight, insurance, and infrastructure. Subsidized loans for priority sectors, preferential rediscount rates, and budgetary subsidies are among the various subsidy policies of several Asian countries.

There are several other kinds of subsidies that are not so obvious. Brazil's rebates of the various taxes, coupled with other forms of assistance, may be viewed as subsidies. Tennessee, Ohio, Michigan, and Illinois, in order to attract foreign automakers to locate their plants in those states, provided such services as highway construction, training of workers, and tax breaks, which are simply subsidies in disguise. Sheltered profit is another kind of subsidy. A country may allow a corporation to shelter its profit from abroad.

In 1971 the USA allowed companies to form domestic international sales corporations (DISCs) even though they cost the US Treasury Department more than $1 billion a year in revenue. GATT, the multilateral treaty, eventually ruled that a DISC was an illegal export subsidy. A new US law then allowed companies that met more stringent requirements to form foreign sales corporations (FSCs). As in the case of Boeing Co., it was the biggest user of this tool, enabling it to avoid $130 million in US taxes in 1998, about 12 per cent of its entire earnings. Ultimately, FSCs were also found to be illegal. The Subsidies Code, technically named the Agreement on Interpretation and Application of Article VI, XVI and XXIII of the General Agreement on Tariffs and Trade, recognizes that government subsidies distort the competitive forces at work in international trade. The rules of the international agreement negotiated during the Tokyo Round of Multilateral Trade Negotiations differentiate between *export subsidies* and *domestic subsidies*.

The Code's rules also differentiate between subsidies paid on *primary products* and those paid on *non-primary products* and primary minerals. A primary product is any product of farm, forest, or fishery in its natural form or that has undergone such processing as is customarily required to prepare it for transportation and marketing in substantial volume in international trade.

The Code prohibits the use of export subsidies on non-primary products and primary mineral products. There is considerable debate over what should be considered manufactured products, since such products are not entitled to any subsidies. For instance, the EU's export subsidies for such manufactured products as pasta and wheat flour are banned by the International Subsidies Code. The EU's position is that pasta and wheat flour are not manufactured products.

Agricultural export subsidies have long been a persistent source of conflict. In 2002, Poland, the Czech Republic, Turkey, and Australia respectively spent $56 million, $35 million, $28 million, and $2 million on agricultural export subsidies. The figures for the following countries are: Switzerland ($292 million), Norway ($128 million), and the USA ($80 million). The EU by itself incredibly spent $5985 million. In 2003, the EU trade ministers applauded an agreement to put limits on the EU's forty-year-old practice of paying farmers subsidies based on the amount of their production. However, the EU has not reduced its $30.5 billion a year paid in production-linked subsidies, nor has it made any changes to its export subsidies–the highest in the world.

Developing countries complain bitterly that these subsidies are harmful to trade by encouraging European farmers to sell their produce abroad. Interestingly, affluent countries have been heavily subsidizing their agricultural businesses.

Their agricultural subsidies total almost $1 a day. While 75 per cent of people in Sub- Saharan Africa live on less than $2 a day, an average European cow receives about $2.50 a day in subsidy. On average, a Japanese cow does even better, receiving about $7 a day in subsidy. The UNCTAD Secretary-General, "six or seven of the top ten agricultural exporters are developed countries, and I don't think they could reach that status without export subidies."

CUSTOMS AND ENTRY PROCEDURES

Customs and Entry Procedures may be Employed as Non-Tariff Barriers. These Restrictions Involve Classification, Valuation, Documentation, License, Inspection, and Health and Safety Regulations.

Classification

How a product is classified can be arbitrary and inconsistent and is often based on a customs officer's judgment, at least at the time of entry. Product classification is important because the way in which a product is classified determines its duty status.

A company can sometimes take action to affect the classification of its product. Sony argued that its PlayStation 2, equipped with a 128-bit microprocessor, a DVD player, and Internet connection, was a big improvement over its PlayStation original and that it should thus qualify as a computer. However, the British customs office chose to continue to classify PlayStation 2 in the video games category, in effect imposing a duty of 2.2 per cent or about $9. Had Sony prevailed in getting the "digital processing units" classification, there would be no import tax.

Valuation

Regardless of how products are classified, each product must still be valued. The value affects the amount of tariffs levied. A customs appraiser is the one who determines the value. The process can be highly subjective, and the valuation of a product may be interpreted in different ways, depending on what value is used and how this value is constructed. In Japan, a commodity tax is applied to the FOB factory price of Japanese cars. Yet American cars are valued on the CIF basis, adding $1000 more to the final retail price of these cars.

Documentation

Documentation can present another problem at entry because many documents and forms are often necessary, and the documents required can be complicated. Japan held up Givenchy's import application because the company left out an apostrophe for its I'Interdit perfume.

Without proper documentation, goods may not be cleared through customs. At the very least, such complicated and lengthy documents serve to slow down product clearance. France, requiring customs documentation to be in French, even held up trucks from other European countries for hours while looking for products' non-French instruction manuals which were banned.

License or Permit

Not all products can be freely imported; controlled imports require licenses or permits. For example, importations of distilled spirits, wines, malt beverages, arms, ammunition, and explosives into the USA require a license issued by the Bureau of Alcohol, Tobacco, and Firearms. India requires a license for all imported goods. It is not always easy to obtain an import license, since many countries will issue one only if goods can be certified as necessary. Japan simplified its licensing procedure in 1986. Previously, a separate license application had been required for any new cosmetic product, even when only a change in shade was involved. The new requirements categorize cosmetics into seventy-eight groups and list permitted ingredients. A marketer simply notifies the government of any new product using those ingredients.

Inspection

Inspection is an integral part of product clearance. Goods must be examined to determine quality and quantity. This step is closely related to other customs and entry procedures. First, inspection classifies and values products for tariff purposes. Second, inspection reveals whether imported items are consistent with those specified in the accompanying documents and whether such items require any licenses.

Third, inspection determines whether products meet health and safety regulations in order to make certain that food products are fit for human consumption or that the products can be operated safely. Fourth, inspection prevents the importation of prohibited articles. Marketers should be careful in stating the amount and quality of products, as well as in providing an accurate description of products.

Any deviation from the statements contained in invoices necessitates further measurements and determination, more delay, and more expenses. Inspection can be used intentionally to discourage imports. Metal baseball bats from the USA, for instance, are required to carry a stamp of consumer safety, and this must be "ascertained" only after expensive on-dock inspection.

Health and Safety Regulations

Many products are subject to health and safety regulations, which are necessary to protect the public health and environment. Health and safety regulations are not restricted to agricultural products.

The regulations also apply to TV receivers, microwave ovens, X-ray devices, cosmetics, chemical substances, and clothing. Concern for safety was used by Japan against aluminum softball bats from the USA. The manufacturing process leaves a small hole in the top which is fitted with a rubber stopper. Japan thus bans the bats on the ground that the stopper might fly out and hurt someone.

PRODUCT REQUIREMENTS

For goods to enter a country, product requirements set by that country must be met. Requirements may apply to product standards and product specifications as well as to packaging, labeling, and marking.

Product Standards

Each country determines its own product standards to protect the health and safety of its consumers. Such standards may also be erected as barriers to prevent or slow down importation of foreign goods. Because of US grade, size, quality, and maturity requirements, many Mexican agricultural commodities are barred from entering the USA. Japanese product standards are even more complex, and they are based on physical characteristics rather than product performance. Such standards make it necessary to repeat the product approval process when a slight product modification occurs, even though the performance of the product in question remains the same. Furthermore, these standards are frequently changed in Japan in order to exclude imports.

Packaging, Labeling, and Marking

Packaging, labeling, and marking are considered together because they are closely interrelated. Many products must be packaged in a certain way for safety and other reasons. Canada requires imported canned foods to be packed in specified can sizes, and instructions contained within or on packages must be in English and French. The Canadian Labeling Act also requires all imported clothing to carry labels in both languages.

Product Testing

Many products must be tested to determine their safety and suitability before they can be marketed. This is another area in which the USA has some trouble in Japan. Although products may have won approval everywhere else for safety and effectiveness, such products as medical equipment and pharmaceuticals must go through elaborate standard testing that can take a few years–just long enough for Japanese companies to develop competing products. Moreover, the reviews take place behind the Health and Welfare Ministry's closed doors. In 1995, Japan's Ministry of International Trade and Industry started requiring imported software products to be certified by agents of the Japan Accreditation Bureau.

The accreditation requirement may reveal how US software is designed while delaying US bids on public contracts. The EU's global approach to testing and certification for product safety provides manufacturers with one set of procedures for certifying product compliance with EU health, safety, and environmental requirements. The various means by which manufacturers can certify product conformance include manufacturer self-declaration of conformity, third-party testing, quality assurance audit, and/or approval by a body authorized by an EU member state and recognized by the EU Commission.

The mark *CE* on the product signifies that all legal requirements concerning product standards have been met. To be legally marketed in the European Union, more than half of American products must bear the CE mark. Unfortunately, certification of product tests and registrations for information technology, medical devices, and certain products can only be carried out in Europe, and the practice is costly and uncompetitive.

Product Specifications

Product specifications, though appearing to be an innocent process, can wreak havoc on imports. Specifications can be written in such a way as to favour local bidders and to keep out foreign suppliers. For example, specifications can be extremely detailed, or they can be written to closely resemble domestic products.

Thus they may be used against foreign suppliers who cannot satisfy the specifications without expensive or lengthy modification. Japan's Nippon Telephone and Telegraph Company (NTT) was able to use product specifications as a built-in barrier when it was forced to accept bids from foreign firms. At one time, it did not even provide any specifications and bidding details in any language apart from Japanese. Its specifications are highly restrictive and written with existing Japanese products in mind. Instead of outlining functional characteristics, NTT specifies physical features right down to the location of ventilation holes, the details of which are almost identical to those of Nippon Electric. For example, NTT requires metal cabinets for modems, whereas most US makers use plastic. Parts must be made by the Japanese to qualify for bidding. In general, NTT goes well beyond specifications for performance. GATT has established procedures for setting product standards using performance standards rather than detailed physical specifications.

QUOTAS

Quotas are a quantity control on imported goods. Generally, they are specific provisions limiting the amount of foreign products imported in order to protect local firms and to conserve foreign currency. Quotas may be used for export control as well. An export quota is sometimes required by national planning to preserve scarce resources. From a policy standpoint, a quota is not as desirable as a tariff since a quota generates no revenues for a country. There are three kinds of quotas: absolute, tariff, and voluntary.

Absolute Quotas

An absolute quota is the most restrictive of all. It limits in absolute terms the amount imported during a quota period. Once filled, further entries are prohibited. Some quotas are global, but others are allocated to specific foreign countries. Japan imposes strict quotas on oranges and beef. To appease the EU, it has lifted quotas on skimmed milk powder and tobacco for Europe. The most extreme of the absolute quota is an embargo, or a zero quota, as shown in the case of the US trade embargoes against Libya and North Korea.

Tariff Quotas

A tariff quota permits the entry of a limited quantity of the quota product at a reduced rate of duty. Quantities in excess of the quota may be imported but are subject to a higher duty rate. Through the use of tariff quotas, a combination of tariffs and quotas is applied with the primary purpose of importing what is needed and discouraging excessive quantities through higher tariffs. When the USA increased tariffs on imported motorcycles in order to protect the US motorcycle industry, it exempted from this tax the first 6000 big motorcycles from Japan and the first 4000–5000 units from Europe.

Voluntary Quotas

A voluntary quota differs from the other two kinds of quota, which are unilaterally imposed. A voluntary quota is a formal agreement between nations, or between a nation and an industry. This agreement usually specifies the limit of supply by product, country, and volume. Two kinds of voluntary quota can be legally distinguished: VER (voluntary export restraint) and OMA (orderly marketing agreement). Whereas an OMA involves negotiation between two governments to specify export management rules, the monitoring of trade volumes, and consultation rights, a VER is a direct agreement between an importing nation's government and a foreign exporting industry. Both enable the importing country to circumvent the GATT's rules that require the country to reciprocate for the quota received and to impose that market safeguard on a most-favored-nation basis. Since this is a gray area, the OMA and VER may be applied in a discriminatory manner to a certain country. In the case of a VER involving private industries, a public disclosure is not necessary.

The largest voluntary quota is the Multi-Fibre Arrangement (MFA) for forty-one export and import countries. This international agreement on textiles allows Western governments to set quotas on imports of low-priced textiles from the Third World. The treaty has been criticized because advanced nations are able to force the agreement on poorer countries. As implied, a country may negotiate to limit voluntarily its export to a particular market. This may sound peculiar because the country appears to be acting against its own self-interest. But a country's unwillingness to accept these unfavorable terms will eventually invite trade retaliation and tougher terms in the form of forced quotas. It is thus voluntary only in the sense that the exporting country tries to avoid alternative trade barriers that are even less desirable. For example, Japan agreed to restrict and reprice some exports within Great Britain. In reality, there is nothing voluntary about a voluntary quota.

FINANCIAL CONTROL

Financial regulations can also function to restrict international trade. These restrictive monetary policies are designed to control capital flow so that currencies can be defended or imports controlled. For example, to defend the weak Italian lira, Italy imposed a 7 per cent tax on the purchase of foreign currencies. There are several forms that financial restrictions can take.

Exchange Control

An exchange control is a technique that limits the amount of the currency that may be taken abroad. The reason exchange controls are usually applied is that the local currency is overvalued, thus causing imports to be paid for in smaller amounts of currency. Purchasers then try to use the relatively cheap foreign exchange to obtain items that are either unavailable or more expensive in the local currency. Exchange controls also limit the length of time and money an exporter may hold for the goods sold. French exporters, for example, must exchange the foreign currencies for francs within one month. By regulating all types of capital outflow in foreign currencies, the government either makes it difficult to obtain imported products or makes such items available only at higher prices.

Multiple Exchange Rates

Multiple exchange rates are another form of exchange regulation or barrier. The objectives of multiple exchange rates are twofold: to encourage exports and imports of certain goods, and to discourage exports and imports of others. This means that there is no single rate for all products or industries, but with the application of multiple exchange rates, some products and industries will benefit and some will not. Spain once used low exchange rates for goods designated for export and high rates for those it desired to retain at home. Multiple exchange rates may also apply to imports.

The high rates may be used for imports of particular goods with the government's approval, whereas low rates may be used for other imports. Since multiple exchange rates are used to bring in hard currencies as well as to restrict imports, this system is condemned by the International Monetary Fund (IMF). The IMF, any unapproved multiple currency practices are a breach of obligations, and the member may become ineligible to use the Fund's resources. In 1985, South Africa, in trying to stem capital outflow, started to require non-residents to transact capital transactions at a separately freely floating exchange rate. The financial rand was much more depreciated than the commercial rand exchange rate. In 1995, as political uncertainty declined, South Africa unified the two exchange rates.

Prior Import Deposits and Credit Restrictions

Financial barriers may also include specific limitations on import restraints, such as prior import deposits and credit restrictions. Both of these barriers operate by imposing certain financial restriction on importers. A government can require prior import deposits that make imports difficult by tying up an importer's capital. In effect, the importer is paying interest for money borrowed without being able to use the money or obtain interest earnings on the money from the government. Importers in Brazil and Italy must deposit a large sum of money with their central banks if they intend to buy foreign goods. To help initiate an aircraft industry, the Brazilian government has required an importer of "flyaway" planes to deposit the full price of the imported aircraft for one year with no interest. Credit restrictions apply only to imports; that is, exporters may be able to obtain loans from the government, usually at very favorable rates, but importers will not be able to receive any credit or financing from the government. Importers must look for loans in the private sector–very likely at significantly higher rates, if such loans are available at all.

Profit Remittance Restrictions

Another form of exchange barrier is the profit remittance restriction. ASEAN countries share a common philosophy in allowing unrestricted repatriation of profits earned by foreign companies. Singapore, in particular, allows the unrestricted movement of capital, but many countries regulate the remittance of profits earned in local operations and sent to a parent organization located abroad. Brazil uses progressive rates in taxing all profits remitted to a parent company abroad, with such rates rising to 60 per cent.

Other countries practice a form of profit remittance restriction by simply having long delays in permission for profit expatriation. To overcome these practices, MNCs have looked to legal loopholes. Many employ various tactics such as counter trading, currency swaps, and other parallel schemes. For example, a multinational firm wanting to repatriate a currency may swap it with another firm which needs that currency, or these firms may lend to each other in the currency desired by each party. Another tactic is to negotiate for a higher value of an investment than the investment's actual worth. By charging its foreign subsidiary higher prices and fees, an MNC is able to increase the equity base from which dividend repatriations are calculated. In addition, compared to profit repatriations, the higher prices and fees are treated as costs or expenses and are thus paid more freely to the parent firm.

PRIVATE BARRIERS

As conventional trade barriers are lowered, governments are shifting their attention to competition policy to address environmental and labour objectives and private barriers. Private barriers are certain business practices or arrangements between or among affiliated firms. Japan's *keiretsu* is a good example of private barriers. The *keiretsu* system deals with cooperative business groups. Such a group includes manufacturers, suppliers, retailers, and customers. Members of the group seek long-term security through interlocking directorates and through owning shares in each other's companies. Toyota Motor Corp. provided $83 million to help out Tomen Corp., a money-losing trading firm. Both belong to the same *keiretsu*, and it is a tradition for members of the *keiretsu* to subsidize each other.

Mitsubishi even arranges for the executives of its affiliated companies to have lunch together so as to discuss business dealings. Naturally, the companies that belong to the same *keiretsu* will grant preferential treatment to the other members. Korea's *chaebol* system also functions in a similar fashion. Private barriers are not unique to Asia.

In Germany, banks are strong and often take a leadership role. In the case of Deutsche Bank, it owns at least 10 per cent of some seventy companies, and its bank executives sit on some 400 corporate boards. As such, it is in a position to encourage its clients to do business with each other–rather than with outsiders. While non-tariff barriers are not as transparent as tariffs, private barriers are the worst in terms of transparency. It is difficult for an outsider to gain business if potential buyers refuse to explain why they do not want to buy from a foreign firm. Certainly, private barriers will be the next significant challenge.

WORLD TRADE ORGANIZATION (WTO)

Virtually all nations seek to pursue their best interests in international trade. The result is that sooner or later international trade and marketing can be disrupted. To prevent or at least alleviate any problems, there is a world organization in Geneva known as the WTO. Created in January 1948, the objective of GATT is to achieve a broad, multilateral, and free worldwide system of trading. For example, its code requires international bidding on major projects. GATT provides the forum for tariff negotiations and the elimination of trade discrimination.

The four basic principles of GATT are:

1. Member countries will *consult* each other concerning trade problems.
2. The agreement provides a framework for *negotiation* and embodies results of negotiations in a legal instrument.
3. Countries should protect domestic industries *only through tariffs*, when needed and if permitted. There should be no other restrictive devices such as quotas prohibiting imports.
4. Trade should be conducted on a *non-discriminatory* basis.

Reductions of barriers should be mutual and reciprocal because any country's import increases caused by such reductions will be offset by export increases caused by other countries' reduction of restrictions. This concept is the basis of the principle of the most favored nation (MFN), which is the cornerstone of GATT. Countries should grant one another treatment as favorable as treatment given to their best trading partners or any other country. For example, reductions accorded France by the USA should be extended to other countries with which the USA exchanges the MFN principle. Likewise, if a country decides to temporarily protect its local industry because that industry is seriously threatened, then the newly erected barriers must apply to all countries even though the threat to its industry may come from only a single nation. The MFN principle thus moves countries away from bilateral bargaining to multilateral bargaining.

Each country must be concerned with the implications that its concessions for one country would mean for other countries. The only exception is that an advanced country should not expect reciprocity from less developed countries. To better reflect actual practice, the MFN principle is now called the NTR by the USA. The USA does not accord MFN status to communist countries that restrict emigration, but this requirement may be waived by the President. After China first received MFN status from the

USA in 1980, mushroom imports from China jumped from nothing to nearly 50 per cent of all US mushroom imports. This increase owed much to the decline of canned mushroom duties, from 45 per cent to 10 per cent. Seven successive rounds of multilateral trade negotiations under GATT auspices produced a decline in average tariff on industrial products in industrial countries from more than 40 per cent in 1947 to about 5 per cent in 1988. The Uruguay round of multilateral trade negotiations, launched in Punta del Este, Uruguay, in September 1986, aimed to liberalize trade further, to strengthen GATT's role, to foster cooperation, and to enhance the interrelationships between trade and other economic policies that affect growth and development.

The Uruguay round attempted to deal with new areas such as services, intellectual property rights, and trade-related investment. Developed nations offered to reduce trade protection to their agriculture and textile industries in exchange for less developed countries' greater imports of services and greater respect for intellectual property. However, the different countries' varying interests repeatedly stalled the talks.

Agricultural disputes even led to violent protests by farmers in France, Japan, South Korea, and others. Not surprisingly, Lee Kuan Yew of Singapore once called GATT the General Agreement to Talk and Talk. Fortunately, delegations from more than a hundred countries were able finally to conclude negotiations at the end of 1993 after seven years of talks. The 109 nations signed the 22,000-page agreement in 1994. This most ambitious and comprehensive global commercial agreement in history provides for a phase-out of the Multi-Fibre Arrangement (MFA) over a ten-year period while reforming trade in agricultural goods.

The agreement also lowers tariffs by more than one-third writes new rules of trade for intellectual property and services, and strengthens the dispute settlement process. Just like the Uruguay round, the 2002 to 2004 Doha round has generated a great deal of controversy and conflict. While the richer economies press the developing countries to open up their markets, the poorer countries have accused the advanced economies of maintaining a very high level of agricultural supports, thus damaging the poor countries' farm-dependent economies. The talks in Cancun in mid-2003 ended up with the delegates from the poorer countries walking out in protest of the advanced economies' insincere efforts to end agriculture subsidies. As a result, the future of the WTO itself could be jeopardized. Hopefully, logic and practicality should ultimately prevail. Because GATT was set up in 1948 as a temporary body, the Uruguay round agreement wanted to replace GATT with the World Trade Organization in 1995.

At the beginning, GATT and the WTO coexisted, but GATT ceased to exist after a one-year period. The WTO, being more permanent and legally secure, will have more authority to settle trade disputes, and will serve along with the International Monetary Fund and the World Bank to monitor trade and resolve disputes.

The WTO will encompass the current GATT structure as well as the Uruguay round agreements. It will provide a single, coordinated mechanism to ensure full, effective implementation of the trading system, and it will also provide a permanent, comprehensive forum to address the new or evolving issues of the global market. The WTO's strengthened dispute settlement system should be better able to limit the scope for unilateral and bilateral actions outside the multilateral system. Under GATT's dispute resolution system, the USA and other members could and indeed did veto the decisions of arbitration boards. As a result, nations could refuse to adopt negative decisions. For example, a GATT panel twice found that the European Union's oilseed subsidies impeded the tariff-free access to the EU market that was promised to the USA in a 1962 trade agreement; yet the EU failed to adequately reform subsidies harmful to US oilseed producers. Under the WTO, a nation's veto of a panel's decision is eliminated.

Other important changes under the new dispute settlement mechanism include:

- Fixed time limits for each stage of the dispute settlement process,
- Automatic adoption of dispute settlement reports,
- Automatic authority to retaliate on request if recommendations are not implemented,
- Creation of a new appellate body to review panel interpretations of WTO agreements, and
- Improved procedural transparency and access to information in the dispute settlement process.

The new procedures yield a panel ruling within sixteen months of requesting consultations. Unfortunately for the USA, one early finding involved a challenge of Venezuela and Brazil concerning an Environmental Protection Agency (EPA) regulation governing US imports of gasoline. The WTO panel ruled that the EPA's treatment of imported gasoline was inconsistent with GATT provisions.

The WTO has 148 members. China, wanting the prestige of being a founding member, tried unsuccessfully to complete its negotiations in 1994 on an accelerated basis. China felt that it should not be held to the same terms which apply to industrialized countries. The USA, however, wanted China to fully observe the WTO rules. After years of negotiation with the EU and the USA, China has finally gained membership. Nepal, one of the poorest countries, became the 148th member in 2003. Supporters of the WTO have long argued that a reduction of trade barriers will boost global trade. However, there is hardly any rigorous empirical investigation of whether the WTO has an impact on trade or trade policy. While one recent study shows that any impact is very little, another IMF study disagrees with that conclusion.

PREFERENTIAL SYSTEMS

GENERALIZED SYSTEM OF PREFERENCES (GSP)

Although the benefits derived from the creation of the WTO are rarely disputed, less developed countries do not necessarily embrace GATT because those countries believe that the benefits are not evenly distributed. Tariff reduction generally favors manufactured goods rather than primary goods. Less developed countries rely mainly on exports of primary products, which are then converted by advanced nations into manufactured products for export back to less developed countries. As a result, a less developed country's exports will usually be lower in value than its imports, thus exacerbating the country's poverty status. In response to less developed countries' needs, the United Nations Conference on Trade and Development (UNCTAD) was created as a permanent organ of the UN General Assembly.

Efforts by the UNCTAD led to the establishment of the New International Economic Order (NIEO) programme. This programme seeks to assist less developed countries through the stabilization of prices of primary products, the expansion of less developed countries' manufacturing capabilities, and the acquisition by less developed countries of advanced technology.

The goal of the UNCTAD is to encourage development in Third World countries and enhance their export positions. This goal led to the establishment of a tariff preference system for less developed countries' manufactured products. In spite of GATT's non-discrimination principle, advanced nations agreed to grant such preferences to less developed countries' goods. The UNCTAD also played a key role in the emergence of a maritime shipping code, special international programmes to help the least developed countries, and international aid targets. Under the generalized system of preferences (GSP), developed countries are allowed to deviate from GATT's traditional non-discrimination principle.

Most developing countries have preferential access to the markets of industrial countries. There are about fifteen such arrangements in effect. Although the lower tariffs help the exports of many low-income countries, they also divert trade from some other countries that may be just as poor. Furthermore, the GSP schemes may perpetuate anti-export biases by undermining incentives to engage in trade liberalization. The US preferential system is known as the generalized system of preferences (GSP). The US Congress passed the Trade Act of 1974, authorizing the initiation of the GSP. The purpose of the act is to aid development by providing duty-free entry on 4000 products from more than thirty developing countries. Products manufactured wholly or substantially in the designated countries are permitted to enter the United Stats duty-free as long as a particular item does not exceed $50.9 million in sales or 50 per cent of all US imports of this product. Not all products qualify for such preferential treatment, however, and one should consult the Harmonized Tariff Schedule of the USA to determine whether a product may enter duty-free.

For a country to qualify, a number of economic variables are considered, such as per capita GNP and living standard. Burma and the Central African Republic had their benefits suspended under the US GSP for failing to meet the labour requirements. Venezuela was challenged as a result of a claim by Occidental Petroleum that its assets were expropriated without compensation. The Four Tigers once receiving almost 60 per cent of the benefits under GSP, were permanently graduated from the programme at the beginning of 1989 as a result of their high degree of economic development and export competitiveness.

Therefore, Black and Decker, which makes electric irons in Singapore, lost more than $3 million a year because of the new duties. Clearly, foreign exporters and American importers can find the GSP system highly advantageous. Among the 140 countries and territories covered by the US GSP programme, Thailand ranks second behind Angola for receiving the highest GSP privileges. Given the fact that GSP is product-specific and that some of Thailand's products have reached their "competitive need" limit, certain benefits will be either reduced or withdrawn. In general, a product that has export sales of $95 million to the USA is not entitled to GSP tariff reductions. In addition, once a country's per capita GNP exceeds $3115, the country will have officially graduated from the US GSP programme.

CARIBBEAN BASIN INITIATIVE (CBI)

Another US preferential system is the Caribbean Basin Initiative (CBI). The Caribbean Basin Economic Recovery Act of 1983 provides trade and tax measures to promote economic revitalization and expanded private sector opportunities in designated countries in the Caribbean Basin region. The main provision of the CBI eliminates US duties on almost all products entering from qualified countries in the Caribbean Basin. The law, however, excludes important products from duty-free status as a safeguard for domestic industry. The Customs and Trade Act of 1990 makes the CBI permanent and provides additional trade benefits for the Caribbean countries. The Act provides a significant advantage to import from the region. The products will benefit by cost reductions through tariff elimination compared with imports from non-CBI countries. American firms producing products in the Caribbean may profit further from exporting to Europe, Canada, and South America, because many Caribbean Basin countries have preferential access to one or more of these other markets. The Act thus encourages US firms to open more labour-intensive assembly plants that export back to North America.

OTHER PREFERENTIAL SYSTEMS

The Andean Trade Preference Act, similar to the CBI, provides trade benefits to Bolivia, Colombia, Ecuador, and Peru. In addition, the USA has passed the African Growth and Opportunity Act to provide reforming African countries with the most liberal access to the US market available to any country with which the USA does not have a free trade agreement. The act has designated thirty-five countries to receive the benefits of lower import duty on an approved list of products entering the US market.

SOME REMARKS ON PROTECTIONISM

Protectionist policies rarely achieve their objectives. As noted by a deputy US trade representative, "The price you pay for protection is inefficiency." Inward looking strategies are based on the *positive externalities* assumption. That is, government intervention is appropriate because the development of a certain industry has a positive impact on a broader segment of the economy. Unfortunately, externalities are usually presumed rather than documented. No nation can dominate all industries. The protection of domestic economies against international competition is responsible for major economic losses for most sub-Saharan African countries. These countries need to open up their economies, and structural adjustment programmes need to be implemented. Most politicians are short-sighted; they simply desire to keep wealth within the home country. The possibility of retaliation is not fully considered. They want the best of both worlds.

Artificial trade barriers reduce the world output of goods and services, and subsequently the world economic welfare; in the end, everyone suffers. The costs of distortions in agricultural trade are large, probably exceeding $120 billion in welfare costs. Countries, developing and industrial, must pay for protectionism.

Elimination of barriers to merchandise trade will result in welfare gains of $250 billion to $620 billion. A country has a choice of opening or closing its borders to trade. If it adopts the open system, it has a much better chance of fostering economic growth and maximizing consumer welfare. By adopting this approach, Hong Kong has been doing well economically.

In response to the first oil price shock in the early 1970s, Brazil and Korea increased protection for domestic industry and got poor economic results. After the second oil price shock in the late 1970s, Korea adopted outward-oriented trade policies and has greatly benefited from international integration and the strong growth of world trade.

Brazil's less outward-oriented policies, in comparison, reduced competitive pressures at home, accelerated inflation, and led to stagnation. The trade regimes are also more restrictive in Africa than in the rest of the world. Nations usually take a short cut and try to have a quick fix for their trade problems.

Preoccupation with immediate problems often makes them lose sight of the long-term objectives. Without proper perspective, they can easily end up with more serious problems later. Trade barriers slow specialization, diversification, investment efficiency, and growth. Government leaders must have political will to resist protectionist measures. Governments must make concerted and determined efforts to publicize the costs of protectionism. Trade policy should include a systematic consideration of such costs.

Openness of an economy is the degree to which foreigners and nationals can transact without government-imposed costs that are not levied on a transaction between two national citizens. One should note that trade openness and financial openness are complementary.

This positive relationship applies both to industrial and developing countries. Even in the case of intra-regional growth, as in China, the evidence shows that the more open areas grow faster than their less open counterparts. The breadth of evidence on openness, growth, and poverty reduction, and the strength of the association between openness and other important determinants of high per capita income, such as the quality of institutions, should give long pause to anyone contemplating the adoption of a novel development strategy that does not center on openness to trade.

CONCLUSION

This stage has discussed various trade barriers that can inhibit international marketing and, in turn, the world economic welfare of all consumers. It is important to understand that these are only some of the many trade barriers–others are not discussed. For example, more and more countries have now turned to "performance requirements" in order to gain trade advantage.

Foreign suppliers are required to use local materials or to do exporting on behalf of an importing nation before they are allowed to sell their products there. Regardless of the inappropriateness or injustice of many of these practices, they are part of international marketing. Although nations have used the WTO to lessen many of these restrictions, others will undoubtedly remain. In fact, most countries in recent years have initiated more protective measures. Since an international marketer has no control over these wide-reaching forces, the best defence is to understand and to be knowledgeable about these trade practices. These barriers may be frustrating but they are not necessarily insurmountable. By understanding them, the marketer can learn what to expect and how to cope. One must always remember that additional problems are often accompanied by additional opportunities–for additional profits.

8

Consumer Behaviour in the International Context

PERSPECTIVES ON CONSUMER BEHAVIOUR

Consumer behaviour may be defined as a study of human behaviour within the consumer role and includes all the steps in the decision-making process. The study must go beyond the explicit act of purchase to include an examination of less observable processes, as well as a discussion of why, where, and how a particular purchase occurs.

Domestically, marketing scholars have employed a variety of techniques and concepts, including the cultural approach, to study consumer behaviour. Yet consumer study on an international basis has employed the cultural approach almost exclusively without much regard for other psychological and social concepts.

This is a very curious approach since it is the norm for virtually all consumer behaviour textbooks to treat culture as only one of the many theoretical concepts which can affect purchase and the other behavioral dimensions.

It is a questionable practice to rely on culture as the sole determinant of behaviour or as the only concept that largely, if not entirely, explains behaviour. Culture undoubtedly affects the psychological and social processes and thus affects consumer behaviour. However, too much emphasis is placed on a single concept. Consumer behaviour research must include international dimensions. Differences in behavioral dimensions among national groups "should not be attributed to differences in culture unless components of culture have been specified." For group mean differences to be meaningful, there should be some explanation as to why these differences should exist. Furthermore, there may be a need to develop an international consumer behaviour model so that studies of consumer behaviour in various countries can be more systematic and better coordinated.

The major behavioral sciences relevant to consumer study are psychology, sociology, and cultural anthropology. Psychology, with the *individual* as its central unit of analysis, is the study of individual and interpersonal behaviour. Behaviour is governed by a person's cognitions, such as values, attitudes, experiences, needs, and other psychological phenomena. Purchase, then, becomes a function of the psychological view of products, and the consumer buys a product not only for consumption but also because of a perception of how a product can be used to communicate with other people.

Some psychological concepts relevant to the study of consumer behaviour are motivation, learning, personality, perception, and attitude. Sociology is the study of groups and human interactions. The unit of analysis is not the individual but rather the *group*. The group, consisting of a set of individuals who interact over time, is important because it can exert a significant influence on a person's preferences and consumption behaviour.

In many instances, it may be useful for a marketer to view consumers as a group. For example, a family, not an individual, often makes a purchase decision that affects all members of the family group. Important sociological concepts are reference group and family. Cultural anthropology is the study of human culture. Thus, the analytic perspective may be quite large. Culture involves an aggregate, social category level and the social categories are significant in the sense that they influence consumers' cognitive and personality development. The concepts from this discipline usually included in the analysis of consumer behaviour are culture, subculture, and social class.

MOTIVATION

Motivation is fundamental in initiating consumer behaviour. Motivation may be viewed as a drive that is directed by a motive formed in relation to a particular goal. Once the motive–drive relationship is developed, the consumer initiates some forms of motivated behaviour to satisfy a previously recognized need.

Consumer motives are determined largely by buying habits, though motives can vary, and it is important to recognize the various types of motives. Motives may be classified as rational and non-rational. Examples of rational motives are price, durability, and economy in operation. Non-rational appeals, in comparison, include prestige, comfort, and pleasure. The problem with the conventional classification is that a consumer may not recognize emotional motives and may have a tendency to rationalize personal behaviour by assigning only rational and socially acceptable motives.

In addition, the process of classification is not always straightforward. Convenience, for instance, can be both rational and non-rational at the same time. In the end, the success of a product is greatly affected by whether its target customers are properly motivated. Whether a motive is rational or irrational is not particularly important. What is important is to identify specific motives relevant for marketing purposes.

A critical task is to select, carefully and properly, a relevant motive for the purpose of product promotion. In addition, the relevance of a particular motive may vary across countries. For example, one study of youths in Hong Kong, Singapore, Canada, and Hawaii compared their beliefs in money, business ethics, *quanxi*, and Machiavellian personality. Surprisingly, Canadians believe that money can work wonders–even more so than their Hong Kong and Singapore counterparts.

LEARNING

Like all habits, food and drink habits are learned. Before World War II, the British were accustomed to drinking tea, not coffee. Then along came the American troops, who brought the American taste for coffee–at first a relatively light, almost blond coffee. Before long, Britons had learned to drink coffee too. In another example, a large lunch with wine presents no problem to a Swiss, but the same will put an American to sleep. On the other hand, American-style cocktails may prove to be too much for Europeans, who are accustomed to milder drinks. Marketers must take these habits into consideration. Motives, cultural norms, and consumption habits are all learned. Therefore, a marketer should understand the learning process. Learning is a change in behaviour that occurs over time relative to a given set of external stimulus conditions.

Baskin-Robbins, as the first fast-food franchise in Vietnam, has to teach the Vietnamese about the concept of fast food. When the ice cream parlor first opened, most Vietnamese customers walked in and sat down, expecting to be waited on. When they were asked to go to the counter, some felt insulted and left. In addition the Vietnamese are accustomed to linger at café tables and are thus not used to having to pay immediately.

Naturally, a number of them got angry and felt that Baskin-Robbins did not trust them by asking them to pay for the ice cream immediately. Interestingly, one learned behaviour is that the rum raisin flavour, not that popular in the plain vanilla US market, is quite popular among the Vietnamese as well as many other Asians. A marketer can play a significant role in facilitating the learning process by using a variety of rewards to encourage learning. Infant formula, as an example, is useful in many non-Western countries for well-to-do women who do not want to bother with breast-feeding. Poor women seek the reward of using this status symbol and of having fatter babies–a benefit implied by this product. Furthermore, young mothers like the prestige of using American or European products.

PERSONALITY

Personality study has long been a subject of interest to marketers due to the assumption that product purchases are an extension of a consumer's personality. Personality, derived from a Latin word meaning "personal" or "relating to person," is the individual characteristics that make a person unique as well as consistent in adjustments to a changing environment. Personality is an integrated system that holds attitude, motivation, and perception together. To study a personality is to study the person as a whole–not only the separate, individual elements that make up a person.

PERSONALITY TRAITS

Personality traits are relatively stable qualities, but they do vary in degree from person to person. Because personality study applies to a person rather than to a group, it is difficult to make generalizations about personality traits among people of a particular country. Nevertheless, it is useful to consider the concept of national character, which states that "people of each nation have a distinctive, enduring pattern of behaviour and/or personality characteristics."

The English, for example, are highly impulse-restrained and unassertive. Despite the difficulty, particular personality traits seem dominant in certain countries. Koreans see themselves as being driven by two complementary passions that are uniquely theirs: *han* (bitterness) and *jong* (devoted love).The interplay of the two explains Korea's ability to be at once intensely productive and violent, to both drive and stall a society, and to be capable simultaneously of love and hate. While both South Korea and Japan display a mixture of ancient and modern Asian cultures, they also differ in a number of ways.

In spite of South Korea's Confucian culture and the bowing, deference, traditions, and formality, the Koreans are also passionate, emotional, intense, energetic, emotional, fun-loving, and impatient. In fact, one of the phrases that is heard most often in South Korea is "balli, balli" (hurry, hurry). Compared to Tokyo, Seoul is more chaotic. One study used the Myers-Briggs Type Inventory to contrast Canadian and Japanese MBA students and found differences in cognitive style. On the judging–perceiving dimension, the Canadians sought fast decisions and rushed to closure on data collection, while such actions may frustrate the Japanese who showed a preference for larger amounts of information. On the thinking–feeling dimension, the Japanese, as expected, preferred forming personal relationships before business was transacted. One personality trait that has gained recent attention is consumer ethnocentrism. Adapted from the general concept of ethnocentrism, consumer ethnocentrism explains that, due to patriotic and nationalistic sentiments as well as a personal level of prejudice against imports, some consumers feel that it is inappropriate or even immoral to buy imported products.

Highly ethnocentric consumers thus tend to buy domestic products. The national markets also possess some other personality characteristics which may affect marketing strategies. Scotland set up Project Galore to develop a strategy to promote the commercial power of Scottishness. Based on the reactions received in Scotland and other parts of the world, tenacity is a true Scottish characteristic. Integrity is another core value, since Scotland and the world believe that Scotland has this attribute to a greater extent than most, if not all, other countries. Spirit is another virtue that defines Scotland. However, although the Scots believe that they have inventiveness, the rest of the world does not seem to subscribe to the same notion, since they do not have enough knowledge of Scotland's inventiveness. While the European Union is unifying markets, it will take time to construct a unified set of European marketing theories. There is still a wide divergence in terms of economic development levels, languages, religions, and legal systems. Generalizations are both difficult and dangerous. Marketers must still consider a country's history, national character, and cognitive styles.

HOFSTEDE'S NATIONAL CULTURES

Hofstede has strongly indicated that ethnocentric management theories are untenable.

Based on his study of work-related values in fifty countries, national cultures have four largely independent dimensions:

1. Individualism vs. collectivism,
2. Large or small power distance,
3. Strong or weak uncertainty avoidance, and
4. Masculinity vs. femininity.

Power distance describes how a society treats unequal people. "Collectivist countries always show large power distance, but individualist countries do not always show small power distance." Regarding uncertainty avoidance, some countries have weak uncertainty avoidance in the sense that they accept uncertainty and they are thus able to take risks easily. In contrast, strong uncertainty avoidance societies create institutions to offer security and avoid risk. With regard to masculinity/ femininity, the classification is derived from whether a society has well-defined roles for men and women. A masculine society clearly expects men to be assertive and dominant and women to assume more service-oriented and caring roles.

This society clearly differentiates between what men should do and what women are supposed to do. Based on Hofstede's research, countries that are low in power distance, masculinity, and uncertainty avoidance include Australia, Canada, Denmark, the United Kingdom, the Netherlands, Norway, New Zealand, Sweden, and the USA. In comparison, those cultures that are low in individualism but high in power distance, masculinity, and uncertainty avoidance include Greece, Mexico, Pakistan, Peru, the Philippines, Taiwan, Thailand, Venezuela, and Japan.

As explained by Hofstede, management is an American invention. However, the practices of management in many parts of the world can deviate greatly from management as practiced in the USA. American management theories emphasize market processes, managers, and individualism–things that assume less significance elsewhere.

In Japan, the emphasis is on workers–not managers. In fact, management as practiced in the USA does not bear much resemblance to management practiced in Japan. A literature review of the five dimensions of national culture led Nakata and Sivakumar to propose that these dimensions affect new product development–both positively and negatively. One study of ten countries and sixty regions found that cultural power distance, cultural individualism, and regional socioeconomics affect brand image strategies. In low power distance countries, people are not too focused on social roles and group affiliation, and it is thus appropriate to use functional brand images that de-emphasize the social, symbolic, sensory, and experiential benefits of products. However, social and/or sensory needs should probably be stressed in a country with a high degree of power distance.

In addition, marketing in high individualism cultures should focus on functional, variety, novelty, and experiential needs, whereas cultures with low individualism may find social brand image strategies to be more appealing. Finally, when regional socioeconomics is high, it is appropriate to focus on social and sensory brand images.

The dimensions of national culture have marketing relevance. A study of TV commercials from Japan, Russia, Sweden, and the USA in terms of the masculine–feminine continuum found that feminine countries showed a higher degree of use of relationships for male and female characters. Since not all cultures share the same values, advertising standardization appears to be strategically unwise.

CLUSTERING: COMMONALITY AND DIVERSITY

The impact of Hofstede's fifty-country study requires no debate. It has spawned a great deal of discussion as well as numerous studies. Another rigorous and large-scale study is just as valuable even though it is yet to attract the same kind of attention.

Project GLOBE based on a collaboration of scholars in all parts of the world, is a study of thousands of middle managers in food processing, finance, and telecommunications industries in sixty-one countries. The study focuses on nine dimensions of national cultures: performance orientation, future orientation, assertiveness, power distance, humane orientation, institutional collectivism, in-group collectivism, uncertainty avoidance, and gender egalitarianism. In the process, six global leadership attributes have been identified. The project uses discriminant analysis to confirm the ten a priori clusters: South Asia, Anglo, Arab, Germanic Europe, Latin Europe, Eastern Europe, Confucian Asia, Latin America, Sub-Saharan Africa, and Nordic Europe. The results offer strong support to the existence of these proposed clusters. Reflecting Latin America's paternalistic orientation, this cluster shows the practices of high power distance, and low performance orientation, uncertainty avoidance, future orientation, and institutional collectivism. The hallmark of the southern Asia cluster is its high power distance and group and family collectivism practices.

Charismatic, team oriented, and humane leadership is highly valued. The members of the Anglo cluster are all developed countries, and their orientation is towards individualist performance. A leader is expected to provide charismatic inspiration and a participative style. The societies found in the Arabic cluster are predominantly Muslim, and they share common literature, architecture, educational background, and religious characteristics.

They are highly group oriented, hierarchical, and masculine while being low on future orientation. The cluster of Germanic Europe is a model of cooperation between labour and capital. Co-determination leads to participative leadership. The Eastern European cluster, reflecting both tradition and transition, stresses high power distance and high family and group collectivism. The Latin Europe cluster scores close to mid-range on all but one dimensions of societal practices on a 7-point measurement scale. The only exception is in terms of a high average of over 5 on power distance. The societies in this cluster attempt to balance the need for competitiveness with their traditional preference for a paternalistic and interventionist government.

PSYCHOGRAPHICS

Because of the disappointing results in using personality to predict purchase behaviour, marketers have turned to other meaningful purchase variables that might be used in conjunction with personality characteristics. This area of purchase behaviour study is known as psychographics, also known as lifestyle or AIO study. Psychographics is a quantitative analysis of consumers' lifestyles and activities with the purpose of relating these variables to buying behaviour. The analysis encompasses both the strength of the qualitative nature of Sigmund Freud's psychoanalytic theory and the statistical and methodological sophistication of trait and factor theories.

As a result, questions are well organized, and responses are subject to numerical representation and multivariate analysis. Questions normally included in psychographic studies are those related to demographics, personality traits, and activities such as media habits, retail patronage, and general interests. People can be classified by their lifestyles and then be contrasted in terms of their consumption habits. For example, respondents from England and Denmark do not view Denmark's furnishing interiors in the same way.

The two cultures have different ideas of appropriate product syntax or how furnishing items could and should be combined. It is generally believed that Japan is so homogeneous that the market should not be segmented and that there will either be a mass response or little response. Actually, psychographics can yield useful information. As an example, the VALS instrument was tailored to the Japanese market.

Ten Japanese segments have been identified: integrators who are well educated and modern, sustainers who are resistant to change, self-innovators who are young and self-directed, self-adapters who are shy and look to self-innovators, *ryoshiki*–"social intelligence"–innovators who are careeroriented and middle-aged, *ryoshiki* adapters who are shy and look to *ryoshiki* innovators, tradition innovators who are middleaged and active in the community, tradition adapters who are young and affluent, high pragmatic who are withdrawn and suspicious and low pragmatic who are attitudinally negative and oriented to inexpensive products. Marketers, in addition to identifying lifestyle variations within a country, may also identify lifestyle groups on a worldwide basis.

Backer Spielvogel Bates Worldwide, there are five distinct groups of consumers worldwide:

1. *Strivers (26 per cent)*: Relatively young people who work very hard and seek convenience and instant gratification,
2. *Achievers (22 per cent)*: Affluent opinion and style leaders who pick brands that make statements about status and quality,
3. *Pressured (13 per cent)*: Predominantly women who contend with economic and family pressures and have little room for pleasure or enjoyment,
4. *Adopters (18 per cent)*: Older consumers who live comfortably in a changing world by respecting new ideas without losing sight of time-honored values, and
5. *Traditionals (16 per cent)*: Those who embody the oldest values of their countries and cultures and resist change while preferring familiar products.

However, 5 per cent of the consumers did not fit into any of these categories.

PERCEPTION

To learn, a person must perceive. Perception goes beyond sensation by providing meaning to sensory stimulations. It is the process of interpreting nervous impulses or stimuli received that the brain must organize and give meaning through cognitive interpretations.

The Chinese, for instance, perceive Coke to look and taste like medicine. One's culture greatly affects one's perception and behaviour. Americans, for example, generally prefer steak on the "rare" side, in order to retain moisture and flavour. Asians, on the other hand, would not dream of eating steak this way, believing meat in that condition to be unsafe. Furthermore,

Americans prefer to cook a big piece of meat, to be cut up or sliced on a serving plate at the dining table when they are ready to eat.

The Chinese, however, prefer to cut the meat into small, bite-sized pieces before cooking and thus have no need for a knife at the dining table.

FORMATION OF PERCEPTION

It is important to keep in mind that perceptions are formed though a highly subjective and selective process. The consumer's cognitive map of the environment is not a photograph of that physical environment. It is instead a partial and personal construction of a situation in which certain cues–selected and given emphasis–are perceived in an individual manner. More precisely, when one forms a perception, one is not a photographer but rather an artist who draws or paints an object in the way one thinks it is or should be.

Therefore, no object or product is ever perceived exactly in the way it actually appears. Because of the selectivity and subjectivity characteristics of perception, people "seeing" the same thing can have vastly different interpretations. In Spain, accepting credit is viewed as an inability to pay–a shameful situation.

While American consumers take it for granted that, if not satisfied, they can simply return a product for a full refund, German consumers are unlikely to share this view. Whether or not a product will be successful depends significantly on how it is perceived. A marketer should provide some cues about a product in order to aid consumers in perceiving the product in the desired manner. Volvo, for example, has done quite well through emphasizing safety features.

COUNTRY OF ORIGIN AND PERCEIVED PRODUCT QUALITY

One of the cues often used by consumers in evaluating products is where a product is made. It is not unusual for consumers to categorize countries and to use these categories to judge product quality. There is evidence of country-category effect in the sense that consumers use stereotyping in typing product classes and brands. At a more specific level, consumers may use country of origin as a guide to product quality. Not only do consumers harbor general images about certain countries, but they also form specific attitudes about products made in those countries. This topic has received a great deal of interest and has been researched in depth. Many empirical studies support the hypothesis that consumers have stereotyped opinions about specific products from particular countries. For example, an investigation of product-country images and ethnocentric behaviours found that Turkish consumers' perceptions of product attributes were influenced by products coming from countries at different levels of socioeconomic and technological development.

When a "made in" designation is not favorably received, a marketer may want to deliberately conceal or not mention the product's origin. Many countries, however, including the USA, require proper origin identification in the form of a tag, label, or other identification means before foreign products can be imported.

The effects of country of origin can be moderated by consumer expertise and the type of attribute information. As shown in one study, when encountering unambiguous attribute information, experts based their evaluations on attribute strength, but novices relied on country of origin. In the case that attribute information was ambiguous, both experts and novices then utilized country of origin stereotypes. Likewise, motivational intensity and direction moderate the effect of information type of country of origin evaluations. When country of origin is salient and when consumers find new information relevant to their judgment, evaluations of the country of origin become more favorable. There is a relationship between consumer ethnocentrism and consumer attitude towards foreign products.

Consumers with high levels of consumer ethnocentrism adopt more favorable attitudes towards products from culturally similar countries when compared to products from culturally dissimilar countries. Country of origin is a multidimensional construct. As such, its effect is neither simple nor straightforward.

Two particular dimensions are country of assembly and country of design. A manufacturer in a newly developed country or less developed country should conceal the identity of its manufacturing locations. However, if its product is *designed* in an advanced country, that fact can improve consumers' ratings of the product. Another study focused on televisions and stereos in terms of the country of origin for parts, assembly, and design. Respondents have more favorable attitudes and higher purchase intention when a product assembled in the USA uses American parts rather than Mexican parts. It should be pointed out that *single-cue* studies created larger country of origin effect sizes than did *multiple-cue studies.*

The effect of country of origin is strongest when it is the only cue, but when other explicit multiple cues are included, the effect weakens. In addition, to use country of origin to a marketer's advantage, the marketer should emphasize high levels of positive attributes and low levels of negative attributes without ignoring the negative attributes. In general, products from less developed countries are less favorably received than those from industrialized countries.

Yet even for high-risk products from less developed countries, consumers are still willing to buy them as long as they carry known brand names, indicating the power of a brand name to moderate the negative influence of a country's negative image. When there is congruence between brand origin and country of manufacture, country of manufacture has impact on product beliefs and brand attitudes.

Incongruence takes place when a branded product is made in a country whose image is not as favorable as that of brand origin. In this case, country of manufacture information adversely affects product evaluations– but only for low equity brands rather than high equity brands. Apparently, a brand can be strong enough to mitigate any negative perceptions derived from country of manufacture information.

In addition, attribute claims become more credible when the products are distributed through a prestigious retailer. Distributors and/or retailers can have an impact on how a brand is perceived. Samsung Electronics Co.'s initial strategy was to use Walmart Stores Inc. to distribute its low-end electronic gadgets. The company has now outgrown that strategy as it pushes towards innovative, higher margin products, such as voice-activated mobile phones that are also digital music players and personal digital assistants. For many consumers, this will be the very first time they try such products, and it will also be the first time they are exposed to brand names associated with these product categories.

So Samsung has an opportunity to create brand equity and loyalty. As a result, it made a tough decision to abandon Walmart in favour of specialty stores. Samsung's strong commitment to its brand strategy has propelled it to be among the world's top fifty brands. In fact, among all brands, Samsung's rise in brand value was the fastest. It may be incorrect to treat country of origin as a halo effect. A country's image varies across product categories. While consumers may prefer Japanese and German cars, they also prefer crystal from Ireland and leather shoes from Italy. Consumer preference is thus a function of product–country match. Consumer willingness to buy a country's particular product increases when the country image is also an important characteristic for that product category. American, Irish, and Mexican consumers are interested in buying a car or watch from Japan, Germany, and the USA because these countries have characteristics which are relevant and important to these products.

In contrast, consumers are less willing to buy Mexican and Hungarian cars and watches because Mexico and Hungary receive poor evaluations on relevant product dimensions. Another study of Bangladeshi consumers and their perceptions of products from nine foreign countries found that they overwhelmingly preferred Westernmade products. At the same time, their perceptions varied across product classes as well as across the sourcing countries. The findings of the various studies have several marketing implications. Because consumers are more wary of products from developing countries, especially when there is a high degree of financial risk, the developing countries naturally need to solve this marketing problem. Because consumers continuously merge product information with country image, quality control is necessary.

The industry association and the government should establish quality standards and provide such incentives as tax benefits and subsidies to exporters who meet the standards, while penalizing those who do not by imposing export taxes or withholding export licenses. To help consumers generalize product information over the country's products, individual marketers can benefit from favorable country image by highlighting products of superior quality from the same country. For example, Mitsubishi may claim that its TV sets are as good as those manufactured by Sony. Alternatively, to prevent consumers from using the country's negative image in product evaluation, marketers should dissociate their products from unsuccessful products manufactured in that country. An international marketer should pay attention to the relationship between country of origin and the perception of product quality.

Country of origin information is more important than price and brand information in affecting product quality assessments. In general, engineering and technical products from Germany, electronics products from Japan, fashion products from France, and tobacco products from the USA are favorably received in most parts of the world. In addition, consumers in less developed countries usually prefer imported or foreign goods, believing that those goods are of higher quality and prestige. A company must keep in mind that a product's image may change if its production facilities are moved from one country to a new location. Lowenbrau lost its image as a prestigious import beer once American drinkers became aware that the beer was licensed to be made by Miller in the USA. Because of the constancy or stability of perceptions, a negative perception associated with a particular country tends to persist.

The failure of Yugoslavia's Yugo automobiles had to do with the negative perception. However, the problem can be overcome if a firm or country perseveres and is determined to improve its product quality. A case in point is Japan. Its initial effort to penetrate the US market after World War II was greeted with the perception that its products were cheap, imitative, and shoddy. Ironically, many consumers, including those in the USA, came to feel that Japanese products are superior to American goods, offering better value for money. South Korea is currently striving to match Japan in this perception game.

In the meantime, its Hyundai automobiles have perception hurdles to overcome. One experiment manipulated the level of warranty coverage and a warrantor's reputation. The findings indicate that warranty strategies can overcome consumers' negative perception about the quality of a company's hybrid product.

ATTITUDE

Attitude is the learned tendency to respond to an object in a consistently favorable or unfavorable way. Attitude is a complex and multidimensional concept. It consists of three components: cognition, affect, and conation. Based on this definition, a few properties of attitude can be identified. First, the relationship between an individual and an object is not neutral: the reaction to the object is either favorable or unfavorable. Most people, for example, have favorable attitudes towards such automobiles as Mercedes-Benz, BMW, and Rolls-Royce, viewing them as status symbols. On the other hand, except for American consumers who have long been conditioned to prefer large automobiles, most consumers have strong reservations about large cars because they look unsightly and are difficult to maneuver on the narrow roads found in most parts of the world, and they are also more uneconomic in terms of fuel consumption. Second, attitudes are relatively enduring and patterned and not temporary or transient.

As a person becomes older, attitudes become more established. This becomes a challenge for international marketers who want to introduce change. A new product often involves a change in a long-held attitude. Finally, attitude is not innate–it must be learned. One's attitude about an object is formed by one's experience of the object, either directly or indirectly. There is a relationship between consumer attitudes and their purchases. For instance, many Singaporeans are out shoppers who go to Malaysia to buy food, beverages, and grocery products due to competitive prices and ample parking space. Compared to their infrequent counterparts, frequent out shoppers perceive fewer secondary costs. In addition, since they engage in outshopping primarily for economic reasons, they do not feel guilty.

Attitude is greatly influenced by culture. Attitudes towards women, for example, vary from country to country. In many countries, women are still considered as a man's property, and a woman must seek her husband's approval before entering into a contract or being allowed to apply for a visa or passport.

In Saudi Arabia, strict Muslim restrictions make it very uncommon for women to work. In Japan, working women are common but rarely have the opportunity to rise to a managerial position. Therefore, when women are portrayed in advertisements, the portrayal should be consistent with the expected role of women in that particular culture. Attitude can affect marketing plans in other ways. Some countries have favorable attitudes towards foreigners, wealth, and change, making it relatively easy for MNCs to introduce new products.

In fact, attitudes towards marketing itself should be considered. In India, marketing is viewed as unnecessary, annoying, and wasteful. Nestlé's infant formula received enormous adverse publicity because of the negative view in less developed countries about the company's marketing activities in poor countries.

One problem firms have in marketing their products overseas involves the negative attitudes towards situations associated with their products and sometimes towards the products themselves. For example, customers may have favorable attitudes towards German machinery but not towards the purchase of such machinery because of the high cost, service, or availability of parts. It is important for a marketer to distinguish between private and public attitudes, because an expressed public attitude can differ widely from a private attitude, especially when the private attitude contradicts the society's cultural norms.

SOCIAL CLASS

Social class implies inequality. Even in the USA, where all are supposed to be equal, some people seem to be much more equal than others. Social class exists because it provides for and ensures the smooth operation of a society. For a society to exist, many functions must be performed–some of which are not very pleasant. In this regard, members of society are not that different from bees in a hive–different types of bees exist for different purposes.

In Japan, even though the government long ago abolished the social caste system to allow for the mixing and reshuffling of people at all social levels, the selective access to higher education still impedes certain individuals from becoming career officials within the government. Many societies see nothing wrong with the existence of a social hierarchy.

In fact, many Asian and Middle East countries view status differences positively. Elders and superiors command respect. Connections with socially acceptable persons are often important in securing business. The criteria used to assign people to social classes vary from country to country. In the USA, relevant characteristics generally used in the construction of a social class index for classification purposes are occupation, source of income, house type, and dwelling area.

In other countries, occupation and/or amount of income are the dominant discriminating variables. In some societies, royalty affiliation is employed as well to distinguish one social class from another. The US social system differs from those of other countries in several respects.

Its greatest representation occurs approximately at the middle of the social class scale. Many developing countries have a very large lower class, and the graphic composition of all social classes resembles a pyramid: the upper class is a small minority group at the top and the vast number of lower-class people occupy the large base at the bottom. Furthermore, the US system allows for social class mobility, while systems elsewhere may be much more rigid. Even when the same distinguishing variable is used in different countries for classification, it may not have the same meaning and does not necessarily yield the same result. If the classification of occupation is considered, in the USA, financial considerations very likely explain why attorneys are accorded the kind of status and prestige rarely found elsewhere. Engineers, on the other hand, are regarded much more highly in societies outside of the USA.

Social class has a great deal of relevance for marketing strategies. It influences store selection, product selection, media selection, advertising appeal selection, and sales promotion selection. Different motives may thus have to be employed for different social classes. Thresher, a British liquor store chain of 990 outlets, used the results of its marketing research to divide its shops into three designations: drinks stores, wine shops, and wine racks. The designations are based on the social status of a neighborhood. The down-market drinks stores are located in working-class areas, and they stock mostly beer. Wine racks, offering a larger selection of wines and champagnes, are found in wealthier locations and have a better educated staff. The middlebrow wine shops are somewhere in between.

GROUP

A group consists of two or more persons who share a set of norms and have certain implicitly or explicitly defined relationships with one another in such a way that their behaviour is interdependent. Group norms influence both general behaviour and consumption behaviour. Originally formed for defence and survival, a group now serves its members more for needs of social and psychological satisfaction. An individual cannot operate well in isolation because all persons are biologically and socially interdependent. An individual needs to belong to a group to interact with those who can provide identification and help to meet needs in a more efficient manner. The influence of a reference group is derived in part from its capacity to disseminate information.

The relevance and strength of influence of a reference group is not constant across product categories. Its influence is determined in part by the conspicuousness of the product in question. A product can be conspicuous in two ways: by having the qualities of visibility and by standing out. The more the product is visible and stands out, the more conspicuous it becomes. Product conspicuousness allows a reference group to operate in exerting its influence on consumer behaviour. For example, Philip Morris's Galaxy brand was perceived at one time as a "diet" cigarette, and for that reason Brazilians became ashamed to be seen with it because social and personal pressures were placed on those who smoked Galaxy.

The relevance of group appeal may be dictated by cultural norms. In contrast to Americans, who are more individually oriented, the Japanese are more committed to group membership and are consensus oriented. Group pressure is very great in Japan. The Fishbein behavioral intentions model was found to reflect cultural differences.The greater importance of subjective norm in Korea and of attitude towards an act in the USA indicates that social pressures, while having a relatively weak influence on Americans, play a major role in the formation of Koreans' behavioral intentions. Therefore, international marketers operating in Confucian cultures should keep in mind that a product may not be evaluated independently of group conformity and face saving. A marketing mix programme should take into account these social factors.

FAMILY

In the USA, the word "family" has a narrow meaning because it encompasses only the husband, wife, and their offspring. This family is known as a nuclear or conjugal family. In other parts of the world, the word has a much broader meaning because it is based on the concept of an extended or consanguine family. A family can be vertically extended when it includes several generations. It can also be horizontally extended when such family members as uncles, aunts, and cousins are included. Thus non-Americans count vertical and horizontal relatives of either the husband or wife or both as part of their family. It is not uncommon for a son to live in his parents' home even after getting married. When his parents become old, it will become his responsibility to take care of his parents, the home, and the business.

In such a country, nursing homes are relatively rare, and the placement of elderly or ill parents in homes for the aged is frowned upon. The Chinese culture emphasizes familial over private self. Attainment of family-oriented goals is a measure of self-realization and self-fulfilment. Boundaries of familial self may include romantic partners and close friends who are "like family."

In family and like-family contexts, there is no need for reciprocity. As a subset and special kind of reference group, the family can be distinguished by its characteristics. First, a family allows its members ample opportunity to interact with one another on a face-to-face basis. In effect, each member operates as both a counselor and an information provider. Second, the family is a consuming unit in the sense that most members share the consumption of many products, especially those that are durables or that affect family budget. Third, individual needs are usually subordinated to family needs. Finally, one member is often assigned the primary duty of buying products for other users, thus acting as a gatekeeper or purchasing agent.

Americans and non-Americans raise their families in very different ways. Americans emphasize individual freedom, and children are taught to be self-sufficient and independent. In Japan and China, the family is the main focal point. Similar to the Hispanics' family orientation, the Japanese feel a strong sense of responsibility and obligation towards their families, and these obligations predominate in family decisions. Because of the emphasis on family orientation, nepotism is an expected and accepted practice in most parts of the world.

The tradition may even be carried on to include business partners. In Japan, close bonds among all members of a manufacturer's distribution channel explain why unprofitable members are not dropped from the system. Pillsbury has to accommodate this different style of doing business in Japan, where the emphasis is on long courtship, trust, sincerity, and Asian "old friends." Joint ventures are akin to a marriage, and a divorce of this kind is strongly frowned upon.

The family tradition also explains why Japanese corporate priorities are employees, suppliers, customers, community, government, bankers, and finally shareholders. A family functions more efficiently when its members specialize in the roles they are most comfortable with or are capable of performing better than other family members. A marketers must determine the kind of decision making that is relevant to the product. Once that fact is known, the marketer can direct promotional effort towards the party making the purchase decision. It is thus useful to consider and to assess the relative influence of each spouse in the decision-making process. A study of two cultures–the USA and China–found that emphasis on joint, husband-dominated, and wife-dominated decisions varied by stage of the decision process as well as by stage–culture interaction.

Compared with the US sample, the Chinese sample exhibited:

- Lower levels of egalitarianism,
- More husband-dominated decisions, and
- Fewer joint decisions.

Similarly, in the case of Hispanic ethnic identification groups, the effect of ethnic identification on marital roles in decision making was found to interact with the phase of the purchase decision process. In addition, there is a positive relationship between ethnic identification and husband dominance in decision making.

OPINION LEADERSHIP

Within each social group, there are some individuals who are able to exert a significant influence on other members in such a way as to affect their thinking and behaviour in a desired direction. These individuals are known as opinion leaders. In the context of consumer behaviour, their opinions about products can affect subsequent purchases made by others. In marketing products overseas, MNCs should attempt to appeal to opinion leaders. In general, these are likely to be people who command respect from others. In Ghana, government health workers gain better cooperation and reception by asking for village witch-doctors' approval before inoculating people or spraying huts to fight malaria.

In developing countries, it is a good strategy to market new ideas to teachers, monks, or priests first, because their opinions influence the acceptance of these ideas by others. When it is doubtful who the opinion leaders are, marketers should try to identify those with influence and affluence. BMW, for example, sells its cars at a discount to diplomats, believing that its target consumers will take notice of the kind of cars driven by those in power. In foreign countries, business periodicals and English-language newspapers are usually an effective means of reaching government and business leaders who are potential opinion leaders.

DIFFUSION PROCESS OF INNOVATIONS

The diffusion process of innovations is an acceptance over time of a product or idea by consumers, linked to a given social structure and a given system of values or culture. Innovators possess certain characteristics that distinguish them from noninnovators. Innovators are frequently opinion leaders, and it is thus desirable to identify and contact innovators. The diffusion process varies from culture to culture.

The conservative business etiquette in South Korea is reflected in Korean firms' organizational structure as well as in their managerial approach, which emphasizes harmony and structure over innovation and experimentation. Diffusion of the Internet differs between the USA and Japan. Japan, as a collectivist culture, values high uncertainty avoidance and has large power distance. As such, Japan has a slower adoption process. One study investigated consumer innovativeness in a cross-cultural context by examining data collected from 2283 consumers in eleven EU countries.

Innovation orientation differs both among consumers and among countries, reflecting the fact that national cultural variables can explain systematic differences in innovativeness between countries. In collectivistic countries, a marketing message should emphasize social acceptance and a product's local origin. In contrast, Australia, New Zealand, the United Kingdom, the USA, and Canada have national cultures that are characterized by low uncertainty avoidance, high individualism, and high masculinity. As such, they are receptive to product innovations.

Culture not only affects the diffusion process in general, but it also exerts a great deal of influence on the adoption of a product in particular. A product that is suitable in one culture may be totally inappropriate elsewhere. The Italian and Asian preference for fresh meat and vegetables has hampered the acceptance of frozen foods. In Italy and Southeast Asia, markets open and close early, and shoppers who wish to select the best items must get to market very early in the morning. By the early afternoon the market is ready to be closed, with only a few inferior items left.

As explained by the international product lifecycle concept, a new product is not adopted at the same time or at the same rate in various countries. It is thus necessary to ask whether innovators should be classified on a national or international basis. If innovators are defined as the first 10 per cent of adopters, how should a consumer be classified if he is not in the first 10 per cent internationally but well within the first 10 per cent of purchasers within his home country? The answer is that the diffusion rate should be based on segmentation criteria for each target market.

Special consideration must be given to certain ethnic groups, age levels, social classes, geographic areas, and so on. Therefore, innovators should be classified as the first 10 per cent of a particular target market, regardless of the percentages of adoption in other countries or on a worldwide scale. It should be pointed out that innovators are small in number and that their influence is not always positive in that they may reject a new product.

Although innovators are important, the evidence suggests that "the basic strategy should be aimed at imitators in the market in order to stimulate demand for the new product. Furthermore, the product should be tailored carefully to the needs and wants of that segment.

CONCLUSION

Consumer behaviour, as a discipline of study, has been researched extensively in the USA at both the macro and micro levels. Surprisingly, it has not been so rigorously and diligently investigated in the international context. All too frequently, studies that compare consumers in various countries attribute differences in consumer characteristics and behaviour to cultural differences.

This convenient approach is inadequate by itself and does not enhance the understanding of consumption behaviour overseas. Instead of explicitly or implicitly attempting to use culture to explain most variations in consumption, researchers should redirect their attention towards smaller units of analysis. This requires a study of psychological concepts as well as social concepts which are not based solely on cultural determinants.

At the psychological level, relevant concepts such as motivation, learning, personality, psychographics, perception, and attitude should be closely examined. Because consumer needs vary across countries, as does the degree of importance attached to a particular need, it is unrealistic to expect consumers everywhere to be motivated in the same way. The varying motives that occur are due in part to individual personality traits and lifestyles.

The learning and perception of a product and the attitude towards it will also affect consumers' motivations in acquiring the product. At the social level, it is redundant to state that consumer behaviour is affected by the cultural environment. It is more important to list specifically the cultural norms in a country and to understand why those norms vary from country to country.

It is thus important to appreciate how these norms are shaped by reference groups, social class, family, opinion leadership, and the diffusion process of innovation. Consumer preference depends in part on how well a product fits into the cultural circumstances and on whether the product will have the approval of a consumer's reference group, social class, and family.

In conclusion, marketers and researchers should guard against using culture as a catch-all term and should not use it on a wholesale basis to explain overseas behaviour. It is necessary to go beyond noticing cultural differences and instead to attempt to understand the underlying causes of cultural variations. This goal requires researchers to be more specific and rigorous in their investigation by extending the application of relevant psychological and social concepts to the international scene. It is time to move away from a vague and generic explanation of consumption behaviour to a more precise and better-focused avenue of research.

9

International Marketing and Trade

International trade is the exchange of capital, goods, and services across international borders or territories. In most countries, such trade represents a significant share of gross domestic product (GDP). While international trade has been present throughout much of history, its economic, social, and political importance has been on the rise in recent centuries. Industrialization, advanced transportation, globalization, multinational corporations, and outsourcing are all having a major impact on the international trade system. Increasing international trade is crucial to the continuance of globalization. Without international trade, nations would be limited to the goods and services produced within their own borders.

International trade is, in principle, not different from domestic trade as the motivation and the behaviour of parties involved in a trade do not change fundamentally regardless of whether trade is across a border or not. The main difference is that international trade is typically more costly than domestic trade. The reason is that a border typically imposes additional costs such as tariffs, time costs due to border delays and costs associated with country differences such as language, the legal system or culture. Another difference between domestic and international trade is that factors of production such as capital and labour are typically more mobile within a country than across countries. Thus international trade is mostly restricted to trade in goods and services, and only to a lesser extent to trade in capital, labour or other factors of production.

Trade in goods and services can serve as a substitute for trade in factors of production. Instead of importing a factor of production, a country can import goods that make intensive use of that factor of production and thus embody it. An example is the import of labour-intensive goods by the United States from China. Instead of importing Chinese labour, the United States imports goods that were produced with Chinese labour. One report in 2010 suggested that international trade was increased when a country hosted a network of immigrants, but the trade effect was weakened when the immigrants became assimilated into their new country. International trade is also a branch of economics, which, together with international finance, forms the larger branch of international economics.

HISTORY

The history of international trade chronicles notable events that have affected the trade between various countries. In the era before the rise of the nation state, the term 'international' trade cannot be literally applied, but simply means trade over long distances; the sort of movement in goods which would represent international trade in the modern world.

MODELS

The following are noted models of international trade.

ADAM SMITH'S MODEL

Adam Smith displays trade taking place on the basis of countries exercising absolute advantage over one another.

RICARDIAN MODEL

The Ricardian model focuses on comparative advantage, which arises due to differences in technology or natural resources. The Ricardian model does not directly consider factor endowments, such as the relative amounts of labour and capital within a country.

The Ricardian model makes the following assumptions:

- Labour is the only primary input to production.
- The relative ratios of labour at which the production of one good can be traded off for another differ between countries and governments

HECKSCHER-OHLIN MODEL

In the early 1900s a theory of international trade was developed by two Swedish economists, Eli Heckscher and Bertil Ohlin. This theory has subsequently been known as the Heckscher-Ohlin model (H-O model). The results of the H-O model are that countries will produce and export goods that require resources (factors) which are relatively abundant and import goods that require resources which are in relative short supply.

In the Heckscher-Ohlin model the pattern of international trade is determined by differences in factor endowments. It predicts that countries will export those goods that make intensive use of locally abundant factors and will import goods that make intensive use of factors that are locally scarce. Empirical problems with the H-O model, such as the Leontief paradox, were noted in empirical tests by Wassily Leontief who found that the United States tended to export labour-intensive goods despite having an abundance of capital.

The H-O model makes the following core assumptions:

- Labour and capital flow freely between sectors

- The amount of labour and capital in two countries differ (difference in endowments)
- Technology is the same among countries (a long-term assumption)
- Tastes are the same.

Reality and Applicability of the Heckscher-Ohlin Model

In 1953, Wassily Leontief published a study in which he tested the validity of the Heckscher-Ohlin theory. The study showed that the U.S was more abundant in capital compared to other countries, therefore the U.S would export capital-intensive goods and import labour-intensive goods. Leontief found out that the U.S's exports were less capital intensive than its imports. After the appearance of Leontief's paradox, many researchers tried to save the Heckscher-Ohlin theory, either by new methods of measurement, or by new interpretations. Leamer emphasized that Leontief did not interpret H-O theory properly and claimed that with a right interpretation, the paradox did not occur.

Brecher and Choudri found that, if Leamer was right, the American workers' consumption per head should be lower than the workers' world average consumption. Many textbook writers, including Krugman and Obstfeld and Bowen, Hollander and Viane, are negative about the validity of H-O model. After examining the long history of empirical research, Bowen, Hollander and Viane concluded: "Recent tests of the factor abundance theory [H-O theory and its developed form into many-commodity and many-factor case] that directly examine the H-O-V equations also indicate the rejection of the theory." In the specific factors model, labour mobility among industries is possible while capital is assumed to be immobile in the short run.

Thus, this model can be interpreted as a short-run version of the Heckscher-Ohlin model. The "specific factors" name refers to the assumption that in the short run, specific factors of production such as physical capital are not easily transferable between industries. The theory suggests that if there is an increase in the price of a good, the owners of the factor of production specific to that good will profit in real terms. Additionally, owners of opposing specific factors of production (*i.e.*, labour and capital) are likely to have opposing agendas when lobbying for controls over immigration of labour. Conversely, both owners of capital and labour profit in real terms from an increase in the capital endowment. This model is ideal for understanding income distribution but awkward for discussing the pattern of trade.

NEW TRADE THEORY

New Trade Theory tries to explain empirical elements of trade that comparative advantage-based models above have difficulty with. These include the fact that most trade is between countries with similar factor endowment and productivity levels, and the large amount of multinational production (*i.e.* foreign direct investment) that exists. New Trade theories are often based on assumptions such as monopolistic competition and increasing returns to scale. One result of these theories is the home-market effect, which asserts that, if an industry tends to cluster in one location because of returns to scale and if that industry faces high transportation costs, the industry will be located in the country with most of its demand, in order to minimize cost. Although new trade theory can explain the growing trend of trade volumes of intermediate goods, Krugman's explanation depends too much on the strict assumption that all firms are symmetrical, meaning that they all have the same production coefficients. Shiozawa, based on much more general model, succeeded in giving a new explanation on why the traded volume increases for intermediate goods when the transport cost decreases.

GRAVITY MODEL

The Gravity model of trade presents a more empirical analysis of trading patterns. The gravity model, in its basic form, predicts trade based on the distance between countries and the interaction of the countries' economic sizes. The model mimics the Newtonian law of gravity which also considers distance and physical size between two objects. The model has been proven to be empirically strong through econometric analysis.

RICARDIAN THEORY OF INTERNATIONAL TRADE (MODERN DEVELOPMENT)

The Ricardian theory of comparative advantage became a basic constituent of neo-classical trade theory. Any under-graduate course in trade theory includes a presentation of Ricardo's example of a two-commodity, two-country model. A common representation of this model is made using an Edgeworth Box. This model has been expanded to many-country and many-commodity cases. Major general results were obtained by McKenzie and Jones, including his famous formula. It is a theorem about the possible trade pattern for N-country N-commodity cases.

Contemporary Theories

Ricardo's idea was even expanded to the case of continuum of goods by Dornbusch, Fischer, and Samuelson This formulation is employed for example by Matsuyama and others. These theories use a special property that is applicable only for the two-country case.

Neo-Ricardian Trade Theory

Inspired by Piero Sraffa, a new strand of trade theory emerged and was named neo-Ricardian trade theory. The main contributors include Ian Steedman (1941–) and Stanley Metcalfe (1946–). They have criticized neo-classical international trade theory, namely the Heckscher-Ohlin model on the basis that the notion of capital as primary factor has no method of measuring it before the determination of profit rate (thus trapped in a logical vicious circle). This was a second round of the Cambridge capital controversy, this time in the field of international trade. The merit of neo-Ricardian trade theory is that input goods are explicitly included. This is in accordance with Sraffa's idea that any commodity is a product made by means of commodities. The limitation of their theory is that the analysis is restricted to small-country cases.

Traded Intermediate Goods

Ricardian trade theory ordinarily assumes that the labour is the unique input. This is a great deficiency as trade theory, for intermediate goods occupy the major part of the world international trade. Yeats found that 30 per cent of world trade in manufacturing involves intermediate inputs. Bardhan and Jafee found that intermediate inputs occupy 37 to 38 per cent of U.S. imports for the years 1992 and 1997, whereas the per centage of intrafirm trade grew from 43 per cent in 1992 to 52 per cent in 1997. McKenzie and Jones emphasized the necessity to expand the Ricardian theory to the cases of traded inputs. In a famous comment McKenzie pointed that "A moment's consideration will convince one that Lancashire would be unlikely to produce cotton cloth if the cotton had to be grown in England." Paul Samuelson coined a term *Sraffa bonus* to name the gains from trade of inputs.

Ricardo-Sraffa Trade Theory

John Chipman observed in his survey that McKenzie stumbled upon the questions of intermediate products and discovered that "introduction of trade in intermediate product necessitates a fundamental alteration in classical analysis." It took many years until Y. Shiozawa succeeded in removing this deficiency. The Ricardian trade theory was now constructed in a form to include intermediate input trade for the most general case of many countries and many goods. This new theory is called Ricardo-Sraffa trade theory. Based on an idea of Takahiro Fujimoto, who is a specialist in automobile industry and a philosopher of the international competitiveness, Fujimoto and Shiozawa developed a discussion in which how the factories of the same multi-national firms compete between them across borders. International *intra-firm competition* reflects a really new aspect of international competition in the age of so-called global competition.

International Production Fragmentation Trade Theory

Fragmentation and International Trade Theory widens the scope for "application of Ricardian comparative advantage." In his chapter entitled *Li & Fung, Ltd.: An agent of global production,* Cheng used Li & Fong Ltd as a case study in the international production fragmentation trade theory through which producers in different countries are allocated a specialized slice or segment of the value chain of the global production. Allocations are determined based on on "technical feasibility" and the ability to keep the lowest final price possible for each product. An example of fragmentation theory in international trade is Li & Fung's garment sector network with yarn purchased in South Korea, woven and dyed in Taiwan, the fabric cut in Bangladesh, pieces assembled in Thailand and the final product sold in the United States and Europe to major brands. In 1995 Li & Fung Ltd purchased Inchcape Buying Services, an established British trading company and widely expanded production in Asia. Li & Fung supplies dozens of major retailers, including Wal-Mart Stores, Inc., branded as Walmart.

INTERNATIONAL BUSINESS

International business comprises all commercial transactions (private and governmental, sales, investments, logistics,and transportation) that take place between two or more regions, countries and nations beyond their political boundaries. Usually, private companies undertake such transactions for profit; governments undertake them for profit and for political reasons. It refers to all those business activities which involve cross border transactions of goods, services, resources between two or more nations. Transaction of economic resources include capital, skills, people etc. for international production of physical goods and services such as finance, banking, insurance, construction etc.

A multinational enterprise (MNE) is a company that has a worldwide approach to markets and production or one with operations in more than a country. An MNE is often called multinational corporation (MNC) or transnational company (TNC). Well known MNCs include fast food companies such as McDonald's and Yum Brands, vehicle manufacturers such as General Motors, Ford Motor Company and Toyota, consumer electronics companies like Samsung, LG and Sony, and energy companies such as ExxonMobil, Shell and BP. Most of the largest corporations operate in multiple national markets.

Areas of study within this topic include differences in legal systems, political systems, economic policy, language, accounting standards, labour standards, living standards, environmental standards, local culture, corporate culture, foreign exchange market, tariffs, import and export regulations, trade agreements, climate, education and many more topics. Each of these factors requires significant changes in how individual business units operate from one country to the next.

PHYSICAL AND SOCIETAL FACTORS OF COMPETITIVE SOCIAL ENVIRONMENT

The conduct of international operations depends on companies' objectives and the means with which they carry them out.

The operations affect and are affected by the physical and societal factors and the competitive environment:

Operations:

- *Objectives*: Sales expansion, resource acquisition, risk minimization, Diversify their revenue stream.

Means:

- *Modes*: Importing and exporting, tourism and transportation, licensing and franchising, turnkey operations, management contracts, direct investment and portfolio investments.
- *Functions*: Marketing, global manufacturing and supply chain management, accounting, finance, human resources.
- *Overlaying Alternatives*: Choice of countries, organization and control mechanisms.

Physical and societal factors:

- Political policies and legal practices
- Cultural factors
- Economic forces
- Geographical influences

Competitive factors:

- Major advantage in price, marketing, innovation or other factors.
- Number and comparative capabilities of competitors.
- Competitive differences by country.
- Local taxes.

Risk:

- Strategic risk
- Operational risk
- Political risk
- Country risk
- Technological Risk
- Environmental Risk
- Economic Risk
- Financial risk
- Terrorism Risk

FACTORS THAT INFLUENCED THE GROWTH IN GLOBALIZATION

There has been growth in globalization in recent decades due to the following eight factors:

1. Technology is expanding, especially in transportation and communications.
2. Governments are removing international business restrictions.

3. Institutions provide services to ease the conduct of international business.
4. Consumers know about and want foreign goods and services.
5. Competition has become more global.
6. Political relationships have improved among some major economic powers.
7. Countries cooperate more on transnational issues.
8. Cross-national cooperation and agreements.

IMPORTANCE INTERNATIONAL BUSINESS EDUCATION

- Most companies are either international or compete with international companies.
- Modes of operation may differ from those used domestically.
- The best way of conducting business may differ by country.
- An understanding helps you make better career decisions.
- An understanding helps you decide what governmental policies to support.

Managers in international business must understand social science disciplines and how they affect all functional business fields.

Importance of Studying International Business

The International Business standards focuses on the following:

- Raising awareness of the interrelatedness of one country's political policies and economic practices on another;
- Learning to improve international business relations through appropriate communication strategies;
- Understanding the global business environment—that is, the interconnected-ness of cultural, political, legal, economic, and ethical systems;
- Exploring basic concepts underlying international finance, management, marketing, and trade relations; and
- Identifying forms of business ownership and international business opportunities.

By focusing on these, students will gain a better understanding Political economy. These are tools that would help future business people bridge the economical and political gap between countries.

There is an increasing amount of demand for business people with an education in International Business. A survey conducted by Thomas Patrick from University of Notre Dame concluded that Bachelor's degree holders and Master's degree holders felt that the training received through education were very practical in the working environment. Business people with an education in International Business also had a significantly higher chance of being sent abroad to work under the international operations of a firm. The following table provides descriptions of higher education in International Business and its benefits.

	Master's	Doctorate
Who is this degree for	People interested in management careers with multinational companies	People who are interested in academic or research careers
Common Career Paths (with approximate median annual salary)	• Chief executives ($167,000)* • General or operations managers ($95,000)*	• University business professors ($75,000)* • Economists ($91,000)*
Time to Completion	1–2 years full-time	3–5 years in addition to master's or other foundational coursework
Common Graduation Requirements	• Roughly 15-20 graduate level courses • Internship or study abroad programme • Foreign language requirement • Dissertation • Teaching requirement	Most (or all) of the master's degree requirements, plus: • At least 12 more graduate level courses • Ph.D. qualifier exams • Dissertation prospectus (proposal)
Prerequisites	Bachelor's degree and work experience, quantitative expertise	Bachelor's or master's degree in business or related field
Online Availability	Yes	Limited

MONOPOLISTIC COMPETITION IN INTERNATIONAL TRADE

Monopolistc competition models are used under the rubric of imperfect competition in International Economics. This model is a derivative of the monopolistic competition model that is part of basic economics. Here it is tailored to international trade.

SETTING UP THE MODEL

Monopolies are not often found in practice, the more usual market format is oligopoly: several firms, each of whom is big enough that a change in their price will affect the price of the other firms, but none with an unchallenged monopoly. When looking at oligopolies the problem of *interdependence* arises.

Interdependence means that the firms will, when setting their prices, consider the effect this price will have on the actions of both consumers and competitors.

For their part, the competitors will consider their expectations of the firm's response to any action they may take in return. Thus, there is a complex game with each side "trying to second guess each others' strategies." The Monopolistic Competition model is used because its simplicity allows the examination of one type of oligopoly while avoiding the issue of interdependence.

BENEFITS OF THE MODEL

The appeal of this model is not its closeness to the real world but its simplicity. What this model accomplishes most is that it shows us the benefits to trade presented by economies of scale.

ASSUMPTIONS OF THE MODEL

- Each firm is presumed to be able *differentiate its product* from that of its rivals. Cars are a good example here; they are very different, yet in direct competition with each other. This means there will be some customer loyalty, which allows for some flexibility for the firm to move to a higher price. In other words, not all of a firm's customers would leave for other products if the firm raised its prices.
- This model dismisses the issue of interdependence when a firm sets its price. The firm will act *as if it were a monopoly* regarding the price it sets, not considering the potential responses from its competitors. The justification is that there are numerous firms in the market, so each receives only scant attention from the others.

Background of the Model

- An industry consisting of a number of firms, each of which produces differentiated products. The firms are monopolists for their products, but depend somewhat of the number of reasonable alternatives available and the price of those alternatives. Each firm within the industry thus faces a demand that is effected by the price and prevalence of reasonable alternatives.
- Generally we expect a firm's sales to increase the stronger the total demand for the industry's product as a whole. Conversely, we expect the firm to sell less if there are a significant number of firms in the industry and/or the higher the firm's price in relation to those competitors. The demand equation for such a firm would be:

$$Q = S \times [1/n - b \times (P - P)]$$

- "Q" = the firm's sales. "*S*" is the total sales of the industry. "n" is the number of firms in the industry, "*b*" is a constant term representing the responsiveness of a firm's sales to its price. "P" is the price charged by the firm itself. "*P*" is the average price charged by its competitors.

- The intuition of this model is:
- If all firms charge the same price their respective market share will be 1/n. Firms charging more get less, firms charging less get more.
- (Note) Assume that lower prices will not bring new consumers into the market. In this model consumers can only be gained at the expense of other firms. This simplifies things, allowing a focus on the competition among firms and also allows the assumption that if *S* represents the market size, and the firms are charging the same price, the market share of each firm will be *S*/n.

INTERNATIONAL TRADE LAW

International trade law includes the appropriate rules and customs for handling trade between countries. However, it is also used in legal writings as trade between private sectors, which is not right.

This branch of law is now an independent field of study as most governments has become part of the world trade, as members of the World Trade Organization (WTO). Since the transaction between private sectors of different countries is an important part of the WTO activities, this latter branch of law is now a very important part of the academic works and is under study in many universities across the world. International trade law should be distinguished from the broader field of international economic law.

The latter could be said to encompass not only WTO law, but also law governing the international monetary system and currency regulation, as well as the law of international development.

The body of rules for transnational trade in the 21st century derives from medieval commercial laws called the *lex mercatoria* and *lex maritima* — respectively, "the law for merchants on land" and "the law for merchants on sea." Modern trade law (extending beyond bilateral treaties) began shortly after the Second World War, with the negotiation of a multilateral treaty to deal with trade in goods: the General Agreement on Tariffs and Trade (GATT).

International trade law is based on theories of economic liberalism developed in Europe and later the United States from the 18th century onwards. International Trade Law is an aggregate of legal rules of "international legislation" and new lex mercatoria, regulating relations in international trade.

"International legislation" – international treaties and acts of international intergovernmental organizations regulating relations in international trade. lex mercatoria - "the law for merchants on land". Alok Narayan defines "lex mercatoria" as "any law relating to businesses" which was criticised by Professor Julius Stone. and lex maritima - "the law for merchants on sea.

WORLD TRADE ORGANIZATION

In 1995, the World Trade Organization, a formal international organization to regulate trade, was established. It is the most important development in the history of international trade law. The purposes and structure of the organization is governed by the *Agreement Establishing The World Trade Organization,* also known as the "Marrakesh Agreement". It does not specify the actual rules that govern international trade in specific areas.

These are found in separate treaties, annexed to the Marrakesh Agreement:

Scope of WTO:

- Provide framework for administration and implemen-tation of agreements;
- Forum for further negotiations;
- Trade policy review mechanism; and
- Promote greater coherence among members economics policies

Principles of the WTO:

- Principle of non-discrimination (most-favoured-nation treatment obligation and the national treatment obligation)
- Market access (reduction of tariff and non-tariff barriers to trade)
- Balancing trade liberalisation and other societal interests
- Harmonisation of national regulation (TRIPS agreement, TBT agreement, SPS agreement)

TRADE IN GOODS

The GATT has been the backbone of international trade law throughout most of the twentieth century. It contains rules relating to "unfair" trading practices — dumping and subsidies.

TRADE AND INTELLECTUAL PROPERTY

The World Trade Organisation Trade Related Intellectual Property Rights (TRIPS) agreement required signatory nations to raise intellectual property rights (also known as intellectual monopoly privileges). This arguably has had a negative impact on access to essential medicines in some nations.

DISPUTE SETTLEMENT

Most prominent in the area of dispute settlement in international trade law is the WTO dispute settlement system. The WTO dispute settlement body is operational since 1995 and has been very active since then with 369 cases in the time between 1 January 1995 and 1 December 2007. Nearly a quarter of disputes reached an amicable solution, in other cases the parties to the dispute resorted to adjudication. The WTO dispute settlement body has exclusive and compulsory jurisdiction over disputes on WTO law.

INTERNATIONAL TRADE: RISKS AND RISK ASSESSMENT

INTERNATIONAL TRADE PRACTICES

All forms of business contain elements of risk, but when it comes to international trade, the risk profile enters a new dimension. Internationally, you seldom have common laws that can support the transaction, as would be the case within one country.

Instead, established trade practices and conventions are used to settle the undertakings made by the parties. The key to successful trade transactions, therefore, depends on a knowledge of these established practices and ensuring that the undertakings in the individual contract are in line with such practices. This is why it is crucial for the seller to have started with a correct risk assessment before finally entering into the transaction.

Sometimes, however, the circumstances in a particular case are so obvious that one hardly thinks of it as a risk assessment, whereas in other situations a thorough risk assessment needs to be done. The main sources for international trade practices are publications issued by the International Chamber of Commerce, which will be referred to many times throughout this book. In every new transaction one has to take it for granted that, from the outset, the parties will have different views about various aspects of the terms of payment. This is quite logical since the most important function of these terms for both seller and buyer is to minimize not only the risks involved, but also the cost of payment and of the financing of the transaction.

The Negotiation Process

The seller will always try to get terms that will maximize the outcome and minimize the risk. However, they must also be prepared to accommodate reasonable demands from the buyer in order to match other competitors and reach a deal that is acceptable to both parties, thereby also developing a good long-term business relationship. Should the seller be inflexible on this point, it could result in an adverse competitive situation with the potential risk of losing the deal. On the other hand, demands from the buyer that are too stringent can have the same result, or be resolved by means of a higher price or some other amendment to the final agreement.

The outcome of these negotiations will depend on past knowledge and experience, which is even more important if the buyer bases their request for tender on simplified or standar-dized terms of payment, usually to their own advantage. In many cases, such terms are adapted to conditions that are not optimal for the seller, compared with what the seller could have reached if they were individually negotiated. In such a case it is important to be able to argue and convince the buyer that there might be other solutions that can satisfy any reasonable demands, in order to find the optimal result for both parties. There is, however, another – and in some countries very common –

way to bridge the gap between the parties, if the seller has to abstain from some demands in negotiations with the buyer.

The seller could approach a third party, often a credit insurance company, in order to reduce the commercial risk which could not be covered through the agreed terms of payment. Finally, it should be noted that the business practices which have been established over time in different countries or regions also create at least a common ground for both parties when starting their payment negotiations, ie choice of currency, form of payment and terms of financing.

Local banks, trade councils and the chambers of commerce in both the seller's and the buyer's country can draw on their experience and give impartial advice on local business practice regarding both the form of payment and the more specific terms of payment, while also taking the size, commodity and other aspects of the potential transaction into account. Such considerations can then be the starting point for negotiations between the parties.

Different Forms of Trade Risk

There are always potential drawbacks in trying to categorize such a general concept as trade risks which could have so many different forms and shapes, but it also has great illustrational advantages, particularly when they also coincide with commonly used business expressions. Figure shows the main risk structure in international trade, which will affect both the seller's and the buyer's view of the terms of payment.

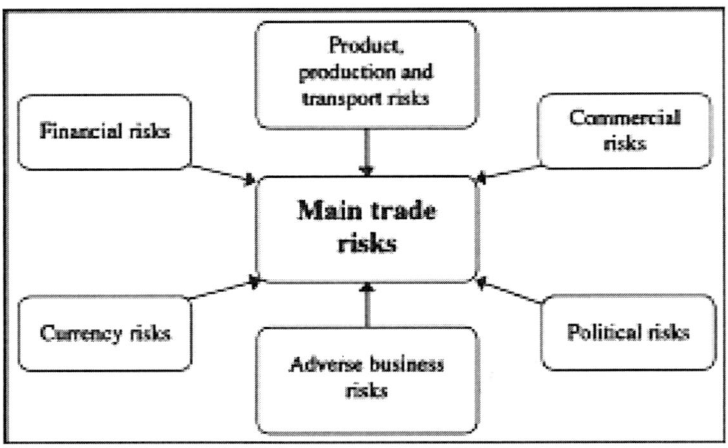

Fig. Different Forms of Risk in International Trade

Obviously, all these risks combined do not often occur in one and the same transaction. For example, a sale to a Norwegian customer in USD may be just a matter of a straight commercial risk on the buyer, whereas delivery of a tailor-made machine to Indonesia has to be risk assessed in quite another way. In quite general terms, the risk structure is directly linked to the obligations undertaken by the seller. This assessment can often be made relatively simple as a commercial risk only, but, in other cases, for example if the transaction also involves assembly, installation, testing or a maintenance responsibility, the assessment has to involve many other aspects as well.

The question of risk is to a large degree a subjective evaluation, but it is still important for both parties to have a good knowledge of these matters in order to carry out a proper and meaningful risk assessment. Only thereafter does the question arise about how to cover these risks through the terms of payment together with other limitations in the contract, if applicable, and together with separate credit risk insurance or guarantees, as the case may be. It should also be noted that most export credit insurance, taken by the seller as additional security, could be impaired or even invalid should the seller themselves not have fulfilled – or been able to fulfil – their obligations according to the contract.

This is another reason why it is so important that the obligations of the seller, according to the contract, are always directly related to those of the buyer. Otherwise the seller may end up in a risk situation that is worse than anticipated at the time of entering into the contract. When all the necessary evaluations have been done, the final decision as to whether the deal is secure enough to be entered into has to be taken. The worst that can happen is finding, after the contract has been signed, that it contains risks that the seller was unaware of at that time. It is then often too late to make changes.

Terms of Delivery and Terms of Payment

The terms of delivery also have to be defined in order to determine when and where the seller has fulfilled the obligations to deliver according to the contract and what is needed in order to do so.

There is a clear connection between these two sets of terms insofar as payment is mostly related to the point at which the risk passes from the seller to the buyer as specified by the terms of delivery; it is to be made either at that particular time or at a specific time thereafter. This connection makes it necessary to outline some basic facts about the different terms of delivery. The standard rules of reference for the interpretation of the most commonly used trade terms in international trade are Incoterms 2000 issued by the International Chamber of Commerce Publication 560.

These rules are now generally recognized throughout the world, so any other unspecified trading terms, which may often have different meanings for companies in different countries, should be avoided. When agreed upon between the parties, these rules and their latest revisions must always be referred to in the sales contract and in all related documentation, for example CIF Hong Kong, Incoterms 2000. The basic purpose of these rules is to define how each Incoterm, as agreed in the sales contract, should be dealt with in terms of delivery, risks and costs, and specify the responsibility of the buyer and seller. For example, who should arrange and pay freight, other transport charges, insurance, duties and taxes?

These aspects are often referred to as the critical points in international trade, detailing at what point the risk is transferred from the seller to the buyer and how the costs involved should be split between the parties. There are presently 13 defined Incoterms, split into four groups, related to the seller's obligation to deliver the goods. Some Incoterms can be used only for maritime transport whereas others can be used for all modes of transport; similarly, some are more suitable than others for use in combination with terms of payment based on 'clean payments' in connection with open account trading, while others are used in combination with 'documentary payments'.

These four groups are:

1. *Group E*: Where the seller has to make the goods available at their premises. The only example is EXW – Ex Works, where the seller must place the goods at the disposal of the buyer at the seller's premises or another named place not cleared for export and not loaded on any collecting vehicle.
2. *Group F*: Where the seller must deliver the goods to a carrier appointed by the buyer. For example, FOB – Free on Board.
3. *Group C*: Where the seller themselves must contract for the carriage of the goods, but without assuming risk of loss of, or damage to, the goods or additional costs due to events occurring after shipment. For example, CIF – Cost Insurance and Freight, where the seller delivers the goods when they pass the ship's rail in the port of shipment and must pay the costs and freight necessary to bring the goods to the named port of destination, but including also the procurement of insurance against the buyer's risk of loss of, or damage to, the goods during carriage.
4. *Group D*: Where the seller also has to bear all costs and risks required to deliver the goods to the place of destination. For example, DDP – Delivered Duty Paid where the seller must deliver the goods to the buyer, cleared for import, and not unloaded at the named place of destination.

When choosing the appropriate terms of delivery, deciding factors include:

- The transportation route, the buyer and the nature of the goods, including the mode of transport;
- Standard practice, if any, in the buyer's country or any regulation set by the authorities of that country to benefit their own transport or insurance industry;

- Procedures, where the seller should avoid terms of delivery, which are dependent on obtaining import licences or clearance of goods to countries they cannot properly judge;
- The competitive situation, where the buyer often suggests their preferred terms of delivery and the seller has to evaluate these terms in relation to the risks involved.

For a standard delivery between established trade partners, neighbouring countries or countries belonging to a common trading area, this question is often easily agreed upon as a matter of standard practice with only an adjustment related to the actual freight and insurance charges, often in connection with open account trading. In these cases, the Incoterms Groups E and F are often used, where the buyer takes the main responsibility for transport and risk of the purchased goods. However, in other cases and when the seller wants to have better control of the delivery process and be able to select transport and/or insurance, the delivery terms C and D are more frequently used.

PRODUCT RISKS

Product risks are risks that the seller automatically has to accept as an integral part of their commitment. First, it is a matter of the product itself, or the agreed delivery; for example, specified performance warranties or agreed maintenance or service obligations. There are many examples of how new and unexpected working conditions in the buyer's country have led to reduced performance of the delivered goods. It could be negligence concerning operating procedures or restrictions, careless treatment, lack of current maintenance, but also damage due to the climate or for environmental reasons. Matters of this nature may well lead to disputes between the parties after the contract has been signed and to increased cost for the delivery as a whole.

It is important for the seller to have the contract, and specifically the terms of payment, worded in such a way that any such changes, which are directly or indirectly due to the actions of the buyer or originating within their country, will automatically include compensation or corresponding changes in the seller's commitments. This can be either in economic terms or in originally agreed time limits, or both. It goes without saying that these risks become even more complicated when it comes to whole projects or larger and more complex contracts. These are often completed over longer periods and involve many more possible combinations of interrelated commitments between the commercial parties, not only between the seller and the buyer, but also often involving other parties in the buyer's country, both commercial and political.

Manufacturing Risks

This risk appears all too frequently when the product is tailor-made or has unique specifications. In these cases there is often no other readily available buyer if the transaction cannot be completed, in which case the seller has to carry the cost of any necessary readjustment, if that is even an option. Risks of this nature occur as early as the product planning phase but may often be difficult to cover from that time owing to the special nature of these products. But they also involve specific risks for the buyer, who often has to enter into payment obligations at an early stage but without the security of the product itself until it has been delivered and installed. In order to safeguard the interests of both parties, the terms of payment are often divided into part-payments related to the production and delivery phases, in combination with separate guarantees, to cover the risks as they occur in different phases of the transaction.

Transport Risks and Cargo Insurance

From a general risk perspective it is not only the product but also the physical movement of the goods from the seller to the buyer that has to be evaluated, based on aspects such as the nature of the product, size of delivery, the buyer and their country, and the actual transportation route. Most goods in international trade, apart from smaller and non-expensive deliveries, are covered by cargo insurance, providing cover against physical loss or damage whilst in transit, either by land, sea or air, or by a combination of these modes of transport. The cover under a cargo or marine cargo policy is almost always defined by standard policy wordings issued by the Institute of London Underwriters.

These are called Institute Cargo Clauses. While there are numerous clauses that will apply to different cargos, the widest cover is provided under Institute Cargo Clauses A or with more restrictive cover under Institute Cargo Clauses B and Institute Cargo Clauses C. Cargo insurance is therefore normally provided through one of these Institute Cargo Clauses A, B or C, plus separate war clauses and strike clauses. The question of who should arrange the insurance is determined by the agreed terms of delivery, as defined by the Incoterms 2000 and described earlier. These terms also define the critical point during transport, where the risk is transferred from the seller to the buyer.

That can be any given point between a named place at the seller's location and a named place at the buyer's location. That specified critical point determines the seller's and the buyer's responsibility to arrange insurance, as required. However, there is another aspect of risk coverage that the seller has to be particularly aware of, and that is the potential risk of the buyer arranging insurance according to some of the terms of delivery. If such a term of delivery is chosen, for example FOB and the buyer fails to insure in a proper and agreed way, the goods may arrive at the destination in a damaged condition and without adequate insurance cover. If, at the same time, the terms of payment allow for payment after delivery, this risk de facto becomes a risk for the seller, who may end up with unpaid for, uninsured and damaged goods at the point of destination.

Such a situation is obviously a consequence of the seller agreeing to terms of payment that did not cover the actual commercial risk, but the insurance risk involved could, in most cases, have been eliminated by separate seller's interest contingency insurance. From the seller's perspective, there are basically three different ways to insure the cargo, either with an open insurance policy covering most or all shipments within the seller's basic trade as agreed in advance with the insurer, or with a specific insurance policy, covering specific shipments on an *ad hoc* basis or those which are outside the set criteria of the open policy.

The open policy is by far the most common in international trade, normally reviewed on an annual basis, and with a 30–60-day cancellation clause, should conditions deteriorate substantially. The open cover is the most cost-effective alternative, but it also has obvious administrative advantages and will automatically secure the actual coverage of all individual shipments under the policy. The third basic form of cargo insurance is seller's interest contingency insurance normally only offered as a complement to the open policy or as integral part of a specific policy, and on an undisclosed basis as far as the buyer is concerned. This insurance covers the risk that the goods may arrive at their destination in a damaged condition, resulting in the buyer's refusal to accept them or they may simply be unable or unwilling to pay for commercial or political reasons, including failure to produce a valid import licence.

In such cases the insurance covers the physical loss of, or damage to, the goods, but it does not cover the credit risk on the buyer, which has to be covered through the terms of payment, in conjunction with any other arrangements. The seller should bear in mind that cargo insurance is a specialized business, where cover and conditions may vary according to the commodity or goods to be shipped, the transportation route and the mode of transport, which is a major reason why open policy cover is the most common in international trade. But normal risk management procedures will always apply: new and adverse conditions and/or additional risks must be reported or approved by the insurer, and the policy normally excludes loss or damage due to wilful misconduct or insufficient, unsuitable or inadequate packing or container stowage by the assured party.

Cargo insurance can be obtained directly from an insurance company or, very often today, directly through the transporting company or the forwarding agent handling the goods. In some countries it is also quite common to use independent cargo insurance brokers, who may be more able to select the most cost-efficient insurance package, based on specific conditions or the trade structure in each individual case. However, the seller should always ensure that the selected insurer has or is part of an established international network for dealing with claims and settlement procedures.

COMMERCIAL RISKS (PURCHASER RISKS)

Commercial risk, also called purchaser risk, is often defined as the risk of the buyer going into bankruptcy or being in any other way incapable of fulfilling the contractual obligations. One might first think of the buyer's payment obligations but it also covers all other obligations of the buyer, according to the contract, necessary for the seller to fulfil their obligations. How does the seller, therefore, evaluate the buyer's ability to fulfil their obligations?

In most industrialized countries within the Organization for Economic Co-operation and Development area, it is relatively easy to obtain a fair picture of potential buyers, either to study their published accounts or to ask for an independent business credit report, which is a more reliable way of dealing with customer risks. This will also give much broader information about the buyer and their business, and not simply some selected economic figures from which the seller often cannot draw any decisive conclusions.

Credit Information

Export trade may be an important factor in the potential growth of business; however, the risks involved in carrying out international business can also be high. In little more than a decade, the world of commerce has changed dramatically. In this commercial environment, the global suppliers of credit information have become a vital source of knowledge and expertise, based on the great wealth of information that they maintain about consumers and how they behave, about businesses and how they perform, and about different markets and how they are changing. The more the seller understands their customers, the more they are able to respond to their individual needs and circumstances.

Credit information suppliers help the seller use information to reach new customers and to build, nurture and maximize lasting customer relationships. Credit information thus forms a vital part of establishing the structure of a potential export transaction and, in particular, the terms of payment to be used. In some cases the information can be provided instantly, inexpensively and in a standardized manner on the internet, but in other cases a more researched profile is required. Each seller must have a policy for obtaining up-to-date information about the commercial risk structure in connection with any new potential buyer or business and with outstanding export receivables.

How this is done may differ depending on the volume and structure of the exports, but it is recommended at least to review the business information systems offered by the larger providers and to choose an alternative that is optimal for the individual seller as to the services and costs involved. The seller should, however, be aware that the contents and accuracy of the business information may vary, depending on the registered information available about the company. The contents can sometimes also be difficult to evaluate and questions always arise about how up to date it really is, particularly when dealing with customers outside the most advanced industrialized countries.

With buyers from non-OECD countries the matter becomes even more complicated. The information, if available, will be much more difficult to evaluate and it will be harder to assess how it has been produced and how it should be analysed. In these cases, the information probably has limited value anyway, because other risk factors, such as the political risk, may be greater – and terms of payment that reflect this combined risk have to be chosen.

The seller may also be able to get assistance abroad through the export or trade council or similar institutions in their country, and/or from the commercial sections of embassies abroad, which can assist with market surveys and other studies in that country. Even banks can participate by issuing introductory letters to their branches or correspondents, enabling the seller to obtain more up-to-date information about the local business conditions and form an opinion about the buyer and their business in connection with the contract negotiations.

ADVERSE BUSINESS RISKS

Adverse business risks include all business practices of a negative nature, which are not only common but also almost endemic in some parts of the world. This could have serious consequences for the individual transaction, but also for the general business and financial standing of the seller, as well as their moral reputation. We are, of course, referring to all sorts of corrupt practices that flourish in many countries, particularly in connection with larger contracts or projects: bribery, money laundering and a variety of facilitation payments:

- Bribery in general can broadly be defined as the receiving or offering of an undue reward by or to any holder of public office or a private employee designed to influence them in the exercise of their duty, and thus to incline them to act contrary to the known rules of honesty and integrity.

This quotation is taken from a UK government body, and even if it is not a legal definition, it gives an accurate description of the problem. If bribery is generally a technique to press the seller for undue rewards, money laundering often has the opposite purpose, which is to invite the seller to do a deal that may on the face of it seem very advantageous, but where the true intention is to disguise or conceal the actual origin of the money involved. It covers criminal activities, corruption and breaches of financial sanctions. It includes the handling, or aiding the handling, of assets, knowing that they are the result of crime, terrorism or illegal drug activities.

Criminal and terrorist organizations generate large sums of cash, which they need to channel into the banking, corporate and trade financial systems, and both banks and traders can innocently fall victim of such activity if not exercising due diligence. A frequently used technique is over-invoicing or inflated transactions, with or without payment to a third party, where the seller may be completely unaware that they could be part of a ruse to launder money. The seller should also be particularly observant in the case of cash payments and be aware that new anti-money laundering regulations must be complied with for such payments in most countries. A reputable business adds respectability to any organization being used for laundering operations, and money launderers will try to use any business, directly through ownership, or indirectly by deceit.

Developing nations are particularly vulnerable to money launderers because they usually have poorly regulated financial systems. These provide the greatest opportunities to criminals. In general terms, a suspicious transaction is one that is outside the normal range of transactions from the seller's point of view, in particular in relation to new customers or where an old customer changes transaction structure in an unusual way.

It can include:

- Unusual payment settlements;
- Unusual transfer instructions;
- Secretiveness;
- Rapid movements in and out of accounts;
- Numerous transfers;
- Complicated accounts structures.

Bribery, money laundering and any other form of corrupt behaviour is bad for business; it distorts the normal trade patterns and gives unfair advantages to those involved in it. It is also extremely harmful for the countries themselves, owing to the damage it causes to the often fragile social fabric; it destroys the economy and is strongly counterproductive for trade and all forms of foreign investments into the country. In the long run, such practices also prevent social and economic stability and development, and it has an especially negative impact on the most disadvantaged parts of the population. Even within the countries where these practices are frequent among individual public and private employees, it is almost always illegal, even if the countries lack the means and the resources to tackle these problems effectively.

The Need for a Strong Policy

The World Bank and the OECD have put a great deal of resources into combating corruption worldwide, and in most countries corruption is now illegal even when committed overseas. The companies also have full responsibility for the wrongdoings of their employees abroad when acting for the company.

As a consequence of the inclusion of anti-corruption laws, it is also incorporated in the procedures of all government departments, for example in the rules of the respective export credit agency. Any violation of the anti-corruption statement that the seller has to give when applying for such insurance could have serious implications for its validity.

It is often not even the threat of prosecution that should most worry the seller. There have been a number of cases in which companies were allegedly involved in corrupt behaviour, but where the true circumstances were not fully disclosed. The allegation could be damaging enough, sometimes based only on rumours emanating from economic groups or political factions within the society to stop or postpone a project or to favour another bidder. Such rumours, true or false, or involving either smaller facilitation payments or large-scale bribery to senior private or public officials, can drag on for years, with economic and detrimental consequences for the company, both overseas and at home.

Every company involved in overseas trade or investments should have a clear anti-corruption policy that is implemented and clearly understood by all its employees, and supervised by the management in an appropriate way. Such a policy is also supported by local laws, which give both the company and its employees a much stronger moral and legal defence against every attempt to extort bribes from them or attempt to induce them into any other form of corrupt practice.

POLITICAL RISKS

Political risk or country risk is often defined as: 'the risk of a separate commercial transaction not being realized in a contractual way due to measures emanating from the government or authority of the buyer's own or any other foreign country'. No matter how reliable the buyer may be in fulfilling their obligations and paying in local currency, their obligations to the seller are nevertheless dependent on the current situation in their own country – or along the route of transport to that country. However, in practice, it may be difficult to separate commercial and political risk because political decisions, or other similar acts by local authorities, also affect the local company and its capabilities of honouring the contract.

For example, some countries may change taxes, import duties or currency regulations, often with immediate effect, which could undermine the basis for contracts already signed. Other common measures include import restrictions or other regulations intended to promote local industry and to save foreign currency. Even with just the risks of such actions, they all have the same negative implications for the transaction and the buyer's possibility of fulfilling their part of the contract.

Seen from a broader perspective, political risk could be divided into different underlying causes, such as:

- Political stability;
- Social stability; and
- Economic stability.

Political stability is often seen as an important criterion of the real political risk. This stability indicates, in general terms, the likelihood or the probability of a country's involvement in, or being affected by, acts of terror, war or internal violence from groupings within the country or sanctions or blockades from other nations. The constant risk of rapid and unexpected change in economic policy or in the form of nationalization or similar measures as a consequence of political instability will have the same effect; they are all extremely damaging for any private commercial economic activity in the country.

Unfortunately, there are presently numerous examples of this political instability in many parts of the world. The social stability of a country is also of great importance, mainly on a long-term basis. However, the developments in many countries, not only developing countries, show all too well how unexpectedly and rapidly social instability can turn into violence or terrorist activity that can paralyse the country or its economy. Economic stability is equally important to maintain the confidence of a country and its economy.

A weak infrastructure, dependence on single export or import commodities, a high debt burden and lack of raw materials are critical factors that, together with other developments, can easily change economic stability in a short time. Even currency restrictions and other more indirect currency regulations such as 'pegging' against other currencies, often USD, could have serious long-term economic consequences, as seen in many countries. The turbulent situation in many developing countries is a constant reminder of the fragility of economic stability in many countries around the world.

Other Forms of Political or Similar Risk

Apart from the real political risks already discussed, there are other measures taken by authorities in the buyer's home country that can affect the buyer and their ability or willingness to fulfil the transaction; for example, demands for product standards, new or changed energy or environmental requirements – measures that could have a genuine purpose or be put in place partly to act as trade barriers to promote sectors or important industries within the country. Irrespective of the purpose, such actions, often called 'non-tariff barriers', could have a negative impact on the signed transaction.

Other, more open measures are sometimes also implemented, often at short notice, as has been seen within the European Union, for example, where the objective has often been to prevent a rapid increase in imports from some emerging market countries, in order to protect the EU's own industry or allow more time to adapt to new trade patterns. But countries involved in the transit of goods have to be considered as well as countries related to subcontractors or suppliers of crucial components. In these cases, perhaps it is not the political risk as defined, but other measures that are more important; for example, the risk of labour market conflicts in the form of strikes or lockouts that could interrupt delivery of components needed for the timely execution of the agreed sales contract.

Not least, the risk involved in ordinary force majeure clauses should be mentioned, even if the background is not political but caused by other factors outside the control of the commercial parties themselves. When used by other parties, such clauses could, for example, release a subcontractor from their delivery obligations during the periods they are applicable, with corresponding effects for the seller. Even bank guarantees and other obligations in favour of the seller could be of limited value during such periods if, as is normally the case, they only cover commitments according to a contract, which may refer to such clauses.

The same goes for presentation of documents under a letter of credit, where the bank will not accept documents that have expired during such interruption of the bank's business. However, when used by the seller, such clauses could protect them against actions for breach of contract, where performance of their contractual obligations is prevented by incidents outside their control.

This is often referred to as 'frustration of contract' and a typical clause might say:

- The Company shall have no liability in respect of any failure or delay in fulfilling any of the Company's obligations to the extent that fulfilment thereof is prevented, frustrated, impeded and/or delayed or rendered uneconomic as a consequence of any fire, flood, earthquake, other natural disaster or Act of God, industrial dispute or other circumstances or event beyond the Company's reasonable control.

Currency Risks

If payment is going to be made in a currency other than that in which the seller incurs their costs, a new currency risk will arise. In most cases, the seller's main costs will be in local currency, which automatically creates such a risk if invoicing in another currency. The size of that risk will depend on the currency and the outstanding period until payment.

Since the introduction of the euro, invoicing in that currency has become increasingly common in European trade and also with sellers outside the euro zone. This development is likely to accelerate with additional countries joining the euro zone. Traditionally, however, the USD has been the preferred third-party currency.

This applies particularly to raw materials and certain commodities in general, and for many other services such as freight and insurance. It is also commonly used in countries where the United States maintains a strong economic or political influence.

Available statistics do not usually show currency distribution for international trade of goods and services, but it can generally be expected that exports invoiced in smaller trade currencies are diminishing in favour of the larger ones, and will probably continue to do so. Most exporters will therefore have to become accustomed to invoicing in foreign currency and to the management of currency risk exposure.

Assessment of Currencies

Traditionally, currencies have been divided into groups of 'strong' and 'weak' currencies, and this view has affected the general conception of preferred trade currencies, even though the highest preference is often for the currency of the home country. Sterling, the yen, the Swiss franc and even the euro and maybe some others would probably be regarded as strong currencies, while others would be seen as neutral, weak or unstable. An evaluation such as this may perhaps have its justification in a longer perspective for currencies where the home countries have maintained economic and political stability over the years, together with a strong economy, low inflation and stable confidence in the future maintenance of this policy.

It should, however, be enough to look at the development of the USD, which has changed its value vis-à-vis other large currencies dramatically over the years to realize that such sweeping statements can have their risks. Furthermore, for most parties it is not the long-term currency development that is most interesting, but rather the shorter perspective, limited to the time-span during which current deals are paid.

Then the situation can be reversed, for in that shorter perspective, a currency can have a development in complete contrast to its long-term trend. In the shorter perspective, other factors, real or expected, may be more important, such as interest rate changes, political news and larger price movements in base commodities, central bank currency interventions, statements and statistics.

All these factors, combined with subjective evaluations by millions of participants in the currency markets, will together constantly create new short-term trends. For those who want to follow short-term currency development, most banks and many other financial or currency institutions publicize information via the internet or e-mail on a regular basis – both retrospectively and actual, together with analysis and evaluations of future trends.

FINANCIAL RISKS

In practice, every international trade transaction contains an element of financial risk. Purchasing, production and shipment all place a financial burden on the transaction that forces the seller to determine how alternative terms of payment would affect liquidity during its different phases until payment – and how this should be financed. And, if the deal is not settled as intended, an additional financial risk occurs.

In the case of subcontractors, who do not share the risks of the transaction and are paid according to separate agreements, the risk increases accordingly and even more so should the seller have to offer a supplier credit for a shorter or longer period. When it comes to larger and more complex transactions, this financial risk aspect is even more obvious. One of the major problems for the seller could be to obtain bankable collateral for the increased need for finance and guarantees.

Even after production and delivery, the seller could still be financially exposed in the case of unforeseen events and delays until final payment. Sometimes the interaction between the seller and the buyer can make it difficult to establish the exact cause for the delay in payment and there are then fewer chances for the seller to refer to a specific breach of contract on the part of the buyer.

On the other hand, if the seller has paid enough attention when drafting the sales contract, including the terms of payment, then it is more likely that any reason for delays will be possible to determine according to the clauses of the contract. There could be numerous reasons for such delays, for example issuing a letter of credit too late, late changes in specification of the goods, late arrival of the vessel, congestion in port, changes in the transport route, to name a few.

The real risk also tends to increase with longer and consequently more costly transport distances. Bureaucratic delays in many countries, as well as delays in the banking system, will have the same result – the final payment to the seller will not be made as anticipated according to the contract. Apart from ordinary overdrafts during production and delivery, the need for finance is also determined by the amount of credit that the seller may have to offer as part of the deal. If so, the financial risk is increased in line with the prolonged commercial and/or political risk.

A careful risk assessment is the first important step to a successfully completed transaction because it is the basis for the seller's own strategy, and for the final decision on what is acceptable in the negotiations with the buyer in order to minimize the risks involved.

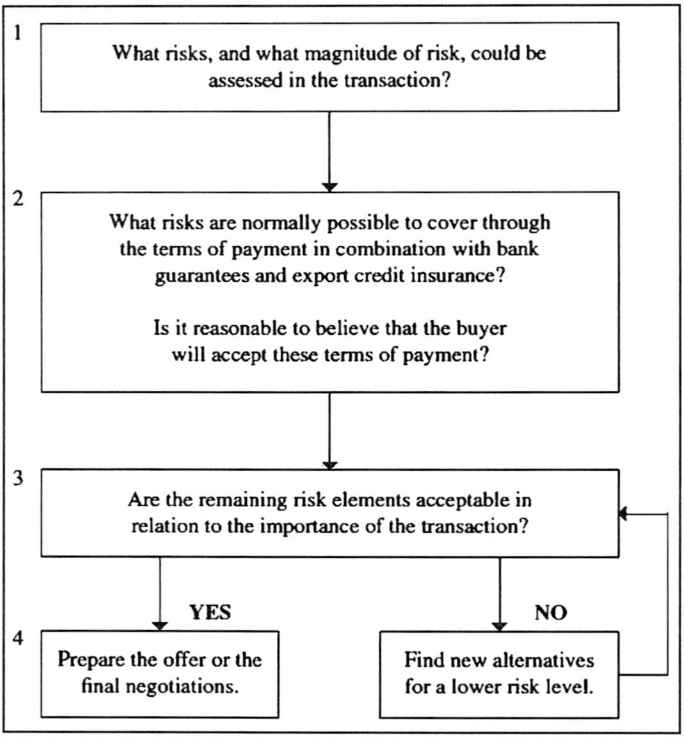

Fig. Risk Assessment – A Summary

Financial Risk and Cash Management

Other forms of financial risk are more obvious but have to be underlined in this context; for example, if the seller misjudges the risks involved in the transaction and becomes exposed through terms of payment that do not cover the real risk situation, or mistakenly enters into the deal without proper risk protection. It goes without saying that such miscalculations can have serious financial consequences, from delays in payment to loss of capital. The financial risks are generally intimately connected to the structure of the terms of payment. The safer they can be made, the more the financial risk will automatically be reduced, the timing of the payments will be more accurate and the liquidity aspect of the transaction better assessed – in fact, the very essence of cash management.

The safer the terms of payment the parties have agreed upon, the more costly they will normally be. And, if they contain bank security, such as a letter of credit or a bank guarantee, that will also reduce available credit limits within the buyer's own bank. However, the buyer is often not prepared to accept higher costs and the use of their own credit limits in order to satisfy what might be seen as excessive demands from the seller, involving methods of payments, which in their opinion, are not normal practice in their country or normally accepted by the company. It is then up to the seller to evaluate the transaction, including potential competition from other suppliers. Eventually, the seller may have to accept the terms of payment offered and try to cover the remaining risks in some other way or to find a compromise by offering compensation to the buyer for the increased bank charges and/or the additional costs incurred by the use of the buyer's existing credit limits.

BUSINESS AND SOCIAL NETWORKS IN INTERNATIONAL TRADE

Nations appear to trade too much with themselves and too little with each other. Jonathan Eaton and Samuel Kortum calculate that "zero gravity" would implya more than fivefold increase in world trade. Attempts to explain this "mystery of the missing trade" have increasingly focused on informal trade barriers, especially weak enforcement of international contracts (James Anderson and Douglas Marcouiller forthcoming) and inadequate information about international trading opportunities. Business and social networks that operate across national borders can help to overcome these kinds of informal trade barriers. For example, Saxenian shows that a transnational community of Indian engineers has facilitated outsourcing of software development from Silicon Valley to regions like Bangalore and Hyderabad.

Research can provide us with insight into *how* transnational networks overcome informal trade barriers, and at the same time can serve to document and even quantify the existence of these barriers. Determining the relative importance of contract enforcement versus informational barriers is especially important since they point to quite different areas of concern for policymakers. Whereas transnational networks have primarily been studied as means of overcoming informal trade barriers, much of the research on the impact of domestic networks on international trade has been motivated byte perception that they constitute informal trade barriers in themselves, with network members colluding to increase their market power by restricting foreign competition. There is also a new line of work that investigates the effect of domestic networks on the composition of international trade.

EXAMPLES AND DEFINITIONS

Empirical research into the impact of networks on international trade has tended to lead theorizing. Most of the empirical work surveyed concerns co ethnic networks and business groups with publicly recorded membership such as the Japanese *keiretsu*. Coethnic networks are communities of individuals or businesses that share a demographic attribute such as ethnicity or religion. Business groups are "sets of firms that are integrated neither completely nor barely at all", and where the lineages of the members can often be traced back to a founding family or small number of allied families. Typical mechanisms serving to integrate the firms include mutual stockholdings and frequent meetings of top executives.

This focus on coethnic networks and business groups is explained by observability rather than primacy of importance: census takers will not record the characteristic "former employee of IBM," yet the fact that many of the key decision makers in the hard disk drive industry shared this characteristic contributed to the rapid spread of popularity of Singapore as a site for FDI, according to industry observers. However ubiquitous networks maybe in the conduct of international trade little can be learned about their impact unless they're observable. In some contexts the keyset re of the networks studied below is that their members are engaged in repeated exchange that helps sustain cooperation/ collusion.

In other contexts the key feature is that network members have thorough knowledge of each others' characteristics, which helps them match with each other or refer each other to outside business opportunities. These key features roughly correspond to two definitions of economic networks used in the sociological literature. The first, based on Joel Podolny and Karen Page, defines an economic network as *a group of agents that pursue repeated, enduring exchange relations with one another*. The second, weaker definition is based on the work of Granovetter: a set of actors who know each others' relevant characteristics or can learn them through referral.

For some purposes these definitions are clearly too broad to be useful. Organized international spot markets do not exist for most traded goods (especially manufactures), so it is entirely possible that systematic micro surveys would reveal that even byte repeated exchange definition most international trade could be viewed as taking place through networks. Egan and Mody, for example, state of trade in bicycles and footwear, "Most U.S. buyers interviewed for this study preferred long-term, stable and direct relationships with both developed and developing country suppliers." This broad definition of the role of networks in international trade may provide insight in some contexts, which suggests that this network view of trade could provide a new way of thinking about the connection between trade and technology transfer.

It clearly will not do, however, when evaluating the claim that networks overcome informal barriers to trade, because it admits networks that were created by trade. This internation-alization may have taken place generations ago, but in this case we will see that it is more accurate to say that these networks are sustained by the trade they're creating than to say that these networks were created by trade. The concentration of empirical research on business groups and co ethnic networks has two unfortunate potential side effects. First, conclusions might be biased byte difficulty of entry into these networks relative to others. Second, the impression might be conveyed that networks are a vestigial or at least culture-bound phenomenon.

This impression would come from the beliefs that co ethnic or co-religious ties are of declining importance in commerce and that business groups are confined to less developed countries (the *grupos económicos* of Latin America or "business houses" of India) or East Asia (the *chaebol* of Korea or *keiretsu* of Japan). Though trends for coethnic networks and business groups need not apply to networks as a whole, we should nevertheless note that the former belief is at least debatable and the latter belief is incorrect: business groups are ubiquitous in the developed countries of continental Europe.

NETWORKS AND OPPORTUNISM

Enforcement of contracts in international trade presents a difficult problem. This part is concerned with how networks facilitate trade across polities by building, or substituting for, trust when contract enforcement is weak to non-existent. Regarding the overseas Chinese network, Maurray Weidenbaum and Samuel Hughes report, "If a business owner violates an agreement, he is blacklisted. This is far worse than being sued, because the entire Chinese network will refrain from doing business with the guilty party." This kind of description suggests that transnational networks deter opportunism in a modern setting, yet the bulk of the more analytical literature has focused on the distant past or extremely underdeveloped environments.

This focus is related to the exclusive reliance of this literature on the tools of theory and case study. An important future task should be collection of data for contemporary networks that facilitate statistical testing of hypotheses. The literature surveyed invariably uses the repeated exchange definition of networks. Its subject is always *trade Diasporas*, which are ethnic or religious groups with settlements at endpoints and transshipment points of a trade route.

According to the survey by Philip Curtin, trade Diasporas dominated cross-cultural trade in most parts of the world until the nineteenth century. Curtin uses the term "cross-cultural" because the term "international" is an anachronism for the period preceding the rise of the nation-state. To some extent trade Diasporas constituted polities in themselves, but their legal enforcement powers were very weak.

Sellers often avoided this problem by traveling with their goods, but agency relations were also prevalent in many trade Diasporas. The use of agency's best documented by Curtin for Armenians and several West African trade Diasporas. Curtin asserts, "Within the [17th–18th century] Armenian community, contracts could be made on a handshake." How were trade Diasporas able to deter opportunistic behaviour and thereby sustain agency? One leading answer is given by Cohen: a trade Diaspora created trust by establishing a "moral community."

An advantage of Cohen's work is that he studies a trade Diaspora, the Hausa in West Africa, that is *contemporary* to the time in which he is writing, which allows him to observe the operation of the Diaspora directly rather than infer it from historical documents. The key actors in Cohen's account are landlord brokers resident in Ibadan, Nigeria, site of the main Hausa trading settlement. These landlord-brokers employed commission agents ("clients") to sell cattle or purchase kola nuts on behalf of dealers located elsewhere in the Diaspora. Opportunistic behaviour byte landlord brokers vis-à-vis the dealers was limited byte fact that they fell under the authority of the chief of the Hausa quarter in Ibadan and by their tradition of accumulating wealth in the form of housing assets: "A landlord cannot sell his houses overnight and leave the community after embezzling the money of traders.

On the other hand, when it is necessary, the Chief can put a great deal of pressure on a landlord in difficulties to sell some of his housing assets in order to meet his financial obligations to traders". No such mechanisms prevented cheating bit he clients of the landlord broker, however, so it is here where development of "moral community" is most crucial. Cohen notes that the relationships between a landlord-broker and his clients constitute a network rather than a hierarchy within the larger network-polity of the Diaspora, not only because there is no binding means of dispute resolution, but also because "the line of demarcation [between landlords and clients] is not rigid but is continually crossed by men moving to the one category or to the other."

He argues that theft was deterred by teeing the repeated economic exchange between a landlord-broker and his clients to building of pseudo-kin relations: "The landlord will tyro marry the client off to... the foster daughters of his wives, or the daughters of his own relatives or of his wives' relatives"; "The landlord can thus be seen as the centre of a network of kinship relations with his clients". Of course this group endogamy was facilitated by the separate identity the Diaspora minority maintained within the host society.

Cohen concludes that "the relationship which thus develops between landlord and client cannot be measured in material or contractual terms alone. It is a relation which cannot be completely reduced to economic or political relations. There is an inescapable moral bond as well." The other leading answer to the question of how trade diasporas were able to sustain agency relations is given by Greif: the threat of collective punishment of deviant agents ball merchants (principals) in the Diaspora substituted for trust. Formally, a repeated game equilibrium in which the strategy of each merchant in a coalition is to refuse forever to deal with an agent who cheats *any* merchant in the coalition sustains a lower efficiency wage premium than a repeated game equilibrium in which each merchant's strategy's to punish only an agent who cheats him.

The higher efficiency wage required to prevent the agent from cheating under a bilateral punishment strategy could be so high as to make agency relations unprofitable. Greif studies the Maghreb traders of the eleventh-century Mediterranean through their documents. Like Cohen in his discussion of landlord-brokers and clients, Greif emphasizes the "horizontal" or non-hierarchical nature of the Maghreb network: "One does not observe the existence of two separate 'classes'... an agents class and a merchants class... the Maghribi traders group was a homogeneous group of middle-class traders and each of them operated as a merchant and as an agent at the same time." He presents evidence for both the transmission of information regarding past conduct of agents throughout the network required byte coalition strategy and for the operation of collective punishment.

For example, when the creditors of Samhun ben Da'ud, a prominent trader from Tunisia, were not paid, he complained that"... their letters filled with condemnation had reached everyone." Regarding collective punishment, Greif reports the following example: "an agent who lived in Jerusalem, Abun ben Zedaka, was accused of embezzling the money of a Maghribi trader. When word of this accusation reached other Maghribi traders, merchants as far away as Sicily canceled their agency relations with him."

Since establishment of a moral community and collective punishment of cheaters are not mutually exclusive mechanisms for discouraging opportunistic behaviour among agents, it seems likely that both were used among the Hausa, Maghreb's, and other trade Diasporas. Indeed, Cohen mentions that the chief of the quarter could resort to "public scandalizing" of a landlord-broker whom he could not punish effectively in other ways. This was accomplished through a special meeting, held in front of the house of the accused man, to which many Hausa dealers who happened to be in the quarter would be invited, ensuring the spread of the scandal throughout the Diaspora. Similarly, kinship ties are not entirely absent from the analysis by Greif, who states that the Maghribi coalition was able to surmount the "endgame" problem because "an old agent would not cheat because he feared that he would be punished through the punishment imposed on his relatives.

Only moral responsibility of relatives was required to enable traders to base their relations upon a reputation mechanism despite the fact that each of them lived for a finite number of years." To some extent it may be that different theoretical perspectives of Cohen and Greif, rather than differences between the Hausa and Maghribi trade Diasporas, caused the former to emphasize moral community and the latter to emphasize collective punishment. On one very important point, however, the two authors are in complete agreement: both the Hausa and the Maghreb's maintained their separate identities *for economic reasons, i.e.*, to facilitate their participation in profitable trade. The efficiency consequences of using networks to solve the problem of opportunism in cross-cultural (or international) trade would seem to be straightforward.

It seems clear that there is net trade creation, which should yield the usual gains from improved allocation of resources, and that the network members themselves should capture a surplus from cooperation. In addition to the theoretical argument of Greif that principals within a repeated exchange network can playa lower wage to their agents, Cohen shows that the Hausa out-competed both the main rival West African ethnic group (the Yoruba) and Europeans in controlling the cattle and kola trades. Greif, however, raises the intriguing possibility that the use of networks to facilitate cross-cultural trade, while statically efficient, is actually dynamically inefficient.

In particular, because an agent from outside the group must be paid a higher wage, the growth of trade handled by a network is hindered by the reluctance of merchants following a "collectivist strategy" to initiate inter economy relations. This is not true for merchants following an "individualist strategy" of bilateral punishment. In my view this argument is not decisive for two reasons. First, the savings to the traders following a collectivist strategy from paying lower wages may finance greater investment and growth in the presence of imperfect capital markets. Second, the network may simply incorporate the trader from the other economy. The exclusiveness of even co ethnic networks can be exaggerated: Cohen notes that "it is possible for some non-Hausa... to become, in effect, Sabo Hausa [Hausa of the Quarter]"; and regarding the overseas Chinese, Constance Lever- Tracyet al. report that "those studied in Australia were proud of trusting relations they had built up with Anglophone Australians."

Of course the process of incorporation requires time and resources, but it may be cheaper in present discounted value terms than paying a higher wage forever. Indeed, part of what the greater savings of traders following a collectivist strategy might finance is precisely investment in cultivation of new network members. Whether or not networks create inefficiencies in expanding trade to new areas or cultures is thus an empirical question. Greif also argues that the use of networks to suppress opportunistic behaviour in international trade was dynamically inefficient in the sense that it hindered institutional innovation designed to accomplish the same purpose. He shows that during the twelfth century the Genoese, whom he identifies as following individualist strategies, "developed an extensive legal system for registration and enforcement of contracts" as well as bookkeeping innovations that made it easier to detect theft of goods being sent overseas.

It certainly seems clear that the use of networks to substitute for formal-legal means of enforcing contracts will hinder the improvement of such means. Improvements in international contract enforcement and other formal-legal means of substituting for trust in international trade have continued to the present day. Two important examples are international commercial arbitration and letters of credit. International commercial arbitration offers a private means of dispute resolution; Laurence Craig, William Park, and Jan Paulsson are the standard reference for International Chamber of Commerce arbitration. Letters of credit allow the trading parties to shift some of their commercial credit risk to the issuing bank and allow the buyer to defer payment until the shipment passes quality inspection.

Such innovations have surely reduced the demand for networks as a means of deterring opportunistic behaviour in international trade and have contributed, along with technological innovations in communication and transport, to "the twilight of the trade diasporas" An important future direction for the literature on transnational networks and opportunism should be to move beyond trade diasporas and to integrate contemporary international trade law and institutions into the analysis as outside options that may influence how the networks operate.

NETWORKS AND OPPORTUNITIES

A more recent literature has emphasized that, in addition to being used to transmit information about past opportunistic business conduct, networks can be used to transmit information about current opportunities for profitable international trade (or investment). The literature surveyed almost always uses the "characteristics knowledge" definition of networks, since the keys knowing the agents' characteristics so as to be able to match them to opportunities.

Transnational networks can facilitate this matching through provision of market information, letting suppliers know that consumers in a particular country will be receptive to their products, or enlightening suppliers on how to adapt their products to consumer preferences in a given country.

Korean wig exports to the United States are an especially well-studied example:

- Korean wig importers' contribution to the Korean wig import business was far greater than their numbers. From these immigrant wig importers, South Korea wig manufacturers could obtain information on new styles and market trends. Since they were not able to develop new styles of their own (prominent U.S. hair designers continuously eloped innovative styles), South Korean wig manufacturers had to depend entirely on Korean immigrant wig importers for information on trends in U.S. wig fashion.

Within a given foreign market, transnational networks can also help producers of consumer goods to find appropriate distributors, assemblers to find the right component suppliers, and investors to find joint-venture partners.

Weidenbaum and Hughes write of the overseas Chinese:

- The members of the bamboo network operate in the interstices of the trading world. They make components, manufacture for others, and perform subassembly work. They are also heavily involved in wholesaling, financing, sourcing, and transporting.... The leading businessmen know each other personally and do deals together, with information spreading through an informal network rather than through more conven-tional channels.

The empirical analyses reviewed below have provided evidence for the trade-creating effects of immigrants and of business groups operating across national borders. Immigrants know the characteristics of many domestic buyers and sellers and carry this knowledge abroad. Foreign direct investment by one or more members of a domestic business group has the same effect. These empirical papers have not been guided by formal theory. The measures of network strength used are *ad hoc,* and the models predicting trade to which they're added are taken "off the shelf."

As a result it is hard to identify the extent to which the estimated coefficients tell us that transnational networks work through provision of market information and matching and referral services as opposed to other means. Readers should therefore keep in mind that all the results reported are open to alternative interpretations. We first consider studies of the impact on bilateral trade of immigrants. An immediate concern is that, rather than a network effect, any positive impact might simply reflect immigrant taste for goods from their countries of origin or the correlation of immigration with country characteristics that promote trade, such as proximity. David Gould allays both concerns by estimating separate equations for exports and imports and including country dummies in his study of the immigrant impact on U.S. bilateral trade with 47 trading partners during the period 1970–86.

His basic estimating framework is Jeffrey Bergstrand's formulation of the gravity equation, to which Gould adds a lagged dependent variable, the stock of immigrants in the United States from each partner, and measures of immigrant skill composition and length of staying the United States. The coefficients on the immigrant stock are positive and highly significant in both the export and import equations, but the coefficients on the immigrant skill composition and length of stay variables are insignificant. The implied long-run elasticity's indicate that a 10-per cent increase in immigrants to the United States will increase U.S. exports to the country of origin by 4.7 per cent and U.S. imports from the country of origin by 8.3 per cent.

A reasonable interpretation of the larger point estimate for the import elasticity's that it combines a taste effect and a network effect, while the export elasticity only reflects a network effect. Keith Head and John Ries essentially repeat Gould's exercise for Canada, investigating the impact of immigrants on Canadian bilateral imports and exports for 136 trading partners during the period 1980–92. Their constant elasticity specification using a lagged dependent variable is closest to that of Gould, the main differences being omission of country dummies and use of a Tobit specification to allow for the many observations of zero on Canadian bilateral exports and imports.

For two different measures of the immigrant stock the estimated coefficients are positive and significant in both the export and import equations. The implied long-run elasticity's for the preferred immigrant stock measure indicate that a 10-per cent increase in immigrants to Canada will increase Canadian exports to the country of origin by 1.3 per cent and Canadian imports from the country of origin by3.3 per cent. The fact that these elasticity's are much lower than those estimated by Gould could be due to the nature of Canadian compared to U.S. trade: Head and Ries point out that "Canada's main export categories, natural resources and United States-bound automotive goods, do not seem likely candidates for transactions cost reductions by immigrants." We turn next to studies of the trade creating effects of business groups operating across national borders. Both studies surveyed are concerned with whether foreign direct investment in manufacturing by assemblers in "vertical" *keiretsu* stimulates exports by other *keiretsu* members.

Having an assembler abroad whose characteristics they know could be helpful to suppliers looking for export opportunities. René Belderbos and Leo Sleuwaegen investigate the 1988 intensity of exports to the European Community (EC) of 86 Japanese firms classified in the electronics or precision machinery industries. They regress the log of the ratio of firm exports to the EC to total sales minus exports to the EC on various firm characteristics plus a dummy for whether the firm is a member of a vertical *keiretsu* for which the assembler operated one or more manufacturing plants in the EC. The *keiretsu* dummy's positive and significant in all specifications. Head and Ries examine total exports of 96 *keiretsu* suppliers in the automobile and electronics industries for the period 1966–90. They regress the log of firm exports on firm characteristics, counts of the firm's foreign distribution and manufacturing investments, and the count of foreign manufacturing investments byte assembler of the vertical *keiretsu* to which the supplier belongs.

The *keiretsu* assembler investment count is positive and highly significant. Rauch and Vitor Trindade (forthcoming) attempt a partial synthesis of the literatures surveyed in this section and the previous one by examining the trade-creating effects of what is, in all probability, the largest transnational network (or set of interlinked national networks) in the world: the overseas Chinese. On the one hand, the overseas Chinese can be seen as a latter day trade Diaspora that deters opportunistic behaviour in international transactions. On the other hand, the overseas Chinese can promote trade by providing market information and matching and referral services because they use co ethnic business societies to keep knowledge of network members' characteristics fresh:

- This networked organizational system also distinguishes ethnic Chinese business patterns from other "personality" methods of conducting business. These types of business patterns developed along with various institutional supports, like clan halls, regional place associations, and "umbrella" organizations such as the Chinese Benevolent Associations in both local and overseas communities. These institutions were primarily involved in maintaining the social "glue" necessary for normative relationships and practices to continue over time and space. The contemporary evolution of these types of institutions has led to new forms of organization, such as the Greater Chinese Entrepreneurs' Conferences, the Chinese Business Fairs, and a number of other international ethnic Chinese conferences devoted primarily to business connections and transactions.

Rauch and Trinidad try to distinguish the trust and business opportunity impacts of the overseas Chinese network on bilateral trade by estimating separate gravity equations for commodities that have "reference prices" and commodities that do not. A reference price is defined as a price that is quoted without mentioning a brand name or other producer identification. Commodities that possess reference prices are taken to be sufficiently homogeneous that if traders see the price differential between two countries' markets is large enough to cover customs and transport costs, they know it is profitable to ship the product.

Commodities that do not possess reference prices are taken to be sufficiently differentiated that prices cannot convey enough of the information relevant for international trade: buyers and sellers must be matched in characteristics space, and hence the thicker information that can be provided byte overseas Chinese network is much more important than for international trade in homogeneous commodities. In contrast, moral community or the threat of collective sanctions should deter equally shipments of rotting fruit or stockings with runs. The same lack of distinction between commodities with and commodities without reference prices should hold for other forms of opportunistic behaviour such as failure to pay for a shipment one has received.

Rauch and Trinidad thus argue that an economically and statistically greater impact of the overseas Chinese network on bilateral trade in commodities without reference prices than in commodities with them establishes a presumption that this network has a quantitatively important effect by matching traders with business opportunities, in addition to its effect through building or substituting for trust. Rauch and Trinidad adapt Jeffrey Frankel's formulation of the gravity equation and begin with his sample of 63 countries. They have data on ethnic Chinese population shares for 57 and 59 of these countries circa 1980 and 1990, respectively, and estimate equations for the log of bilateral trade (sum of exports and imports) for each year separately.

The strength of the overseas Chinese network for any two trading partners is measured byte product of their ethnic Chinese population shares, which gives the probability that, if we select an individual at random from each country, both will be ethnic Chinese. The gravity equation estimates to compute the per centage increases in bilateral trade attributable to the overseas Chinese network, evaluating all variables at their mean values. As we would expect, the network impact is much larger for trade between countries with ethnic Chinese population shares at the levels prevailing in Southeast Asia than for all other country pairs.

The per centage increases in bilateral trade attributable to direct and indirect colonial ties are also provided as a standard for comparison, where an indirect colonial tie exists between two countries that had the same colonial power. The integration of commercial interests that prevailed during colonial periods should have established a common business language or lingua franca and a set of business contacts, facilitating the search by producers for the right distributors, by assemblers for the right suppliers, and so on. The differences across commodity groups reported in table are all statistically significant, and confirm that the increase in bilateral trade attributable to the overseas Chinese network is larger for differentiated than for homogeneous products.

We see that the impact on bilateral trade of both the overseas Chinese network and direct and indirect colonial ties is lower in 1990 than in 1980 for both the homogeneous and the differentiated commodity groups. This could reflect strengthening of international contract enforcement mechanisms and improvements in communications technology, or it could reflect weakening of ethnic bonds and direct colonial ties and the spread of English as a common business language. Countering these (possible) trends are two tendencies that should increase rather than decrease the importance of networks for international trade.

First, the information intensity of trade is increasing: Rauch finds that differentiated products have increased their share of world trade from 56.5 per cent in 1970 to 67.1 per cent in 1990, and it seems likely that product differentiation itself is becoming ever finer. Second, supply of the other transnational networks covered by studies in this section is increasing: a rising flow of migrants, especially from poor to rich countries, has resulted in the foreign-born accounting for a growing share of the population of most rich countries, and business groups are increasingly spread across national borders. The implications for economic efficiency of transnational networks that provide information about profitable trading opportunities can be evaluated using the model of Rauch and Alessandra Casella.

In their model production takes place as follows: producers match pair wise, and if the match is acceptable an internationally immobile resource ("labour") is employed to realize the productive opportunity. Domestic matching is characterized by complete information—every producer knows the type of every other—while international matching is hampered by incomplete information: because producers' types are not observable to foreigners, matching is effectively random. However, each producer has access only to the labour in his own country, so domestic matches must employ domestic labour, while international matches can employ labour in whichever country it is cheaper. International matches can thus serve to transfer labour demand (producer services) from the country where labour is scarce to where it is abundant, yielding the standard gains from trade. insurance, the delivery terms C and D are more frequently used.

Rauch and Casella model a transnational network as extending to the international market the complete information that prevails for non-members only in the domestic market: each network member knows the types of all other network members in both countries. This facilitates the transfer of labour demand and increases the extent to which the countries' factor endowment ratios can differ without ruling out achievement of full efficiency. In this respect the network acts like an improvement in the matching technology between countries. The network differs from such an improvement, however, in that it only reduces informational barriers for a subset of producers, so that distributive effects between network member and non-member producers can arise.

Rauch and Casella find that in equilibrium where full efficiency's not achieved the network may cause aggregate profits of producers who are not members to fall even though world wages and world profits as a whole increase. Moreover, although the network must (weakly) increase the value of world output in a two-country model, Rauch and Casella show that this need not be true if there is more than one international market so that the network does not necessarily link the countries with the largest difference in factor endowment ratios: they demonstrate that in a three-country model a network can have an effect analogous to harmful "trade diversion."

NETWORKS AS MARKET STRUCTURE

Whereas transnational networks can help to overcome informal barriers to international trade, domestic networks can create informal barriers by facilitating collusion to restrict the market access of foreign firms. The dominant strand of the literature surveyed in this section investigates whether *keiretsu* act this way. The repeated exchange definition of networks is always used in this work. A new line of research covered at the end of this section moves away from investigation of the relationship between networks and informal trade barriers to examine how the market structure created by domestic business groups influences the *composition* of trade. Studies of whether *keiretsu* act as barriers to imports (especially from the United States) are surveyed by Lawrence and Gary Saxon house.

Two influential papers are K. C. Fung and Lawrence. Fung examines U.S. net exports to Japan for 22 industries in 1980. In various specifications he consistently finds a negative, highly statistically significant, but quantitatively small effect of either the per centage of industry sales or the per centage of industry employment accounted for by *keiretsu*-affiliated companies. Collusion by *keiretsu* members to restrict imports is certainly not the only possible explanation for this result, and Lawrence is especially concerned about the alternative explanation that efficiency gains realized by *keiretsu* reduce the competitiveness of imports. He reasons that the latter explanation should imply that *keiretsu* increase industry exports as well as reduce imports. He examines the ratio of imports to Japanese domestic demand

and the ratio of Japanese exports to total world exports for 37 industries in 1985.

The per centage of industry sales accounted for by *keiretsu*-affiliated firms is negatively and significantly related to import penetration, consistent with the findings of Fung, and is insignificantly related to the Japanese world export share. The *keiretsu* impact on imports found by Lawrence is quantitatively large, unlike that found beefing; setting the *keiretsu* sales per centage to zero would roughly double the average import share. When Lawrence splits the *keiretsu* variable into the per centage of industry sales accounted for by firms affiliated with "horizontal" versus vertical keiretsu, both are still negatively associated with import share but the vertical *keiretsu* variable has a positive and weakly significant effect on export share.

If vertical *keiretsu* do indeed reduce imports and increase exports because of efficiency gains, it is most likely because the long-term supply relationships that exist within these repeated exchange networks encourage relationship specific investments. Barbara Spencer and LarryQiu model relationship specific investments by *keiretsu* suppliers in a paper designed to shed light on the United States-Japan auto parts dispute. In their model *keiretsu* auto parts suppliers make no verifiable investments that create rents for the *keiretsu* assembler, perhaps by reducing assembly costs by improving the "fit" with other *keiretsu* parts. Payments to the suppliers cannot be based on their investments and instead the assembler engages in simultaneous Nash bargaining over price with each supplier, where if bargaining breaks down the supplier does not produce and the assembler purchases a "generic" part, which could be produced by a U.S. supplier. Note that the equilibrium price exclusive of the rent to the assembler could exceed the price of the generic part.

Spencer and Qiu use their model to show how a number of equilibrium *keiretsu* behaviours could yield a false impression of collusion to restrict U.S. market access. First, under the reasonable assumption that the rents to the assembler generated by relationship specific investments are unobservable outside the *keiretsu*, it could appear that the assembler is sourcing parts from within the *keiretsu* even though prices are higher than those charged by outside suppliers. Second, if relationship-specific investments are more valuable to the assembler for parts with higher cost shares, imports could be restricted to lower value parts.

Third, a reduction in trade barriers or prices charged by U.S. auto parts suppliers could lead to an expansion of Japanese auto production without any corresponding rise in imports by improving the bargaining power of the assembler with *keiretsu* suppliers. Moreover, as shown by Qiu and Spencer (forthcoming), a policy that directly requires an increase in the U.S. content of Japanese autos could paradoxically reduce the value of U.S. auto parts exports to Japan by reducing Japanese auto output due to lost benefits from relationship-specific investment. Suppose for the sake of argument that the model of Spencer and Qiu captures the true state of affairs regarding vertical *keiretsu*.

The question of whether vertical *keiretsu* or similarly organized business groups in other countries act as trade barriers then comes down to whether more efficient foreign suppliers can become members of the network. This is another version of the unanswered empirical question that arose in connection with evaluation of Greif's claim of dynamic inefficiency in the ability of transnational networks to overcome trade barriers. The work surveyed so far, in its focus on whether business groups (specifically, *keiretsu*) are "efficient or exclusionist," has nothing to say about the numbers or sizes of business groups, which could be important features of domestic market structure that influence foreign trade. In a series of papers and a book manuscript, Robert Feenstra, GaryHamilton, and coauthors have explored the implications for international trade of the differences between the size distributions and average "internalization" of Korean versus Taiwanese business groups.

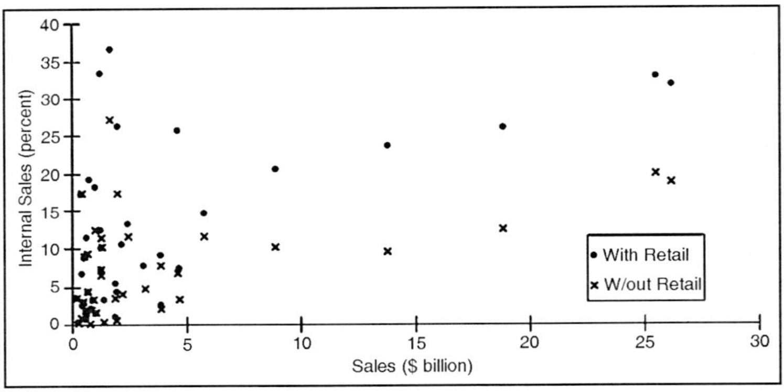

Fig. Korean Business Group.

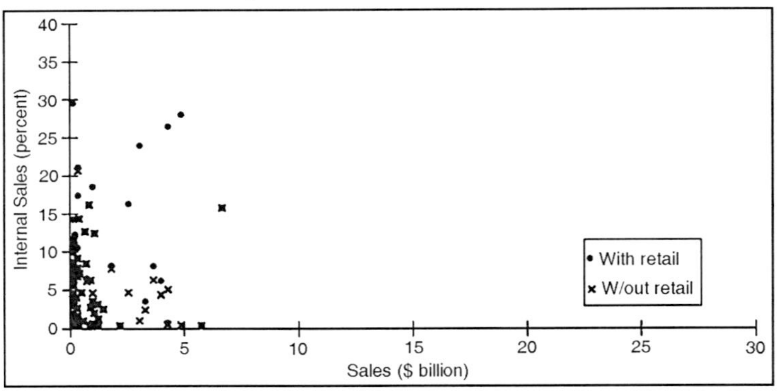

Fig. Tiawanese Business Group.

Figures show the size and internalization of the 44 largest business groups (known as chaebol) in Korea in 1989 and the eighty largest business groups in Taiwan in 1994 for which data on internal transactions are available. The vertical axis measures internalization by the ratio of sales to other firms in each group to total group sales. The points labeled "without retail" exclude the purchases from other firms within the group of group trading companies and all other group firms within the wholesale and retail sector. We see that in Korea there exist five very large business groups, the smallest of which is larger than the largest business group in Taiwan.

The weighted average internal sales ratios, with and without retail, respectively, are 22.1 and 12.2 per cent for the Korean sample versus 9.5 and 4.5 per cent for the Taiwanese sample. With their large size and high internalization the Korean groups are well suited to realization of economies of scale through long production runs of standardized products, whereas Taiwanese groups are better suited to serving niche markets by changing product design to meet the demands of overseas customers. Feenstra, Tzu-Han Yang, and Hamilton thus predict that U.S. imports from Taiwan will display greater within-industry product variety than U.S. imports from Korea.

This prediction is generally confirmed for the periods 1978–82 and 1983–88 in that the U.S. expenditure share within a five digit SIC industry on country varieties that are *not* supplied by *both* countries tends to be greater for Taiwan than Korea, except in a few intermediate goods industries where some of the largest and most internalized Taiwanese business groups are located. Feenstra, Yang, and Hamilton also find for these two periods that within intermediate goods industries the United States tended to import higher-priced varieties from Taiwan than from Korea, whereas the opposite was true within final goods industries. Taking price as a proxy for quality, they interpret these results as supporting the hypothesis of Dani Rodrik that, if reputations for quality tend to spill over to all exporters from a given country, large business groups will be better able to internalize this externality and hence have a greater incentive to produce high-quality goods.

Feenstra, Deng-Shing Huang, and Hamilton and Feenstra, Hamilton, and Huang develop a theoretical model of multiple business groups. They offset the complexity of dealing with many rather than one business group by dispensing with the view of business groups as networks and instead modeling them as hierarchies: each business group is a centrally organized set of firms that maximizes joint profits. The two papers begin with a model in which there is monopolistic competition in supply of both intermediate and final goods. This generates an incentive for business groups (vertically integrated firms) to form and eliminate the markups on intermediate goods in internal group transactions, each group trading off increased collective profits against a fixed "governance cost" for the group as a whole.

For most parameter values the papers find two stable equilibrium: a low concentration equilibrium with a large number of low-internalization groups that sell to outsiders at low markups, and a high-concentration equilibrium with a small number of high-internalization groups that sell to outsiders at high markups. The intuition for the existence of multiple stable equilibrium is as follows. Start in the low-concentration equilibrium and artificially raise markups charged to outsiders for intermediate goods. This creates an incentive for existing groups to expand and incorporate more product varieties, but the market can only support a smaller number of these larger groups, the result being greater concentration that validates the higher markups.

Feenstra and Hamilton (forthcoming) argue that cultural and historical factors pushed Taiwan towards the low-concentration and Korea towards the high-concentration equilibrium. Due to the existence of low markups and greater product variety, consumer welfare is greater in the low-concentration (Taiwan) equilibrium. Whereas the literature surveyed in this section has a lot to say about the efficiency consequences of business groups, it is virtually silent on the question of whether business groups will become more or less important for international trade. Many writers on business groups in a context other than international trade take the functionalist position that they're responses to various "market imperfections," and that these market imperfections will ultimately vanish with economic development, taking business groups along with them.

The fate of business groups is, of course, bound up with the fate of the network form of organization in general, which at one time was widely believed to be a transitional stage on the way to the centrally administered multidivisional firm but now seems to be gaining ground against that hierarchical form. Entering this debate would take us well beyond the scope of this survey. For example, past investments by *keiretsu* suppliers to adapt their products to the specifications of assemblers in the home country could give them an advantage even over equally knowledgeable competing suppliers when the assembler establishes facilities abroad, providing an alternative explanation for the trade-creating effect of such foreign direct investment.

Similarly, the East Asian business groups might be solving problems of weak contract enforcement or lack of information regarding business opportunities in a purely domestic context. Taken as a whole, the international trade literature on business groups also needs to outgrow its exclusive focus on East Asia. Not only does this convey the misleading impression that business groups are not important for international trade elsewhere, but it may lead to biased inferences about the typical impact of business groups on trade. Another important step for this literature is micro-level studies of the openness of business groups to membership by foreign firms or of how business groups engage in importing and exporting. With firm-level empirical studies proliferating in the international trade field, there is less and less excuse for treating business groups as empirical (though not theoretical) black boxes. In particular, a great deal of insight into the questions of whether business groups exclude imports or how they provide variety and quality in exports could be had by studying the trading companies that are at the center of many groups.

NETWORK INTERMEDIARIES

Suppose that a firm looking for foreign buyers or sellers does not belong to an appropriate network. Conventional search is an option, but often a poor one if what the firm is searching for is not sufficiently homogeneous to have an informative price. An alternative is to engage a network intermediary, *i.e.*, an agent who sells access to and use of his network, typically for a commission on the value of the transactions realized. These intermediaries go byte names agent, broker, trader, etc., but not all actors so labeled should be considered network intermediaries.

Network intermediaries are distinguished by what Yung Rhee and Christine Soulier call their "deep knowledge" of the capabilities and preferences of the sellers or buyers in their networks:

- As highlighted in our Hong Kong survey, the most important resource that ETCs (export trading companies) have is their deep knowledge about external markets/buyers and local production capabilities/producers. Without such information, ETCs can hardly be effective in matching potential overseas buyers to local producers... the effectiveness of Japanese, Korean, and Hong Kong GTCs (general trading companies) has been based on the depth of their product-market knowledge and of the supplier-buyer network.

The networks to which these intermediaries sell access may consist of densely interconnected firms, such as business groups, or of firms that do virtually no business with each other, so that if one removed the intermediary they would not constitute a network at all. Descriptions of the activities of the former type of intermediaries suggest that thyrne e crucial to both the ability of small, low-internalization business groups to provide product variety and the ability of large, high internalization business groups to realize economies of scale in the production of standardized goods. Of trading companies for groups of fashion shoe producers in Taiwan, You-tien Hsing writes, "A typical shoe trading company usually had 12–15 partner manufacturers.

To offset limited demand for each order, trading companies coordinated and allocated orders in accordance with the specialty of individual factories." Describing the large, general trading companies at the heart of many *keiretsu*, the *sogo shosha* of Japan, M. Y. Yoshino and Thomas Lifson state, "the *sogo shosha*'s uniqueness lies in its capacity to provide essential links between stages in a product system for a client firm." Studies of network intermediaries that sell access to unconnected firms have mainly concerned buyers who provide less developed country manufacturers with access to sets of developed country retailers. The principal interest of these studies is in how such network intermediaries translate the preferences of retailers into product designs and models and provide other technical assistance to the (low-tech) manufacturers.

The apparent importance of belonging to these transnational business and social networks does not prove that network intermediation is undersupplied, however, because the costs of establishing each of these transnational networks were sunk for purposes other than creating trade: it could be that the costs of setting up new network intermediaries would outweigh the benefits of the additional trade they would create. A crucial input to any evaluation of the case for market failure in provision of network intermediation is knowledge of the determinants of supply: how do actors become network intermediaries?

The literature is virtually silent on this question, but there exist many suggestive anecdotes: a former mergers and acquisitions officer for Chase Manhattan in Hong Kong who now matches leisure-related, California-based businesses with Asian partners; an industrial engineering consultant who had designed factory layouts throughout Asia who now matches U.S. toy designers with Chinese toy manufacturers; a leader of Daewoo's team of machine installation specialists and production line experts assigned to Bangladesh who subsequently opened a firm "engaged exclusively with the import and export trade of Bangladesh's new garment factories".

Such anecdotes, and intuition, suggest that actors become network intermediaries by accumulating "deep knowledge" of buyers and sellers through working with them in a non-intermediary capacity, then selling access to those with whom they formerly worked when this becomes more profitable. At the very least, it seems unlikely that this process will supply intermediaries whose networks span many industries. Realization of business opportunities often requires coordination across several industries, however. An entrepreneur seeking many component s to assemble into a final product for which he has a buyer, for example, could employ many specialized intermediaries, but this is likely to be cumbersome.

More importantly, the components need to be matched not only to the client but to each other, so only diversified intermediary could put together an attractive package. If diversified network intermediaries are not generated as a by-product of non-intermediary activity could an adequate supply result from more planned accumulation of contacts by actors who have already dedicated them to intermediation? There is good reason to believe that this kind of investment will fall short of the socially optimal level, because the intermediary may not be able to garner a large enough share of the surplus he creates for his clients to recover his investment.

The fact that the intermediary needs deep knowledge of the members of his network in order to know which is the best match for his client means that the quality of service he provides his client is inherently noncontractible. In the absence of an enforceable contract based on payment for surplus created the intermediary must rely on his bargaining power, but this is limited because the specificity of each match leaves the intermediary with poor alternative transactions if bargaining breaks down. In addition to this contracting problem, there is a difficulty if one needs to be actually involved in the production process in order to acquire deep knowledge.

It is one thing to leave a career in production to become an intermediary when the opportunity to earn a better living presents itself, and quite another to participate in production with the plan of augmenting the network to which one will sell access as an intermediary, given the risk that by the time one has learned enough, markets or technology will have changed so as to destroy the synergy with one's existing network. The case for undersupply of network intermediation thus appears to be strongest for large diversified intermediaries. Some governments have evidently come to the same conclusion:

Rauch describes how the aforementioned *sogo shosha* and their imitators, the general trading companies (GTCs) of Korea and the foreign trade companies (FTCs) of Turkey, all benefited from implicit or explicit government subsidies during their start-up years, after which they became viable without subsidies. This evidence that government policy can be used, in effect, to promote the formation of transnational networks is intriguing, but failed attempts to establish general trading companies in Taiwan and the United States make it clear that much further theoretical and empirical research is required before reliable policy recommendations can be formulated.

LEARNING IN NETWORKS

Economists have often modeled international technology transfer as an arm's-length phenomenon. Firms are not *taught* the new technology. Rather they engage in purposive imitative activity on their own, employ machinery and equipment that embodies foreign knowledge, license the new technology, and so on.

However, it is difficult to learn new technology through these mechanisms. There is a growing body of evidence that for less developed country(LDC) firms in particular a major and perhaps predominant source of technology transfer (and transfer of managerial know-how) is instruction by developed country buyers: producers seeking cheaper suppliers of inputs and distributors seeking cheaper suppliers of final goods.

Pack and John Page state:

- The motivation of the purchasers is to obtain still lower-cost, better quality products from major suppliers whose products account for a significant per centage of profits. To achieve this they're willing to transmit tacit and occasionally proprietary knowledge from their other OECD suppliers. Such transfers of knowledge are more likely to characterize simpler production sectors such as clothing and footwear or more generally those older technologies that are not hedged by restrictions adopted to increase appro-priability, such as patents and trade secrets.

These buyer– seller relationships are long-term and thus fit our repeated exchange definition of networks. One example of such evidence is a study by Egan and Mody , who surveyed U.S. buyers operating in LDCs, including "manufacturers, retailers, importers, buyers' agents, and joint venture partners".

They found:

- Buyers also render long-term benefits to suppliers in the form of information on production technology. This occurs principally through various forms of in-plant training. The buyer may send international experts to train local workers and supervisors .
- Buyers may also arrange short-term worker training in a developed country plant.

Rhee, Bruce Ross-Larson, and Garry Pursell surveyed Korean exporters of manufactures.

Their findings were similar to those of Egan and Mody:

- The relations between Korean firms and the foreign buyers went far beyond the negotiation and fulfillment of contracts. Almost half the firms said they had directly benefited from the technical information foreign buyers provided: through visits to their plants by engineers or other technical staff of the foreign buyers, through visits by their engineering staff to the foreign buyers . . .

The Rhee, Ross-Larson, and Pursell survey was conducted in 1975. More recently Korea and the other advanced East Asian countries have played the role for LDCs that foreign buyers used to play for them. The role of Korea in developing garment exports from Bangladesh is an especially interesting case that is studied in Rhee. This case is part of the broader phenomenon of "triangle manufacturing" in East Asia: countries such as Korea and Taiwan continue to accept and fulfill the orders of developed country buyers for labour-intensive goods, but have "outsourced" the actual production to countries with lower wages. This process of learning foreign technology can be thought of as taking place within international production networks or "global commodity chains". This theoretical framework predicts that once LDC firms are incorporated into the "bottoms" of the chains, their learning will continue by movement up the chains. There are two types of chains: "producer driven" and "buyer-driven," which are illustrated in figure .

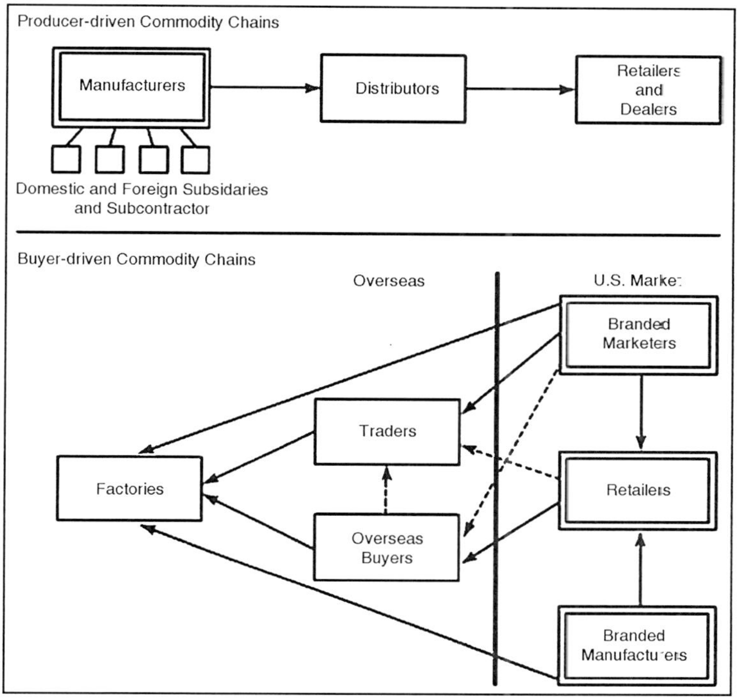

In the former, large manufacturers play the central roles in coordinating the production networks. Producer-driven chains are typical in capital- and technology-intensive industries such as automobiles, aircraft, semiconductors, and heavy machinery . In the latter, large retailers, branded marketers, and branded manufacturers play the coordinating roles. Buyer driven commodity chains are typical in labour-intensive, consumer goods industries such as garments, footwear, toys, house wares, and consumer electronics. Profitability is highest at the tops of the chains where barriers to entry are greatest: scale and technology in producer driven chains, design and marketing expertise in buyer-driven chains. In buyer-driven commodity chains, one mode through which learning is predicted to continue is *organizational succession*: from assembler to original equipment manufacturer (OEM) to original brand-name manufacturer (OBM), which is from more subordinate, competitive, and low-profit positions to more controlling, oligopolistic, high-profit positions.

In the apparel industry, Gereffi finds that LDC firms that have parts provided to them for assembly learn how to find on their own the parts needed to make the product according to the design specified by the buyer (and may then subcontract the assembly); firms that have reached this level learn how to design and sell their own merchandise, becoming branded manufacturers (and may then subcontract the production, becoming branded marketers). Additional study's needed to determine whether this pattern of learning is common in other consumer goods industries, and what kind of learning modes might be present in producer-driven commodity chains.

REVIEW OF MAIN THEMES AND ISSUES FOR FUTURE RESEARCH

Numerous statistical and case studies provide evidence that transnational business and social networks promote international trade by alleviating problems of contract enforcement and providing information about trading opportunities. Some studies established a large quantitative importance for these network effects. Developments in the demand for networks will probably tend to reduce this quantitative importance in the future, while trends in the supply of networks will probably tend to increase it. On the demand side, institutional developments such as international commercial arbitration and letters of credit and technological improvements in communication reduce the need for networks, although this effect is offset by the increased share of differentiated products in international trade.

On the supply side, increased migration and increased foreign direct investment are extending ever more domestic networks across international borders. Perhaps the biggest unknown is the impact of e-commerce on the importance of networks for international trade. Certainly the use of search engines is likely to reduce the demand for networks, but this effect could be limited if, as it is said, the internet disseminates information but not understanding. New technology could interact with networks in surprising ways: for example, e-mail probably retards the decay of established networks. The efficiency implications of transnational networks would appear to be straightforward: they improve the allocation of resources by creating trade, and they generate surplus from cooperation for their members. Closer theoretical examination, however, raises three caveats.

First, less desirable network members may choose to enter the anonymous international market where their characteristics are not known, harming non-members even though the existence of a transnational network still increases world output in the aggregate. Second, a transnational network can have an effect analogous to harmful trade diversion if it links the "wrong" countries. Third, organization of international trade through networks may hinder its growth if transnational networks tend to be closed to new members. This last caveat is an especially important topic for empirical research because the openness of networks is also the key to whether otherwise efficiency-enhancing *domestic* networks *impede* international trade.

As little as we know about the ability of existing transnational (or domestic) networks to incorporate new members, we know even less about how entirely new transnational networks are formed. This survey has discussed how domestic networks, when spread across international boundaries by migration or foreign direct investment, promote trade, and also how trade can help to maintain transnational networks once they're established, but nothing has been said about if and how trade *creates* transnational networks. An important question for future research is whether formation of new business and social networks can help us understand apparent hysteretic effects in bilateral trade, such as those found by Barry Eichengreen and Douglas Irwin.

INTERNATIONAL TRADE POLICY

UNDERSTANDING THE TRADE POLICY

Trade policy is a collection of rules and regulations which pertain to trade. Every nation has some form of trade policy in place, with public officials formulating the policy which they think would be most appropriate for their country. The purpose of trade policy is to help a nation's international trade run more smoothly, by setting clear standards and goals which can be understood by potential trading partners. In many regions, groups of nations work together to create mutually beneficial trade policies. Things like import and export taxes, tariffs, inspection regulations, and quotas can all be part of a nation's trade policy. Some nations attempt to protect their local industries with trade policies which place a heavy burden on importers, allowing domestic producers of goods and services to get ahead in the market with lower prices or more availability.

Others eschew trade barriers, promoting free trade, in which domestic producers are given no special treatment, and international producers are free to bring in their products. Safety is sometimes an issue in trade policy. Different nations have different regulations about product safety, and when goods are imported into a country with stiff standards, representatives of that nation may demand the right to inspect the goods, to confirm that they conform with the product safety standards which have been laid out.

Security is also an issue, with nations wanting to protect themselves from potential threats while maintaining good foreign relations with frequent trading partners. When nations trade with each other regularly, they often establish trade agreements. Trade agreements smooth the way for trading, spelling out the desires of both sides to create a stronger, more effective trading relationship.

Many trade agreements are designed to accommodate a desire for free trade, with signatories to such agreements making certain concessions to each other to establish a good trading relationship. Regular meetings may also be held to discuss changes in the financial climate, and to make adjustments to trade policy accordingly. For lay people, understanding trade policy can get quite complex.

The relevant rules, regulations, agreements, and treaties are often scattered across numerous government documents and departments, from State Departments which handle foreign policy to economic departments which deal with the nuts and bolts of things like converting currency. Often, the best resource for information is documents pertaining to specific trade agreements, such as the North American Free Trade Agreement. These documents spell out the trade policy of the nations involved in one convenient location, although the language used can become very complex.

BALANCE OF TRADE

Trade balance is the difference between a country's imports and exports. When a country's imports surpass its exports over a period of time, it is called a trade deficit. A country's balance of trade is its largest component when it comes to payments. The value of balance of trade is expressed in domestic currency and is denoted by the symbol, 'NX'.

Understanding Trade Balance

Trade balance is a reflection of a country's international market and its domestic consumption. A country's balance of trade comprises a major segment of balance of payments. This is an effective mechanism to quantify a country's overall economic transactions with the rest of the world. It also affects the country's overall GDP for that particular period. What happens when a country's exports exceed the total imports during a given period? Then, the balance of trade is termed as trade surplus or favourable balance of trade.

Composition of Trade Balance

For a given country, trade balance comprises those products that a country trades on with other countries.

Factors that affect trade balance are:

- *Demand and Supply*: The demand and supply trend defines the cost of domestic products to be sold in the international market.
- *Domestic Business*: Sound, domestic policies are required to boost production and international trade. Some countries like the US provide subsidies to local manufacturers for exported goods and services.
- *Trade Agreements*: Bilateral agreements govern international trade and define the products and their prices in the global context.
- *External Pressures*: Many countries export items that face heavy competition in international market. This results in market segmentation and low pricing. Countries that are mostly oil exporters or IT hubs tend to generate favourable trade balance due to less competition in the international market. External pressures also work in the form of trade bans. These bans are enforced by either individual countries or international organizations such as the WTO or IMF.

- *Exchange Rate*: For nations with low exchange rate values, balance of trade tends to remain unfavourable.

Proactive market policies are required to ensure that a country's trade balance remains favourable. A sound trade balance represents an important benchmark as it reflects economic stability between nations. It fortifies trade ties with other countries and generates immense possibilities to stem job losses, inflation and unemployment.

Economic Impact

Conditions where Trade Imbalances may be Problematic

Those who ignore the effects of long run trade deficits may be confusing David Ricardo's principle of comparative advantage with Adam Smith's principle of absolute advantage, specifically ignoring the latter. The economist Paul Craig Roberts notes that the comparative advantage principles developed by David Ricardo do not hold where the factors of production are internationally mobile. Global labour arbitrage, a phenomenon described by economist Stephen S. Roach, where one country exploits the cheap labour of another, would be a case of absolute advantage that is not mutually beneficial. Since the stagflation of the 1970s, the U.S. economy has been characterized by slower GDP growth.

In 1985, the U.S. began its growing trade deficit with China. Over the long run, nations with trade surpluses tend also to have a savings surplus. The U.S. generally has lower savings rates than its trading partners which tend to have trade surpluses. Germany, France, Japan, and Canada have maintained higher savings rates than the U.S. over the long run. Few economists believe that GDP and employment can be dragged down by an over-large deficit over the long run. Others believe that trade deficits are good for the economy. The opportunity cost of a forgone tax base may outweigh perceived gains, especially where artificial currency pegs and manipulations are present to distort trade.

Wealth-producing primary sector jobs in the U.S. such as those in manufacturing and computer software have often been replaced by much lower paying wealth-consuming jobs such those in retail and government in the service sector when the economy recovered from recessions. Some economists contend that the U.S. is borrowing to fund consumption of imports while accumulating unsustainable amounts of debt. In 2006, the primary economic concerns centered around: high national debt, high non-bank corporate debt, high mortgage debt, high financial institution debt, high unfunded Medicare liability, high unfunded Social Security liability, high external debt and a serious deterioration in the United States net international investment position, high trade deficits, and a rise in illegal immigration.

These issues have raised concerns among economists and unfunded liabilities were mentioned as a serious problem facing the United States in the President's 2006 State of the Union address. On June 26, 2009, Jeff Immelt, the CEO of General Electric, called for the U.S. to increase its manufacturing base employment to 20 per cent of the workforce, commenting that the U.S. has outsourced too much in some areas and can no longer rely on the financial sector and consumer spending to drive demand.

Conditions where Trade Imbalances may Not be Problematic

Small trade deficits are generally not considered to be harmful to either the importing or exporting economy. However, when a national trade imbalance expands beyond prudence, adjustments tend to occur. While unsustainable imbalances may persist for long periods, the distortions likely to be caused by large flows of wealth out of one economy and into another tend to become intolerable. In simple terms, trade deficits are paid for out of foreign exchange reserves, and may continue until such reserves are depleted. At such a point, the importer can no longer continue to purchase more than is sold abroad.

This is likely to have exchange rate implications: a sharp loss of value in the deficit economy's exchange rate with the surplus economy's currency will change the relative price of tradable goods, and facilitate a return to balance or an over-shooting into surplus the other direction. More complexly, an economy may be unable to export enough goods to pay for its imports, but is able to find funds elsewhere. Service exports, for example, are more than sufficient to pay for Hong Kong's domestic goods export shortfall. In poorer countries, foreign aid may fill the gap while in rapidly developing economies a capital account surplus often off-sets a current-account deficit. Finally, there are some economies where transfers from nationals working abroad contribute significantly to paying for imports. The Philippines, Bangladesh and Mexico are examples of transfer-rich economies.

Adam Smith on Trade Deficits

"In the foregoing part of this chapter I have endeavoured to show, even upon the principles of the commercial system, how unnecessary it is to lay extraordinary restraints upon the importation of goods from those countries with which the balance of trade is supposed to be disadvantageous. Nothing, however, can be more absurd than this whole doctrine of the balance of trade, upon which, not only these restraints, but almost all the other regulations of commerce are founded. When two places trade with one another, this [absurd] doctrine supposes that, if the balance be even, neither of them either loses or gains; but if it leans in any degree to one side, that one of them loses and the other gains in proportion to its declension from the exact equilibrium."

Milton Friedman on Trade Deficits

In the 1980s, Milton Friedman, the Nobel Prize-winning economist and father of Monetarism, contended that some of the concerns of trade deficits are unfair criticisms in an attempt to push macroeconomic policies favourable to exporting industries. Prof. Friedman argued that trade deficits are not necessarily important as high exports raise the value of the currency, reducing aforementioned exports, and vise versa for imports, thus naturally removing trade deficits not due to investment.

Milton Friedman's son, David D. Friedman, shares this view and cites the comparative advantage concepts of David Ricardo. In the late 1970s and early 1980s, the U.S. had experienced high inflation and Friedman's policy positions tended to defend the stronger dollar at that time. He stated his belief that these trade deficits were not necessarily harmful to the economy at the time since the currency comes back to the country. However, it may be in one form or another including the possible tradeoff of foreign control of assets. In his view, the "worst case scenario" of the currency never returning to the country of origin was actually the best possible outcome: the country actually purchased its goods by exchanging them for pieces of cheaply-made paper.

As Friedman put it, this would be the same result as if the exporting country burned the dollars it earned, never returning it to market circulation. This position is a more refined version of the theorem first discovered by David Hume. Hume argued that England could not permanently gain from exports, because hoarding gold would make gold more plentiful in England; therefore, the prices of English goods would rise, making them less attractive exports and making foreign goods more attractive imports.

In this way, countries' trade balances would balance out. Friedman believed that deficits would be corrected by free markets as floating currency rates rise or fall with time to encourage or discourage imports in favour of the exports, reversing again in favour of imports as the currency gains strength. In the real world, a potential difficulty is that currency markets are far from a free market, with government and central banks being major players, and this is unlikely to change within the foreseeable future.

Nevertheless, recent developments have shown that the global economy is undergoing a fundamental shift. For many years, the U.S. has borrowed and bought while in general, the rest of the world has lent and sold. However, as Friedman predicted, this paradigm appears to be changing. As of October 2007, the U.S. dollar weakened against the euro, British pound, and many other currencies. For instance, the euro hit $1.42 in October 2007, the strongest it has been since its birth in 1999. Against this backdrop, American exporters are finding quite favourable overseas markets for their products and U.S. consumers are responding to their general housing slowdown by slowing their spending.

Furthermore, China, the Middle East, central Europe and Africa are absorbing more of the world's imports which in the end may result in a world economy that is more evenly balanced. All of this could well add up to a major readjustment of the U.S. trade deficit, which as a per centage of GDP, began in 1991. Friedman and other economists have pointed out that a large trade deficit signals that the country's currency is strong and desirable.

To Friedman, a trade deficit simply meant that consumers had opportunity to purchase and enjoy more goods at lower prices; conversely, a trade surplus implied that a country was exporting goods its own citizens did not get to consume or enjoy, while paying high prices for the goods they actually received. Friedman contended that the structure of the balance of payments was misleading. In an interview with Charlie Rose, he stated that "on the books" the US is a net borrower of funds, using those funds to pay for goods and services. He essentially claimed that the foreign assets were not carried on the books at their higher, truer value. Friedman presented his analysis of the balance of trade in Free to Choose, widely considered his most significant popular work.

Frédéric Bastiat on the Fallacy of Trade Deficits

The 19th century economist and philosopher Frédéric Bastiat expressed the idea that trade deficits actually were a manifestation of profit, rather than a loss. He proposed as an example to suppose that he, a Frenchman, exported French wine and imported British coal, turning a profit. He supposed he was in France, and sent a cask of wine which was worth 50 francs to England. The customhouse would record an export of 50 francs. If, in England, the wine sold for 70 francs, which he then used to buy coal, which he imported into France, and was found to be worth 90 francs in France, he would have made a profit of 40 francs. But the customhouse would say that the value of imports exceeded that of exports and was trade deficit against the ledger of France. By reductio ad absurdum, Bastiat argued that the national trade deficit was an indicator of a successful economy, rather than a failing one. Bastiat predicted that a successful, growing economy would result in greater trade deficits, and an unsuccessful, shrinking economy would result in lower trade deficits. This was later, in the 20th century, affirmed by economist Milton Friedman.

Warren Buffett on Trade Deficits

The successful American businessman and investor Warren Buffett was quoted in the Associated Press as saying "The U.S trade deficit is a bigger threat to the domestic economy than either the federal budget deficit or consumer debt and could lead to political turmoil... Right now, the rest of the world owns $3 trillion more of us than we own of them." Buffett has proposed a tool called Import Certificates as a solution to the United States' problem and ensure balanced trade.

John Maynard Keynes on the Balance of Trade

In the last few years of his life, John Maynard Keynes was much preoccupied with the question of balance in international trade. He was the leader of the British delegation to the United Nations Monetary and Financial Conference in 1944 that established the Bretton Woods system of international currency management. He was the principal author of a proposal — the so-called Keynes Plan — for an International Clearing Union. The two governing principles of the plan were that the problem of settling outstanding balances should be solved by 'creating' additional 'international money', and that debtor and creditor should be treated almost alike as disturbers of equilibrium.

In the event, though, the plans were rejected, in part because "American opinion was naturally reluctant to accept the principal of equality of treatment so novel in debtor-creditor relationships". His view, supported by many economists and commentators at the time, was that creditor nations may be just as responsible as debtor nations for disequilibrium in exchanges and that both should be under an obligation to bring trade back into a state of balance. Failure for them to do so could have serious consequences. In the words of Geoffrey Crowther, then editor of The Economist, "If the economic relationships between nations are not, by one means or another, brought fairly close to balance, then there is no set of financial arrangements that can rescue the world from the impoverishing results of chaos."

These ideas were informed by events prior to the Great Depression when — in the opinion of Keynes and others — international lending, primarily by the U.S., exceeded the capacity of sound investment and so got diverted into non-productive and speculative uses, which in turn invited default and a sudden stop to the process of lending. Influenced by Keynes, economics texts in the immediate post-war period put a significant emphasis on balance in trade. For example, the second edition of the popular introductory textbook, An Outline of Money, devoted the last three of its ten chapters to questions of foreign exchange management and in particular the 'problem of balance'.

However, in more recent years, since the end of the Bretton Woods system in 1971, with the increasing influence of Monetarist schools of thought in the 1980s, and particularly in the face of large sustained trade imbalances, these concerns — and particularly concerns about the destabilising effects of large trade surpluses — have largely disappeared from mainstream economics discourse and Keynes' insights have slipped from view. They are receiving some attention again in the wake of the Financial crisis of 2007–2010.

Physical balance of trade

Monetary balance of trade is different from physical balance of trade. Developed countries usually import a lot of primary raw materials from developing countries at low prices. Often, these materials are then converted into finished products, and a significant amount of value is added. Although for instance the EU has a balanced monetary balance of trade, its physical trade balance is negative, meaning that a lot less material is exported than imported. For this reason, activists talk about the issue of ecological debt which implies a sort of predatory economic system. The nature of the trade balance statistics is such that is conceals distorted material flow.

TARIFF

A tariff is a tax placed on imported goods. Each country has separate tariff regulations. The five main types of tariffs include revenue, ad valorem, specific, prohibitive and protective. A revenue tariff increases government funds. For example, countries that do not grow bananas may create a tariff on importing bananas. The government would then make money from businesses that import bananas. An ad valorem tariff means that the tariff applies to a per centage of the import's value such as a set number of cents on every dollar of value. A specific tariff, on the other hand, means that the tariff is not concerned with the estimated value of the imported goods, but rather is based on specific amount of the goods.

A specific tariff may apply to the number of goods imported or to the weight, volume or other measurement of the goods. A prohibitive tariff is one that is such as high cost that it keeps the item from being imported. A protective tariff is used to raise the price of imported goods as a protective measure against the competition from foreign markets. A higher tariff allows a local company to compete with foreign competition. Protective tariffs can be advantageous as they can help foster the local economy, but sometimes they can also make the price of the item so expensive that companies must charge more. For example, when gas prices become too high, industries such as the trucking industry may have to charge retailers more for delivering products.

The retail industry then has to mark up their items to allow for their increased transportation costs in order to make the same profit they once did. The end result is that consumers pay more for the goods. When no tariff or other restrictions are placed on imported goods, it is called free trade. Some people consider free trade to allow increased economic growth potential. Others counter that the removal of tariffs to permit free trade only makes the economy have to depend on global markets rather than increase the stability of domestic markets.

Kinds of Tariff

There are various types of tariffs:

- An ad valorem tariff is a set per centage of the value of the good that is being imported. Sometimes these are problematic, as when the international price of a good falls, so does the tariff, and domestic industries become more vulnerable to competition. Conversely, when the price of a good rises on the international market so does the tariff, but a country is often less interested in protection when the price is high.

They also face the problem of inappropriate transfer pricing where a company declares a value for goods being traded which differs from the market price, aimed at reducing overall taxes due.

- A specific tariff, is a tariff of a specific amount of money that does not vary with the price of the good. These tariffs are vulnerable to changes in the market or inflation unless updated periodically.
- A revenue tariff is a set of rates designed primarily to raise money for the government. A tariff on coffee imports imposed by countries where coffee cannot be grown, for example raises a steady flow of revenue.
- A prohibitive tariff is one so high that nearly no one imports any of that item.
- A protective tariff is intended to artificially inflate prices of imports and protect domestic industries from foreign competition especially from competitors whose host nations allow them to operate under conditions that are illegal in the protected nation, or who subsidize their exports.
- An environmental tariff, similar to a 'protective' tariff, is also known as a 'green' tariff or 'eco-tariff', and is placed on products being imported from, and also being sent to countries with substandard environmental pollution controls.
- A retaliatory tariff is one placed against a country who already charges tariffs against the country charging the retaliatory tariff. These are usually used in an attempt to get other tariffs rescinded.

Tariffs, in the 20th century, are set by a Tariff Commission based on terms of reference obtained from the government or local authority and suo motu studies of industry structure. Tax, tariff and trade rules in modern times are usually set together because of their common impact on industrial policy, investment policy, and agricultural policy. A trade bloc is a group of allied countries agreeing to minimize or eliminate tariffs and other barriers against trade with each other, and possibly to impose protective tariffs on imports from outside the bloc. A customs union has a common external tariff, and, according to an agreed formula, the participating countries share the revenues from tariffs on goods entering the customs union.

If a country's major industries lose to foreign competition, the loss of jobs and tax revenue can severely impair parts of that country's economy and increase poverty. If a nation's standard of living or industrial regulations are too great, it is impossible for domestic industries to survive unprotected trade with inferior nations without compromising them; this compromise consists of a global race to the bottom. Protective tariffs have historically been used as a measure against this possibility. However, protective tariffs have disadvantages as well.

The most notable is that they prevent the price of the good subject to the tariff from undercutting local competition, disadvantaging consumers of that good or manufacturers who use that good to produce something else: for example a tariff on food can increase poverty, while a tariff on steel can make automobile manufacture less competitive. They can also backfire if countries whose trade is disadvantaged by the tariff impose tariffs of their own, resulting in a trade war and, according to free trade theorists, disadvantaging both sides.

CUSTOMS WAR

A Customs war which is also known as a toll war or tariff war is a kind of economical variance flanked by two or extra states. In regulate to anxiety one of the states, the extra raises taxes or tariffs for a number of the products of that state. The latter state may also increase the tariffs. One of the latest toll wars happened in 1920's and 1930's between the Weimar Republic and Poland. The earlier state, led by Gustav Stresemann wanted to force Poland by creating an economic crisis to give up its territory and increased the tolls for coal and steel products developed there. As a reprisal, the Poles increased toll rates for many German products. This led to fast development of the port of Gdynia, which was the only way Poland could export its goods to Western Europe without having to transport them through Germany.

In September 1922 the Fordney-McCumber Tariff was signed by President Warren Harding. In the end, the tariff law raised the average American ad valorem tariff rate to 38 per cent. Trading partners complained immediately. Those injured by World War I said that, without access by their exports to the American market, they would not be able to make payments to America on war loans. But others saw that this tariff increase would have broader deleterious effects. Democratic Representative Cordell Hall said, "Our foreign markets depend both on the efficiency of our production and the tariffs of countries in which we would sell. Our own [high] tariffs are an important factor in each.

They injure the former and invite the latter." Five years after the passage of the tariff, American trading partners had raised their own tariffs by a significant degree. France raised its tariffs on automobiles from 45 per cent to 100 per cent, Spain raised tariffs on American goods by 40 per cent, and Germany and Italy raised tariffs on wheat.. One can argue that the spiral of increasing tariffs was one of the main causes of the Great Depression. To avoid customs wars which are considered harmful to the world's economy, the World Trade Organization was created.

FREE TRADE

Free trade is a system in which goods, capital, and labour flow freely between nations, without barriers which could hinder the trade process. Many nations have free trade agreements, and several international organizations promote free trade between their members. There are a number of arguments both for and against this practice, from a range of economists, politicians, industries, and social scientists. A number of barriers to trade are struck down in a free trade agreement. Taxes, tariffs, and import quotas are all eliminated, as are subsidies, tax breaks, and other forms of support to domestic producers. Restrictions on the flow of currency are also lifted, as are regulations which could be considered a barrier to free trade.

Put simply, free trade enables foreign companies to trade just as efficiently, easily, and effectively as domestic producers The idea behind free trade is that it will lower prices for goods and services by promoting competition. Domestic producers will not longer be able to rely on government subsidies and other forms of assistance, including quotas which essentially force citizens to buy from domestic producers, while foreign companies can make inroads on new markets when barriers to trade are lifted. In addition to reducing prices, free trade is also supposed to encourage innovation, since competition between companies sparks a need to come up with innovative products and solutions to capture market share. Free trade can also foster international cooperation, by encouraging nations to freely exchange goods and citizens.

Agreements between trading partners can also promote educational advantages, such as sending engineers to train with people in the top of the engineering field in one nation, or sending agriculture experts to rural areas to teach people about new farming techniques and food safety practices. Opponents of free trade often argue that it hurts domestic producers by opening up competition to companies which operate in nations with less stringent labour laws. In the European Union, for example, there are specific rules about working hours, fair rates of pay, working conditions, and so forth, which drive up the cost of production for companies which operate in the European Union. By contrast, labour laws in many developing nations like Honduras are much more lax, allowing companies to produce products at low cost, because they have low overhead costs.

Free trade has also raised concerns about product safety among some consumer advocates. A series of scandals in the early 21st century involving tainted food products from China highlighted the issue of purchasing goods from countries with inefficient or incomplete regulatory systems. Other people have suggested that free trade encourages companies to relocate, because when barriers to foreign trade are lifted, domestic companies have no reason not to move operations overseas to take advantage of cheaper labour, inexpensive supplies, and lax regulatory systems.

Skin of free trade

Free trade implies the following features:

- Trade of goods without taxes or other trade barriers.
- Trade in services without taxes or other trade barriers.
- The absence of "trade-distorting" policies that give some firms, households, or factors of production an advantage over others.
- Free access to markets.
- Free access to market information.
- Inability of firms to distort markets through government-imposed monopoly or oligopoly power.
- The free movement of labour between and within countries.
- The free movement of capital between and within countries.

Current status of Free Trade

Most countries in the world are members of the World Trade Organization, which limits in certain ways but does not eliminate tariffs and other trade barriers. Most countries are also members of regional free trade areas which lower trade barriers among participating countries. Most countries prohibit foreign airlines from cabotage and foreign landing rights are generally restricted, but open skies agreements have become more common. Notable contemporary trade barriers include ongoing tariffs, import quotas, sanctions and embargoes, currency manipulation of the Chinese yuan with respect to the U.S. dollar, agricultural subsidies in developed countries, and buy American laws.

Economics of free trade

Economic Models

Two simple ways to understand the potential benefits of free trade are through David Ricardo's theory of comparative advantage and by analyzing the impact of a tariff or import quota. A simple economic analysis using the law of supply and demand and the economic effects of a tax can be used to show the theoretical benefits of free trade.

Trade Diversion

According to mainstream economic theory, global free trade is a net benefit to society, but the selective application of free trade agreements to some countries and tariffs on others can sometimes lead to economic inefficiency through the process of trade diversion. It is economically efficient for a good to be produced by the country which is the lowest cost producer, but this will not always take place if a high cost producer has a free trade agreement while the low cost producer faces a high tariff. Applying free trade to the high cost producer can lead to trade diversion and a net economic loss. This is why many economists place such high importance on negotiations for global tariff reductions, such as the Doha Round.

Opinion of Economists

The literature analysing the economics of free trade is extremely rich with extensive work having been done on the theoretical and empirical effects. Though it creates winners and losers, the broad consensus among members of the economics profession in the U.S. is that free trade is a large and unambiguous net gain for society. In a 2006 survey of American economists, "87.5 per cent agree that the U.S. should eliminate remaining tariffs and other barriers to trade" and "90.1 per cent disagree with the suggestion that the U.S. should restrict employers from outsourcing work to foreign countries." Quoting Harvard economics professor N. Gregory Mankiw, "Few propositions command as much consensus among professional economists as that open world trade increases economic growth and raises living standards."

Nonetheless, quoting Prof. Peter Soderbaum of Malardalen University, Sweden, "This neo-classical trade theory focuses on one dimension, *i.e.*, the price at which a commodity can be delivered and is extremely narrow in cutting off a large number of other considerations about impacts on employment in different parts of the world, about environmental impacts and on culture." Most free traders would agree that there are winners and losers from free trade, but argue that this is not a reason to argue against free trade, because free trade is supposed to bring overall gain due to idea that the winners have gained enough to make up for the losses of the losers and then some.

Chang argues otherwise, saying that the economy could shrink as a result, and that some people being worse off due to trade displacement without recourse to welfare assistance to find a better job is not acceptable. In an assessment of the literature on the theory and empirical research relating to the benefits of free trade, Sonali Deraniyagala and Ben Fine found that much of the work was flawed, and concluded that the extent to which free trade benefits economic development is unknown. Theoretical arguments are largely dependent upon specific empirical assumptions which may or may not hold true. In the empirical literature, many studies suggest the relationship is ambiguous, and the data and econometrics underlying a set of empirical papers showing positive results have been critiqued.

The best of these papers use a simplified model, and the worst involve the regression of an index of economic performance on an index of openness to trade, with a mix of these two approaches common. In some cases, Deraniyagala and Fine claim, these indexes of openness actually reflect trade volume rather than policy orientation. They also observe that it is difficult to disentangle the effects of reverse causality and numerous exogenous variables. In Kicking Away the Ladder, Ha-Joon Chang reviews the history of free trade policies and economic growth, and notes that many of the now-industrialized countries had significant barriers to trade throughout their history.

Protectionism under the auspices of the infant industry argument was first pursued by Alexander Hamilton in the 1790s in opposition to the admonition of Adam Smith, who advised that the United States focus on agriculture, where it had a comparative advantage. In the 1840s Friedrich List, known as the father of the infant industry argument,: advocated the infant industry argument for Germany. Chang's research shows that the United States and Britain, sometimes considered to be the homes of free trade policy, were aggressive protectionists. Britain did end its protectionism when it achieved technological superiority in the late 1850s with the repeal of the Corn Laws, but tariffs on manufactured products had returned to 23 per cent by 1950.

The United States maintained weighted average tariffs on manufactured products of approximately 40-50 per cent up until the 1950s, augmented by the natural protectionism of high transportation costs in the 19th century.: The most consistent practitioners of free trade have been Switzerland, the Netherlands, and to a lesser degree Belgium.: Chang describes the export-oriented industrialization policies of the Asian Tigers as "far more sophisticated and fine-tuned than their historical equivalents".

Opposition

The relative costs, benefits and beneficiaries of free trade are debated by academics, governments and interest groups. A number of arguments for and against in the ongoing public debate can be seen in the free trade debate article. Arguments for protectionism fall into the economic category or the moral category; a general argument against free trade is that it is colonialism or imperialism in disguise. The moral category is wide, including concerns of income inequality, environmental degradation, supporting child labour and sweatshops, race to the bottom, wage slavery, accentuating poverty in poor countries, harming national defence, and forcing cultural change. Free trade is often opposed by domestic industries that would have their profits and market share reduced by lower prices for imported goods.

For example, if United States tariffs on imported sugar were reduced, U.S. sugar producers would receive lower prices and profits, while U.S. sugar consumers would spend less for the same amount of sugar because of those same lower prices. The economic theory of David Ricardo holds that consumers would necessarily gain more than producers would lose. Since each of those few domestic sugar producers would lose a lot while each of a great number of consumers would gain only a little, domestic producers are more likely to mobilize against the lifting of tariffs. More generally, producers often favour domestic subsidies and tariffs on imports in their home countries, while objecting to subsidies and tariffs in their export markets. Socialists frequently oppose free trade on the ground that it allows maximum exploitation of workers by capital.

For example, Karl Marx wrote in The Communist Manifesto, "The bourgeoisie... has set up that single, unconscionable freedom — Free Trade. In one word, for exploitation, veiled by religious and political illusions, it has substituted naked, shameless, direct, brutal exploitation." Nonetheless, Marx favoured free trade solely because he felt that it would hasten the social revolution. To those who oppose socialism, this becomes an argument against free trade. "Free trade" is opposed by many anti-globalization groups, based on their assertion that free trade agreements generally do not increase the economic freedom of the poor or the working class, and frequently make them poorer.

Where the foreign supplier allows de facto exploitation of labour, domestic free-labour is unfairly forced to compete with the foreign exploited labour, and thus the domestic "working class would gradually be forced down to the level of helotry." To this extent, free trade is seen as nothing more than an end-run around laws that protect individual liberty, such as the Thirteenth Amendment to the United States Constitution. In this regard, protective trade policies are seen, not so much as protecting domestic producers, but rather, as protecting liberty itself. This argument actually comports with the economic analysis of Free Trade to the extent that "slavery and perfect competition equilibria are Pareto optimal."

Thus, while admitting that some gain in efficiency might be realized in the short-term by implementation of free trade policies, the long-term question of the cost of that efficiency in terms of loss of liberty remains. It is important to distinguish between arguments against free trade theory, and free trade agreements as applied. Some opponents of NAFTA see the agreement as being materially harmful to the common people, but some of the arguments are actually against the particulars of government-managed trade, rather than against free trade *per se*.

For example, it is argued that it would be wrong to let subsidized corn from the U.S. into Mexico freely under NAFTA at prices well below production cost because of its ruinous effects to Mexican farmers. Of course, such subsidies violate free trade theory, so this argument is not actually against the principle of free trade, but rather its selective implementation. Latin America performed poorly since tariff cuts in 1980s and 1990s, compared to protectionist China and Southeast Asia. According to Samuelson, it is wrong to assume a necessary surplus of winnings over losings. The paper, "Will inventions A or B lower or raise the new market-clearing real wage rates that sustain high-to-full employment" condemned "economists' over-simple complacency about globalization" and said that workers don't always win. Some economists try to emphasize that trade barriers should exist to help poor nations build domestic industries and give rich nations time to retrain workers.

Colonialism

It has long been argued that free trade is a form of colonialism or imperialism, a position taken by various proponents of economic nationalism and the school of mercantilism. In the 19th century these criticized British calls for free trade as cover for British Empire, notably in the works of American Henry Clay, architect of the American System and by German American economist Friedrich List. More recently, Ecuadorian President Rafael Correa has denounced the "sophistry of free trade" in an introduction he wrote for a book titled The Hidden Face of Free Trade Accords, written in part by Correa's current Energy Minister Alberto Acosta. Citing as his source the book Kicking Away the Ladder, written by Ha-Joon Chang, Correa identified the difference between an "American system" opposed to a "British System" of free trade. The latter, he says, was explicitly viewed by the Americans as "part of the British imperialist system." According to Correa, Chang showed that it was Treasury Secretary Alexander Hamilton, and not Friedrich List, who was the first to present a systematic argument defending industrial protectionism.

TRADE PACT

A trade pact is a wide ranging tax, tariff and trade pact that often includes investment guarantees. The most common trade pacts are of the preferential and free trade types are concluded in order to reduce tariffs, quotas and other trade restrictions on items traded between the signatories.

Definition of Trade Pact

An agreement between countries that seeks to increase the level of free trade. This is done by creating special tax, tariff and trade regulations that can reduce barriers. A trade pact can also come with a guarantee of an investment in one country by another, such as foreign direct investment. It is a form of economic integration.

Classification of trade pacts

By Number and Type of Signatories

A trade agreement is classified as bilateral when signed between two sides, where each side could be a country, a trade bloc or an informal group of countries. A trade agreement signed between more than two sides is classified as multilateral.

By Sophistication

There are a variety of trade agreements; with some being quite complex, while others are less intensive.

The resulting level of economic integration depends on the specific type of trade pacts and policies adopted by the trade bloc:

- Separate
  - Trade and Investment Framework Agreement
  - Bilateral Investment Treaty
  - *Preferential Trade Arrangement:* Limited scope and depth of tariffs reduction between the customs territories.
    i. *Free Trade Agreement Establishing a Free Trade Area:* Extensive reduction or elimination of tariffs on substantially all trade allowing for the free movement of goods and in more advanced agreements also reduction of restrictions on investment and establishment allowing for the free movement of capital and free movement of services
    ii. *Common Market:* FTA with significantly reduced or eliminated restrictions on the freedom of movement of all factors of production, including free movement of labour and of enterprise; and coordination in economic policy
  - Currency union - sharing the same currency
- Composite
  - *Customs Union:* FTA with common external tariffs of all signatories in respect to non-signatory countries
    i. *Customs and Monetary Union:* Customs union with Currency union
    ii. *Economic Union:* Customs union with Common market
    iii. *Economic and Monetary Union:* Economic union with Currency Union
    iv. *Fiscal Union:* Common coordination of substantial parts of the fiscal policies

Special Agreements

- World Trade Organization treaty
  - Agreements in the WTO framework
- The now defunct Multilateral Agreement on Investment

By the World Trade Organization

Typically the benefits and obligations of the trade agreements apply only to their signatories. In the framework of the World Trade Organization a different agreement types are concluded, whose terms apply to all WTO members on the so-called most-favoured basis, which means that benefitial terms agreed bilaterally with one trading partner will apply also to the rest of the WTO members. All agreements concluded outside of the WTO framework are called preferential by the WTO. According to WTO rules these agreements are subject to certain requirements such as notification to the WTO and general reciprocity where unilateral preferences are allowed only under exceptional circumstances and as temporary measure.

The trade agreements called preferential by the WTO are also known as regional, despite not necessarily concluded by countries within a certain region. There are currently 205 agreements in force as of July 2007. Over 300 have been reported to the WTO. The number of FTA has increased significantly over the last decade. Between 1948 to 1994, the General Agreement on Tariffs and Trade, the predecessor to the WTO, received 124 notifications. Since 1995 over 300 trade agreements have been enacted.

The WTO is further classifying these agreements in the following types:

- Goods covering:
  - Basic preferential trade agreement
  - Free trade agreement
  - Customs union
- Services covering:
  - Economic Integration Agreement - any agreement, including a PTA, that covers services

Reaction

Trade pacts are frequently politically contentious since they may change economic customs and deepen interdependence with trade partners. Increasing efficiency through "free trade" is a common goal. For the most part, governments are supportive of further trade agreements. There have been however some concerns expressed by the WTO. According to Pascal Lamy, Director-General of the WTO, the proliferation of RTA "...is breeding concern — concern about incoherence, confusion, exponential increase of costs for business, unpredictability and even unfairness in trade relations." The position of the WTO is that while the typical trade agreements are useful to a degree, it is much more beneficial to focus on global agreements in the WTO framework such as the negotiations of the current Doha round. The anti-globalization movement opposes such agreements almost by definition, but some groups normally allied within that movement, *e.g.* green parties, seek fair trade or safe trade provisions that moderate what they perceive to be the ill effects of globalization.

10

Relation of Finance to Distribution Channels and International Marketing

In order to create values through the performance of marketing activities, various costs must be incurred and all of them must be financed. The functions of exchange and physical supply, as well as other facilitating functions, are possible only through adequate financing with suitable types or kinds of capital or credit facilities. The nature and problems of the types of financing that are necessary for the successful performance of marketing functions in channels of trade, as well as those that are used to facilitate the process of ultimate consumption.

RELATION OF FINANCE TO DISTRIBUTION CHANNELS

The financial strength of a vendor has a decided influence upon his channels of distribution. Some canners of fruit and vegetables dispose of their entire output through selling agents to whom they are financially obligated. A similar reason is often advanced for the employment of selling agents in the textile trades although another marketing specialist, the factor, is often used for purely financial assistance.

Whether or not a firm shall embark upon a method of distribution involving the elimination of the wholesaler or even the retailer may hinge largely or entirely upon the extent of its financial resources. Few manufacturers, indeed, can muster the capital required for establishing their own retail stores. Many of them cannot even afford to establish a sales organization to sell directly to retailers, or to maintain the warehouses necessary to furnish prompt delivery. This is one of the important reasons for the utilization of the wholesaler in the channel of distribution. One reason for the employment of manufacturers' agents is the inability of sellers to finance their own sales force.

This problem may be viewed, with results not dissimilar, from the standpoint of the buyer. Relatively few retailers can afford to purchase their merchandise requirements directly from manufacturers. Most independent druggists and hardware merchants use wholesalers not only as a source of supply for merchandise but also as a source of capital for financing inventories through trade credit.

FINANCE AND MARKETING POLICY

Market finance also exercises a profound influence on the adoption of certain marketing policies. Obviously, no marketing institution can operate on a credit basis, whether it be retailer, manufacturer, or wholesale middleman, without adequate financial resources. As certain leading general merchandise chains diversified their lines in the late 1950's, by adding durable goods and higher unit value fashion merchandise, they found it necessary to depart from a traditional cash-and-carry policy and to offer the type of credit services which consumers expect in connection with the purchases of such items.

This, of course, involved substantial new financial requirements. The adoption of brands, manufacturers' or private, is largely dependent upon the concern's financial ability to advertise them effectively and to organize and maintain the proper sales machinery. In selling goods on consignment, financial strength is the most important prerequisite. Other policies, including the rendering of certain services, are equally dependent, in varying degrees, upon the company's financial ability to justify their adoption.

CAPITAL NEEDS IN MARKETING

To carry on the necessary marketing activities, an enterprise needs at least two major types of funds, one for permanent investment and the other for temporary or short-term financial requirements.

Permanent Capital

Permanent or long-term capital must be supplied for the purchase and acquisition of fixed assets such as land, buildings, delivery equipment, furniture and fixtures, warehousing equipment, and other assets of a more or less permanent nature. A sufficient amount must also be provided in this manner for normal working capital. This may be termed permanent working capital; it constitutes that portion of the funds of a business enterprise which is required from week to week and from month to month. It is the sum needed to carry normal or at least minimum inventories of merchandise and supplies, to provide for the carrying of a normal or minimum investment in accounts and notes receivable, and to insure that there will be adequate funds on hand to meet payrolls and provide for other operating expense disbursements such as advertising, rental payments, insurance premiums, etc.

The funds required for long-term investment purposes may be secured through investment by the parties engaged in the marketing operations or through long-term borrowing. Unincorporated enterprises, including the sole proprietorships and the partnerships, make provision for at least a major portion of the long-term capital investment out of their own personal funds. Corporations, on the other hand, raise equity capital by the sale of stock. Both corporations and unincorporated enterprises resort to the use of investment credit, namely, they secure loans for purely investment purposes through the issue of relatively long-term obligations. These obligations take the form of bonds, real estate mortgages, chattel mortgages, and long-term promissory notes. These are all promises to pay definite sums of principal either in a lump amount of at certain intervals.

While it is *desirable* for a firm to obtain all of its permanent capital requirements from equity or long-term sources, this is a *practical* impossibility for most of them, especially small business enterprises. Consequently, it is rather common to provide for a substantial portion of the permanent capital needed for inventories, accounts receivable, and other assets through reliance upon financial institutions or trade creditors.

Temporary Financial Requirements

Every merchandising enterprise requires temporary additions to its long-term needs and for a variety of circumstances. One of the most important is *seasonal fluctuations* in marketing activity. Purchases of goods for resale are seldom distributed evenly throughout the year, nor do seasons of heavy buying necessarily coincide with those of peak sales. Seasonal conditions of form-utility production or of consumption require large advance expenditures for stock. Wholesale grocers, for example, often purchase a full year's supply of canned goods during the canning season. Retailers of ready-to-wear apparel must concentrate stocks of all fall merchandise in the summer in order to show it in advance of the peak autumn selling season. Pronounced seasonal peaks in sales volume place a heavy financial burden upon merchandising firms, since they are followed by proportionately heavy increases in accounts receivable. The seasonal aspect in marketing is sometimes accentuated as a result of unusually slow transitions. When a season is "slow," goods do not sell in quantity until late, thereby tying up some capital in excessive premature inventories. There is also much "frozen credit," because under these conditions purchasers fail to pay their bills promptly, and it is exceedingly difficult to realise on many receivables outstanding.

All marketing organizations are affected by *cyclical fluctuations* business conditions. Periods of prosperity or recession may be characterized, respectively, by upward or downward price movements. Purchases are always heavier in anticipation of rising prices and correspondingly light when prices take a downward trend. Similarly, buyers hold off the market during periods of price uncertainty. Even when prices are stable and remain at a given level for any length of time, the needs for current financing will vary with the condition of the times.

There are other situations that may require varying amounts of temporary capital. Exceptionally favorable opportunities to purchase goods in larger than usual quantities may present themselves, or it may become advisable to take advantage of cash discounts by paying merchandise creditors before the bills become due.

SOURCES OF CURRENT MARKETING CAPITAL

Most of the temporary capital requirements and varying proportions of the long-term capital needed for investment in current assets are obtained by business firms through the use of relatively short-term credit. This credit may be obtained from commercial banks, other specialized financial agencies, or trade credit sources.

Commercial Banks

Commercial bank credit may be defined as the power that enables commercial banking institutions to attract funds of depositors, to create obligations through the issue of paper money, and to make loans.

Uses

One of the purposes of bank credit is to make loans to individuals or firms for relatively short periods of time. Sellers borrow from banks in order to help them carry their accounts and notes receivable, while purchasers of merchandise resort to bank loans as a means of securing funds for the payment of bills upon the insistence of creditors or for the purpose of taking advantage of cash discounts. Such loans may be unsecured when the basis for granting them is the general credit standing of the borrower, or they may be secured by assignment of accounts receivable, warehouse receipts, or other collateral. Another use of bank credit is financing purchases of machinery and equipment through instalment loans to business. Such loans are usually secured by a chattel mortgage and are amortized by regular instalment payments, ordinarily over a period of 24 to 36 months or, in the case of very expensive machinery or equipment with a long life expectancy, over periods ranging up to 60 monthly payments.

Limitations

An important limitation that often prevents businessmen from relying heavily upon bank credit is the length of the credit period. Except for the instalment loans just noted, this usually varies from 30 to 90 days. The 90-day limitation is rather common because only those notes that mature within such time can be rediscounted by member banks at the Federal Reserve Banks.

This limitation applies to all types of commercial paper arising out of the domestic production or trade in manufactured goods. Notes based upon loans for agricultural purposes or those that arise out of foreign trade transactions may be rediscounted through the Federal Reserve banking system even if for longer periods of time. An even more significant reason for the short term of bank credit lies in the reason for its existence.

A commercial bank has the function of helping businesses to carry the peak of the load at the time they are paying for their purchases and waiting for remittance from their own customers. It does not aim to supply permanent working capital, although it is not uncommon for banks to extend loans to acceptable risks for periods much longer than 90 days, usually by the process of renewal. Since banks, however, desire their customers to clear their accounts at certain intervals, most businesses cannot place too much reliance upon this source for permanent working capital.

Factors

Among the oldest of the special types of financial institutions used in connection with the marketing process are factors. They have given continuous financial support to the textile industry and apparel trades for over a century and a half and have, in recent decades, spread their services to such other lines of trade as paper, glassware, shoes, petroleum, cosmetics, chemicals, furniture, and furs.

Services

The principal service of the factor is that of financing accounts receivable. After sales are made, the factor functions by buying or discounting sales invoices. A seller, in this manner, obtains immediate cash for current operations and does not suffer from delay in receipt of payment for goods. Factors usually make outright purchases of accounts receivables (i.e., purchase without recourse) and thus assume all collection risks and responsibilities.

Clients of the factor usually notify their customers that the account has been "factored" and instruct them to make payment to the factoring company. This is normally done by stamping payment instructions on the customer's invoice. In some cases, factoring is handled on a nonnotification basis. This variation is for the benefit of clients who do not want their customers to know that the account has been sold to a factor. In this case, the client's customers pay their accounts to him, and he in turn forwards such payments to the factor immediately upon receipt.

For this type of financing service, the factor receives income in two ways. The first is an interest charge based on all advances, usually at the rate of 6 per cent per annum. The second part is a charge or commission that is made for the services of advising clients on the selection of risks and for collecting the accounts when they become due. This service charge, as distinct from the interest rate charged for the use of money, varies from a fraction of 1 per cent to 3 per cent of the face amount of the invoice. Because the money invested in receivables is usually turned over several times a year, the effective rate implicit in the service charge often runs into a considerable percentage figure.

For example, if a 2 per cent service charge is made upon an advance that matures within 60 days, the effective annual rate is 12 per cent since there are six 60-day periods in a year. When this rate is added to the first part of the factor's compensation, say an interest rate of 6 per cent per annum, the factor may be able to earn a gross return of approximately 18 per cent upon the capital used in his business. The rates for the service charge are not highly standardized, however, but are a matter of individual negotiation based upon the type of customers, whether the factor assumes the risk of noncollection, amounts of money advances, length of the credit period, and the number and kind of other services rendered.

Conditions Relating to Use

The factor's financial service is often regarded by his clients as superior to that of the commercial bank, for he advances a larger percentage of the value of the accounts receivable from customers, assumes the risk of credit losses, and takes over much of the routine bookkeeping work associated with a credit department. Wide knowledge of particular lines of business makes it possible for him to do this, also to serve as a valuable and skilled adviser to his clients. Furthermore, his risks are widely distributed, thereby warranting him to assume hazards that might spell ruin to a single manufacturer with only a few customers, each of which required large amounts of goods on credit. In addition, the credit department of the factor prevents frauds and impositions by buyers, who fear to impair their credit standing with this specialized type of banker known to control the credits of a number of possible sources of supply.

Sellers of goods must meet certain qualifications, however, before the factor can be called upon for financial assistance. The client must have a generally good reputation for reliable merchandise, prompt shipment, and a good class of customers. The client's customers must be well established and not seriously affected by changes in business conditions.

Open Accounts Receivable Financing

Factoring, as described above, is to be distinguished from open accounts receivable financing as carried on by banks and other financial institutions. In open account financing, accounts are assigned without notification and with recourse, so that the seller retains responsibility for credit-granting, collection, and the risk of credit losses. Another form of such financing consists of promissory notes which are secured by accounts pledged as collateral.

Sales Finance Companies

Sales finance companies such as the General Motors Acceptance Corporation, the Universal CIT Credit Corporation, the Commercial Credit Company, and hundreds of other smaller and less well-known similar organizations are important principally for their activities in financing instalment purchases of automobiles and other durable goods by ultimate consumers. In this connection, their services are discussed in a following major section which deals with consumer credit.

Many of the sales finance companies also engage in business financing. Some of them acquire open accounts receivable, in a manner similar to factors. Another service consists of instalment lien obligations in connection with the purchase, by merchants and manufacturers, of items of machinery, fixtures, or equipment that are used in the conduct of business.

One of the principal business financing services of sales finance companies is what is generally known as floor planning. This is a method of financing inventories of automobiles and other types of high unit value durable goods, especially major household appliances and certain types of industrial equipment sold through distributors. The practice may be illustrated with reference to the automobile industry. Automobile manufacturers normally expect cash payment upon delivery of cars to the dealer. Few dealers have the capital necessary to stock a large assortment of automobiles.

The commercial bank's standards of credit and maturity length of loans have been too strict to be of great value to the average dealer, who has therefore turned to the sales finance company for aid in carrying adequate inventories. Under the floor plan method, the dealer acquires new cars, stores or displays them, and executes a trust receipt for the benefit of the finance company. In this manner, the dealer has physical possession of the merchandise and can display and attempt to sell it, but he does not have legal title to it. Title to the automobiles is vested in the finance company, the dealer merely holding the goods in trust. In some companies, chattel mortgages are used to secure the loans upon cars in storage rather than a trust receipt.

When a sale is made, the proceeds must be immediately turned over to the finance company before the car can be moved from the dealer's premises. In many instances, this is largely in the nature of a bookkeeping transaction rather than a transfer of cash funds, for the same sales finance company often finances the major part of the ultimate consumer's purchase price. The amount loaned to dealers under the floor plan method usually does not exceed 90 per cent of the cost of the article from the manufacturer.

Financing Through Warehouse Receipts

Every public warehouse issues to depositors receipts for goods placed in storage, and these warehouse receipts are used as a basis for securing advances on the stored goods from commercial banks and, to some extent, also from finance companies. The owner may receive a *negotiable* warehouse receipt executed in his name and which he may endorse to the order of his bank or other lending institution, or he may obtain a *nonnegotiable* receipt issued originally in the name of the lender. Either type of receipt is regarded as sound collateral. Loans amounting to 60 or 70 per cent of the market value of the merchandise are often made on the basis of such security. Until the loan is repaid, the borrower cannot regain possession of the merchandise. If the loan is defaulted, the bank can claim the merchandise and have it sold to satisfy the obligation. When the borrower wishes to make a partial withdrawal of the merchandise which is so pledged, arrangements can easily be made to repay part of the loan or to pledge additional security of an equally satisfactory character.

Field Warehousing

A natural development of the principle of using warehouse receipts as a basis for outside financing is field warehousing. The idea is simply that warehouse receipts normally issued on goods stored in a public warehouse shall be made available for financing the storage of merchandise on the premises of the manufacturer or whoever owns the goods. The warehouse is in effect moved to the owner's plant or warehouse. The owner of the goods actually leases a portion of his storage facilities to a licensed warehouseman who places a representative in charge, posts signs stating that a designated portion of the warehouse is in charge of the outside organization, and adds to or takes from stock as directed by the banker who has the stock as collateral.

The field warehouse representative may actually be a regular employee of the owner of the pledged inventory, but must be covered by a fidelity bond commensurate with the degree of financial responsibility involved. Under this arrangement, such a representative can continue with the performance of his normal responsibilities, so that there is very small personnel expense connected with the warehousing. Field warehousing is thus, in reality, more of a credit arrangement than a strictly storage operation. Experience has shown that collateral so warehoused is just as secure as when it is placed in a public warehouse.

Typical illustrations of the plan in use are manifold. A paint manufacturer found himself with an overstock. Three options existed. He could cut the price, take a large loss, and perhaps move it into the market. He could deposit the merchandise in a public warehouse and borrow on it, but that was too expensive. The third plan, that of assigning a part of the stock to a field warehouseman, was adopted with success and economy. Manufacturers of tin cans store them in canners' warehouses until they are needed by the canner, when he makes the required payment before they are released by the manufacturer.

He thus reduces the time for his loans to a few days, for as soon as they are filled they become the basis of another loan, as they can be at once turned over to the same field warehouseman who had them while they were empty. A steel pipe manufacturer has used the plan for carrying reserve stocks in three widely scattered cities. Farm implement manufacturers find it equally useful in connection with the accumulation of inventory for seasonal selling peaks. In fact, any manufacturer or middleman with substantial stocks of standardized goods which are in ready demand can use the plan for addtional financing.

The advantages of field warehousing are several. First, it is economical, since it is unnecessary to move the stock to a public warehouse for deposit. Liquids can be left in their natural containers, cans of food need not be cased or labeled until their buyer is determined and is ready to pay for them, and in some cases goods to be further processed can be left adjacent to their next step of production, thus eliminating the two-way trip to a public warehouse. Second, banks are ready to quote a lower rate of interest on loans so secured than on loans based on an open line of credit, for the notes can be rediscounted with a reserve bank. Third, if the manufacturer cannot be supplied with funds locally, paper secured by field warehouse receipts can be more readily sold in a nation-wide commercial paper market.

The principal limitation is the cost of arranging for field warehousing services. Service fees must be charged to cover the cost of segregating the warehouse area involved, providing locks and signs, bonding a warehouse representative, and making periodic audits of goods held in storage. Such charges are relatively small when inventories of large value are involved but are prohibitive in connection with very small-scale financing. The minimum loan which is considered economically practical for a field warehousing company to handle is about $10,000.

Mercantile Credit

Mercantile credit is the credit one businessman extends to another when selling goods on time for resale or for commercial use. It includes all postponements of payment involved in the purchase of goods throughout the process of distribution, from the time they are in the state of raw materials until they reach the hands of the retailer or business user. Its purpose is to facilitate the marketing of goods through channels of trade.

Terms of Sale

The terms of sale in mercantile credit commonly comprise two distinct elements—the net credit period and the cash discount. The length of time for which credit is extended is called the *net credit period.* Wholesalers and manufacturers adjust their credit periods to different lines of business, but great differences are sometimes observed in the same line and even within individual establishments when granting credit to different customers. In general, the length of the credit period tends to conform roughly to the receipt of income, on the part of buyers, from the sale of goods and services. The rate of turnover of the purchaser's stock of goods is the most fundamental and determining factor as to the amount of time involved. In the wholesale tobacco trade, where the typical customer's rate of stock turnover is very high, wholesalers' terms to retailers are usually 7 to 10 days, but in the jewelry trade, where retail stock turnover is ordinarily very slow, terms ranging from 60 to 120 days, or even longer, are usual.

While the rate of stock turnover is the fundamental consideration, other factors modify this relationship and sometimes obscure it completely. Longer periods are common when customers are located at a considerable distance from the seller, and when goods must be in transit for extended periods. In some instances, the credit period offered to particular buyers is governed by the length of the credit period granted by preceding sellers. If customers of the purchaser receive income seasonably, as in farming areas, the retailers' credit requirements are magnified and longer periods are common. *Cash discounts* are generally granted in the mercantile field whenever goods are sold on credit, as a means of stimulating advance payment of bills.

Cash discounts are premiums for advance payment, at a rate which is considerably higher than the prevailing rate of interest, because of advantages that accrue to the seller from such a procedure. An illustration of this may be afforded by the following terms which are more or less common in certain lines of trade. Assume that a bill of goods is purchased on terms of 2/10, net 30 days. This means that if the purchaser pays for the goods within 10 days from date of the shipment or date of the invoice (which are usually synonymous), he will receive a 2 per cent discount to be deducted from the amount billed on the invoice. If, on the other hand, he waits the full 30 days and pays his bill at expiration of the net credit period, he must pay the full amount of the bill. Thus, by deferring payment for 20 days beyond the 10-day period, the purchaser sacrifices 2 per cent of the full amount involved. Receiving a 2 per cent discount for a period of 20 days is the equivalent of earning interest on the amount involved in the transaction at the rate of 36 per cent per annum. This is true because the discount is paid for a period of time which is approximately one-eighteenth of a year.

The seller justifies this discount policy on the ground that it gives him quicker possession of the money, which can be turned over again, and also reduces the credit and moral risks. Immediate possession of the money from the sale of goods tends to increase the rate of working capital turnover, furnishes adequate funds to operate the business, obviates the necessity for elaborate credit and collection machinery, reduces losses from bad debts, and tends to promote a spirit of good will between seller and customer through the elimination of some occasions for friction.

While the cash discount is generally regarded as a premium for payment in advance of due date, it is very often difficult to distinguish it from trade discounts or deductions from list prices quoted to the trade.

The same procedure may be used in order to ascertain the effective rate of interest involved in any cash discount, provided the length of the credit period is known. This may be generalized as follows:

- Subtract the number of days in the cash discount period from the number of days in the credit period. The result is the length of the period for which the discount is granted.
- Divide 360 days (the number of days assumed to represent an interest year) by the answer to 1, above. This shows the number of comparable periods in a year.
- Multiply the answer to 2, above, by the cash discount percentage.

The result is the effective annual rate of interest. This procedure may be illustrated with respect to terms of 3/10, net 60:

- 60 (credit period) minus 10 (cash discount period) equals 50 days.
- 360 divided by 50 equals 7.2 such periods per year.
- 7.2X3percent equals an effective annual rate of interest of 21.6 per cent.

Large so-called cash discounts are offered, they are expected to be generally taken. Consequently, the seller prices his merchandise accordingly, so that the true price equals the invoiced price less the portion of the discount which constitutes *in fact* a trade discount.

Limitations

Most sellers establish quantitative credit limits which state the maximum amount of credit that may be allowed to be outstanding on each individual customer's account. Such limits are approximate ceilings that reflect the considered judgment of the selling company as to the amount of credit that may be extended safely to a given purchaser. It is an amount which a careful analysis of the character, capacity, capital, and conditions surrounding the business of the purchaser reveals to be in proper proportion to other aspects of the subject's business. There are other limitations to the use of mercantile credit. Some customers, because of their poor credit standing, may not be able to secure any credit accommodations whatever from their sources of supply, or may be granted exceedingly small amounts and for limited periods of time. Some types of suppliers sell only on a cash basis. Finally, when relatively large cash discounts are available, failure to take advantage of them makes mercantile credit an expensive form of outside financing. This causes many buyers to seek other sources of capital, in order to take cash discounts, and thereby to avoid undue dependence upon trade credit.

Mercantile Credit Agencies

In analyzing a credit risk, either an active or prospective account, the seller must secure essential information on the risk's character, capacity, and capital standing, as well as on the general business and economic conditions affecting the risk. The most common source of such data is the mercantile agency, the best known of which is Dun & Bradstreet, Inc. In many manufacturing and wholesaling businesses, by far the largest percentage of orders is checked for credit principally or entirely on the basis of information obtained from mercantile agencies through their rating books, special reports or both. Mercantile agencies are institutions formed for the primary purpose of gathering information concerning the credit standing of businessmen and disseminating that information to their subscribers.

FINANCING THE CONSUMER

To facilitate the process of consumption, some goods are sold to the ultimate consumer on credit, or loans of cash are made to him. The subject was analyzed as one determinant of consumer behaviour. At this point, consumer finance is treated as a marketing activity, with attention given both to its business and social implications.

Nature of Consumer Credit

The credit granted to ultimate consumers for the purpose of facilitating the process of consumption is known as consumer credit. Theoretically, it is the power which an individual uses in obtaining goods and services, or in borrowing money, for consumption purposes, on the promise to repay an equivalent at an agreed future time. Broadly conceived, consumer credit includes all credit extensions for personal use, whether granted by manufacturers that sell directly to consumers, by retailers, professional men, service businesses, or by the various types of financial institutions. Reasons for and Basic Types of Consumer Credit From the standpoint of creditors, the principal reason for credit is profit. To the retailer, credit spells increased sales volume and remunerative business; to the money lender, it means a worth-while return on his investment. To the ultimate consumer, however, the matter is not so simple.

In general, however, the consumer is prompted to use credit by one or more of three sets of motives: *convenience, a desire for immediate improvement in his standard of living,* and *necessity*. Each of these motives constitutes, in the main, the fundamental explanation for a different type of consumer credit: *the charge account, instalment sale credit, and consumer cash credit, respectively.*

Importance and Composition of Consumer Credit

The importance of consumer credit may be judged in several ways. First, it may be pointed out that about one-third of all retail store sales is made on a credit basis, with about two-thirds of such credit sales being made on a charge account basis and about one-third on some type of instalment credit arrangement. The importance of credit sales varies considerably among different lines of trade, being of greatest significance to large establishments, with a wide range of merchandise classifications, serving a relatively permanent clientele.

For example, department stores, which account for only 6.7 per cent of retail store sales, hold 19 per cent of the total consumer indebtedness arising out of the use of charge accounts in all retail stores, including credit card plans. Another indication of the importance of consumer credit is the volume of credit outstanding at a particular time. Such data, which are published regularly in very comprehensive fashion, measure the amount due creditors as of a particular date rather than the volume of credit granted during a particular period. Nevertheless, trends in such data at least reflect increasing or decreasing use of various means of financing consumption through credit.

In 1960, for example, consumers owed $54 billion in connection with previous uses of all forms of short-term and intermediateerm instalment credit. This was the equivalent of 15 per cent of total disposable personal income during that year. On an annual basis, consumer credit outstanding (debt) has tended to increase gradually but consistently, from 9.2 per cent in 1950 to 15 per cent of disposable personal income in 1960. Greater use of consumer credit, as so measured, is explained by a variety of factors, including:

- Growing acceptance of credit as an institution of modern society, as opposed to a puritanical aversion to indebtedness;
- Increasing levels of per family income which has enhanced the demand for types of goods commonly sold on a credit basis and caused a larger proportion of the population to qualify as acceptable credit risks;
- A wider variety of credit or financing arrangements, available from a growing number of marketing and financial institutions, especially designed to meet the particular needs of families in different income groups and financial circumstances.

Of total consumer indebtedness in 1960, 78 per cent arose out of the use of one form or another of instalment credit and 22 per cent reflected noninstalment credit. Instalment debt was, however, only 11.7 per cent, or less than one-eighth, of total annual disposable personal income. It appears, therefore, that the total population could safely carry considerably larger amounts of instalment financial obligations, without impairing its ability to repay on a reasonable basis, provided such debt is of high quality by virtue of being wisely extended in the vast number of individual cases that comprise the aggregate.

The composition of consumer credit, in terms of debt outstanding. These data do not correspond with the magnitude of consumer expenditures made on a credit basis since expenditures which involve long-term financing tend to be overstated in terms of marketing significance and those which are short-term obligations tend to be understated. However, provide a frame of reference for appraising the composition of consumer credit by major parts or uses and by various sources of credit (holders), and do serve as a background for discussion of types of credit and kinds of financial institutions which are discussed below.

Charge Accounts

Consumers utilize charge accounts chiefly because it is convenient for them to obtain goods on that basis. Orders can be placed by telephone, better service can be obtained from stores, several members of a family may buy on an account, home budgeting may be facilitated, and family budgeting may be controlled through monthly payments.

Merchants who operate on a charge account basis do so for several reasons. It is claimed that charge accounts serve to build regular customers who tend to concentrate their purchases and to buy more merchandise. Credit customers are believed to be less resistant to sales and advertising appeals and are more likely to buy on considerations of quality and style rather than price. Stores extending charge account credit also have a more uniform distribution of sales than do cash stores which experience pronounced peaks in business on and following paydays and lulls in activity between such times.

In spite of the advantages explained above, many stores do not choose to make charge accounts available to their customers. If the basic appeal of an establishment is price, all services, including credit, are usually minimized. Charge accounts are not usually used in the sale of goods of low unit value, as in the case of variety store items, for which customers are accustomed to paying cash. Furthermore, merchants with limited financial resources are often forced to operate on a cash basis because charge accounts involve financing consumer purchases for periods of 50 or 60 days on the average.

Retail store charge accounts have tended to be a relatively stable or declining component of total consumer credit out standings, but service credit, which is closely akin to charge accounts, has increased significantly in the post-World War II era. Service credit consists principally of amounts owed to doctors, hospitals, and public utility companies. Its steady growth reflects wider acceptance of credit financing of medical and household operation expenses, but is also partly attributable to the increased relative significance of service expenditures in the typical family budget.

Most charge accounts involve a relationship between an individual retail store and an individual consumer; however, some group arrangements are of interest. In some cities, numerous independent retailers and service establishments sell on credit through bank charge account plans. Usually a number of stores are affiliated with a given bank; the bank makes credit investigations and approves the accounts; customers may make charge purchases in any of the participating stores; the retailer receives cash for the sale, minus a service charge, at the daily presentation of the sales checks to the bank; and the bank bills the customer monthly for all purchases he made in all participating stores. Major oil companies have promoted the use of credit cards or credit check books which are accepted by any of the independent dealers associated with the company and by the dealers of other affiliated companies. National credit card plans, such as Carte Blanche of Hilton Hotels Corporation and the American Express Company Credit Card, are similar in many respects but are used to a greater extent for handling business travel and entertainment expense than for financing ultimate consumption. Such group arrangements have made it possible for many individual firms to offer charge account services when they would otherwise have found it impossible or uneconomical to do so.

Instalment Sale Credit

Instalment sale credit differs from charge account credit in one major way. Instead of paying the full amount of the bill at the end of a given period of time, the purchaser, when using instalment credit, agrees to pay his obligation in fixed portions or instalments at stated intervals. Other common, although not universal, distinctions are that a down payment is often made on instalment transactions and that a finance charge is levied on the unpaid balance.

Although it is an old business practice, the instalment method did not evoke much attention until about the middle of the 1920's when its use was greatly extended together with the expansion of the automobile market. During the 1930's the method became more common as it was extended to numerous types of durable goods and even to "soft" goods which have been later sold extensively on deferred multiple payment plans. Instalment sale credit accounts for about one-third of total credit sales of retail establishments in nonwar years. During war years and periods of national emergency marked by scarcities of durable goods, the total volume of instalment sale credit has been as little as one-fourth of total credit sales and as low as less than 5 per cent of the total sales of retail establishments. More than one-half of the *instalment sale* credit *extended* annually represents automobile financing. Other lines of business in which instalment sale credit is of great significance are furniture stores, household appliance stores, jewelry stores, automobile tire and accessory stores, and department stores.

Instalment selling has also been applied to the marketing of various kinds of services. Airlines, for example, have made it possible for consumers to take expensive vacation trips which are financed over a number of months. Similarly, many doctors, dentists, and hospitals have made arrangements with financing institutions so that people with limited incomes may finance major medical expenses on definite instalment arrangements.

Sales Finance Companies and Instalment Sale Credit

Finance companies are of two types: *consumer* or *personal finance companies* engaged chiefly in making cash loans and which are discussed at a later point, and *sales finance companies* engaged principally in financing the sale of products. Sales finance companies, in turn, may be divided into two principal classes: manufactured-owned companies, such as General Motors Acceptance Corporation, and independent financial institutions, as illustrated by Commercial Credit Corporation. Regardless of ownership, both types of companies do the bulk of their business in connection with automotive sales, but both types also are heavily engaged in financing sales of appliances, electronic products, furniture, and other durable goods. The nature of their operations may be illustrated with respect to automobile financing.

When an automobile is sold on the instalment plan (and the same applies to other articles financed by sales finance companies), a promissory note covering the transaction is made out by the purchaser. The note, secured by a chattel mortgage on the car, or by a conditional sales contract, is indorsed by the dealer, with or without recourse, as the case may be, and is then discounted by the finance company. Prior to acceptance of the risk by the finance company, a credit investigation is made in order to determine the purchaser's willingness and ability to meet the instalments when due. An agreement must be reached on the amount of down payment and the number of, and the amount of time between, instalment payments.

On automobiles, the usual down payment required has, from time to time, varied from about 10 per cent to 15 per cent to onethird of the purchase price; the time interval between payments is generally one month; and the number of payments has varied from about 12 to 36. In some cases, however, automobiles are sold on terms involving no down payment and with terms of 48 months.

In determining the amount to be paid under the instalment sales contract a regular service charge is added to the unpaid balance. This charge, which is all too often confused and compared with pure interest rates, must cover interest on the money lent, credit and collection expense of the lending agency, a reasonable allowance for bad debt losses, allowance for expenses involved in repossession, reconditioning, and sale of cars of delinquents, and certain types of insurance as specified.

This charge is quoted in terms of a *nominal* rate, i.e., the amount of service charge expressed as a percentage of the total unpaid amount on a per annum basis, that is, on the total initial unpaid balance. The *actual* effective rate of charge is generally about twice the nominal rate because the debtor is constantly decreasing the outstanding balance by monthly payments made throughout the period.

Instalment Credit Handled by Retailers

Instalment credit is generally used in many types of retail stores that operate without assistance from sales finance companies. Department stores, mail order companies, furniture stores, and home appliance stores are some of the major types of establishments that maintain their own instalment credit departments, make credit investigations, and handle collections, which are accepted at accounts receivables offices in the store or are made by consumers by mail. Many of these stores finance their receivables through commercial banks or other financial institutions. Some large-scale retailers have subsidiary corporations which have been established to handle their time-sales financing activities and which operate in the same manner as sales finance companies.

Durable goods items of high unit value are usually sold on straight instalment contracts which customarily involve a down payment and payments of a specified amount for a definite number of weeks or months. Since about the middle 1940's, various types of "budget," "revolving" or "optional" credit plans have been adopted extensively by department stores, mail order companies, and apparel retailers, to facilitate the sale of soft goods on instalments. According to a common arrangement, the consumer contracts to pay a certain amount each month and thus is granted a credit limit which is a multiple of the monthly payment. In a 12-month revolving account, if the customer contracts to pay $20 per month the credit limit is set at $240. The consumer can make purchases of any kind of goods sold by the store, so long as the credit limit is not exceeded. Each month a carrying charge is added to the outstanding balance as of the end of the month.

The "optional" or multiple-purpose account used by many retailers serves either as a regular charge account or as a deferred payment account. If the customer wishes to pay the total amount of the monthly billing, he may do so, and there is no service charge. On the other hand, if the billing is large (e.g., owing to seasonal purchases such as at school opening time, Christmas, or Easter) payments may be spread over several or many months, with a service charge added to the outstanding balance, as in the case of revolving credit. The various forms of revolving credit are classified, for statistical purposes, along with regular instalment credit. Their popularity in the 1950's and early 1960's has resulted in the shifting of some debt balances from the category of charge account to instalment.

Arguments for Instalment Credit

The real nature of instalment credit can be but little understood merely from a knowledge that it involves periodic payments. Instalment credit is not merely a technique; rather it is a pervasive influence and an explanation of its nature must be sought in the effects it has upon all whom it touches. These effects are reputedly both beneficial and detrimental.

The advantages of instalment credit may be considered from the standpoint of the business establishments that use it as a selling technique and from the view of the consumer and society in general. To merchants selling on the instalment plan, it is not a matter of conjecture that the plan tends to increase sales volume. It does increase the total demand for goods of the type that may be sold on this plan, as is shown below, and it brings people into stores at frequent intervals to make payments. Each such call is an opportunity to make additional sales, with payments for one purchase leading to still additional purchases and greater familiarity with the credit-granting establishment.

From the standpoint of society, the instalment plan is desirable, first, because it *enables people to obtain, without delay, many commodities of high unit value and much usefulness,* without the necessity of waiting long periods before they are acquired, or of doing without them altogether. The buyer is thus enabled to use the article while paying for it; as a result he can enjoy life more fully than would otherwise be possible.

A second social advantage, and one contrary to much popular opinion, is that instalment buying *tends to encourage thrift.* It is an enforced form of saving, *provided* that the terms of payment are such that the consumer's equity in the purchased article is increased at a rate greater than the rate at which the article is used up or consumed. Many people will economize in order to be able to meet instalments when they come due, even though they may be unable, or lack the discipline, to economize merely for the sake of accumulating money for future use. Third, *because instalment credit has widened the market for the type of consumer goods sold in this manner, it has contributed to lower prices on such goods.*

Most of the industries manufacturing durable goods of high unit value operate on a decreasing cost basis; consequently, as their output is increased, the unit cost is materially reduced. The advantage of lower prices resulting from market expansions attributable to consumer credit inures to the benefit, therefore, of cash and credit customers alike. There can be no doubt, furthermore, that instalment credit *has contributed to a substantially higher standard of living for large segments of the consuming public.*

This argument is a natural corollary of the two just stated, in that it results both from the savings feature of the plan and the broadening of the market through price reductions of many types of goods. Standards of living are judged in large measure by the number and kinds of durable goods and costly articles in the possession of consumers, as well as by the consumption of items yielding cultural and aesthetic satisfaction. Much of the income that is now used for purchasing automobiles, television, radios, dishwashers, washing machines, garbage disposals, vacuum cleaners, floor coverings, furniture, and refrigerators would be expended upon highly perishable satisfactions in the absence of instalment credit. Furthermore, in the absence of economies of scale enjoyed by industries manufacturing such goods, unit prices would necessarily be much higher and at such a level that it would be impossible for the masses to purchase items of this kind.

Objections to Instalment Credit

Instalment credit is sufficiently well established as a business practice that it is only upon rare occasions that objections to it arise from within the business community. Some strong arguments have been set forth against it, however, by those who view the subject from a consumer or social standpoint. Most such objections are either made by those who have no understanding of this type of credit, or objections are directed to abuses rather than to sound applications of it. Among the most common criticisms is that it causes people to live beyond their means by the consumption of luxuries to which they are not entitled on the basis of current income. Tastes and desires of different individuals vary so much, however, as to make any attempt to dictate that one commodity be purchased instead of another, or that it be bought on a certain basis, the height of absurdity.

A second and somewhat related objection is that instalment credit has led consumers to mortgage their future incomes, both through the consumption of luxuries and overconsumption in general, to the extent that the slightest interruption in normal earnings would effect a very serious and straitened condition in their ability to meet obligations. Such criticisms are apparently based upon two assumptions:

- That a person's income is static
- That instalment purchases are made on top of what would be normally bought in the absence of such purchases. In numerous individual cases the person who bought an expensive article on the instalment plan may justly expect an increase in his present earnings during the life of the contract. Again, he may so reapportion and redirect his purchases that less of other types of goods will be bought, or he may have been saving to the extent that this distribution of his income can be modified without impairing his security. Furthermore, many buyers on the instalment plan have resources other than their immediate income, which can be converted into cash if desired or necessary in order to meet obligations.

One of the most serious objections to instalment credit is its costliness. In operating on a charge account basis, there is but one collection to be made for purchases during the credit period and, ordinarily, only one chance that payment will be delayed or not made at all. From the standpoint of the store or finance company, there are repetitive chances that the instalment purchaser will become delinquent. Elaborate collection machinery must be established to insure that payments are kept forthcoming and that the purchaser remains satisfied with the goods and the service of the selling establishment. In addition to collection expenses, carrying charges must also include, as previously indicated, interest on the funds used, bookkeeping and clerical costs, credit investigation expense, reserves for bad debt losses, and allowances for the cost of repossession and resale of articles.

An objection voiced by many is that charges are exorbitant, that is, even greater than warranted by actual costs of carrying instalment accounts. This criticism arises in part from misunderstanding and in part because certain less reputable vendors have taken advantage of the ignorance of some consumers. All too often the carrying charge on instalment purchases is inappropriately related to the economic concept of interest which involves merely a price paid for the use of money.

Learning that the actual rate of instalment charge per annum on a given transaction is, for example, 12 or 18 per cent per annum, a consumer may unrealistically compare this rate with a rate of interest, say 3 or 4 per cent, that his funds will yield if deposited in a savings account. The conclusion may be drawn that the charge is exorbitant, without cognizance of the fact that interest is only a fraction of the total charge which must cover all of the various costs detailed in the preceding paragraph. In other cases, the charge of exorbitance results from the practice of certain vendors who do not quote any percentage rate of instalment charge, but emphasize in the sales presentation merely the amount of the down payment and the amount of the periodic payments.

Apparently there are many consumers who are unable or too indifferent to figure the cost of purchasing on the instalment plan at the time purchases are made if the amount of the monthly or weekly payment is something they feel they can reasonably afford. Consequently, certain stores have been able to make very high charges on instalment transactions and under such circumstances that the amount of the charge is not actually known by many customers. Fortunately, this is a practice that has never been common among more reputable dealers. A fifth important criticism of instalment credit is concerned solely with *abuses,* as for example, when carrying charges are not disclosed or are misrepresented.

Many vendors and finance companies have quoted only nominal rather than actual rates of charge per annum and, even so, have failed to indicate whether the rate applied to the unpaid balance after the deduction of the down payment or to the full purchase price of the article. With respect to this criticism, it is significant that steps have been taken in the direction of regulation relating to the use of clear forms of instalment contracts which reveal just what the customer gets and how much he is paying for the product and how much for the financing of it.

Cash Credit as a Supplement to Instalment Sale Credit

Consumer cash credit may be distinguished from instalment sale credit in that consumers obtain cash funds, rather than merchandise, in exchange for a promised future repayment. A large proportion of such credit has its origin in human want and misery and is explained by the urgent need for immediate funds in order to cope with emergency situations. To an important extent, however, cash credit is a supplement to instalment sale credit; and in this respect it is of great significance as a factor in the marketing of goods. There are numerous instances in which a consumer has a choice as to the type of credit he might use.

For example, in buying a major electrical appliance, he might make the purchase on the instalment plan, arranging for payments with the store from which the purchase is made. On the other hand, he might obtain a cash loan from a lending agency, pay cash to the store selling the merchandise, and repay the loan to the lending agency in periodic instalments. In some instances, the latter procedure may be used to circumvent the down payment that is required by the store selling on the instalment plan. There are no statistics that reveal the extent to which cash credit directly supplements instalment sale credit and to what extent it is used for emergency purposes arising out of unforeseen events or from past financial mismanagement. That cash credit is of considerable significance in facilitating the sale of goods is, however, generally recognized, both by marketing authorities and by those engaged in the cash-lending business.The principal sources of consumer cash credit are as follows:

- Consumer or personal finance companies: These are lending agencies licensed under state laws to engage in the business of lending money to consumers. Typical examples are Household Finance Company, Personal Finance Company, and City Loan Company.
- Banks: Most commercial and industrial banks have consumer loan departments. In general, they make loans of larger amounts at lower rates of instalment payment charges than is the case with personal finance companies, owing to their tendency to confine lending activities to high-grade credit risks.
- Credit Unions: Cooperative organizations formed for the purpose of encouraging thrift among members and making loans to them at relatively low rates are known as credit unions. Such organizations are chartered under, and regulated by, state or federal law. Members are ordinarily otherwise affiliated in some way, as employees of a particular company or members of the same church, labour union, or lodge. Since much of the work of the credit union is done by members without compensation, because its facilities are often subsidized by employers or other associated institutions, and because of certain tax advantages owing to status as cooperatives, loans are made at lower rates than are available from financial institutions. Credit is, however, available only to members.

Control of Consumer Credit

As consumer credit has grown in stature in the course of this century, it has led to ever-broadening concepts of its social and economic significance. Consumer credit, particularly of the instalment sale or instalment cash type, has been, accordingly, the subject of increasing control and regulation by state and federal government. This control is of two types, quality and quantity control.

Quality Control

Regulations pertaining to the quality of consumer credit are designed to prevent usurious, deceptive, unfair, or monopolistic practices by credit-granting agencies.

At the beginning of this century, many consumers in need of cash funds were forced to look to illegal lenders or "loan sharks" as a source for loans, and had to pay exorbitant rates. The reason for this was that the usury laws of most states limited interest rates to 6 per cent per annum or, in the presence of a special contract, to 8 per cent. Such rates were inadequate to attract agencies to make consumer loans in small amounts at inevitable high costs. After making a thorough study, the Russell Sage Foundation, a philanthropic organization working for the improvement of social conditions, drafted a model bill for submission to state legislatures in 1916. This Uniform Small Loan Law, has subsequently been enacted, in some cases with modifications, in 44 states.

The main provisions of the law permit specially authorized rates on loans up to $300. A charge of 3 ½ per cent per month on unpaid balances of $100 or less and 2 ½ per cent per month on the remainder up to the $300 limit is recommended. The law provides that no special fees may be collected on the loans, nor may any charges be made other than the rates applying on the unpaid balance. Companies operating under the law are licensed and bonded and are subject to state inspection.

State laws concerning the control of instalment sale credit were first enacted in the 1930's but have since been passed in more than 30 states containing more than three-fourths of the population. Some of these laws pertain solely to automobile financing whereas others cover all kinds and types of instalment sale credit. Practically all of them are intended to combat excessive finance charges and nonprice abuses by requiring instalment sellers to provide written contracts that give a dollar itemization of the following: commodity price, down payment, finance charge, and insurance and/or other charges, if any. In a few states, such laws have specific provisions establishing maximum allowable finance charges.

The broadening interest in the quality of available instalment sale credit is also evident from a code of fair trade practices covering certain aspects of automobile sale financing. Rules promulgated by the Federal Trade

Commission Trade Commission in 1951 prohibited a variety of abusive or deceptive practices which had become somewhat common among less scrupulous automotive dealers. These rules apply, of course, only to dealers engaged in interstate commerce and subject to the jurisdiction of the FTC.

From time to time there has been considerable sentiment in favour of a federal law which would prescribe standard conditions of disclosure of credit terms in all cash and sale instalment credit transactions. One proposal bill, the improperly designated "Truth in Lending Act," was the subject of much publicity in 1961. If enacted, it would require that the instalment charge in every transaction be stated in terms of simple "interest" per annum. Owing to the wide variety of instalment plans in use, it would be practically impossible to comply with the terms of such a law in each particular retail transaction. Moreover, referring to such a charge as "interest" is fallacious when due consideration is given to the other, and quantitatively more significant, types of clerical and operating costs which must be recovered in instalment finance charges. Such a law would, furthermore, greatly extend federal control of local and retail business activity and duplicate to a substantial extent the provisions of numerous and increasing state laws on the same subject but which, significantly, require disclosure of finance charges only in amounts or in some other simple fashion.

11

Benchmarking the World Stock Markets

Interest in foreign stock markets has significantly increased during the last two decades, particularly during the 1980s when international portfolio investments seem to have increased substantially. Evidence of this interest is reflected in the increasing literature on the subject. While advances have been made in both the theory and the empirical analysis of international portfolio investments, significant and fundamental research is still needed on several fronts to advance our understanding of the establishment, functioning, growth and interaction of stock markets with the economies in which they operate.

This understanding is critical in order to confidently provide policy recommendations leading to the further development of world stock markets. Studies of international stock markets have often been born by extending the concepts and the knowledge on the functioning of domestic stock markets. Because of this, the recent domestic markets literature. Particularly relevant contributions are those analysing the functioning of stock markets and their interaction with economic variables and policies.

Different stages of economic development appear to impinge on stock market development. With this notion, a subset of the literature has focused on emerging markets, *i.e.* those operating in developing economies. The bulk of the substantive literature, however, has focused on developed markets, *i.e.* those operating in developed economies. Stock markets, on the other hand, do not work in isolation as they form part of the financial system and arise as a consequence of the international monetary system. To the extent that they were considered relevant, studies in these areas that could throw some light on the development of international stock markets are also briefly reviewed.

Central to the study of the world stock markets is also the controversy between integration and segmentation of capital markets, which by necessity needs to be considered also. The international stock markets, with special attention paid to identifying possible policy implications. The study does not pretend to be exhaustive. A special effort is made to highlight issues that may provoke further research which would advance our understanding of stock markets.Basically descriptive and only attempts to be analytical on certain relevant theoretical issues. Such understanding is essential for providing policy recommendations leading to further development of international stock markets.

The following section focuses on the international asset pricing literature. The assumptions of CAPMs that have been extended to international markets are examined in detail, with special attention to possible violations of these assumptions in the case of international markets. Possible avenues for further research to develop a general international equilibrium model are briefly discussed; and some of the limitations of these models for providing policy recommendations are examined.

In the third section we review the macroeconomics literature, including international monetary economics papers dealing with capital and monetary flows and the relevant determinants of such flows. Also, contributions on the interaction of security markets with the economy are also examined. The need for disaggregating non-monetary assets in macroeconomic models and the behaviour of such assets under certain policy variables are also reviewed. It is argued that Tobin's open economy macro model provides the basis for further developing our understanding of stock markets with the economy. Focusing more on overall financial systems and economic development in the fourth section, the possible implications for the development of stock market activities with an economic development perspective and its potential contri-bution to economic growth are reviewed. The impact of foreign aid in the development of domestic savings and investments is also briefly mentioned.

Extending the discussions of the fourth section, the specific literature on emerging markets is examined in the fifth section. The particular characteristics of emerging markets in contrast with those already developed is presented. The potential role that governments could play in promoting stock markets in developed economies is discussed.

The sixth section examines in particular three relevant issues of international stock markets:

- The controversy of integration versus segmentation;
- Foreign direct investments as an alternative to constrained portfolio investments; and
- The capital flight debate.

The concluding section evaluates the current knowledge of international stock markets and advocates further research aiming to identify potential policy guidelines for the development of stock markets. The underlying premise is that stock market growth would improve the allocable efficiency of resources internationally and induce further economic growth on a world-wide scale.

INTERNATIONAL ASSET PRICING AND DIVERSIFICATION

The interest in foreign stock markets since the seminal paper has been largely motivated by the expected benefits to be accrued by investors from diversifying their portfolios in world markets. Under different comparative advantages, and thus different economic structures, financial assets issued in different countries are subject to a valuation process determined by each country's economic and business cycle as well as its fiscal, financial and monetary policies.

Policy differences aside, the non-synchronous economic and business cycles are the basis for internationally diversifying equity portfolios. This economic reality is the basis for selecting stocks or portfolios with weakly correlated international returns, which has been greatly emphasized in the international asset pricing models literature. In extending domestic portfolio theory into the interna-tional arena, it is often implicitly assumed that all domestic equity markets in the world, except for the eventuality of following different business cycles, have the same attributes and similar characteristics regarding their performance and asset pricing. By further assuming that all individuals have homogeneous preferences and beliefs and that markets are complete and perfect, an optimal allocation of world wealth is determined at the theoretical level.

All the standard assumptions of CAPMs which are often applied to international markets can be encompassed in the general notion of perfect, complete, homogeneous consumption, tastes and beliefs; stable, efficient and integrated capital markets whereby efficient markets include at least three different aspects, *i.e.* exchange or operational, production or allocable and informational efficiency.

Violations of these assumptions result in unbalanced non-equilibrium portfolios, or ineffi cient world market portfolios. Therefore, by extending CAPMs to the international environment where domestic markets are considered part of an integrated world market, the underlying assumptions of such models need to be re-examined.

A long list of assumptions and valuation criteria of CAPMs are still questionable in the international arena. Several financial economists and contributions in the literature suggest that in the international market, more so than within a single domestic market, participants are heterogeneous. For example, deviations from PPP lead to heterogeneity among international investors. Also based on the comparative advantage of their country and their individual wealth, market participants may have different tastes and perceptions, and thus different expectations and attitudes towards risks.

Even from a domestic perspective, that interpersonal differences in the perception of and the attitudes towards risk and uncertainty are perhaps the single most important factor in the forming of capital markets. The following points are also important: firms issuing securities in world markets may not be price-takers; non-competitive behaviour, exclusive technologies and the limited number of firms are sources of non-optimality of stock market allocation under economies of scale and industrial structures where economic groups have market power, particularly those in small economies, not all investors may maximize single-period expected utility based only on mean and variance returns; given the small capitalization of certain markets and companies, investors may not be able to buy or sell as much of every security without affecting prices; all investors, particularly in small countries, may not be able to borrow or lend an unlimited amount of risk-free assets; based on different rates of economic growth, the expected real return on assets may differ and the supply of securities may not be fixed, and so the relative prices of assets may be unstable thereby preventing markets reaching equilibrium conditions; given the small number of listed securities in several countries and their small market capitalization, investors may find it attractive to buy and sell assets outside organized markets; given capital flow restrictions, capital mobility is impaired, limiting the integration of world markets and creating additional interna-tional capital market imperfections; other imperfections-such as information, transaction costs and taxes -abound in world markets.

Subject to different fiscal, financial and monetary policies that affect relative asset prices and their stability, world markets may not be in equilibrium and are subject to a sovereign risk which though largely ignored at the domestic level is relevant internationally. The risk of policy changes in individual markets needs to be explicitly taken into account in international investments. In addition, while violating perfect market conditions, the monopoly of firms (particularly of MNCs) may not permit the separation of production and financial decisions. Under these conditions, production and financial markets may not be Pareto optimal, and therefore the allocation of resources may not be efficient. Also, if international markets are incomplete, it would be relevant to analyse the consequences of opening new international markets. A case where, in providing new opportunities to trade (*i.e.* new markets), investors do not recognize the interdependence between the gains from trade at different times, and their utilities, and thus their welfare, are reduced. In particular, it would be relevant to determine what the world-wide wealth effects are when domestic markets or partial international markets are extended to a full world capital market by introducing (or 'opening') the rest of the world market. Besides possible violations of CAPM's assumptions, overriding questions remain open regarding the criteria to be used for valuing international assets and regarding the controversy of integration versus segmentation of world markets.

An extensive body of the literature has focused on the valuation of assets based on domestic versus international factors; and is therefore concerned also with the foreign exchange risk faced by international investors. If PPP does not hold, investors are subject to an exchange risk. Based on homogeneous beliefs and investors' access to home-country risk-free assets, Solnik has argued that foreign exchange risk is neutralized by holding investors' own-country risk-free assets. While Solnik's assumptions are questionable, the different but preferred consumption basket of investors may result in foreign exchange risks.

Undoubtedly, for a better understanding of such risks there is still a need to develop an acceptable theory of foreign exchange rate determination which so far has eluded us. A general equilibrium model of international capital markets with heterogeneous consumption tastes would require as yet unknown procedures for computing equilibrium prices. Thus, such a general equilibrium model would also require an optimal allocation of foreign exchange risk-bearing among international investors. The rationale for such an allocation of exchange risk still needs to be worked out in the context of international asset pricing models. Given their different purchasing power, investors from different countries (unless they have decreasing absolute risk aversion, *i.e.* they have logarithmic utilities) will differ in identifying an efficient portfolio and therefore the measure-ment of returns in any single currency unit could not serve as a benchmark for valuation. Heterogeneous investors, could value assets relative to each other but then the market portfolio becomes unobservable. Thus, resolving the problem of portfolio choice when investors' real returns differ is a necessary first step towards a truly international CAPM. Because of these limitations, as Adler and Dumas have pointed out, besides the descriptive value of the statistics, the available international CAPM 'results offer neither guidelines for the construction of optimally diversified portfolios nor the basis for evaluating the benefits or value of such diversification'.

The issue of integration versus segmentation of markets still remains a controversial issue in the empirical analysis of world markets. While further research is required to determine the extent of world market integration, the overriding evidence of restrictions and lack of information regarding a substantial number of individual markets suggests that they are not perfectly integrated world-wide. As in Lee and Sachdeva, a capital market is segmented when certain groups of investors limit their investments to a subset of the universe of all possible asset claims.

Such market segmentation can occur because of ignorance about the universe of possible asset claims or because of transaction costs (brokerage costs, taxes, or information acquisition costs), or because of legal impediments.

Without examining in detail other market imperfections, it is evident that very little is known about world markets. Only recently has the full structure of world markets started to be analysed. On the basis of this limited information, *a priori* it is anticipated that world markets are segmented. If emerging markets are ignored, it is plausible that developed markets may be more closely related given their openness to trade and the influence of monetary and economic variables. Such interrelation, however, could be limited by different government policies and real return divergences. So far, the advances in CAPM theory permit us to deal with incomplete markets, heterogeneous investors (but with the same beliefs) and B taste parameters (the universal separation theorem). Under such assumptions the equilibrium rates of return will be determined as if the securities markets were complete and, desite differences in wealth, utility of present consumption, rate of patience and A taste parameters, the optimal portfolio of risky securities (the market portfolio) will be the same for all individuals. Nevertheless, if the universal separation theorem holds, incomplete markets are also operational (exchange) and production (allocable) efficient.

In addition, in markets where the universal separation theorem holds or where a composite individual can be constructed, equilibrium rates of return are insensitive to the population and to the distribution of resources among individuals. This is particularly relevant for emerging markets and, if such assumptions hold in international markets, Branson's (1970) international capital flows determination as a function of wealth becomes questionable. So, if international markets are susceptible to be represented by a composite individual, this implies that investors will hold a proportion of the market capitalization of individual countries similar to the proportion that they represent in world markets, *i.e.* they would hold the world market portfolio. It is plausible, however, that by introducing transactions and information costs which may be high in small capitalized markets or in markets with a significant number of small firms, the revised optimal world market portfolio may not include investments in certain emerging markets. Thus, the transaction and information differential costs and their impact in world portfolio choices needs to be determined and empirically validated.

Therefore, if investors hold the world market portfolio, the capitalization of individual stock markets, and particularly of emerging markets, will not increase by the flow of investments from rich countries but by increasing stock investments within their own economies. Thus, even with fully open economies, the flow of foreign investments would be mainly determined by the growth of individual domestic markets. This is a relevant empirical question that could help policy-makers to determine whether fiscal, financial and monetary policies could be aimed to attract international investments. If the universal separation theorem holds, however, interference by policy-makers that alters rates of return will lead to a non-optimal allocation of resources.

The main stumbling block for extending the universal separation theorem to international markets is the B taste parameter, which is expected to be different between investors from different countries. This represents what Adler and Dumas (1983) have identified as the main constraint for computing equilibrium prices. Nevertheless, if international investors have logarithmic utilities, returns measured in any currency could serve as a benchmark for valuation.

In searching for a complete international CAPM, two avenues of research become obvious. The first is theoretical and would be to search for a general equilibrium model with heterogeneity in consumption tastes. The second is empirical and would be to determine to what extent international investors have different consumption tastes or if they have logarithmic utilities. While Dumas (1977) briefly discussed studies that found similarities of consumption tastes in developed countries, such studies need to be extended to both developed and developing economies. Differences in wealth, the consumption opportunity set and stages of economic development suggest that consumption tastes between developed and developing markets may differ; this, however, remains an open issue. Assuming that markets are fully integrated, Stulz (1981b) has already developed a model dealing with temporary different consumption opportunity sets in (but not across) different countries where the real expected return on a risky asset is proportional to the covariance of that asset with changes in the world real consumption rate. If a country's real consumption closely correlates with the world real consumption, differences in consumption opportunity sets are apparently not likely to matter for studies of international asset pricing. This appears to imply that, even with different investor tastes, world markets would be integrated and therefore could be modelled on the basis of a simple international asset pricing model with returns valued in real terms. However, differences in consumption opportunity sets can create significant differences in asset holdings across countries. While violation of PPP would limit the results of this model, some premises about non-observability of foreign prices question the full integration assumption. But before examining the correlation of real asset returns in world markets, additional research is needed to determine to what extent world investors evaluate returns based on nominal versus real returns.

Therefore, the empirical line of research focuses on the determination of consumption or taste differences which may still permit analysis of international asset pricing with existing models. In contrast, if the search for a theoretical general equilibrium model with different consumption tastes is successful, it is necessary to analyse the extent to which violations of the CAPM's assumptions would affect equilibrium returns. After finding this general equilibrium model, the relaxation of assumptions (regarding imperfections, inefficiencies, segmentation, changing supply of securities etc.) could be studied following Stapleton and Subrahmanyam's (1980) approach.

Therefore, only if empirical studies support the use of existing models of international asset pricing or if new theoretical developments lead to a general equilibrium model with different consumption tastes could we be confident of existing guidelines, or of those that would be developed based on the new general equilibrium model for the construction of optimally diversified international portfolios or of the benefits of such diversification.

Until further research provides support for existing guidelines and models, caution must be exercised in their application and use. As Stulz has pointed out: 'Buying the market portfolio in a foreign country might just be buying a highly inefficient portfolio for domestic investors'. Users of existing models and guidelines may help the development of future research by documenting their experience so as to point out the path that could help to develop an acceptable theory of international finance. Perhaps by examining actual foreign portfolio investments in world markets, investment patterns may be identified that could help explain portfolio choices and international asset pricing and that could permit testing of existing and future international asset pricing models.

While a complete international security pricing model would be relevant for determining the world stock market portfolio and for analysing the informational efficiency of organized world markets, such a model would have to be expanded to include other assets to study the exchange (operational) and allocable (production) efficiency of world markets. The inclusion of other financial assets and securities traded in non-organized markets in a broad and complete international CAPM would throw some light on the overall efficiency of organized world securities markets.

While the determination of a broad and complete international asset pricing model is relevant, it still belongs to the realm of partial analysis where most variables are exogenously determined. Thus, such models would not permit an analysis of possible feedback effects of changes in the economic and financial setting and therefore they would be limited to providing recommendations or guidelines for policy-makers.

These policy recommendations may come through in developing and examining general equilibrium macroeconomic models, where financial markets, and stock markets in particular, would be integrated into open economies. Such developments are still in their infancy and much more remains to be done to analyse international asset pricing models in the context of open economies and under changing fiscal, financial and monetary policies.

MACROECONOMIC ANALYSIS

At the macro level most of the literature has focused on the implications of capital flows (mainly long-term loans or bonds) on balance of payments, trade balances, foreign exchange rates and equalization of factors of production. Particularly influential has been the work, who identified stock and flow effects in determining international capital move-ments. Under a partial analysis framework, Branson identified the major determinants (*i.e.* total wealth of home-country investors, the level of domestic and foreign interest rates, risk considerations and the level of other variables such as exports) of total assets held abroad. Of these determinants, given their relative magnitude, wealth considerations are most relevant. Under acceptable risk levels, and great discrepancies in domestic and foreign interest rates, the wealthier the country the larger would be the value of total assets held abroad by its residents.

The movements of capital in response to changes in the differential between foreign and domestic interest rates are a consequence of pure stock adjustments. The larger the portfolio and the interest differentials, the larger the magnitude of stock adjustments and therefore of capital movements.

Continued capital movements, on the other hand, are mainly ascribable to the portfolio's growth (the flow effect) which relative to stock effects is considered to be small. Therefore, interest differentials would be more important than growth in explaining capital movements. But in a world of changing interest rates and growing portfolios, observed capital movements reflect the combined result of both stock and flow effects.

Branson's empirical analysis, however, did not separate equities and long-term claims on foreigners. They were lumped together and determined as a residual of total US claims on foreigners exclusive of foreign direct investment, short-term claims and long-term banking claims. Disregarding well-known differences between equities and loans, Branson's approach implies that the major determinants for movements of both types of assets are the same, or alternatively that equities and loans would be perfect substitutes. These implicit assumptions, however, are questionable and need to be validated. Unless perfect substitutability of equities and loans can be proved or a clear transmission process by which interest rates determine stock prices is identified, movements of equities and loans need to be disaggregated and explained. Branson's straightforward model determines major factors affecting loan movements but his partial analysis needs to be reassessed in an open economy macroeconomic model where different types of assets are recognized.

Extending Branson's model to a general equilibrium model of financial markets in an open economy, but still ignoring foreign exchange rate fluctuations and differences in asset type, changes in income are highly significant in explaining capital flows. Thus, in contrast to Branson's emphasis, capital flows reflect divergent growth rates and cyclical phases between countries. Kouri and Porter further claim that the more basic sources of capital flows are fluctuations in money demand and supply.

A dynamic international asset pricing model where stock portfolios grow with the economy in which they are held, Branson's wealth relevance for international portfolios is at odds with a truly international asset pricing model. If Branson's view were applicable to stock markets, investors of wealthier countries would have a larger share of foreign stocks than those determined by the international market portfolio. A resolution of these divergent views is particularly relevant for policy-makers interested in attracting foreign capital.

If Branson's views hold, policy-makers could expect a significant flow of investments from wealthier countries. But if the international asset pricing models are correct, such an inflow would be largely determined by the size and growth of the domestic market relative to world markets.

Evidently the impact of monetary policies for attracting foreign capital in one case would be more relevant than in the other. So additional studies need to be made for determining the factors explaining international investments in stock markets.

Under a portfolio approach, the demand for financial assets (bonds and money) as determined by income, the world interest rate and wealth. Assuming perfect capital mobility and fixed exchange rates, an increase in the stock of either bonds or money will stimulate a readjustment of portfolios. Under constant portfolios, there would be no investment demand or supply of assets and thus no capital movements. In a growing economy, portfolio equilibrium would require world issuance of new assets at the rate of growth of the world economy. Zero balance of payments and zero net capital flows would be consistent with new issuance of bonds and currency in each country at the same rate as its economic growth. Thus, a different pattern of growth among countries would result in portfolio adjustments and capital flows due mainly to wealth effects.

While focusing on the determinants of the net factors income from abroad, along the lines of Allen, that the movements of capital can be explained by the same determinants that explain the growth of an economy. As the net factors income from abroad only measures the net aggregate revenues of both investments and services from abroad, and is usually determined as a residual between GDP and GNP calculations, Borts and Kopecky's results are suspicious and not particularly illuminating.

Overall, capital movements and their implications regarding equity investments in world markets have been largely ignored in the open economy macroeconomics literature. While some authors claim that 'international capital flows improve the efficiency of resource allocation in the world and thereby raise world output and welfare' empirical studies to validate this hypothesis need to be developed. Saving-investment correlation, by implication, casts doubts on the allocable efficiency of capital markets. They conclude that even if international financial markets are integrated so as to equalize financial expected returns, the expected returns on physical capital are not equalized. Under such segmentation between financial and physical assets it is doubtful that international financial resources are efficiently allocated, and therefore that world output and welfare are increased. At the theoretical level and with a domestic perspective, if capital markets are somewhat less than perfect, the private allocation of investment in general is inconsistent with the social welfare and social wealth optimum allocation. In this regard, income redistribution effects of international portfolio investments need to be examined also. Therefore, substantial research is still needed to review the allocable efficiency of capital markets, and in particular that of equity markets.

Except for money and credit type instruments, other financial assets have also been largely ignored even in the closed economy macroeconomics literature. Despite the implicit relationship between macroeconomic aggregates and financial markets, most macroeconomic analyses focus primarily-if not exclusively-on money, and more recently on long-term financial instruments or credit aggregates. Perhaps, because of specialization and differences in curricula, there is a divorce between financial economists and macroeconomists which has stinted the integration of financial markets in macroeconomic models.

Although empirical studies have analysed the relationship of stock prices and certain economic indicators, except for Tobin's and Gavin's work briefly discussed below and a more limited model by For an increasing understanding of international capital flows within equity markets, and their impact on world-wide economic and business activities, the relationship of domestic equity markets and economic variables is of primary importance and needs clear identification.

If such a relationship is established, perhaps the body of the theory of economics may be easily adapted for analysing the behaviour of financial markets. With a domestic perspective, the best descriptive relationship of security markets and the economy, or economic aggregates, so far has been provided. In Davidson's view, if monetary policy does not accommodate the growth of investments in real assets, *ceteris paribus,* the supply of stocks increases while the demand and stock prices drop, limiting the rate of capital accumulation and therefore reducing economic growth.

Central to this view is the relationship of stock prices and money supply which remains an unresolved and controversial issue. Based on the informational efficiency of stock markets, it has been argued that stock prices or returns anticipate (lead) changes in money growth rates. Pearce's views are based on the behaviour between the movements of stock price indices and the index of industrial production. He found that stock prices usually lead industrial production activity in the USA. However, this relationship was weaker in the UK and Canada and absent in West Germany and France; no explanation was given and no theoretical basis was provided to account for the differences.

In contrast, Gray analyses the correlation of stock return risk premia over bond yields. Based on a partial model of stock prices, he found a positive correlation between the expected and actual risk premia and projected stock prices and returns for the 1978 and 1988 period. The analyses are based on the Data Resources Incorporated forecasting model. Along the lines that increases in stock prices increase household wealth, which induces greater consumer spending and investments in real assets by making it cheaper to issue new securities and more expensive to acquire capacity by mergers and acquisitions.

In the absence of a complete macroeconomic model explaining the interaction of macroeconomic variables and stock markets, applied factor analysis to search for a set of macroeconomic variables that systematically influenced stock market returns and to study the implication of this influence in asset pricing. The results of their study, however, were inconclusive. Perhaps the interaction and simultaneous determination of certain macroeconomic variables could limit the success of factor analysis for finding the correct set of variables affecting stock market behaviour.

In this regard, the extension of Tobin's model discussed below may be more promising. An extremely significant breakthrough, which apparently has been largely unrecognized. Based on his previous work, extended the standard macro model that limits itself to two asset categories-money and everything else-by including foreign currency assets and, for the first time, equities. This is apparently the first macro model that provides the level of disaggregation necessary to study the stock market and its interaction with an open economy seriously while examining policy implications and feedbacks into other economic variables. As Tobin recognizes, an essential part of macroeconomic activity is the dynamics of flows and stocks, investment and capital, saving and wealth and the specific forms of saving and asset stocks; transactions which are the sources of variation of money stocks make a difference, particularly if such transactions alter the wealth and portfolio position of the participants in the economy.

In Tobin's model it is also assumed that the initial wealth and portfolio composition of economic agents are given; otherwise they would have to be endogenously determined. Tobin also recognizes that financial and capital markets are highly imperfect co-ordinators of saving and investment. This imperfection is a source of macroeconomic instability but an opportunity for macroeconomic policies of stabilization.

As Tobin has pointed out, the innovation of his model is to integrate saving and portfolio decisions in a macroeconomic model. The markets which determine asset prices and interest rates co-ordinate these demand flows with the supply flows arising from real investment, the government deficit and the external current account. Tobin's model simultaneously handles the flows arising from saving and asset accumulation and those from portfolio adjustments. Government's financing requirements immediately affect financial markets.

Aside from the general policy implication of Tobin's model regarding fiscal and monetary policies under a flexible exchange rate, the foreign exchange rate is determined by markets in which demands and supplies for current and capital accounts are combined. While this approach is effective for analysing the impact of total international flows on the foreign exchange rate, it hinders the analysis for flows arising from trade and those from stock investments. By disaggregating such flows, an extension of Tobin's model could provide insights not yet available on the impact of foreign investments in domestic markets of equities (stocks). Tobin's model may also be relevant for studying the impact and determination of foreign exchange risks. Under sticky exchange rate expectations and exchange appreciations, Tobin's analysis in his Keynesian version determines that expansionary fiscal and monetary policies are effective. In a fiscal expansion, exchange appreciation reduces the demand for money because the wealth held in foreign investments is lower while the return of such investments is higher. Again within the Keynesian version, the number of possible substitution patterns of financial assets creates ambiguities that need to be resolved. The results of the model are determined contingent on certain substitution patterns.

Under the classical variant where prices are endogenously determined, the monetary expansion is not neutral. It lowers real interest rates and shifts the composition of output from consumption to investment. Central to Tobin's model is its own *q*-theory which establishes the relationship between changes in individual stocks as a function of the market value of the firm and the replacement cost of its fixed assets. While this relationship is still subject to further analysis, a plausible alternative linking investments in real assets with the issuance of securities still needs to be identified.

This in itself is an area that needs further investigation and which points to a weakness in investment theory. What are the determinants for enterprises to identify and undertake investments in real assets? While no theory has yet provided a satisfactory answer to this question, once a behavioural equation is developed, the financing of such undertakings could be left open to determine the composition of debt and equity as a function of cost and risk differences.

Among the recommendations for extending his model, Tobin suggests including a complete foreign sector where its demands for all local assets are introduced, as opposed to specifying all foreign transactions through the balance-of-payments equation. Tobin and Braga De Macedo (1980) have already made some inroads in extending this model to the international arena. Unfortunately, equities and bonds were considered perfect substitutes, preventing focus on the equities market alone. By disaggregating equity markets, the effect of macroeconomic policies and other assets on open economies linked by trade, capital markets and floating exchange rates could be analysed. Perhaps another useful extension would be the introduction of short-term financial assets which would permit economic agents to invest in very liquid interest-earning assets as opposed to long-term financial investments in bonds or equities which are usually less liquid. This would resemble real world financial markets more. Even without these extensions, Tobin's model is rich and provides the necessary framework for carefully studying the implications of fiscal, financial and monetary policies on equity markets.

While the empirical testing of Tobin's model would be practically limited by data constraints perhaps to the US economy, the richness of the model could permit theoretical extensions for increasing our understanding of the behaviour and functioning of world equity markets. Therefore, such theoretical extensions and empirical studies to test the basic model and its extensions should be encouraged.

The IS-LM closed economy model by assuming that asset values, rather than interest rates, are the main determinants of aggregate demand and output. Assuming further that stocks and short- and long-term bonds are perfect substitutes, and that agents are satisfied with the proportion of money in their portfolios, the effect of a change either in current policy or in anticipated policy is a discrete change in the stock market due to the change in the anticipated sequence of profits and real rate of interest.

Perhaps the perfect asset substitution assumption obscures the policy effects on stock markets and indirectly increases their relevance in the economy which may vary in different economies. Gavin extended Blanchard's closed economy model to an open small economy model in which the stock market determines domestic aggregate demand. He found that if stock market effects are important enough, then a monetary expansion can result in real exchange rate appreciation, rather than depreciation.

Also, Gavin's results regarding the effective-ness of fiscal expansion. If the favourable effects on future productivity lead to strong enough stock market effects, an anticipated fiscal expansion can lead to an output expansion rather than a contraction. Similar to Blanchard and Tobin's models, Gavin's model is restricted by substitutable assets but is less disaggregated than that of Tobin and therefore more limited. Furthermore, by assuming strong stock market effects, Gavin's model may not resemble the actual relevance of stock markets in economic activity. While his model still permits the analysis of stronger influences such as the real exchange rate, the relative relevance of financial markets and their effect on economic variables may be better analysed by Tobin's model and the suggested extensions.

A general equilibrium macroeco-nomic model which includes stock markets. However, under certainty conditions and other simplifying assumptions, including no differentials in net yields between domestic and foreign equities, and based on Tobin's *q*-theory, the so-called equities are redundant and are practically a mirror image of real capital accumulation, so the results and the analysis are not particularly useful. Informational inefficiencies, particularly of equity markets, determine macroeconomic cyclical behaviour.

Their models focus primarily on the behaviour of firms regarding output. Informational inefficiencies determine large fluctuations in the cost of capital which in turn determine observed cyclical variations in firms' investments and prices. The interpretation of such models in a full macroeconomic model may shed some light on the behaviour of equity markets under certain fiscal, financial and monetary policies. Such developments, however, remain a challenge for further research.

Evidently, the analysis of the interaction between financial markets and the economy is an open field that needs to be closely explored. In this regard, Tobin's contributions provide a strong base under which future analysis could be developed. The interaction between financial markets and the economy would be helpful for determining investors' portfolio adjust-ments based on current and expected economic activity, studying market feedback effects on the economy, asset pricing (including risks) relative to real assets, price levels, capital flows and monetary, credit and fiscal policies, as well as the functioning of different financial intermediaries and markets. By further studying the interaction of markets and the economy at the domestic level and extending such models under an open economy framework we would be better able to understand the determinants of international capital flows and their impact on the world economy.

As Tobin has Pointed Out

The traditional aggregation of all non-monetary assets into a single asset with a common interest rate does not permit analysis of some important policies, institutional structures and events.... Asset disaggregation is essential for analyzing, among other phenomena, financing of capital accumulation and government deficits, details of monetary and debt management policies, international capital movements and foreign exchange markets, and financial intermediation... what transactions are the source of variation of money stocks makes a difference, depending on how they alter the wealth and portfolio positions of economic agents. The incorporation of equities in open economy macroeconomic models could help us to understand the impact of fiscal, financial and monetary policies in the functioning, growth, asset pricing, determination of optimal portfolios, portfolio adjustments, substitution patterns with other financial assets, risks, international movements, allocable efficiency and welfare implications of equity markets, their impact on other macroeconomic aggregates and their contribution to economic growth. Such an analysis is nowadays more relevant for policy-makers adopting policy reforms aimed to correct economic external and internal imbalances, or to promote the development of equity markets, or to simultaneously achieve both objectives in the medium term.

ECONOMIC DEVELOPMENT

A different subset of the literature has focused on the relationship of financial markets and economic development. Most of this literature, including empirical studies regarding financial repression, has been recently surveyed. Therefore, only an overview is presented below. Except for the financial repression studies, most of these contributions are largely descriptive and inductive.

Largely focusing on financial markets as a relevant mechanism for economic growth, the significance of this body of the literature lies on the analysis of the major determinants of the growtfinancial markets and the introduction of concepts and measurements to characterize it. While the real rates of interest and government controls are identified as major determinants of financial market growth, the financial deepening (shallow finance) and financial repression concepts and ratio measure-ments have been introduced to describe the development status of financial markets in different economies. While there is consensus on the view that financial development leads to economic development, no conclusive evidence has been provided so far. The validity of such claims and suggest that financial factors are important if they are very distorted; otherwise, probably they do not make much difference to the level of per capita GNP.

The comparative analysis presented in a few studies indicates that financial markets in developing countries have a much narrower range of institutions and instruments and are much smaller with respect to the size of their economies than those of developed countries. Lacking a full macroe-conomic model where most financial market variables are integrated with real economic activity, the majority of the theoretical discussions evolve around the national and flow of funds accounts with particular emphasis on savings, investments and money, and as a consequence on credit markets.

Particular attention is paid to fiscal, financial and monetary policies that affect the growth of overall financial markets. The most salient policy instrument determining the growth of savings and investments, and thus determining financial liberalization, is the real rate of interest. In discussing financial markets in aggregation, with limited data and smaller capital markets in relation to the total financial system, the explicit role and the functioning of stock markets are practically ignored. Wai however, concludes that the development impact of capital markets in developing countries has been small, and that although they can play a positive and increasing role in development, their contributions would remain modest. Further studies are required to determine the benefits of well-developed equity markets for economic development. But first, methods to determine how economic growth can be attributed to financial markets need to be designed.

The relatively small size of stock markets *vis-à-vis* their economies (even in the case of industrialized countries) and the limited number of market participants, may continue to constrain the impact of stock markets on economic growth. The relative developmental impact of stock markets in developing countries may be increased, however, by reducing market imperfections and increasing their allocable efficiency. Nevertheless, the analyses of particular imperfections and their consequences are still needed.

Studies on the flow of savings into different financial markets and the effects of such flows on monetary and economic variables would also help policy-makers to adopt policies leading to the further development of financial markets, enhancement of their allocable efficiency and enhancement of their role in allocating the bearing of risks. The prospect for further increasing the stock markets' developmental impact also needs to be re-examined in the light of the growth and increasing integration and efficiency of world capital markets. Financial markets' developmental impact, however, is not expected to overshadow the relevance of sound and stable macroeconomic policies. On the contrary, the financial markets' contribution to economic growth will be determined by government policies.

The recent experience of financial liberalization and the limited success in developing more efficient financial markets is examined. The high specialization of developing economies and the historically excessive regulation of financial systems are identified as the main constraints for financial market development. Economic specialization limits the potential diversification for market participants and the excessive regulation of financial systems is not conducive to promoting rational and prudent credit decisions. It is implicitly suggested that excessive controls have not helped to develop the necessary experience and skills of investors and financial institutions to operate in a freer financial environment. Among other measures for the success of financial liberalization and for maintaining the stability of financial institutions, Dooley and Mathieson suggest limiting their parvalue liabilities, including foreign exchange exposure, and adopting prudent regulation and supervision.

A subset of the economic development literature has also focused on the impact of capital inflows in monetary aggregates and in economic growth and savings. To control monetary aggregates, adjusting and co-ordinating changes in exchange and interest rates while initially reducing the domestic component of base money. Gupta and Anisul (1983) on the other hand empirically examine the impact of foreign capital inflows on economic growth and domestic savings.

Their study confirms that, although foreign capital makes a positive contribution to growth, domestic savings are more important. The impact of foreign capital differs by type. While the evidence is mixed, Gupta and Anisul concluded that foreign aid is more productive for economic growth than foreign private capital. Perhaps this could be explained by the conditionality usually imposed on foreign aid which is commonly provided for financing economically beneficial investments.

In contrast, they found that foreign aid has a negative effect on domestic savings while the impact of foreign private capital in a few cases is positive. Gupta and Anisul suggest that the negative impact of foreign aid on savings could be a result of the recipient government relaxing its efforts to mobilize resources domestically, expecting that the foreign aid inflow would cover the savings gap.

The development of a complete macroeconomic model for an open economy where disaggregated financial markets are integrated with real economic activity would also help for re-examining the impact of financial markets in economic growth as well as for reviewing the effect of fiscal, financial and monetary policies on the growth of domestic savings. In addition, such a model would help in an analysis of the effect of foreign capital flows on economic and domestic savings growth. Thus the development of such a model *à la* Tobin with a complete disaggregation of financial markets (where the impact of stock markets could also be analysed) is long overdue and remains a challenge for future research. Perhaps only through this model can different policies be evaluated for confidently making policy recommendations that would help to further develop financial markets and the economies where they operate.

EMERGING MARKETS

The bulk of portfolio theory, market performance and asset pricing literature which has mostly been developed with a domestic perspective and has mainly focused on (or implicitly assumed) developed equity markets is well known and abundant. In contrast, the literature examining the organization and institutional structure, the functioning and performance, the growth constraints, the savings mobilization role, its world market integration and the macroeconomic, welfare and developmental impact of emerging markets and their response to different fiscal, financial and monetary policies is extremely limited, fragmented and often of doubtful quality. Most of the limited emerging market literature is generally descriptive and usually follows a case approach which prevents the development of generalizations.

Overall, the results of this literature (often focused on overall capital markets as opposed to stock markets alone) indicate that the establishment, growth and functioning of emerging markets are bound by historical circumstances, cultural factors, economic and financial development, economic and financial market structures and government policies. Because of this, generalizations about all emerging markets also need to be considered with caution and an in-depth analysis of individual emerging markets is required for providing adequate policy recommendations for their development. Furthermore, given data limitations and information of doubtful quality, most of the studies in this body of the literature have usually been qualified, often considered preliminary and tentative. Therefore, the same word of caution applies to this review.

The general view of this subset of the literature is that, with very few exceptions, securities markets in developing countries are characterized to be small relative to the economies where they operate, particularly when the representation of the industrial sector in stock markets is not proportional to its contribution to economic activity; thin, with little or no trading and with insignificant amounts of new issues by private companies and therefore with limited liquidity; and less efficient and usually riskier than securities markets in developed countries.

Securities markets in developing countries are further characterized by having strong risk-averse investors, who lack the confidence to participate in a market subject to insider dealings and manipulations, and a limited supply of securities, in particular through organized stock exchanges. Nevertheless, in a few cases and in particular instances a limited number of emerging markets have performed rather well, occasionally outperforming developed markets. Beset by policies that have resulted in repressed and shallow financial markets, emerging markets are not expected to function similarly to developed markets. In this light, it is most likely that emerging markets, more so than developed markets, are incomplete and imperfect. While this is still subject to further analyses, it is clear that functional differences between markets result in internationally segmented markets and as a corollary in a suboptimal allocation of wealth on a world-wide basis.

Regarding relative riskiness, perhaps due to market imperfections in the real sector and in the industrial organization of developing countries, it has been suggested that large companies in developing markets may have a smaller risk than those of developed countries. Such riskiness only focuses on the low variability of prices and not on the market power of some companies which may permit stock market manipulation, thereby representing a higher risk for investors. The market portfolio of developed markets, on the other hand, with a wider number of investment opportunities is usually less risky than the market portfolio of emerging markets. Despite the capital flights controversy, the potential for international diversification and its benefits is nevertheless also available to emerging markets.

With a limited understanding on all aspects of emerging markets, an incomplete theoretical framework and scarce empirical investigations, domestic and international investors, international organizations and policy-makers practically operate in a vacuum that may prevent them achieving their objectives. The intuition that emerging markets need to be promoted in most economies, for example, still needs to be validated by rigorous and systematic studies of the underlying economic structure and policy framework under which such markets operate. With the limited understanding of the functioning of stock markets in the context of the macroeconomy, policy recommendations regarding the development, functioning, openness and control of emerging markets are suspect and need to be re-examined in the context of a general macroeconomic model which is still awaiting development.

A significant controversy exists about the role that governments should play in the establishment, promotion and control of stock markets. While some writers suggest that, for promoting the development of stock markets, governments should decide on the role those markets would play *vis-à-vis* other methods for financing development, others support the premise that the allocation of savings through such markets should be determined by economic forces. Generally it is recommended that the establishment of stock markets should be motivated by economic reasons rather than, as in some instances, political reasons.

In practice some government officials from some developing countries have been ambivalent and indifferent in promoting stock markets and suspicious of foreign influences and controls. This may in part be explained by the expected limited impact of stock markets on economic development. Stock markets nevertheless may still increase the efficiency of allocating domestic and foreign savings. In some instances, stock markets have been used to promote the indigenization of foreign companies.

Furthermore, in the 1980s they have been considered as a serious alternative in attracting foreign investments and are considered to be instrumental in the privatization of government-owned corporations and in the reduction of foreign debt through debt-to-equity conver-sion mechanisms. In contrast, some suggest that the promotion of stock markets is not always recommended, particularly when market imperfections abound and in the case of emerging markets as stock markets would exacerbate the uneven distribution of wealth and income in developing countries.

While certain conditions should exist for developing stock markets, such as a vigourous and healthy private sector, sufficient domestic savings, a stable economic and financial environment, an adequate legal and regulatory framework and adequate fiscal, financial and monetary policies, in general it is suggested that the participation of governments in the securities market should be limited and perhaps concentrated on enhancing the protection of investors.

Controls need to be in place for avoiding insider trading, manipulation and occasional speculative splurges that have ended in several cases in a crash that has eliminated the interest of market investors and thus reverted markets to a lethargic state. However, the emphasis should be on developing strong and transparent capital market organizations and institutions rather than on stringent controls and bureaucratic procedures.

Policies to increase the liquidity and yields while reducing risks of securities have been adopted in several countries. In some cases fiscal policies through tax incentives apparently yielded positive results but the effects are not as positive as expected. Overall, however, systematic analysis of the effectiveness of those policies still needs to be carried out. Again the soundness of policy recommendations can be better evaluated by using a general equilibrium open economy macroeconomic model. Perhaps in its absence, warnings are commonly offered for the potential negative effects of policies aimed to develop capital markets further.

It is usually recommended that such markets should not be developed if there is no real demand for the services they can provide and when their development may lead to an unsustainable growth, particularly in the early stages. Differences of opinion exist in terms of the speed by which policy-makers should promote securities markets.

While some recommend fast policy actions with errors in judgement to be corrected with experience, others recommend a positive but gradual approach for policy actions. Undoubtedly, the preferred approach needs to be selected considering the particular characteristics of the economy and culture where those markets would operate. The limited evidence shows that errors in judgement in the developing securities markets usually do not provide, except in the long run, second chances for correcting wrong policies and decisions.

As several writers suggest, the process for developing securities markets is costly and risky. Therefore, policy recommendations should be analysed in depth and when adopted they should be decisively implemented. Other policy objectives recommended in this subset of the literature are to increase savings in the economy, to foster more even distribution of wealth and income and to eliminate barriers for the free allocation of savings. A diversity of financial institutions particularly of the institutional investor type, should be promoted and encouraged to participate in the securities market.

The timely and adequate availability of information should be encouraged and the training and sophistication of market participants needs to be increased. The fundamental development of emerging markets is a continuous process and much more remains to be done to complete their development and to exploit their potential fully.

To achieve these objectives, further developments of the theory and empirical work on emerging equity markets and international capital flows needs to be encouraged. There are particular questions that need to be answered to understand the functioning and inherent limitations of emerging markets better. If emerging markets are thin and therefore illiquid, would they still be able to attract international investors? For this assessment, international CAPMs that take into account liquidity risks need to be developed.

In the context of the standard CAPMs it is claimed that international investors are in a better position to incur additional risks than domestic investors, but such risks refer to market and not to liquidity risks. Thus, even if emerging markets could open up additional investment opportunities, their liquidity risks may be so high that international investors may not be willing to participate in such markets. Externalities in the information about the behaviour of other decision-makers, and uncertainty about the environment, generate a demand for liquidity which may be exacerbated in the case of emerging markets.

At the theoretical level, Lintner (1970) and Litzenberger and Budd (1972) have shown that the risk premium and the market price of risk, subject to the class of investors' utility functions, varies with the growth in per capita national wealth, the size of the market and the number of market participants. This would help to explain the higher risks of emerging markets which could then be reduced by increasing the number of market participants and market capitalization. Risk premium, however, may increase with per capita wealth increases, *i.e.* with economic growth.

If so, this would limit the feasible rate of growth of the economy. In addition to the thinness and limited diversification of emerging markets, the risks determined by the stages of economic development and growth may explain why emerging markets are more volatile than developed markets.

In this regard, the stability of economic policies for reducing the volatility of emerging markets is more relevant in developing than developed countries. Given the limited research on emerging markets it is not surprising that the Lintner and Litzenberger and Budd theories have not been subjected to empirical testing. Besides testing these theories, additional efforts should be made to develop the theory of stock market growth, in particular with regard to relative growth with respect to the economy.

Other aspects of emerging markets also remain open for further analysis. Are emerging markets of very small economies able to provide sufficient and increasing investment opportunities to justify relatively high information costs? Or is the supply of investment opportunities in those markets basically fixed, thereby exacerbating those costs? While international CAPMs assume a fixed number of securities, they vary in practice.

It is expected that the number of securities in emerging markets may be subject to change more than in the case of developed countries; thus, the effect of changes in the supply of securities on capital asset pricing and portfolio choices needs to be evaluated. If the economic growth of developing countries is higher than the growth of developed economies, are emerging markets able to provide sufficient investment opportunities and stocks commensurate with the high economic growth to attract substantial foreign portfolio investment?

Or is the market capitalization of emerging markets so small that it inhibits international flows despite the higher economic growth and potential profitability? Are there minimum economy sizes and number of market participants below which stock markets are inoperative? If so, what are the alternatives for small economies for improving the allocation of resources and the exchange of assets? Given the smallness of emerging markets relative to world markets, would emerging markets provide higher average returns than large developed markets in a similar way to the small-firm size effect in developed markets? If so, could that explain potential higher returns but also higher risks? Is the size effect of small companies also present within emerging markets? With very few exceptions, the analysis of emerging markets has eluded the interest of renowned financial and macro economists. Also owing to severe information constraints, low levels of market capitalization, high volatility and unfamiliarity, emerging markets have not significantly attracted international investors and research houses of financial institutions.

Only recently, as a result of the breakdown of the international financial intermediation process after 1982 and the related global debt crisis, has the role of emerging markets in the reduction of debt, as a vehicle to attract financial resources and as an alternative to term lending for financing development, attracted the attention of international organizations, policy-makers and the interna-tional financial community. Significant efforts are still needed to develop our understanding of emerging markets and to design adequate policies for their development.

To help in this endeavour, the development of a complete survey and statistical information of world markets on a timely basis needs to be made available on a consistent and comparable basis. Also, to study international flows further, disaggregated information on different types of capital flows, particularly on foreign portfolio investments, needs to be made available. In this regard, the IMF balance-of-payments statistics could be expanded to include disaggregated types of capital flows. The IMF financial statistics are well known and widely disseminated and thus could make this information available to both researchers and international investors.

INTEGRATION AND CAPITAL FLOWS

Central to the study of international financial systems, particularly regarding stock markets, is the controversy on the integration versus segmentation of markets. While a number of international capital asset pricing and macroeconomic models implicitly assume integrated markets, a subset of the literature specifically focuses on this controversy.

Assuming that segmentation of stock markets is mainly a result of government controls, some researchers have suggested that foreign direct investments are a plausible alternative to attain the diversification benefits not available if stock markets are segmented. In the middle of the integration versus segmentation controversy lies the study of capital flight and its economic and welfare implications. Given the relevance of these issues in the study of stock markets, specific studies on these subjects and other aspects not covered before are succinctly discussed below.

World Stock Markets and Segmentation

The apparent ignorance about the universe of possible asset claims in world markets. Except for a recent paper by Calderón-Rossell, no study that analyses total world markets where emerging markets are taken into account is known to the author.

Most studies of international markets are usually concentrated on developed markets, and so no concept of a full world stock market exists. Data limitations, which include unavailability or untimeliness, inconsistent information and high cost, and the relative smallness of emerging markets may have contributed to a partial view of world markets. Under these constraints and based on this apparent ignorance, world markets would be segmented.

Empirical methods so far have not successfully determi-ned if world capital markets are segmented or integrated. However, even if capital markets are perfectly integrated, the high levels of uncertainty motivated in part by untimely information may constrain the diversification of the optimal world portfolio and therefore lead to ignoring the *true* world capital market. If so, asset allocation in world markets may not be efficient. The optimal asset allocation depends on the investment universe. The constrained optimal portfolio choice under incomplete information in total world markets is also an area that needs to be further developed.

Furthermore, while the absence of information resembles the absence of markets, particularly in limiting an optimal allocation of resources, the big difference between these scenarios is that the former may be corrected by investing in obtaining information but the latter is beyond the control of investors. Both domestic theoretical models and empirical research on portfolio choices under such constraints need to be extended to the international arena. The determination of segmentation versus integration of capital markets, the absence of a complete world market perspective and the uncertainty due to the lack of information or other causes are relevant factors that affect a world-wide optimal allocation of wealth. Therefore, besides determining the overall efficiency of capital markets (particularly of emerging stock markets) and their role in the allocation of world wealth, policy-makers need to adopt policies that enhance the integration of equity markets (and thus develop home-country stock markets). This would permit increasing world welfare and growth.

Besides fully open economy policies, multiple listings and electronic linkages are areas that could enhance the integration of world markets and should be explored in detail. However, it appears that multiple listings face similar questions to those of MNCs in their alternative role for portfolio investments that is discussed below. The existing technical advances in interna-tional communications would permit a drastic reduction in information gaps, would substantially increase the efficiency of world markets and would permit an optimal and timely allocation of world resources which are expected to increase world welfare.

The electronic linkages of world markets would require a massive and tremendous effort for modernizing the policy-making process in individual markets, the development of consistent information and data analysis (including stock markets data and accounting information), new clearing procedures and controls and a complete change in the way that transactions take place. Perhaps international institutional investors and international organizations can take the lead in promoting these developments.

It is possible that the integration of markets in the EC that is expected to take place in the 1990s and the introduction of Globex, a computer system for trading futures on a worldwide basis designed by the Chicago Mercantile Exchange and Reuters Holding, may provide lessons to take into account for the full integration of world markets. Therefore, such experiences need to be closely watched. For the integration of world markets and the necessary development of individual and international markets, further developments of theories and empirical work and the additional training of macroeconomists and policy-makers in these matters remain fundamental and priority tasks. Largely because of the lack of a universal understanding on how stock markets operate and the weaknesses of curricula for training economists, policies focusing on the development of stock markets have not been forthcoming.

Universities and international organiza-tions can fulfil a useful role in this regard. Supporting research in this area, strengthening curricula and transferring this knowledge and future developments to policy-makers, particularly those in emerging markets, may help to focus their attention on stock markets and on adopting policies for their development, thereby improving the allocation of resources and world welfare.

Foreign Direct Investment as a Vehicle for Portfolio Investments

The role of MNCs in providing an indirect diversification vehicle in segmented international markets has been examined. Although foreign direct investments are more closely related to markets in real assets and corporate control, it has been claimed that they provide a diversification potential which may not otherwise be available to international investors. In its own right, at both the micro and macro level, as well as from different perspectives, particular attention has been given to foreign direct investments. No attempt is made here to cover this literature.

In the context of the international capital asset pricing theory, but introducing barriers for international portfolio investments in certain markets, the portfolio diversification potential through MNCs needs to be evaluated by distinguishing between international portfolio investments versus foreign direct investments. But first, significant questions regarding the market valuation of MNCs in domestic markets need to be resolved.

To what extent is multinationality reflected in the domestic the MNC's home country) market price of MNCs? Are MNC shares evaluated in the context of a pure domestic risk-return relationship or are they evaluated from an implicit but unspecified segmented international risk-return relationship?

Besides the effect of increasing the number of shares in the domestic market, is the market price line of pure domestic firms affected by the inclusion of MNC shares? If MNCs provide additional diversifications to those available in large domestic stock markets, is such diversification recognized in domestic asset pricings? If such additional diversification exists, stock markets may not be Pareto production efficient in view of the monopolistic competi-tiveness of MNCs. And if such larger diversification exists but is not recognized by domestic markets, the lack of Pareto production efficiency of markets would be exacerbated by informational inefficiencies.

Lacking information about the relative merits of different international investment opportunities and the relative probabilities of events, prices would simply be random.

On the other hand, if MNCs' monopolistic competitive position is determined by the comparative advantages of the economic structure at home, it is unlikely that by investing abroad they can provide the same diversification potential of international portfolio investments. Foreign portfolios provide additional investment opportunities based on the economic structure of foreign countries. Unless we are able to answer these questions, the diversification potential of MNCs remains a moot question.

Capital Flight Controversy

Extraneously enough, differences in wealth between developed and emerging markets have created biases and an asymmetry in value judgements regarding international capital flows. The social welfare of an individual country is not necessarily the same as the world welfare. Flows arising from investors of developed markets considered as a positive development are cast in the framework of international portfolio diversifications. In contrast, flows from emerging markets perceived as a negative process are commonly referred to as capital flights. So investors from developed markets are *good knights* while those from emerging markets are *evil knights*. Under that perspective, international investments and diversification opportunities should be available only to *good knights* but not to *evil knights*.

As Cumby and Levich have remarked, 'the notion that capital flight represents a source of disutility focuses on a nationalistic measure of social utility' (1987:31). This perspective, however, goes against the notion that open economies would lead to an increase in world output and welfare.

Focusing on controls, Dooley (1986) has proposed that capital flights should be considered as those not reported in the balance of payments. The presumption is that such flows would be illegal and perhaps motivated by tax avoidance and controls.

Aside of legal considerations, attention should be paid to the determinants of such unreported transactions. Perhaps they are motivated by the underlying perception and risk aversion of investors who are attempting to circumvent expected restrictions on wealth and capital movements and are therefore seeking to diversify their portfolios internatio-nally. Such potential restrictions may reduce or eliminate the benefits of future investment opportunities with obvious implications on individual welfare.

Are the country policies adequate? What are the income redistribution effects of capital flows? To evaluate government policies and the income redistribution effects of capital flows, improvements may be needed in the national accounts and balance-of-payments statistics for obtaining sufficiently disaggregated information on all international transactions and capital movements.

CUSTOMER MANAGEMENT SYSTEMS

Companies need a method for viewing all customer and marketing-related information in an integrated way. Often marketing organizations maintain multiple databases for each business and marketing activity with data that is not easily integrated for strategic or operational purposes. A new generation of software that is Internet based gathers information from customer service, Web sites, direct mail operations, telemarketing, field sales, customer service, distributors, retailers and suppliers for the purpose of managing marketing, sales and customer service activities.

The major applications families are commonly referred to as sales force automation (SFA) and customer relationship management (CRM) systems.

Some CRM systems are fully integrated with SFA applications and some are standalone. The worldwide market for such systems is projected to grow five times faster than the overall software market, from $5 billion in 1999 to more than $22 billion in 2003.

Sales Force Automation

SFA is a customer management tool that is one of the fastest growing elements of the MkIS. SFA applications are often integrated with the CRM system. SFA involves the application of information technology to the sales function or, more appropriately, to the activities leading to a sale. These activities include acquiring sales leads, managing the sales opportunity, closing the sale and managing the customer relationship. The historic role of personal selling has been to move the product—to generate transactions.

As selling has become increasingly more professional, sales people emphasize building relationships with customers that will generate loyalty-based repeat transactions over time. Relationship building often necessitates that the sales person has consultative and advisory skills in addition to product knowledge and sales abilities. Team-based selling places emphasis on role specialization, collaboration and coordination. Customers have become more sophisticated as well.

Requirements for customised solutions, rapid response times and the need for concurrent and post-sale service have greatly increased the need for information technology in the sales process. The goals of SFA are to increase the effectiveness of the sales organization, improve its efficiency and to create superior value for the customer. Sales effectiveness focuses on getting the sale by improving lead generation, qualifying prospects, coordinating sales efforts, and tracking commitments.

Effectiveness is a function of improving the sales process. Sales efficiency is evaluated by measuring the return on sales efforts. SFA can improve sales efficiency by reducing sales cycle time, by managing workflow, and tracking the current status of critical activities related to the sale.

Proposal generation, opportunity management, fulfillment, and follow up are facilitated by SFA. Superior customer value is achieved when the customer expectations are exceeded. It is a primary determinant of customer satisfaction. SFA enables better understanding of customer expectations and management of the customer account.

The Sales Process

The typical field sales process consists of a series of steps that are designed to lead to a sale. The typical role of the MkIS is to support the sales process steps of lead generation, sales process management, and account management.

- *Lead generation*: Leads represent potential customers. The identification of a lead is the beginning of the sales cycle. After leads are identified, they must be qualified. This process involves gathering information about the lead and comparing the result against qualifying criteria. The lead generation process is becoming more automated with regard to obtaining more pre-qualifying information directly from the lead and augmenting it from commercial and other databases such as credit bureaus. The advent of Web-based technologies is driving this trend. Qualified leads are then distributed to the sales force.
- *Sales Process Management*: This process starts when the sales person receives the lead information. The primary information system need is for a convenient method to track the process and store data the data generated at each stage. There are a number of sub-steps to this stage of the process.
  - *Verification of the opportunity*: The sales person usually contacts the lead and attempts to verify the existence and nature of an opportunity including its size, timing, and appropriateness of the products and services of the selling company. Sales people will also desire to verify the lead's ability to purchase, identify the names of key decision-makers and influencers, and the level of budget authority. This information is entered into the sales database.
  - *The Sales Call*: If the lead is amenable and the opportunity justifies it, a sales call is scheduled. Information may be sent to the prospect and a custom presentation may be created. The SFA system is used to provide a single point of interface for the sales person to coordinate the activities leading up to the sales call. After the call, the SFA system is updated with customer requirements, new information and commitments made by the sales person.
  - *Opportunity Management*: If the sales person is successful, the next step is typically the receipt of a request for proposal (RFP) from the prospective customer. The RFP will generally state the customer's requirements and the date for the final submission. Follow-on visits may be necessary to clear up or identify new requirements. The prospect may want to visit the seller's manufacturing site. The final product of this stage is the creation of a proposal and price quote to be presented to the prospect. This document should build a sound economic case for the purchase. All these interactions, requirements, commitments, and competitor information are tracked by the SFA system that

provides the database, tools and templates to generate the proposal.

- *Closing the Sale*: The presentation of the proposal and the price quote is the start of the closing process. Even if the sales person has done a good job of presenting the business case, further negotiations may be necessary to close the sale. If all objections are met and the proposal is accepted the close is successful. If not, the sales team will need to debrief the sessions learned to determine why the proposal was not accepted. The outcomes are recorded in the SFA system.

- *Account Management*: The automation of the sales process may result in a standalone system that is not integrated with other management systems. However, SFA is increasingly being integrated with the overall CRM system. This is especially true of the account management function. Since the primary goal of the CRM system is to manage the customer relationship in order to generate repeat sales, a good sales person will want to keep track of the status of a new account and how well the customer is being served. This is especially true if the account is to become "referenceable" to other prospects. The account management function of the CRM system enables the sales person to track order entry, order processing, shipment, and installation. The sales person may need to ensure that post-sales service is delivered or monitor the results of and installation and track the customer's satisfaction. The ability to track outcomes and interact with the customer in order to reassess needs and create new opportunities is a major benefit that flows from effective account management.

Sales Force Automation Tools

SFA tools consist of software applications that enable the salesperson to better target sales opportunities and manage the sales cycle. The tools are increasingly available bundled as integrated suites that are Internet enabled, accessible through a browser and linked to the CRM system.

The software applications may be categorized as:

- *Document management tools*: These tools support all stages of the sales process. They include word processors, graphics programmes, spreadsheets, e-mail, expense reports, proposal generators, and "product configurators." A Web-accessible sales library or encyclopedia of previously developed product information, brochures, product demonstrations, presentations, financial information, price lists, white documents, and public relations materials is a key resource for sales force productivity.

- *Personal management tools*: These tools focus on increasing the efficiency and effectiveness of the sales teams efforts. They typically include calendar and scheduling programmes, contact management systems, and call reporting capabilities.
- *Process management tools:* These tools are used to keep track of customer requirements and sales commitments. They include opportunity management systems, project management systems, account management systems, order-entry systems, telemarketing systems, team-selling systems.

Increasingly, with the rise of Web-based hosting and the application service provider (ASP) industry, SFA applications and databases are being hosted by third-party specialists and accessed remotely on the Internet. With the ASP model, client companies are essentially outsourcing all or part of there IS function. Remote hosting raises issues of security and scalability. The advantages of an ASP approach are its browser-based simplicity, rapid implementation, and lower cost of deployment. Most ASP applications use a subscription-based pricing model. Some vendors are proposing that renting the application or paying by the transaction may become the pricing model of the future.

Customer Relationship Management

The Internet has facilitated a fundamental shift in market power from sellers to buyers. Customers, newly endowed with the power of market information, have much different expectations than before. Customers can easily move their business to another vendor with the click of a mouse. They have access to the same cost data as their suppliers and they demand 24x7 customer service.

Customers now have almost unlimited ability for interactions with organizations through the Web in addition to the traditional phone and mail methods. Company web sites facilitate information search, shopping and customer support. E-mail communication can target specific offers on a one-to-one basis. Understanding and meeting demanding expectations has placed a renewed emphasis on managing customer relationships. The primary goal of CRM systems is to increase the return on marketing expenditures by enabling the understanding of the complete history of a firm's interactions with its customers.

CRM applications can deliver targeted solutions that promote customer loyalty as measured by increased response to promotions, purchase frequencies and volume, and minimizes the time between orders. CRM systems are able to target marketing communications to likely buyers, facilitate sales efforts and deliver customer service. CRM systems increase revenue, lower costs and optimize customer lifetime value.

Customer Relationship Management Design Principles

The CRM field is rapidly evolving into an integrated discipline that manages all of a company's touches with the customer.

Accordingly, several design principles have evolved as the foundation for CRM development:

- The CRM system should offer the customer multiple channels for communication such as the telephone, e-mail, fax, on-line or some combination. Each channel should lead to an interaction that satisfies customer expectations. Customers must be able to choose the method that best meets their needs on each occasion.
- Each CRM interaction should deliver value to the customer. The CRM system must be able to determine what value is required and deliver it quickly whether it is a product or service transaction or a customer service request.
- The CRM system integrates the customer throughout the firm's value chain. Customers should be able to reach into all necessary functions of the organization not just to the sales organization, or customer service, but to manufacturing and even the CEO. Better integration of the customer into the process can lead to higher levels of trust, loyalty and repeat purchases. The cost of acquiring a new customer often far exceeds that of retaining existing ones.
- Knowledge is captured during each CRM interaction. The CRM system should capture knowledge about the customer and the customer's relationship with the company over time. Sales and customer support histories should be analysed for indications of how well the vendor is doing in meeting customers' needs and how valuable the customer is to the marketer.

Customer Relationship Management Functions

CRM applications provide the customer-related information that is necessary to drive a firm's ebusiness activities. Better customer information enables more effective demand forecasting, product launches and marketing campaigns. CRM functions are sometimes referred to as the company's "front office."

CRM functionality includes:

- E-commerce support
- Sales force automation
- Telesales and call centre automation
- Direct mail and catalog sales
- E-mail and e-newsletter response
- Web sales and personalization

- Analysis of Web generated data
- Traditional customer support and service
- On-line support and customer service
- Mobile support through laptops, handheld devices.
- Training

Modern CRM systems are fully integrated with the "back office" elements of the enterprise resource planning (ERP) system such as accounting, manufacturing, project management, and human resources. This integration enables the sharing of customer information that can impact the operations of the enterprise and vice versa. Common customer definitions, price lists, employee definitions, service requests, call histories, order histories, contracts, service level agreements are accessible by all who need them. Correspondingly, marketing can access information on items such as new product development, product costs, order status, delivery dates and backorders.

TYPES OF BUSINESS PURCHASE DECISIONS

While it would appear business customers face the same four purchase situations faced by consumers (Minor New Purchase, Minor Re-Purchase, Major New Purchase, Major Re-Purchase), the nature of the business market noted above has led many marketing academics to group business purchase situations into only three categories. The reason is that the idea of a minor order may not hold as well in the business market, where buyers tend to place larger orders and where suppliers' marketing efforts are directed toward the most profitable buyers.

- *Straight Re-Purchase*: These purchase situations involve routine ordering. In most cases buyers simply reorder the same products or services that were previously purchased. In fact, many larger companies have programmed re-purchases into an automated ordering system that initiates electronic orders when inventory falls below a certain pre-determined level. For the supplier benefiting from the re-purchase this situation is ideal since the purchaser is not looking to evaluate other products. For competitors who are not getting the order it may require extensive marketing efforts to persuade the buyer to consider other product or service options.
- *Modified Re-Purchase*: These purchases occur when products or services previously considered a straight re-purchase are for some reason now under a re-evaluation process. There are many reasons why a product is moved to the status of a modified re-purchase. Some of these reasons include: end of purchase contract period, change in who is involved in making the purchase, supplier is removed from an approved suppliers list, mandate from top level of

organization to re-evaluate all purchasing, or strong marketing effort by competitors. In this circumstance the incumbent supplier faces the same challenges they may have faced when they initially convinced the buyer to make the purchase. For competitors the door is now open and they must work hard to make sure their message is heard by those in charge of the purchase decision.

- *New Task Purchase*: As the name suggests, these purchases are ones the buyer has never or rarely made before. In some ways new task purchases can be considered as either minor or major depending on the total cost or overall importance of the purchase. In either case the buyer will spend considerably more time evaluating alternatives. For example, if faced with a major new task purchase, which often involves complex items, such as computer systems, buildings, robotic assembly lines, etc., the purchase cycle from first recognizing the need to placement of the order may be months or even years. The business market we now look at how purchasing decisions are made. Business purchasing follows the same five-step buying process faced by consumers:
  - Need Recognition
  - Search:
  - Evaluate Options
  - Purchase
  - After-Purchase Evaluation.

While the steps are the same as consumer purchasing, the activities occurring within each step are quite different as we discuss below.

NEED RECOGNITION

In a business environment needs arise from just about anywhere within the organization. The Buying Centre concept shows that Initiators are the first organizational members to recognize a need. In most situations the Initiator is also the User or Buyer. Users are inclined to identify the need for new solutions (i.e., new products) while Buyers are more likely to identify the need to re-purchase products.

But marketers should also understand that more companies are replacing human involvement in re-purchase decisions with automated methods, thus making it more challenging for competitors to replace currently purchased products. In straight re-purchase situations, whether there is human intervention or not, the purchasing process often jumps from Need Recognition to Purchase and little search activity is performed. As part of this step, a specifications document may be generated that lays out the requirements of the product or service to be purchased. Several members of the Buying Centre may be involved in creation of the specifications. For the marketer, establishing close contact with those who draw up the specifications may help position the marketer's product for inclusion in the search phase.

SEARCH

The search for alternatives to consider as potential solutions to recognized needs is one of the most significant differences between consumer and business purchasing. Much of this has to do with an organization's motive to reduce costs. While a consumer will probably not search hard to save two cents a gallon on gas, a company that has a large fleet of cars or trucks certainly will. In fact, this step in the purchase process is where professional buyers make their mark.

The primary intention of their search efforts is to identify multiple suppliers who meet product specifications and then, through a screening process, offer a selected group the opportunity to present their products to members of the Buying Centre. Although in some industries, such as chemicals, online marketplaces and auction sites offer buyers another option for selecting suppliers that may not include supplier presentations. For suppliers, the key to this step of the purchase process is to make sure they are included within the search activities of the Buyer or others in the Buying Centre. In some instances this may require that a supplier work to be included within an approved suppliers list. In the case of online marketplaces and auction sites, suppliers should work to be included within relevant sites.

EVALUATE OPTION

Once the search has produced options, members of the Buying Centre may then choose among the alternatives. In more advanced purchase situations, members of the Buying Centre may evaluate each option using a checklist of features and benefits sought by the buyer. Each feature/benefit is assigned a weight that corresponds to its importance to the purchase decision. In many cases, especially when dealing with Government and Not-For-Profit markets, suppliers must submit bids with the lowest bidder often being awarded the order, assuming products or services meet specifications.

PURCHASE

To actually place the order may require the completion of paperwork (or electronic documents) such as a purchase order. Acquiring the necessary approvals can delay the order for an extended period of time. And for very large purchases, such as buildings or large equipment, financing options may need to be explored.

AFTER-PURCHASE EVALUATION

After the order is received the purchasing company may spend time reviewing the results of the purchase. This may involve the Buyer discussing product performance issues with Users. If the product is well received it may end up moving to a straight re-purchase status thus eliminating much of the evaluation process on future purchases.

MEANING AND CONCEPT OF CONSUMER BEHAVIOUR

Through the application of sociology, psychology and demographics, marketers can begin to understand why consumers form attitudes and make decisions to purchase. Consumer-behaviour studies inform marketers, advertisers and public agencies how product and service selection is influenced by personality, perception, values and beliefs. For marketing, these influences are studied in the context of demographics, which includes ethnicity, age, marital status, size of family, income, education and employment.

PERCEPTION

Perception is how information is collected and categorized. Perception is affected by the amount of exposure to a stimulus and by individual interpretation. For example, a consumer who hears—once—that dairy herds contribute to greenhouse gas would not take the statement seriously. If the same consumer encountered that information often and from many sources, then the consumer's attitude towards dairy products might change enough to influence how often the consumer chose yogurt as a breakfast food.

PERSONALITY

Personality is a weak component of consumer behaviour. Personality means a pattern of behaviour founded on an individual's outlook and internal traits. In this use, outlook means point-of-view and traits mean the consumer's usual manner of responding to the environment. An example of outlook is the effect of a recessionary economy on consumer confidence. Examples of traits are introversion or extroversion, ambition or complacency, aggressiveness or timidity and compulsiveness or pragmatism. A consumer whose decision to purchase is influenced by extroversion or compulsiveness, might choose to be less innovative during an economic downturn because confidence is lower.

VALUES

Values are the consumer's set of standards about conduct that arise from learned culture. A "terminal value" is a long-term goal or role model, as when a consumer strives for a particular lifestyle, such as healthful diet and exercise. An "instrumental" value is a flexible and negotiable action that is exercised daily, such as when a consumer makes a decision to purchase either organic or nonorganic products.

BELIEFS

In consumer behaviour study, "beliefs" are specific beliefs about products in the marketplace. Consumer belief is a combination of knowledge, emotions and actual actions to purchase or not purchase. For example, if a consumer has a negative or prejudiced set of beliefs about Yugoslavia, then marketing an automobile manufactured in Yugoslavia would have to focus on changing those beliefs.

ATTITUDE

Consumer attitude is a combination of perceptions, values and beliefs. The consumer must first perceive the product and then focus values and beliefs onto the product and make a decision to purchase or not to purchase.

Beliefs are more vulnerable to marketing than values are, because beliefs are subject to knowledge and emotion. For example, positive facts can inform a consumer's knowledge about automobile manufacturing in Yugoslavia. A marketer might decide what demographic group can best afford a Yugoslavian automobile and then generate positive emotion by associating the automobile with music towards which that demographic group feels positive.

BUSINESS VS CONSUMER MARKETS

For marketers, the selling environment of business markets present uniquely different circumstances when compared to selling to consumers.

At the beginning of this tutorial we saw two ways in which consumer and business markets differ:

- Business markets are more likely to be price driven than brand driven, and
- Demand in business markets tends to be more volatile than consumer markets.

However, the two markets are dissimilar in other ways requiring marketers to take a different approach when selling to business customers than to consumers.

These differences include:

- How Decisions Are Made
- Existence of Experienced Purchasers
- Time Needed to Make Buying Decision
- Size of Purchases
- Number of Buyers
- Type of Promotional Effort Needed to Reach Buyer

BUYING DIFFERENCES

Buying Centre Decisions

In the consumer market a very large percentage of purchase decisions are made by a single person. As we discussed in the Consumer Buying Behaviour tutorial, there are situations in which multiple people may be involved in a consumer purchase decision, such as a child influencing a parent to choose a certain brand of cereal or a husband and wife deciding together to buy a house, but most of the time purchases are individual decisions. The business market is significantly different. While single person purchasing is not unusual, especially within a small company, a significant percentage of business buying, especially within larger organizations, requires the input of many.

In the marketing literature those associated with the purchase decision are known to be part of a Buying Centre, which consists of individuals within an organization that perform one or more of the following roles:

- *Buyer*: Responsible for dealing with suppliers and placing orders
- *Decider*: Has the power to make the final purchase decision
- *Influencer*: Has the ability to affect what is ordered such as setting order specifications
- *User*: Those who will actually use the product when it is received
- *Initiator*: Any Buying Centre member who is the first to determine that a need exists
- *Gatekeeper*: Anyone who controls access to other Buying Centre members

For marketers confronting a Buying Centre it is important to first identify who plays what role. Once identified the marketer must address the needs of each member, which may differ significantly. For instance, the Decider, who may be the company president wants to make sure the purchase will not negatively affect the company's bottom line while the Buyer wants to be assured the product will be delivered on time. Thus, the way each Buying Centre member is approached and marketed to requires careful planning in order to address the unique needs of each member.

Experienced Purchasers

As noted in the discussion of the Buying Centre, organizations often employ purchasing agents or professional buyers whose job is to negotiate the best deals for their company. Unlike consumers, who often lack information when making purchase decisions, professional buyers are generally as knowledgeable about the product and the industry as the marketer who is selling to them.

Decision Making Time

Depending on the product, business purchase decisions can drag on for an extensive period. Unlike consumer markets where impulse purchasing is rampant, the number of people involved in business purchase decisions results in decisions taking weeks, months or even years.

Size of Purchases

For products that are regularly used and frequently purchased, businesses will often buy a larger volume at one time compared to consumer purchases. Because of this business purchasers often demand price breaks for higher order levels.

Type of Promotions

Companies who primarily target consumers often use mass advertising methods to reach an often widely dispersed market. For business-to-business marketers the size of individual orders, along with a smaller number of buyers, makes person-to-person contact by sales representatives a more effective means of promotion.

Index

N

O

P

R

S

T

U

W